The Message

A Translation of the Glorious Qur'an

"... a Book which We have sent down to you so that you may bring the people out of the darkness and into the light..." (Qur'an 14:1)

FIFTH REVISION

The Monotheist Group

Brainbow Press
United States of America

The Message: A Translation of the Glorious Qur'an

For information:

www.Free-Minds.Org
www.Brainbowpress.Com
www.ProgressiveMuslims.Org

ISBN-13: 978-0-9796715-4-8 (pbk)
ISBN-13: 978-0-9796715-2-4 (cloth)

ISBN-10: 0-9796715-4-x (pbk)
ISBN-10: 0-9796715-2-3 (cloth)

Printed in the United States of America

This work represents a translation of the divine words as revealed by the Almighty over 1,400 years ago and in no way is the translation itself divine or perfect. Any shortcomings are purely due to human error and the reader is always advised to independently **verify** what he/she reads.

"And do not uphold what you have no knowledge of; for the hearing, and eyesight, and mind—all these you are responsible for."
(Qur'an 17:36)

Errata Notice:

As the Qur'an translation is a human effort, you may occasionally note a discrepancy in our interpretation or an error in translation. We are working hard to have the most accurate translation available, and thus will be regularly updating the work. The print version may be slightly behind in updates compared to the online version. The online version may be found at (www.free-minds.org/quran). Should you find an error, please notify us at (free@free-minds.org).

'Our Lord, forgive us our sins and our shortcomings in our responsibility, and make firm our foothold, and grant us victory over the rejecting people.'(Qur'an 3:147)

CONTENTS

PREFACE

With so many English translations of the Qur'an available, it is inevitable that the reader would ask "why make another one?" The answer to that question lays in the current structure of the Islamic faith itself, and the fact that, for many centuries, Islam has been primarily subcategorized as either "Sunni" or "Shia" or one of the many other denominations that have emerged over the years.

As such, all translators have belonged to one school of thought or another which clearly comes across in the interpretation of and choice of translation for specific words or verses.

The Message: A Translation of the Glorious Qur'an is an attempt to be free from the influences of sectarianism, delivering to the reader a rendition as close to the pure message of the Qur'an as possible.

> *"Those who have divided their system and become sects, you are not with them in anything. Their matter will be with God, then He will inform them of what they had done." (Qur'an 6:159)*

The Message: A Translation of the Glorious Qur'an is the result of a group effort by people who do not belong to any denomination, and, for the first time in many centuries, are simply proud to call themselves "Muslims," submitting to God alone.

> *"And strive for God a genuine striving. He is the One who has chosen you, and He has made no hardship for you in the system, the creed of your father Abraham; He is the One who named you 'those who have submitted' (Muslimeen) from before and in this. So let the messenger be witness over you and you be witness over the people. So hold the Connection and contribute towards purification and hold tight to God, He is your patron. What an excellent Patron, and what an excellent Supporter." (Qur'an 22:78)*

The Message: A Translation of the Glorious Qur'an is unique in the fact that it uses neither footnotes nor comments letting the text speak for itself and delivering to the reader a rendition of the pure message of the Qur'an which is in itself a 'fully detailed' Book.

> *"'Shall I seek other than God as a judge when He has sent down*

to you the Book fully detailed?' Those to whom We have given the Book know it is sent down from your Lord with the truth; so do not be of those who have doubt. And the word of your Lord is completed with truth and justice; there is no changing His words. He is the Hearer, the Knower." (Qur'an 6:114-115)

Finally, no matter how much can be said about this translation or any other, it is imperative to point out that guidance cannot come from any text or human being, rather, true knowledge and guidance can only come from the One who initiated the heavens and the earth. It is God alone that we seek for help.

"You alone we serve, and You alone we seek for help." (Qur'an 1:5)

Welcome to the path of God Alone.

Welcome to *The Message.*

A. METHODOLOGY FOR THIS TRANSLATION

This work is the culmination of years of group research and study into the Qur'an and its nature, and is an attempt to reintroduce people to the words of God with authenticity and objectivity.

The most significant points that the reader needs to be aware of with regards to this translation are as follows:

1. CHAPTER HEADINGS

In reviewing the oldest written records of the Qur'an, it was found that no actual chapter names as used in current printed editions ever existed (e.g. 'the cow, the family of Imran, the women, etc.') and that they were later insertions to ease reference.

Image from chapter 10 of the Sanaa
Qur'an dated around 800 AD.[1] which shows
no chapter name/heading

While this translation does use numeric chapter headings to ease reader reference, the removal of the 'names' has been done to maintain authenticity of the revealed text.

---

1. UNESCO http://portal.unesco.org/ci/photos/showphoto.php/photo/3355

2. THE 'BASMALLAH'

Current printed editions of the Qur'an record the 'Basmallah' (the title which reads: 'In the name of God, the Almighty, the Merciful') at the start of each chapter/sura (with the exception of chapter/sura 9). However, what is peculiar is that the Basmallah is only counted as a verse at the beginning of the Qur'an in 1:1, while all the remaining Basmallah's that prefix other chapters/suras are unnumbered.

Research into this matter by looking at the older texts has been unable to yield the background or rationale into this different treatment for the Basmallah, however, what is apparent is that even with the oldest surviving copies, the Basmallah prefixes nearly all chapters/suras.

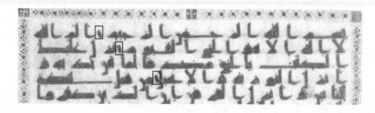

Image from chapter 3 of the Gold Qur'an
dated around 800 AD.[2] which shows the
'Basmallah' followed by a verse stop

This translation has included the Basmallah's in nearly all chapters while following the common convention of not numbering them with the exception of 1:1.

3. HAFS VS. WARSH

One of the least known facts regarding the Qur'an is the existence of slight variations between existing printed versions (up to ten copies exist with minor variations, with the two most prominent being known under the names of 'Hafs' and 'Warsh')[3].

While there is no variation with regards to the bulk text of the Qur'an (i.e. nearly the same number of words, and sequence of words,

---

2. All scans of Gold Qur'an are made available by John Hopkins University (http://goldkoran.mse.jhu.edu/).
3. Al-Qiraat Al-Ashr Al-Mutawatira, by Allawi Mohammed Balfaqeeh (Published by Dar Al-Mahajir)

in all versions), there is a slight difference in some of the spelling of certain words as well as the issue of the location of verse 'stops' which significantly differ from one version to the other.

Although the 'Warsh' style of separating the verses is found to be more in-line with the older surviving texts, the approach of this translation has been to remain with the common 'Hafs' numbering of verses as being the most prevalent among Muslims (Warsh being limited mainly to parts of North Africa).

4. THE MISSING 'BASMALLAH'

Another noticeable aspect of the printed Qur'an is the lack of a 'Basmallah' at the beginning of chapter/sura 9. Information written regarding this subject does not provide the rationale behind such treatment, while some of the discussion revolve around the structure of the Qur'an perhaps being 113 chapters rather than 114 (this is argued on the basis of combining chapters 8 and 9 due to the lack of the Basmallah).

In reviewing the older written texts, it was found that the older texts indeed do not carry a Basmallah for chapter 9, and that the ability to realize the separation between chapters 8 and 9 is achieved through a man-made injection of the chapter detail to highlight the beginning of a new chapter.

Image from chapter 9 of the Gold Qur'an showing inserted chapter detail to mark separation

Although no definitive answer to this issue has been found, it is being pointed out for the sake of transparency that this translation is following the common convention of having 114 chapters, without a Basmallah for chapter 9.

B. The Qur'an Initials

A unique feature of the Qur'an is the presence of 14 initials at the outset of 29 out of the total 114 chapters:

No.	Chapter No.	Quaranic Initials
1	2	A.L.M.
2	3	A.L.M.
3	7	A.L.M.S'.
4	10	A.L.R.
5	11	A.L.R.
6	12	A.L.R.
7	13	A.L.M.R.
8	14	A.L.R.
9	15	A.L.R.
10	19	K.H'.Y.A'.S'.
11	20	T'.H'.
12	26	T'.S.M.
13	27	T'.S.
14	28	T'.S.M.
15	29	A.L.M.
16	30	A.L.M.
17	31	A.L.M.
18	32	A.L.M.
19	36	Y.S.
20	38	S'.
21	40	H.M.
22	41	H.M.
23	42	H.M,A'.S.Q.
24	43	H.M.
25	44	H.M.
26	45	H.M.
27	46	H.M.
28	50	Q.
29	68	N.

The meaning ascribed to these initials has been speculated over the centuries, with the most contemporary being that they are mathematical keys designed to preserve the authenticity of the Qur'an, or that the 14 letters represent the differentiation between the "Muhkam" and "Mutashabih" verses outlined in 3:7.

We leave it to the reader to examine this phenomenon and come to his/her own conclusions.

C. How to Study the Qur'an

If you are one of those who wish to seek knowledge and improve on your understanding of the Qur'an, then we have identified seven key study points which may be put to use by both novices and experts. These points will appear to be quite obvious once you read them, but sometimes, being reminded, benefits us all.

1. Language is Not a Barrier

The first point of contention in the study of the Qur'an typically is language. Many of the people who want to uphold the Qur'an have been informed that the Book of God can only be recited or studied in the original Arabic language, and that any translation will not give the proper meaning. The flip-side is that these same "experts" will then tell the Arabic speakers that the Qur'an is "too difficult" for them to understand and that they should leave its understanding to the scholars!

Of course, the Qur'an itself says that language is not a barrier to its understanding as God is the One who is making it understood to people who open their hearts to Him and become purified.

> *"And had We made it a Qur'an that was non-Arabic, they would have said: 'If only its verses were made clear!' Non-Arabic or Arabic, say: 'For those who believe, it is a guide and healing. As for those who disbelieve, there is deafness in their ears, and they are blind to it. These will be called from a place far away.'" (Qur'an 41:44)*

> *"It is an honorable Qur'an. In a protected Book. None can grasp it except those purified. A revelation from the Lord of the worlds." (Qur'an 56:77-80)*

2. LOOK AT THE FULL VERSE

Quoting the Qur'an out of context is by far the biggest error that even seasoned students continue to fall into. Such method can be used to justify any desire or any view no matter how ungodly it may appear.

To take an example, a favorite quote which is repeated by many unknowledgeable groups is that the Qur'an promotes killing and violence as evidenced by the verse:

> *"And you may kill them wherever you engage them..." (Qur'an 2:191).*

However, once we use the method of *full context*, then a totally different picture appears regarding the same issue:

> *"And you may kill them wherever you engage them, and expel them from where they expelled you, and know that persecution is worse than being killed. And do not fight them at the restricted Temple unless they fight you in it; if they fight you then kill them, thus is the recompense of the rejecters." (Qur'an 2:191)*

Here we have a case of warfare being engaged in, and the people who were driven out being allowed to fight and reclaim their land/territory... A far cry from the sporadic killing that is implied when quoting out of context.

3. THE QUR'AN EXPLAINS ITSELF

The Arabic language, as with any other language, has undergone some subtle changes over the centuries where words may not still retain their original meanings, and where the common spoken and written form have diverted to become the standard. When faced with a choice where there appears to be a discrepancy in a given meaning, let the other verses of the Qur'an, where such word is used, be your guide:

> [Yusuf Ali Translation]: *"Those who follow the messenger, the unlettered (Ummy) Prophet, whom they find mentioned in their own (scriptures),- in the law and the Gospel;- for he commands them what is just and forbids them what is evil; he allows them as lawful what is good (and pure) and prohibits them from what is bad (and impure); He releases them from their heavy burdens and from the yokes that are upon them..." (Qur'an 7:157)*

The word 'Ummy' in today's Arabic dictionaries and common use refers to a person who: 'cannot read or write.' Therefore, when reading the Qur'an, the understanding given is that the Prophet was an illiterate man who delivered this magnificent text from inspiration, and had it recorded by scribes! However, when we look at the use of the word in other verses of the Qur'an, we find that its use gives the meaning of: 'Gentiles,' who had no knowledge of any previous scriptures:

"If they debate with you, then say: "I have submitted myself to God, as well as those who follow me." And say to those who have received the Book and the gentiles (Ummyeen): *"Have you submitted?" If they have submitted then they are guided, and if they turn away, then you are only to deliver, and God is Seer over the servants." (Qur'an 3:20)*

Another word that has had its meaning diverted over time is the name of God: 'Al-Rahman,' which has come to indicate 'Most Gracious/All Merciful/Beneficent.' This name is thought to be a synonym of the other name widely used in the Qur'an 'Al-Raheem', however, we know from the Qur'an that the Arab speakers of the time did not recognize this name, let alone its meaning:'

"And if they are told: "Prostrate to (Al-Rahman)." *They say: "And what is* (Al-Rahman)? *Shall we prostrate to what you order us?" And it increases their aversion. (Qur'an 25:60)*

The word use of the Qur'an gives us a completely different meaning for this name, indicating that it is a name of power and might, used to instil fear in God's enemies—not mercy and compassion—best translated as 'The Almighty':

"So she took a veil to separate her from them, so We sent Our Spirit to her, and he took on the shape of a mortal in all similarity. She said: "I seek refuge with the Almighty (Al-Rahman) *from you if you are righteous." (Qur'an 19:17-18)*

"My father, do not serve the devil. For the devil was ever disobedient to the Almighty (Al-Rahman). *My father, I fear that a retribution will inflict you from the Almighty* (Al-Rahman) *and that you will become an ally to the devil." (Qur'an 19:44-45)*

4. Be Aware of the Context

Some Arabic words, like in English, can have slightly different meanings depending on the context they are placed in. One such example is the word 'Daraba' which has a natural meaning of *putting forth* or *positioning* as can be seen in the verses below:

"Did you not note how God puts forth (Daraba) *the example that a good word is like a good tree, whose root is firm and whose branches are in the sky." (Qur'an 14:24)*

"For the poor who face hardship in the cause of God, they cannot go forth (Darban) *in the land; the ignorant ones think they are rich from their modesty; you know them by their features, they do not ask the people repeatedly. And what you spend out of goodness, God is fully aware of it." (Qur'an 2:273)*

"Shall We withdraw (NaDrib) *the reminder from you, because you are a transgressing people?" (Qur'an 43:5)*

*"O you who believe, if you go forth (*Darabtum*) in the cause of God, you shall investigate carefully. And do not say to those who greet you with peace: "You are not a believer!" You are seeking the vanity of this world; but with God are many riches. That is how you were before, but God favored you, so investigate carefully. God is expert over what you do." (Qur'an 4:94)*

However, there are certain cases where this word can give the meaning of *'strike/beat'* as the act of striking involves the hand being put forth:

*"So how will it be when their lives are terminated by the angels, while striking (*Yadriboona*) their faces and their backs?" (Qur'an 47:27)*

While this may not appear as a big issue, not looking at the context can have serious consequences as we can see in the meaning that has ascribed to the word 'Daraba' by the majority of translators for verse 4:34:

[Yusuf Ali Translation]: *Men are the protectors and maintainers of women, because Allah has given the one more (strength) than the other, and because they support them from their means. Therefore the righteous women are devoutly obedient, and guard in (the husband's)*

x

absence what Allah would have them guard. As to those women on whose part ye fear disloyalty and ill-conduct , admonish them (first), (Next), refuse to share their beds, (And last) beat them – "Idribuhun" (lightly); but if they return to obedience, seek not against them Means (of annoyance): For Allah is Most High, great (above you all)." (Qur'an 4:34)

As a result of the choice of words, we have generations of men who believe that it is their God given right to '*beat*' their wives into obedience!

The correct approach would have been to understand the context of the verse (in this case, it deals with the subject of a woman who rebels against her duties and/or her husband "Nushooz⁴") and thus the word "Idribuhun" is one of the three suggested steps to deal with the situation (the others steps being to talk it out, and to abstain from sexual contact).

"The men are to support the women with what God has bestowed upon them over one another and for what they spend of their money. The upright females are dutiful; keeping private the personal matters for what God keeps watch over. As for those females from whom you fear rebellion (Nushooz), then you shall advise them, and abandon them in the bedchambers, and withdraw from them (Idribuhun); if they obey you, then do not seek a way over them; God is Most High, Great." (Qur'an 4:34)

As such, which meaning of "Idribuhun" would make the most sense: letting the wife become isolated and temporarily withdrawing from her to let her reflect on her actions, or, beating an already aggravated person into submission and inflaming an already tense situation?

The answer as always is to follow the *best* meaning derived...

"The ones who listen to what is being said, and then follow the best of it. These are the ones whom God has guided, and these are the ones who possess intelligence." (Qur'an 39:18)

5. ARRANGE SIMILAR TOPIC VERSES TOGETHER

A study point of crucial importance is to arrange the verses of the Qur'an by order of subject/topic to seek its meaning.

---

4. Nushooz is correctly understood by translators as being 'ill-conduct/rebellion' as can be seen in its use in 4:34, and it can also apply to a man as seen in 4:128.

Looking to the example of 'divorce,' we find that the subject is scattered in three different chapters (chapter 2, chapter 33, and chapter 65) which, when placed together, provide a more extensive picture of the proceedings and laws regarding divorce...

"And those divorced shall wait for three menstruation periods; and it is not permissible for them to conceal what God has created in their wombs, if they believe in God and the Last Day. And their husbands have a greater right to return them in this, if they wish to reconcile. And for them are rights similar to those owed by them. And the men will have a degree over them. And God is Noble, Wise." (Qur'an 2:228)

"The divorce may occur twice. So, either they remain together equitably, or part ways with goodness. And it is not permissible for you to take back anything you have given them unless you fear that they will not uphold the boundaries of God. So if you fear that they will not uphold the boundaries of God, then there is no sin upon them for what is given back. These are the boundaries of God so do not transgress them. And whoever shall transgress the boundaries of God, then these are the wicked." (Qur'an 2:229)

"If he then divorces her: she will not be permissible for him until after she has married a different husband. If he were to divorce her; then there is no sin that they come back together if they think they will uphold the boundaries of God. These are the boundaries of God, He clarifies them for a people who know." (Qur'an 2:230)

"And if you have divorced the women, and they have reached their required interim period, then either you remain together equitably, or part ways equitably. And do not reconcile with them so you can harm them out of animosity; whoever does so is doing wrong to his soul; and do not take the revelations of God as mockery. And remember the blessings of God upon you, and what was sent down to you of the Book and the wisdom, He warns you with it. And be aware of God and know that God is knowledgeable of all things." (Qur'an 2:231)

"And if you divorce the women, and they reach their required interim period, then do not make difficulty for them if they wish to remarry their husbands if they have amicably agreed among themselves out of what is best. This is to remind any of you who believe in God and the Last Day, this is better for you and purer; and God knows while you do not know." (Qur'an 2:232)

"O you who believe, if you marry the believing females, then divorce them before having intercourse with them, then there is no interim required of them. You shall compensate them, and let them go in an amicable manner." (Qur'an 33:49)

"O prophet, if any of you divorce the women, then divorce them while ensuring their required interim is fulfilled, and keep count of the interim. You shall reverence God your Lord, and do not evict them from their homes, nor should they leave, unless they commit an evident immorality. And these are the boundaries of God. And anyone who transgresses the boundaries of God has wronged his soul. You never know; perhaps God will make something come out of this." (Qur'an 65:1)

"Then, once the interim is fulfilled, either you remain together equitably, or part ways equitably and have it witnessed by two just people from among you; and give the testimony for God. This is to enlighten those who believe in God and the Last Day. And whoever reverences God, He will create a solution for him." (Qur'an 65:2)

"And He will provide for him whence he never expected. Anyone who puts his trust in God, then He suffices him. The commands of God will be done. God has decreed for everything its fate." (Qur'an 65:3)

"As for those who have reached menopause from your women, if you have any doubts, their interim shall be three months. As for those whose menstruation has ceased, and are already pregnant, their interim is until they give birth. And anyone who reverences God, He makes his matters easy for him." (Qur'an 65:4)

"You shall let them reside in the dwelling you were in when you were together, and do not coerce them to make them leave. And if they are pregnant, you shall spend on them until they give birth. Then, if they nurse the infant, you shall give them their due payment. And you shall maintain the amicable relations between you. If you disagree, then another woman may nurse the child." (Qur'an 65:6)

Here is the summary when arranging all similar verses:

- If the couple insist on divorce, then, from the declaration of divorce, the couple must wait for the interim period. (65:1)
- In the interim period, the wife remains in her husband's home. (65:1)

- The interim period required is three menstruation periods. The interim for women who do not menstruate or have reached menopause is three months. The interim for pregnant women is until they deliver. There is no interim if the couple has never had intercourse with each other. (2:228, 65:4, 33:49)
- If the couple reconcile, then divorce may be retracted and cancelled at any point during the interim period. (2:229)
- If the couple still wishes to follow through with the divorce after the end of the interim period, then two witnesses are required to complete the process. (65:2)
- If this is the third divorce, then the couple may not remarry each other unless the woman marries another man and then divorces from him. (2:230)

As shown in the example above, the simple step of examining all related verses gives a very detailed account that can be applied in any civil society.

6. LOOK TO EXAMPLES IN THE QUR'AN

Once a meaning is derived, the final accuracy test is to compare such a meaning to the stories related in the Qur'an if such a story can be found. The reason being is that the stories related in the Qur'an are 'live' examples for us to learn from and compare situations.

> "We narrate to you the best stories through what We have inspired to you in this Qur'an; and before it you were of those who were unaware." (Qur'an 12:3)

One example for using this method is in dealing with the issue of 'theft'.

> [Yusuf Ali Translation]: As to the thief, Male or female, cut off (Iqta) his or her hands: a punishment by way of example, from Allah, for their crime: and Allah is Exalted in power. (Qur'an 5:38)

If we had based our opinion solely on verse 5:38 as shown above, then our understanding would be that the hands of thieves are to be severed completely. If this is indeed what God has commanded, then we have no option but to hear and obey.

However, in this particular case, we find that a small check against the real life example given in the Qur'an of Joseph and his brothers and how they dealt with the issue of theft leads us to a completely different conclusion:

> *"They said: 'By God, you know we have not come to cause corruption in the land, and we are not thieves!' They said: 'What shall be the punishment, if you are liars?' They said: 'The punishment is that he in whose saddlebag it is found will himself serve as the punishment. It is so that we punish the wicked.'" (Qur'an 12:73-75)*

The law of God that Joseph applied against his brother in the matter of theft did not lead to any amputation of the hand or any other mindless act of violence. It did, however, lead to the brother being made to remain behind and work as a penalty against that which he was accused of stealing.

Looking back at verse 5:38 with the correct translation we see a completely different understanding from that found by Yusuf Ali:

> *"And the male thief, and the female thief, you shall cut their resources— as a penalty for what they have earned—to be made an example of from God. God is Noble, Wise." (Qur'an 5:38)*

The correct understanding of the verse not only matches the live example given in the Qur'an, but it also comes in-line with the other checks and balances that God has given such as the punishment not exceeding the crime (16:126).

7. BE PATIENT AND SEEK THE HELP OF GOD

Even with all the skill and knowledge we may possess, the study of the Qur'an will always be lacking if God is not sought for help and assistance. After all, He is the ultimate teacher in all things, especially the Qur'an.

> *"When you read the Qur'an, you shall seek refuge with God from the outcast devil. He has no authority over those who believe, and who put their trust in their Lord. His authority is over those who follow him, and set him up as a partner." (Qur'an 16:98-100)*

Also, do not be scared or confused if your findings or understandings do not conform to what others have said or taught for years or centuries… Truth does not need to conform to the majority to be truth.

> *"And if you obey most of those on the earth they will lead you away*

from the path of God; that is because they follow conjecture, and that is because they only guess." (Qur'an 6:116)

Finally, remember we are here on this planet to serve God and walk in His path, and not to serve our own agendas and our own egos:

"You alone we serve, and You alone we seek for help." (Qur'an 1:5)

CONCLUSION

You now should have the necessary tools to educate yourself with the Qur'an by holding the best methods for deriving its meanings and laws...Try to make it a habit of seeking the answers for yourself through the guidance of God... Do not be quick to ask 'others' what God says regarding this or that matter, but try to establish the bond with God directly yourself...It is only through this self-awareness that people can have a defence mechanism against the misinformation and ignorance that has been taught for many generations.

Learn to let God be the focus of your actions and your life, and let His words be your guide to success in this life and the next..What will count is not how much wealth we accumulate or how powerful we become, but how we use our wealth to help others and how we use our power and position to help mankind towards purification.

"O you who believe, do not be distracted by your money and your children from the remembrance of God. And those who do this, then they are the losers. And give from that which We have provided to you, before death comes to one of you, then he says: 'My Lord, if only You could delay this for a short while, I would then be charitable and join the righteous!' And God will not delay any soul if its time has come. And God is Expert in all that you do. " (Qur'an 63:9-11)

We are certain that upon reading and studying the Qur'an you will find more than what you expected. For, although it is 'finite' in its words and pages, it is 'infinite' in its knowledge and lessons.

The Monotheist Group

www.Free-Minds.Org

www.ProgressiveMuslims.Org

CHAPTER 1

1:1   In the name of God, the Almighty, the Merciful.

1:2   Praise be to God, Lord of the worlds.

1:3   The Almighty, the Merciful.

1:4   Sovereign of the Day of Judgment.

1:5   You alone we serve, and You alone we seek for help.

1:6   Guide us to the straight path.

1:7   The path of those You have graced, not of those who have incurred the wrath, nor the misguided.

CHAPTER 2

2:0   In the name of God, the Almighty, the Merciful.

2:1   ALM.

2:2   That is the book, which is without doubt—a guide for the righteous.

2:3   The ones who believe in the unseen, and hold the Connection, and from Our provisions to them they spend.

2:4   And the ones who believe in what was sent down to you, and what was sent down before you, and regarding the Hereafter they are certain.

2:5   Those are the ones guided by their Lord, and those are the successful ones.

2:6   As for those who reject, whether you warn them or do not warn them, they will not believe.

2:7   God has sealed their hearts and their ears, and over their eyes are covers. They will incur a great retribution.

2:8   And from the people are those who say: "We believe in God and in the Last Day," but they are not believers.

2:9   They seek to deceive God and those who believe, but they only deceive themselves without noticing.

2:10   In their hearts is a disease, so God increases their disease, and they will have a painful retribution for what they have denied.

2:11   And if they are told: "Do not make corruption in the land," they say: "But we are reformers!"

2:12   No, they are the corrupters, but they do not perceive.

2:13   And if they are told: "Believe, as the people have believed," they say: "Shall we believe like the foolish have believed?" No, they are the foolish but they do not know.

2:14   And if they come across those who have believed, they say: "We believe," and when they are alone with their devils they say: "We are with you, we were only mocking."

2:15   God mocks them, and leaves them in their transgression, blundering.

2:16   These are the ones who have purchased straying with guidance; their trade did not profit them, nor were they guided.

2:17   Their example is like the one who lights a fire, so when it illuminates what is around him, God takes away his light and leaves him in the darkness not seeing.

2:18   Deaf, dumb, and blind, they will not return.

2:19   Or like a storm from the sky, in it is darkness and thunder and lightning. They place their fingers in their ears from the thunderbolts for fear of death; and God is aware of the rejecters.

2:20   The lightning nearly snatches their sight, whenever it lights the path they walk in it, and when it becomes dark for them they stand. Had God willed, He would have taken their hearing and their sight; God is capable of all things.

2:21   O people, serve your Lord who has created you and those before you that you may be righteous.

2:22   The One who has made the earth a resting place, and the sky a shelter, and He sent down from the sky water with which He brought out fruits as a gift to you. So do not set up any equals with God while you know.

2:23   And if you are in doubt as to what We have sent down to Our servant, then bring a chapter like this, and call upon your witnesses other than God if you are truthful.

2:24   And if you cannot do this; and you will not be able to do this;

then beware the Fire whose fuel is people and rocks, it has been prepared for the rejecters.

2:25   And give good news to those who believe and do good works that they will have estates with rivers flowing beneath them. Every time they receive a provision of its fruit, they say: "This is what we have been provisioned before," and they are given its likeness. And there they will have pure mates, and in it they will abide.

2:26   God does not shy away from putting forth the example of a mosquito, or anything above it. As for those who believe, they know that it is the truth from their Lord. As for the rejecters, they say: "What does God intend with this example?" He strays many by it, and He guides many by it; but He only strays by it the wicked.

2:27   The ones who break the pledge to God after making its covenant, and they sever what God had ordered to be delivered, and they make corruption on the earth; these are the losers.

2:28   How can you reject God when you were dead and He brought you to life? Then He makes you die, then He brings you to life, then to Him you return.

2:29   He is the One who has created for you all that is on the earth, then He attended to the heaven and has made it seven heavens, and He is aware of all things.

2:30   And your Lord said to the angels: "I am placing a successor on the earth." They said: "Will You place in it he who would make corruption in it, and spill blood; while we glorify Your praise, and exalt to You?" He said: "I know what you do not know."

2:31   And He taught Adam the names of all things, then He displayed them to the angels and said: "Inform Me of the names of these if you are truthful."

2:32   They said: "Glory to You, we have no knowledge except that which You have taught us, You are the Knowledgeable, the Wise."

2:33   He said: "O Adam, inform them of their names," so when he informed them of their names, He said: "Did I not tell you that I know the unseen of the heavens and the earth, and that I know what you reveal and what you are hiding?"

2:34   And We said to the angels: "Yield to Adam," so they yielded except for Satan, he refused and became arrogant, and became of the rejecters.

3

2:35 And We said: "O Adam, reside you and your mate in the paradise, and eat from it bountifully as you both wish, and do not come near this tree, else you will be of those who have wronged."

2:36 So, the devil caused them to slip from it, and he brought them out from what they were in, and We said: "Descend; for you are enemies to one another; and on the earth you will have residence and provisions until the appointed time."

2:37 Adam then received words from his Lord, so He forgave him; He is the Forgiver, the Merciful.

2:38 We said: "Descend from it all of you, so when the guidance comes from Me, then whoever follows My guidance, they will have nothing to fear, nor will they grieve."

2:39 And those who disbelieve and deny Our revelations, they are the dwellers of Hell, in it they will abide.

2:40 O Children of Israel, remember My favor that I had bestowed upon you, and fulfill your pledge to Me that I may fulfill My pledge to you, and reverence Me alone.

2:41 And believe in what I have sent down, affirming what is with you, and do not be the first to disbelieve in it! And do not purchase with My revelations a cheap gain, and of Me you shall be aware.

2:42 And do not confound the truth with falsehood, nor keep the truth secret while you know.

2:43 And hold the Connection, and contribute towards purification, and kneel with those who kneel.

2:44 Do you exhort the people to do good, but forget yourselves, while you are reciting the Book? Do you not comprehend?

2:45 And seek help through patience and through the Connection. It is a difficult thing, but not so for the humble.

2:46 The ones who conceive that they will meet their Lord and that to Him they will return.

2:47 O Children of Israel, remember My favor that I had bestowed upon you, and that I had preferred you over all the worlds.

2:48 And beware of a Day when no soul can avail another soul, nor will any intercession be accepted from it, nor will any ransom be taken, nor will they have supporters.

2:49 And We saved you from the people of Pharaoh, they were afflicting you with the worst punishment; they used to slaughter your children, and rape your women. In that was a great test from your Lord.

2:50 And We parted the sea for you, thus We saved you and drowned the people of Pharaoh while you were watching.

2:51 And We appointed a meeting time for Moses of forty nights, but then you took the calf after him while you were wicked.

2:52 Then We pardoned you after that, perhaps you would be thankful.

2:53 And We gave Moses the Book and the Criterion, perhaps you would be guided.

2:54 And Moses said to his people: "O my people, you have wronged yourselves by taking the calf, so repent to your Maker, and slay yourselves; that is better for you with your Maker, so He would forgive you. He is the Forgiving, the Merciful."

2:55 And you said: "O Moses, we will not believe you until we see God openly!" So the thunderbolt took you while you were still staring.

2:56 Then We revived you after your death that you may be thankful.

2:57 And We shaded you with clouds, and sent down to you manna and quails: "Eat from the goodness of the provisions We have provided you." They did not wrong Us, but it was their souls that they wronged.

2:58 And We said: "Enter this town, and eat from it as you wish bountifully. And enter the passageway by crouching, and say: "Our load is removed," so that your wrongdoings will be forgiven, and We will increase for the good doers."

2:59 But the wicked altered what was said to them to a different saying, thus We sent down upon the wicked an affliction from the heavens for what wickedness they were in.

2:60 And Moses was seeking water for his people, so We said: "Strike the rock with your staff." Thus twelve springs exploded out of it; each people then knew from where to drink. "Eat and drink from the provisions of God, and do not roam the earth as corrupters."

2:61 And you said: "O Moses, we will not be patient to one type of food, so call for us your Lord that He may bring forth what the earth grows of its beans, cucumbers, garlic, lentils, and onions."

He said: "Would you trade that which is lowly with that which is good?" Descend Egypt, you will have in it what you have asked for. And they were stricken with humiliation and disgrace, and they remained under the wrath of God for they were disbelieving in the revelations of God, and killing the prophets without right; this is for what they have disobeyed and transgressed.

2:62　Surely those who believe; and those who are Jewish, and the Nazarenes, and the Sabians, whoever of them believes in God and the Last Day and does good works; they will have their recompense with their Lord, and there is no fear upon them, nor will they grieve.

2:63　And We took your covenant, and raised the mount above you: "Take what We have given you with strength, and remember what is in it that you may be righteous."

2:64　Then you turned away after this. And had it not been for the grace of God upon you and His mercy, you would have been of the losers.

2:65　You have come to know who it was among you that transgressed the Sabbath, We said to them: "Be despicable apes!"

2:66　So it was that We made it burdensome for what had happened in it and also afterwards, and as a reminder to the righteous.

2:67　And Moses said to his people: "God orders you to slaughter a heifer." They said: "Do you mock us?" He said: "I seek refuge with God that I not be of the ignorant ones."

2:68　They said: "Call upon your Lord for us that He may clarify which it is." He said: "He says it is a heifer neither too old nor too young, an age between that. So now do as you are commanded."

2:69　They said: "Call upon your Lord for us that He may clarify what color it is." He said: "He says it is a yellow heifer with a strong color, pleasing to those who see it."

2:70　They said: "Call upon your Lord for us that He may clarify which one it is, for the heifers all look alike to us and we will, God willing, be guided."

2:71　He said: "He says it is a heifer which was never subjugated to plough the land, or water the crops, without any patch." They said: "Now you have come with the truth." And they slaughtered it, though they had nearly not done so.

2:72   And you had murdered a person, then disputed in the matter; God was to bring out what you were keeping secret.

2:73   We said: "Strike him with part of it." It is thus that God brings the dead to life, and He shows you His signs that you may comprehend.

2:74   Then your hearts became hardened after that, they became like rocks or even harder; but even from the rocks there are rivers that burst forth, and from them are those that crack so that the water comes forth, and from them are what descends from concern towards God; and God is not unaware of what you do.

2:75   Did you expect that they would believe with you, when a group of them had heard the words of God then altered them knowingly after having understood?

2:76   And when they come across those who believe, they say: "We believe!" And when they are alone with each other they say: "Why do you inform them of what God has said to us? Then they would use it in argument against us at your Lord. Do you not comprehend?"

2:77   Do they not know that God knows what they conceal and what they declare?

2:78   And among them are gentiles who do not know the Book except by hearsay, and they only conjecture.

2:79   So woe to those who write the Book with their hands then say: "This is from God," so that they can purchase with it a cheap price! Woe to them for what their hands have written and woe to them for what they gained.

2:80   And they said: "The Fire will not touch us except for a number of days." Say: "Have you taken a pledge with God? If so, then God will not break His pledge. Or do you say about God what you do not know?"

2:81   Indeed, whoever gains a sin, and is surrounded by his mistakes; those are the people of the Fire, in it they will abide.

2:82   And those who believe and do good works, they are the people of Paradise, in it they will abide.

2:83   And We took the covenant of the Children of Israel: "You shall not serve except God, and do good to your parents, and regard the relatives, and the orphans, and the needy, and say kind things to the people, and hold the Connection, and contribute towards purification." But then you turned away, except for a few of you; you were objecting.

2:84 And We have taken a covenant with you: "You shall not spill the blood of each other, nor drive each other out from your homes." And you agreed to this while bearing witness.

2:85 But then, here you are slaying yourselves, and driving out a group of you from their homes; you act towards them with sin and animosity. And if they come to you as prisoners, you demand ransom for them, while it was forbidden for you to drive them out! Do you believe in part of the Book and disbelieve in part? The punishment for those among you who do so is humiliation in this worldly life, and on the Day of Resurrection they will be delivered to the most severe retribution. God is not unaware of what you do.

2:86 These are the ones who have purchased this worldly life instead of the Hereafter. The retribution will not be reduced for them, nor will they be supported.

2:87 And We gave Moses the Book, and after him We sent the messengers. And We gave Jesus, son of Mary, the clear proofs, and We supported him with the Holy Spirit. Is it that every time a messenger comes to you with what your souls do not desire, you become arrogant? A group of them you deny, and a group of them you kill!

2:88 And they said: "Our hearts are sealed!" No, it is God who has cursed them for their rejection, for very little do they believe.

2:89 And when a Book came to them from God, affirming what is with them; while before that they were mocking those who rejected; so when what they knew came to them, they rejected it! The curse of God be upon the rejecters.

2:90 Miserable indeed is what they purchase with their souls, that they disbelieve in what God has sent down as a resentment that God would send down from His grace to whom He pleases of His servants; thus they have incurred wrath upon wrath. And the rejecters will have a humiliating retribution.

2:91 And if it is said to them: "Believe in what God has sent down;" they say: "We believe only in what was sent down to us," and they reject what came after it, while it is the truth affirming what is with them. Say: "Why then did you kill the prophets of God if you were believers?"

2:92   And Moses had come to you with clear proofs, then you took the calf after him; you were wicked!

2:93   And We took your covenant, and raised the mount above you: "Take what We have given you with strength, and listen." They said: "We hear and disobey!" And they had consumed the calf inside their hearts by their disbelief. Say: "Miserable indeed is what your belief orders of you if you are believers!"

2:94   Say: "If the abode of the Hereafter has been set exclusively for you with God, to the exception of all other people, then you should wish for death if you are truthful!"

2:95   They will never wish for it because of what their hands have delivered; and God is aware of the wicked.

2:96   And you will find them the most obsessive people regarding longevity; even more than the polytheists; each one of them wishes that he could live a thousand years. It will not change for him the retribution even if he lived so long, God is watchful over what you do.

2:97   Say: "Whoever is an enemy to Gabriel, then know that he has sent it down into your heart with the permission of God, affirming what is with him, and a guide and good news for the believers."

2:98   "Whoever is an enemy to God and His angels, and His messengers, and Gabriel, and Michael, then so God is the enemy to the disbelievers."

2:99   We have sent down to you clear revelations; only the wicked would disbelieve in them.

2:100   Is it that each time they make a pledge, a group of them breaks it? Alas, most of them do not believe.

2:101   And when a messenger came to them from God, affirming what was with them, a group of those who had already received the Book placed the Book of God behind their backs as if they did not know.

2:102   And they followed what the devils recited regarding the kingship of Solomon. Solomon did not reject, but it was the devils who rejected; teaching people magic and what was sent down on the two angels in Babylon: Haroot and Maroot. Though these two did not teach anyone until they said: "We are but a trial, so do not renounce!" Thus they learn from them what can separate between a person and his mate; but they cannot harm anyone except with the permission of God. And they learn what harms them and does not benefit them, and they have known that he who purchases such has no place in the Hereafter. Miserable indeed is what they purchased with their souls if only they knew!

2:103 And had they believed and been righteous, it would have brought them a reward from God which is far better if only they knew!

2:104 O you who believe, do not say: "Shepherd us," but say: "Be patient with us," and listen. For the rejecters is a painful retribution.

2:105 Neither do those who have rejected from among the people of the Book, nor from among the polytheists, wish that any good comes down to you from your Lord. But God chooses with His mercy whom He wishes; and from God is the greatest grace.

2:106 We do not duplicate a sign, or make it forgotten, unless We bring one which is like it or even greater. Did you not know that God is capable of all things?

2:107 Did you not know that to God is the kingship of the heavens and the earth, and that you do not have besides God any guardian or supporter?

2:108 Or do you want to ask your messenger as Moses was asked before? Whoever replaces belief with rejection, he has indeed strayed from the right path.

2:109 Many of the people of the Book have wished that they could return you to being rejecters after your believing, out of envy from their souls after the truth was made clear to them. You shall forgive them and overlook until God brings His will. God is capable of all things.

2:110 And hold the Connection, and contribute towards purification; and what you bring forth of good for your souls you will find it with God. God is watching what you do.

2:111 And they said: "None shall enter Paradise except those who are Jewish or Nazarenes;" this is what they wish! Say: "Bring forth your proof if you are truthful."

2:112 No; whoever submits himself to God, while doing good, he will have his recompense with his Lord. There will be no fear over them, nor will they grieve.

2:113 And the Jews say: "The Nazarenes have no basis," and the Nazarenes say: "The Jews have no basis," while they are both reciting the Book! Similarly, those who do not know have said the same thing. God will judge between them on the Day of Resurrection in what they dispute.

2:114 And who are more wicked than those who prevent the temples of God that His name be mentioned in them; and they seek their destruction? They will not be able to enter them except in fear; they will have humiliation in this world and in the Hereafter a painful retribution.

2:115 And to God belongs the east and the west, so wherever you turn, there is the face of God. God is Encompassing, Knowledgeable.

2:116 And they said: "God has taken a son!" Be He glorified. To Him is all that is in the heavens and the earth, all are dutiful to Him.

2:117 Initiator of the heavens and the earth, when He decrees a command, He merely says to it: 'Be,' and it is.

2:118 And those who do not know said: "If only God would speak to us, or a sign would come to us." It is the same thing that the people before them have said, their hearts are so similar! We have clarified the signs for a people who comprehend.

2:119 We have sent you with the truth as a bearer of good news and a warner. You will not be questioned about the people of Hell.

2:120 Neither the Jews nor the Nazarenes will be pleased with you until you follow their creed. Say: "The guidance is the guidance of God." And if you follow their desires after the knowledge that has come to you, then there is none who can help or protect you against God.

2:121 Those to whom We gave the Book, they recite it as it truthfully deserves to be recited; they believe in it. As for those who disbelieve in it, they are the losers.

2:122 O Children of Israel, remember My favor that I had bestowed upon you, and that I had preferred you over all the worlds.

2:123 And beware of a Day when no soul can avail another soul, nor will any amendment be accepted from it, nor will any intercession help it; they will not be supported.

2:124 And it was so, that Abram was tested by commands from his Lord, which he fulfilled. He said: "I will make you a leader for

11

the people." He said: "And also from my progeny?" He said: "My pledge will not encompass the wicked."

2:125 And it was so, that We have made the House to be a model for the people and a place of safety. And you shall take the station of Abram as an orientation for connecting. And We made a pledge to Abram and Ishmael: "You shall purify My House for those who visit, and those who are devoted, and the kneeling, the prostrating."

2:126 And it was so, that Abram said: "My Lord, make this a land of peace, and provide for its inhabitants of the fruits for whoever believes in God and the Last Day." He said: "As for he who rejects, I will let him enjoy for a while, then I will force him to the retribution of the Fire. What a miserable destiny!"

2:127 And it was so, that Abram was raising the foundations for the House, and Ishmael: "Our Lord accept this from us, You are the Hearer, the Knowledgeable."

2:128 "Our Lord, and let us submit to You and from our progeny a nation submitting to You, and show us our rites, and forgive us; You are the Forgiver, the Merciful."

2:129 "Our Lord, and send among them a messenger from among themselves, that he may recite to them Your revelations and teach them the Book and the wisdom, and purify them. You are the Noble, the Wise."

2:130 And who would abandon the creed of Abram except one who fools himself? We have selected him in this world, and in the Hereafter he is of the righteous.

2:131 When his Lord said to him: "Submit," he said: "I submit to the Lord of the worlds."

2:132 And Abram enjoined his sons and Jacob: "O my sons, God has selected the system for you, so do not die except as ones who have submitted."

2:133 Or were you present when death came to Jacob and he said to his sons: "Who shall you serve from after me?" They said: "Your god, and the god of your fathers Abram, and Ishmael, and Isaac; One god and to Him we submit."

2:134 That is a nation that has passed away; to them is what they have earned, and to you is what you have earned; and you will not be asked regarding what they did.

2:135 And they said: "Be Jewish or Nazarenes so that you may be guided!" Say: "No, rather the creed of Abram, monotheism; for he was not of the polytheists."

2:136 Say: "We believe in God and in what was sent down to us and what was sent down to Abram, and Ishmael, and Isaac, and Jacob, and the Patriarchs, and what was given to Moses and Jesus, and what was given to the prophets from their Lord; we do not make a distinction between any of them and to Him we submit."

2:137 So, if they believe exactly as you have believed, then they are guided; but if they turn away, then they are in opposition and God will suffice you against them, and He is the Hearer, the Knower.

2:138 Such is the coloring of God, and who is better than God in coloring? And to Him we are in service.

2:139 Say: "Do you debate with us regarding God? He is our Lord and your Lord, and we have our works and you have your works, and to Him we are believers."

2:140 "Or do you say that Abram and Ishmael and Isaac and Jacob and the Patriarchs were Jewish or Nazarenes?" Say: "Are you more knowledgeable or is God?" Who is more wicked than the one who conceals a testimony with him from God? God is not unaware of what you do.

2:141 That is a nation that has passed away; to them is what they have earned, and to you is what you have earned; and you will not be asked regarding what they did.

2:142 The foolish from among the people will say: "What has turned them away from the focal point that they were on?" Say: "To God is the east and the west, He guides whomsoever He wishes to a straight path."

2:143 And as such, We have made you a balanced nation so that you may be witness over the people, and that the messenger may be witness over you. And We did not make the focal point that you came on except that We may know who is following the messenger from those who will turn on their heels. It was a great thing indeed except for those whom God had guided; God was not to waste your belief. God is Merciful and Compassionate over the people.

2:144 We see the shifting of your face in the heaven; We will set for you a focal point that will be pleasing to you: "You shall set your face towards the restricted Temple; and wherever you may be, you shall all set your faces towards it." Those who have been given the Book know it is the truth from their Lord. And God is not unaware of what you do.

2:145 And if you come to those who have been given the Book with every sign they will not follow your focal point, nor will you follow their focal point, nor will some of them even follow each others focal point. And if you were to follow their desires after the knowledge that has come to you, then you would be one of the wicked.

2:146 Those to whom We have given the Book know it as they know their own children; and a group of them hides the truth while they know.

2:147 The truth is from your Lord, so do not be one of those who doubt.

2:148 And to each is a direction that he will take, so you shall race towards good deeds. Wherever you may be, God will bring you all together. God is capable of all things.

2:149 And from wherever you go out, you shall set your face towards the restricted Temple; it is the truth from your Lord; and God is not unaware of what you do.

2:150 And from wherever you go out, you shall set your face towards the restricted Temple. And wherever you may be, you shall all set your faces towards it; that the people will have no room for debate with you, except those of them who are wicked. You shall not be concerned by them, but be concerned by Me; so that I may complete My blessings upon you and that you may be guided.

2:151 As We have sent a messenger to you from among yourselves to recite Our revelations to you, and purify you, and teach you the Book and the wisdom, and teach you what you did not know.

2:152 So remember Me that I may remember you, and be thankful to Me and do not disbelieve.

2:153 O you who believe, seek help through patience and through the Connection, God is with the patient ones.

2:154 And do not say of those who are killed in the cause of God that they are dead; no, they are alive but you do not perceive.

2:155 And We will test you with some fear and hunger, and a shortage in money and lives and fruits. And give good news to those who are patient.

2:156   The ones who, when afflicted with adversity, they say: "We are to God and to Him we will return."

2:157   For those there will be connections from their Lord and a mercy, they are the guided ones.

2:158   The stone and the rock outcropping are amongst the symbols of God. So whoever makes Pilgrimage to the House, or is merely visiting, commits no error should he traverse them. And whoever donates in goodness, then God is Thankful, Knowledgeable.

2:159   Surely those who conceal what We have sent down to them of the clarities and the guidance, after We had made it clear for the people in the Book; these will be cursed by God and be cursed by those who curse.

2:160   Except those who repent and amend and clarify; for those I will accept their repentance, for I am the One who accepts repentance, the Merciful.

2:161   Surely, those who have disbelieved and then died as disbelievers; they will be cursed by God, and the angels, and all the people.

2:162   They will abide therein, where the retribution will not be lightened for them, nor will they be reprieved.

2:163   And your god is but One god, there is no god except He; the Almighty, the Merciful.

2:164   Surely, in the creation of the heavens and the earth, and the differences between the night and the day, and the ships that sail in the sea for the benefit of the people, and what God has sent down of water from the sky so He brings the earth back to life after it had died, and He sent forth from it every creature, and the dispatching of the winds and the clouds that have been commissioned between the earth and the sky are signs for a people who comprehend.

2:165   And from among the people are some who take other than God as equals to Him, they love them as they love God; but those who believe love God more strongly; and when those who were wicked see the retribution, they will see that all power belongs to God, and that God is severe in retribution.

2:166   When those who were followed will disown those who followed them, and they will see the retribution, and all excuses will abandon them.

2:167   And those who followed them said: "If we only could have a chance to disown them as they have disowned us." It is such that

15

God will show them their works which will be regretted by them; they will not leave the Fire.

2:168 O people, eat from what is on the earth as good and permissible, and do not follow in the footsteps of the devil. He is to you a clear enemy.

2:169 He only orders you to evil and immorality, and that you may say about God what you do not know.

2:170 And if they are told: "Follow what God has sent down," they say: "No, we will follow what we found our fathers doing!" What if their fathers did not comprehend anything and were not guided?

2:171 And the example of those who disbelieve is like one who repeats what he has heard of calls and cries; deaf, dumb, and blind, they do not comprehend.

2:172 O you who believe, eat from the good things We have provided for you, and be thankful to God; if it is Him you serve.

2:173 He has only forbidden for you that which is already dead, and blood, and the meat of pig, and what was sacrificed with to other than God. Whoever finds himself forced out of need, without seeking disobedience or transgression, then there is no sin upon him. God is Forgiving, Merciful.

2:174 Surely, those who conceal what God has sent down of the Book, and they purchase with it a cheap price; they will not eat in their bellies except the Fire, and God will not speak to them on the Day of Resurrection, nor will He purify them, and they will have a painful retribution.

2:175 These are the ones who have purchased straying with guidance, and retribution for forgiveness; they have no patience towards the Fire.

2:176 This is because God has sent down the Book with the truth; and those who have disputed about the Book are in far opposition.

2:177 Piety is not to turn your faces towards the east and the west, but pious is one who believes in God and the Last Day, and the angels, and the Book, and the prophets, and he gives money out of love to the relatives, and the orphans, and the needy, and the wayfarer, and those who ask, and to free the slaves; and he holds the Connection, and contributes towards purification; and those who keep their pledges when they make a pledge, and those who are patient in the face of adversity and hardship and when in despair. These are the ones who have been truthful, and these are the righteous.

2:178   O you who believe, impartiality has been decreed for you in the case of those who are killed; the free as the free, and the slave as the slave, and the female as the female. Whoever is forgiven anything by his brother, then it is to be followed with kindness and goodness towards him; that is an alleviation from your Lord, and a mercy. Whoever transgresses after that, he will have a painful retribution.

2:179   And through impartiality you will be protecting life, O you who possess intelligence, that you may be righteous.

2:180   It is decreed for you that if death should come to any of you, that it is best if he leaves a will for his family and relatives out of goodness; this is a truth for the righteous.

2:181   Whoever alters it after having heard it, then the sin will be upon those who alter it. God is Hearer, Knowledgeable.

2:182   If anyone fears harm or sin from his beneficiary, and reconciles between them, there is no sin upon him. God is Forgiving, Merciful.

2:183   O you who believe, fasting has been decreed for you as it was decreed for those before you, perhaps you may be righteous.

2:184   A few number of days. Whoever of you is ill or traveling, then the same count from different days; and as for those who can do so but with difficulty, they may redeem by feeding the needy. And whoever does good voluntarily, then it is better for him. And if you fast it is better for you if only you knew.

2:185   The month of Ramadhan, in which the Qur'an was sent down as a guide to the people and a clarification of the guidance and the Criterion. Those of you who witness the month shall fast therein; and whoever is ill or traveling, then the same count from different days. God wants to bring you ease and not to bring you hardship; and so that you may complete the count, and magnify God for what He has guided you to, and that you may be thankful.

2:186   And if My servants ask you about Me, I am near answering the calls of those who call to Me. So let them respond to Me and believe in Me that they may be guided.

2:187   It has been made permissible for you during the night of fasting to approach your women sexually. They are a garment for you and

17

you are a garment for them. God knew that you used to betray your souls, so He has redeemed you, and forgiven you; now you may approach them and seek what God has written for you. And you may eat and drink until the white thread is distinct from the black thread of dawn; then you shall complete the fast until night; and do not approach them while you are devoted in the temples. These are the boundaries of God, so do not transgress them. It is thus that God clarifies His revelations to the people that they may be righteous.

2:188 And do not consume your money between you unjustly by bribing the decision makers so that you may consume a part of the money of other people sinfully while you know!

2:189 They ask you regarding the crescents, say: "They provide a timing mechanism for the people and the Pilgrimage." And piety is not that you would enter a home from its back, but piety is whoever is righteous and comes to the homes from their main doors. And be aware of God that you may succeed.

2:190 And fight in the cause of God against those who fight you, but do not aggress, God does not love the aggressors.

2:191 And you may kill them wherever you engage them, and expel them from where they expelled you, and know that persecution is worse than being killed. And do not fight them at the restricted Temple unless they fight you in it; if they fight you then kill them, thus is the recompense of the rejecters.

2:192 And if they cease, then God is Forgiving, Merciful.

2:193 And fight them so there is no more persecution, and so that the system is for God. If they cease, then there will be no aggression except against the wicked.

2:194 The restricted Month shall be met in the restricted Month, and the prohibitions shall be impartial. Whoever attacks you, then you shall attack him the same as he attacked you; and be aware of God, and know that God is with the righteous.

2:195 And spend in the cause of God, but do not throw your resources to disaster. And do good, for God loves those who do good.

2:196 And conclude the Pilgrimage and the visit for God. But, if you are prevented, then provide what offering is affordable; and do not shave your heads until the offering reaches its destination. Whoever of you is ill or has an ailment to his head, then he may redeem by fasting or giving a charity or a rite. When you are secure, then whoever enjoys the visit until the Pilgrimage, then he shall provide what offering is affordable; but for he who cannot find anything, then the fast of three days during the Pilgrimage and seven when he returns; this will make a complete ten—this is for those whose family is not present at the restricted Temple. And be aware of God, and know that God is severe in retribution.

2:197   The Pilgrimage is in the appointed months; so whoever decides to perform the Pilgrimage in them, then there shall be no sexual approach, nor wickedness, nor baseless argument in the Pilgrimage. And any good that you do, God is aware of it; and bring provisions for yourselves, though the best provision is righteousness; and be aware of Me O you who possess intelligence.

2:198   There is no sin upon you to seek goodness from your Lord. So when you disperse from the elevated place, then remember God at the symbol which is restricted, and remember Him as He has guided you; for you were straying before that.

2:199   Then you shall disperse from where the people dispersed, and seek the forgiveness of God; God is surely Forgiving, Merciful.

2:200   When you have completed your rites, then remember God as you remember your fathers or even greater. From among the people is he who says: "Our Lord, give us from this world!" But in the Hereafter he has no part.

2:201   And some of them say: "Our Lord, give us good in this world, and good in the Hereafter, and spare us from the retribution of the Fire."

2:202   These will have a share for what they have earned; and God is swift in reckoning.

2:203   And remember God during a few number of days. Whoever hurries to two days, there is no sin upon him; and whoever delays, there is no sin upon him if he is being righteous. And be aware of God, and know that it is to Him that you will be gathered.

2:204   And from among the people are those whose words you admire in this worldly life, but God is witness as to what is in his heart, for he is the worst in opposition.

2:205   And if he gains power, he seeks to corrupt the earth and destroy its crops, and the lineage. God does not love corruption.

2:206   And if he is told: "Be aware of God," his pride leads him to more sin. Hell shall be sufficient for him; what a miserable abode!

2:207   And from among the people is he who sells his soul seeking the grace of God; God is kind to His servants.

2:208   O you who believe, join in peace, all of you, and do not follow in the footsteps of the devil. He is to you a clear enemy.

2:209   But if you slip after the clarity has come to you, then know that God is Noble, Wise.

2:210   Are they waiting for God to come to them shadowed in clouds with the angels? The matter would then be finished! And to God all matters are returned.

2:211   Ask the Children of Israel how many clear signs did We give them? And whoever changes the grace of God after it has come to him, then God is Mighty in retribution.

2:212   This worldly life has been made pleasing to the disbelievers, and they mock those who believe. And those who are righteous will be above them on the Day of Resurrection; God provides for whoever He wishes without reckoning.

2:213   The people used to be one nation, then God sent the prophets as bearers of good news and warners, and He sent down with them the Book with the truth so that they may judge between the people in what they were disputing. But after receiving the clarity, the people disputed in it due to animosity between them. And God guided those who believed with His permission regarding what they disputed in of the truth. And God guides whoever He wishes to a straight path.

2:214   Or did you expect that you would enter Paradise, while the example of those who were before you came to you; they were stricken with adversity and hardship, and they were shaken until the messenger and those who believed with him said: "When is the victory of God?" Yes indeed, the victory of God is near.

2:215   They ask you what they should spend, say: "What you spend out of goodness should go to your family and the relatives and the orphans, and the needy, and the wayfarer. And any good you do, God is fully aware of it."

2:216   Warfare has been decreed for you while you hate it; and perhaps you may hate something while it is good for you, and perhaps you may love something while it is bad for you; and God knows while you do not know.

2:217   They ask you about the restricted Month: "Is there fighting in it?"

Say: "Much fighting is in it, and to repel from the path of God and to disbelieve in it, and the restricted Temple, to drive its inhabitants out from it is far greater with God, and persecution is worse than being killed." And they still will fight you until they turn you back from your system if they are able. And whoever of you turns back from his system, and he dies while disbelieving, then these have nullified their works in this world and the next; these are the people of the Fire, in it they will abide!

2:218 Indeed, those who believe, and those who have immigrated and strived in the cause of God—these are seeking the mercy of God, and God is Forgiving, Merciful.

2:219 They ask you about intoxicants and gambling. Say: "In them is much sin, and a benefit for the people; but their sin is greater than their benefit." And they ask you how much they are to give, say: "The excess." It is thus that God clarifies for you the revelations that you may think.

2:220 In this world and the next; and they ask you regarding the orphans, say: "To fix their situation is best, and if you are to mix with them, then they are your brothers." And God knows the corrupt from the good, and if God had wished He could have made things difficult. God is Noble, Wise.

2:221 And do not marry the female polytheists until they believe; for a believing servant is better than a polytheist, even if she is pleasing to you. And do not give in marriage to the male polytheists until they believe; for a believing servant is better than a polytheist, even if he is pleasing to you. These invite to the Fire, while God is inviting to Paradise and forgiveness by His consent. He clarifies His revelations for the people that they may remember.

2:222 And they ask you about the menstruations? Say: "It is harmful, so retire yourselves sexually from the women during the menstruations, and do not approach them until they are purified. When they are purified, then you may approach them as God has commanded you." God loves the repenters and He loves the purified.

2:223 Your women are a cultivation for you. So approach your cultivation as you wish towards goodness. And be aware of God and know that you will meet Him, and give good news to the believers.

2:224 And do not make God the subject of your casual oaths. Be pious and righteous and reconcile among the people; and God is Hearer, Knower.

21

2:225   God will not call you to account for your casual oaths, but He will call you to account for what has entered your hearts. God is Forgiving, Compassionate.

2:226   For those who abstain from their wives, they shall be given four months. If they renounce, then God is Forgiving, Merciful.

2:227   And if they insist on the divorce, then God is Hearer, Knowledgeable.

2:228   And those divorced shall wait for three menstruation periods; and it is not permissible for them to conceal what God has created in their wombs, if they believe in God and the Last Day. And their husbands have a greater right to return them in this, if they wish to reconcile. And for them are rights similar to those owed by them. And the men will have a degree over them. And God is Noble, Wise.

2:229   The divorce may occur twice. So, either they remain together equitably, or part ways with goodness. And it is not permissible for you to take back anything you have given them unless you fear that they will not uphold the boundaries of God. So if you fear that they will not uphold the boundaries of God, then there is no sin upon them for what is given back. These are the boundaries of God so do not transgress them. And whoever shall transgress the boundaries of God, then these are the wicked.

2:230   If he then divorces her, she will not be permissible for him until after she has married a different husband. If he were to divorce her; then there is no sin that they come back together if they think they will uphold the boundaries of God. These are the boundaries of God, He clarifies them for a people who know.

2:231   And if you have divorced the women, and they have reached their required interim period, then either you remain together equitably, or part ways equitably. And do not reconcile with them so you can harm them out of animosity; whoever does so is doing wrong to his soul; and do not take the revelations of God as mockery. And remember the blessings of God upon you, and what was sent down to you of the Book and the wisdom, He warns you with it. And be aware of God and know that God is knowledgeable of all things.

2:232   And if you divorce the women, and they reach their required interim period, then do not make difficulty for them if they wish to remarry their husbands if they have amicably agreed among themselves out of what is best. This is to remind any of you who believe in God and the Last Day, this is better for you and purer;

and God knows while you do not know.

2:233 And the birth mothers may suckle their children two full cycles, if they wish to complete the suckling. And the man for whom the child is born is responsible for both their provisions and clothing equitably. A soul is not burdened except with what it can bear. No mother shall be harmed because of her child, nor shall a father be harmed because of his child. And for the guardian is the same requirement. So if they wish to separate out of mutual agreement and counsel, then there is no sin upon them. And if you want to hire nursing mothers, then there is no sin upon you if you return what you have been given equitably. And be aware of God, and know that God is watching over what you do.

2:234 And those of you whose lives are terminated, and they leave wives behind, they will have a required interim period of four months and ten. So when they reach their required interim, then there is no sin upon you for what they do with themselves in goodness. And God is Expert to what you do.

2:235 And there is no sin upon you if you openly propose marriage to the women, or you keep it between yourselves. God knows that you will be thinking about them, but do not meet them secretly, unless you have something righteous to say. And do not finalize the marriage contract until the interim in the book is reached. And know that God knows what is in your souls, so be aware of Him, and know that God is Forgiving, Compassionate.

2:236 There is no sin upon you if you divorce the women before having sexual intercourse with them, or before setting the dowry for them. Let them have recompense, the rich according to his means, and the poor according to his means. A recompense in goodness, a responsibility for the good doers.

2:237 And if you divorce them before having sexual intercourse with them, but you have already set the dowry for them; then you must give half of what you have agreed, unless they forgive or the guardian over the marriage contract forgives. And if you forgive, it is closer to righteousness. And do not forget the favor between you; God is Seer of what you do.

2:238 Maintain the Connections, and the central Connection; and stand dutifully for God.

2:239 But if you are fearful, then you may do so while walking or riding. If you become secure, then remember God as He has taught you what you did not know.

2:240 And those of you whose lives are terminated, and they leave wives behind, a decree to their wives that they be provided with support for one cycle, if they do not leave. If they leave then there is no sin upon you for what they do with themselves of goodness; and God is Noble, Wise.

2:241 And for those divorced, to have support in goodness is an obligation upon the righteous.

2:242 It is such that God clarifies for you His revelations that you may comprehend.

2:243 Did you not note those who left their homes in groups, all the while they were fearful of death; so God said to them: "Die," then He resurrected them. God has bestowed a great grace over the people, but most of the people are not thankful.

2:244 And fight in the cause of God and know that God is the Hearer, the Knowledgeable.

2:245 Who will lend God a loan of righteousness that He may multiply it for him many times over? God collects and He distributes, and to Him you will return.

2:246 Did you not note the leaders of the Children of Israel after Moses, they said to their prophet: "Send us a king that we may fight in the cause of God;" he said: "Are you not concerned that if fighting is decreed for you, you will then not fight?" They said: "And why should we not fight in the cause of God when we have been expelled from our homes along with our children." So it was, that when fighting was decreed for them they turned away, except for a few of them! God is fully aware of the wicked.

2:247 And their prophet said to them: "God has sent Saul to you as a king." They said: "How can he have the kingship when we are more deserving than him, and he has not been given an abundance of wealth?" He said: "God has chosen him over you and increased him in knowledge and physical stature." God grants His sovereignty to whom He chooses; and God is Encompassing, Knowledgeable.

2:248 And their prophet said to them: "The sign of his kingship shall be that he brings to you the ark in which there is tranquility from your Lord and the legacy of what was left behind by the descendants of Moses and the descendants of Aaron being carried by the angels. In this is a sign for you if you are believers."

2:249 So when Saul set out with the soldiers, he said: "God will test you with a river, whoever drinks from it is not with me, and whoever does not taste from it except one scoop with his hand is with me." They all drank from it, except for a few of them. So when he and those who believed with him crossed it, they said: "We have no power today against Goliath and his soldiers!" But the ones who understood that they would meet God said: "How many a time has a small group beaten a large group with the permission of God, and God is with the patient ones!"

2:250 And when they came forth to Goliath and his soldiers, they said: "Our Lord grant us patience, and make firm our foothold, and grant us victory over the disbelieving people."

2:251 So they defeated them with the permission of God, and David killed Goliath, and God gave him the kingship and the wisdom and taught him what he wished. And if it were not for God defending the people against themselves, then the earth would have long been corrupted; but God has bestowed grace upon the worlds.

2:252 These are the revelations of God, We recite them to you with the truth, and you are one of the messengers.

2:253 Such messengers, We have preferred some over others; some of them talked to God, and He raised some of them in rank, and We gave Jesus, son of Mary, the clear proofs and We supported him with the Holy Spirit. And had God wished, the people after them would not have fought after the proofs had come to them, but they disputed, some of them believed and some of them rejected. If God had wished they would not have fought, but God does what He pleases.

2:254 O you who believe, spend from what We have provided for you before a Day comes when there is no trade, nor friendship, nor intercession; and the rejecters are the wicked.

2:255 God, there is no god except He, the Living, the Eternal. No slumber or sleep overtakes Him; to Him belongs all that is in the heavens and the earth. Who will intercede with Him except with His permission? He knows their present and their future, and they have none of His knowledge except for what He wishes. His Throne encompasses all of the heavens and the earth and it is easy for Him to preserve them. He is the Most High, the Great.

2:256 There is no compulsion in the system; the proper way has been clarified from the wrong way. Whoever rejects evil, and believes in God, indeed he has taken grasp of the strongest hold that will never break. God is Hearer, Knower.

2:257 God is the ally of those who believe, He brings them out of the darkness and into the light. As for those who reject, their allies are the evil ones, they bring them out of the light and into the darkness; these are the people of the Fire, in it they will abide.

2:258 Have you not noted him who debated with Abram regarding his Lord, while God had given him a kingship? Abram said: "My Lord is the One who gives life and death," he said: "I bring life and death." Abram said: "God brings the sun from the east, so you bring it from the west." The one who rejected was baffled! And God does not guide the wicked people.

2:259 Or the one who passed through a town which had become ruins. He said: "How can God possibly revive this after it had died?" So God put him to death for one hundred calendar years, then He resurrected him. He said: "How long have you stayed here?" He said: "I have stayed here a day or part of a day." He said: "No, you have stayed here for one hundred calendar years! Look at your food and drink, they have not changed, but look at your donkey! And We will make you a sign for the people; and look at the bones how We let them arise, then We cover them with flesh." So when it was clear to him what happened, he said: "I now know that God is capable of all things!"

2:260 And Abram said: "My Lord, show me how You resurrect the dead." He said: "Do you not already believe?" He said: "I do, but it is so my heart can be relieved." He said: "Choose four birds, then cut them, then place parts of the birds on each mountain, then call them to you; they will come racing towards you. And know that God is Noble, Wise."

2:261 The example of those who spend their money in the cause of God is like a seed that sprouts forth seven pods, in each pod there is one hundred seeds; and God multiplies for whoever He chooses, and God is Encompassing, Knowledgeable.

2:262 Those who spend their money in the cause of God, then they do not follow what they have spent with either insult or harm; they will have their recompense with their Lord, there is no fear over them nor will they grieve.

2:263 Kind words and forgiveness are far better than a charity that is followed by harm. God is Rich, Compassionate.

2:264 O you who believe, do not nullify your charities with insult and harm; like one who spends his money to show off to the people, and he does not believe in God and the Last Day. His example is like a stone on which there is dust, then it is subjected to a heavy rain which leaves it bare. They cannot do anything with what they have earned; and God does not guide the rejecting people.

2:265 And the example of those who spend their money seeking the grace of God, and to save their souls, is like the example of a garden that is on a high ground and is subjected to a heavy rain, and because of that it produces double its crop. And if no heavy rain comes, then it still gives enough. And God is Seer of what you do.

2:266 Does anyone of you desire that he has an estate with palm trees and grapevines, and rivers flowing beneath it, and in it for him are all kinds of fruits, then he is afflicted with old age and his progeny is weak, and a firestorm strikes it and it all burns? It is thus that God makes clear for you the signs that you may reflect.

2:267 O you who believe, spend from the good things that you have earned, and from what We have brought forth from the earth. And do not select the rotten from it to give, while you would not take it yourselves unless you closed your eyes regarding it. And know that God is Rich, Praiseworthy.

2:268 The devil promises you poverty and orders you to immorality, while God promises forgiveness from Him and grace. God is Encompassing, Knowledgeable.

2:269 He grants wisdom to whom He chooses, and whoever is granted wisdom has been given much good. Only those who possess intelligence will remember.

2:270 And whatever you spend out of your monies, or whatever you pledge as a promise, then God knows it. The wicked have no supporters.

2:271 If you openly give charities, then it is acceptable; but if you conceal them and give them to the poor, then that is better for you. And He cancels some of your sins; and God is Expert to all that you do.

2:272 You are not responsible for their guidance, but it is God who will guide whoever He wishes. And whatever you spend out of goodness is for your own souls. And anything you spend should be in seeking the face of God. And whatever you spend out of goodness will be returned to you, and you will not be wronged.

2:273　For the poor who face hardship in the cause of God, they cannot go forth in the land; the ignorant ones think they are rich from their modesty; you know them by their features, they do not ask the people repeatedly. And what you spend out of goodness, God is fully aware of it.

2:274　Those who spend their money in the night and in the day, secretly and openly, they will have their recompense with their Lord, there is no fear over them nor will they grieve.

2:275　Those who consume usury do not rise except as one being influenced by the touch of the devil. That is because they have said: "Trade is the same as usury." While God has made trade permissible, and He has made usury forbidden. Whoever has received understanding from his Lord and ceases, then he will be forgiven for what was before this and his case will be with God. But whoever returns, then they are the people of the Fire, in it they will abide.

2:276　God condemns usury, and He grants growth to the charities. And God does not love any wicked sinner.

2:277　Those who believe and do good works, and hold the Connection, and contribute towards purification; they will have their recompense with their Lord and there is no fear over them nor will they grieve.

2:278　O you who believe, be aware of God and give up what is left from usury, if you truly are believers.

2:279　And if you will not do this, then be informed of a war from God and His messenger; but if you repent, then you will have back your principal money, you will not be wronged nor will you wrong.

2:280　If the person is facing insolvency, then you shall wait until he becomes able. And if you relinquish it as a charity it is better for you if only you knew.

2:281　And be aware of a Day when you will be returned to God, then every soul will be paid what it has earned, and they will not be wronged.

2:282　O you who believe, if you borrow for a future period, then you shall record it. And let a scribe of justice record it for you; and let not the scribe refuse to record as God has taught him. Let him record and let the person who is borrowing dictate to him, and let him be aware of God, and let him not reduce from it anything.

If the one who is borrowing is immature or weak or he cannot dictate himself, then let his guardian dictate with justice; and bring two witnesses from among your men; if there are not two men, then a man and two women from whom you will accept their testimony, so that if one of them becomes blindsided, then the one can remind the other. And let the witnesses not refuse to come if they are called. And do not fail to record it no matter how small or large until its maturity, that is more just with God and better for the testimony, and better that you do not have doubts. Exempt is trade done on the spot between you, then there is no sin upon you if you do not record it—and have evidence if you trade. No scribe shall be harmed nor any witness; for if you do so then it is a wickedness on your part, and be aware of God and God teaches you and God is aware of all things.

2:283 And if you are traveling or do not find a scribe, then a pledge of collateral. So, if you have entrusted each other in this manner, then let the one who was entrusted deliver his trust, and let him be aware of God his Lord. And do not hold back the testimony. And whoever holds it back, then he has sinned in his heart, and God is aware of what you do.

2:284 To God is what is in the heavens and in the earth, and whether you declare what is in your souls or hide it, God will call you to account for it. He will forgive whom He wishes, and punish whom He wishes, and God is capable of all things.

2:285 The messenger believes in what was sent down to him from his Lord; and the believers, all who believe in God, and His angels, and His Books, and His messengers: "We do not make a distinction between any of His messengers;" and they said: "We hear and obey, forgive us our Lord, and to You is our destiny."

2:286 God does not burden a soul except with what it can bear. For it is what it earns, and against it is what it earns. "Our Lord, do not mind us if we forget or make mistakes; our Lord, do not place a burden upon us as You have placed upon those before us; our Lord, do not place upon us what we cannot bear; pardon us, and forgive us, and have mercy on us; You are our patron, so grant us victory over the rejecting people."

CHAPTER 3

3:0 In the name of God, the Almighty, the Merciful.

3:1 ALM.

3:2 God, there is no god except He, the Living, the Eternal.

3:3 He sent down to you the Book with the truth, affirming what is between his hands; and He sent down the Torah and the Gospel.

3:4 From before as a guidance for the people, and He sent down the Criterion. Those who rejected the revelations of God, they will have a severe retribution, and God is Noble, exacting in Revenge.

3:5 For God nothing is hidden on the earth or in the heavens.

3:6 He is the One who pictures you in the wombs as He pleases. There is no god except He, the Noble, the Wise.

3:7 He is the One who sent down to you the Book, from which there are fixed verses—they are the Mother of the Book—and others which are comparable. As for those who have a disease in their hearts, they follow that of it which is comparable, seeking to confuse, and seeking to derive an interpretation. But none know its interpretation except God, and those who are well founded in knowledge; they say: "We believe in it, all is from our Lord." And none will remember except those who possess intelligence.

3:8 "Our Lord, do not make our hearts deviate after You have guided us, and grant us from You a mercy. Indeed, You are the Grantor."

3:9 "Our Lord, You will gather the people for a Day in which there is no doubt; God does not break His appointment."

3:10 As for those who rejected, neither their money nor their children will avail them anything from God. They are the fuel of the Fire.

3:11 Like the behavior of the people of Pharaoh and those before them. They rejected Our signs so God took them for their sins. God is awesome in retribution.

3:12 Say to those who have rejected: "You will be defeated and gathered towards Hell, what a miserable abode!"

3:13 There was a sign for you in the two groups that met. One was fighting in the cause of God, and the other was rejecting. They thus saw them as twice their number with their eyes. And God supports with His victory whom He wills. In this is a lesson for those with vision.

3:14 It has been adorned for people to love the desire of women; and to want sons, and ornaments made from gold and silver, and trained horses, and hoofed animals, and fields. These are the enjoyment of the world, and with God is the best abode.

3:15 Say: "Shall I inform you of what is greater than all this? For those who believe in their Lord will be estates with rivers flowing beneath them; abiding therein, and with pure mates, and an acceptance from God. And God is Seer over the servants."

3:16 The ones who say: "Our Lord, we believe, so forgive us our sins, and spare us the retribution of the Fire."

3:17 The patient, and the truthful, and the devout, and the givers, and the seekers of forgiveness in the late hours of the night.

3:18 God bears witness that there is no god except He, as do the angels, and those with knowledge, He is standing with justice. There is no god except He, the Noble, the Wise.

3:19 The system with God is submission, and those who received the Book did not dispute except after the knowledge came to them out of jealousy between them. And whoever rejects the revelations of God, then God is swift in reckoning.

3:20 If they debate with you, then say: "I have submitted myself to God, as well as those who follow me." And say to those who have received the Book and the gentiles: "Have you submitted?" If they have submitted then they are guided, and if they turn away, then you are only to deliver, and God is Seer over the servants.

3:21 Those who reject the revelations of God and kill the prophets without right, and kill those who order justice from among the people; inform them of a painful retribution.

3:22 These are the ones whose works will be lost in this world, and in the Hereafter they will have no supporters.

3:23 Did you not note those who were given a portion of the Book being invited to the Book of God to judge between them, then a group of them turns away while they are adverse?

3:24 That is because they said: "The Fire will not touch us except for a few number of days," and they were arrogant by what they invented in their system.

3:25 How shall it be when We gather them on the Day in which there is no doubt; and every soul shall receive what it has earned, and they will not be wronged.

3:26 Say: "Our god, Possessor of kingship; You grant kingship to whom You please, and revoke kingship from whom You please, and honor whom You please, and humiliate whom You please; in Your hand is goodness. You are capable of all things."

3:27 "You blend the night into the day, and You blend the day into the night; and You bring the living out of the dead, and You bring the dead out of the living; and You provide for whom You wish without reckoning."

3:28 Let not the believers take the rejecters as allies instead of the believers. And whoever does so will have nothing with God; for you are to be cautious of them as they deserve. And God warns you of Himself, and to God is the destiny.

3:29 Say: "Whether you hide what is in your chests or you reveal it, God will know." And He knows what is in the heavens and the earth; and God is capable of all things.

3:30 The Day every soul will find what good it had done present; and what bad it had done, it will wish that between them was a great distance. And God warns you of Himself, and God is Compassionate towards the servants.

3:31 Say: "If you love God then follow me so God will love you and forgive your sins." God is Forgiver, Merciful.

3:32 Say: "Obey God and the messenger." But if they turn away, then God does not love the rejecters.

3:33 God has selected Adam, and Noah, and the family of Abraham, and the family of Imran over the worlds.

3:34 A progeny each from the other, and God is Hearer, Knower.

3:35 When the wife of Imran said: "My Lord, I have vowed to You what is in my womb, completely, so accept from me, You are the Hearer, the Knower."

3:36 So when she had delivered she said: "My Lord, I have delivered a female," and God is fully aware of what she delivered, "And the male is not like the female, and I have named her Mary, and I seek refuge for her and her progeny with You from the outcast devil."

3:37 So her Lord accepted her a good acceptance, and made her grow into a good growth, and charged Zechariah with her. Every time Zechariah entered upon her in the enclosure, he found provisions with her. He said: "O Mary, from where did you get this?" She said: "It is from God, for God provides for whom He wishes without reckoning."

3:38 It was then that Zechariah implored his Lord; he said: "My Lord, grant me from You a good progeny. You are the Hearer of prayer."

3:39 So the angels called to him while he was standing, connecting, in the enclosure: "God gives you glad tidings of John, affirming the word from God, and a master, and steadfast, and a prophet from the upright."

3:40 He said: "My Lord, how can I have a boy when old age has reached me and my wife is infertile?" He said: "It is as such that God does what He pleases."

3:41 He said: "My Lord, make for me a sign." He said: "Your sign is not to speak to the people for three days except by symbol, and remember your Lord greatly, and glorify at dusk and dawn."

3:42 And the angels said: "O Mary, God has selected you and purified you, and He has selected you over all the women of the worlds."

3:43 "O Mary, be dutiful to your Lord and prostrate and kneel with those who kneel."

3:44 This is from the news of the unseen that We inspire to you. You were not with them when they drew straws as to which one of them will be charged with Mary; you were not with them when they disputed.

3:45 And the angels said: "O Mary, God gives you glad tidings of a word from Him. His name is the Messiah, Jesus, son of Mary. Honorable in this world and in the Hereafter, and from among those who are made close."

3:46 "And he will speak to the people from the cradle and to middle-age, and is from among the upright."

3:47 She said: "My Lord, how can I have a son when no mortal has been with me?" He said: "It is thus that God creates what He wills, when He decrees a command, He merely says to it 'Be,' and it is."

3:48 And He teaches him the Book and the Wisdom and the Torah and the Gospel.

3:49 And as a messenger to the Children of Israel: "I have come to you with a sign from your Lord; that I create for you from clay the form of a bird, then I blow into it and it becomes a bird with the permission of God, and I heal the blind and the lepers, and give life to the dead with the permission of God, and I prophesize for you what you shall eat and what to store in your homes. In that is a sign for you if you are believers."

3:50 "And affirming what is between my hands of the Torah, and to make permissible some of that which was made forbidden to you; and I have come to you with a sign from your Lord, so be aware of God and obey me."

3:51 "God is my Lord and your Lord, so serve Him, this is a straight path."

3:52 So when Jesus felt their rejection, he said: "Who are my supporters to God?" The disciples said: "We are the supporters of God, we believe in God and we bear witness that we have submitted."

3:53 "Our Lord, we believe in what You have sent down, and followed the messenger, so record us with those who bear witness."

3:54 And they schemed and God schemed, but God is the best schemer.

3:55 For God said: "O Jesus, I will terminate your life, and raise you to Me, and purify you of those who have rejected, and make those who have followed you above those who have rejected until the Day of Resurrection. Then to Me is your return, all of you, so I will judge between you in what it was that you disputed."

3:56 "As for those who have rejected, I will punish them severely in this world and in the Hereafter, they will have no supporters."

3:57 "And as for those who believe and have done good works, We will pay them their recompense; God does not love the wicked."

3:58 This We recite to you from the revelations and the wise reminder.

3:59 The example of Jesus with God is similar to that of Adam; He created him from dust, then He said to him "Be" and he was.

3:60 The truth is from your Lord, so do not be of those who doubt.

3:61 Whoever debates with you in this after the knowledge has come to you, then say: "Let us call our children and your children, our women and your women, ourselves and yourselves, then, let us invoke and make the curse of God upon the liars."

3:62   This is the narration of truth, there is no god except God; and God is the Noble, the Wise.

3:63   And if they turn away, then God is aware of the corrupters.

3:64   Say: "O people of the Book, let us come to a mutual understanding between us and between you; that we serve none except God, and that we do not set up anything with Him, and that none of us takes each other as patrons besides God." If they turn away, then say: "Bear witness that we have submitted."

3:65   "O people of the Book, why do you debate with us regarding Abraham when the Torah and the Gospel were not sent down except after him? Do you not comprehend?"

3:66   Here you have debated in what you knew; so why then do you debate in what you do not know? And God knows while you do not know.

3:67   Abraham was neither a Jew nor a Nazarene, but he was a monotheist who submitted; he was not of the polytheists.

3:68   The most legitimate people to Abraham are those who followed him; and this prophet, and those who believed; and God is the supporter of the believers.

3:69   A group from the people of the Book wished that they could misguide you, but they only misguide themselves and they do not notice.

3:70   "O people of the Book, why do you reject the revelations of God while you are bearing witness?"

3:71   "O people of the Book, why do you confound the truth with falsehood and conceal the truth while you know?"

3:72   And a group from among the people of the Book said: "Believe in what was sent down to those who believe during the beginning of the day, and reject it by the end of it, perhaps they will return."

3:73   "And do not believe except in he who follows your system." Say: "The guidance is the guidance of God." That anyone should be given similar to what you have been given, or that they debate with you at your Lord. Say: "The bounty is in the hand of God, He gives it to whom He chooses, and God is Encompassing, Knowledgeable."

3:74   He singles out with His mercy whom He chooses, and God is with

Great Bounty.

3:75 And from among the people of the Book are those whom if you entrust him with a large amount he gives it back to you, and there are those whom if you entrust with one gold coin he will not return it to you unless you are standing over him. That is because they said: "We have no obligation towards the gentiles." They say about God lies while they know.

3:76 Indeed, anyone who fulfils his pledge and is righteous, then God loves the righteous.

3:77 The ones who purchase with the pledge of God and their oaths a cheap price, those will have no portion in the Hereafter, and God will not speak to them, nor will He look at them on the Day of Resurrection, nor will He purify them, and they will have a painful retribution.

3:78 And from among them is a group who twist their tongues using the Book so that you may think it is from the Book, while it is not from the Book, and they say it is from God while it is not from God, and they say about God lies while they know.

3:79 It is not for any mortal that God would give him the Book and the authority and the prophethood, then he would say to the people: "Be servants to me rather than God!" Rather: "Be devotees for what you have been taught of the Book, and of what you have studied."

3:80 Nor does He order you that you take the angels and the prophets as patrons. Would He order you to rejection after you have submitted?

3:81 And God took a covenant from the prophets: "For what I have given you of the Book and wisdom, then a messenger will come to you affirming what is with you. You will believe in him and support him." He said: "Do you testify, and agree to this burden?" They said: "We testify." He said: "Then bear witness, and I am with you bearing witness."

3:82 Whoever turns away after that, then they are the wicked.

3:83 Is it other than the system of God that they desire, when those in the heavens and the earth have submitted to Him voluntarily or by force? And to Him they will be returned.

3:84 Say: "We believe in God and what was sent down to us and what was sent down to Abraham and Ishmael and Isaac and Jacob and the Patriarchs, and what was given to Moses and Jesus and the prophets from their Lord. We do not make a distinction between any of them, and to Him we submit."

3:85 And whoever follows other than submission as a system, it will not be accepted from him, and in the Hereafter he is of the losers.

3:86 How can God guide a people who had rejected after believing, and had witnessed that the messenger was true, and the clear evidences had come to them? God does not guide the wicked people.

3:87 To these the punishment will be that the curse of God will be upon them and that of the angels and the people all together!

3:88 Abiding therein, the retribution will not be lightened for them, nor will they be reprieved.

3:89 Except those who repent after this and make amends, then God is Forgiver, Merciful.

3:90 Those who have rejected after their belief, then increased in rejection, their repentance will not be accepted, they are the strayers.

3:91 Those who have rejected and died while they were rejecters, if the earth full of gold were to be ransomed with it would not be accepted from any of them. For these there will be a painful retribution and they will have no supporters.

3:92 You will not reach piety until you spend from what you love; and whatever you spend, God is aware of it.

3:93 All the food was made permissible to the Children of Israel except what Israel forbade for himself before the Torah was sent down. Say: "Bring the Torah and recite it if you are truthful."

3:94 Whoever invents lies about God after this, these are the wicked.

3:95 Say: "God bears truth. Follow the creed of Abraham, monotheism, and he was not of the polytheists."

3:96 The first House established for the people is the one in Bakk'a, blessed, and a guidance for the worlds.

3:97 In it are clear signs: the station of Abraham. And whoever enters it will have safety. And God is owed from the people to make Pilgrimage to the House, whoever can make a way to it. And whoever rejects, then God has no need of the worlds.

3:98 Say: "O people of the Book, why do you reject the revelations of God, while God is witness over what you do?"

3:99 Say: "O people of the Book, why do you repel from the path of God those who believe? You wish to twist it while you are witnesses. And God is not unaware of what you do."

3:100 O you who believe, if you obey a group of those who received the Book they will turn you after your belief into rejecters!

3:101 And how can you reject when the revelations of God are being recited to you and with you is His messenger? And whoever holds firmly to God has been guided to the straight path.

3:102 O you who believe, reverence God as He deserves to be reverenced, and do not die except as ones who have submitted.

3:103 And hold firmly to the rope of God, all of you, and do not be separated. And remember the blessing of God upon you when you were enemies and He united your hearts. Then you became, with His blessing, brothers; and you were on the edge of a pit of fire and He saved you from it; it is thus that God clarifies for you His signs that you may be guided.

3:104 And let there be a nation from among you who calls towards righteousness, and advocate for good and prohibit vice. And these are the successful ones.

3:105 And do not be like those who separated and differed after the clarity had come to them. And for them is a painful retribution.

3:106 The Day on which faces will be lightened and faces will be darkened; as for those whose faces will be darkened: "Did you reject after believing? Taste the retribution for what you rejected."

3:107 As for those whose faces will be lightened, they are in the mercy of God, in it they abide.

3:108 These are the revelations of God, We recite them to you with the truth. God does not want wickedness for the worlds.

3:109 And to God is all that is in the heavens and the earth; and to God all matters are returned.

3:110 You were the best nation that emerged for the people, you advocated for good and prohibited vice, and believed in God. If the people of the Book believed it would have been better for them; from among them are the believers, but the majority are the wicked.

3:111   They will not harm you except in being an annoyance, and if they fight you they will turn and flee, then they will not be supported.

3:112   They are struck with humiliation wherever they are engaged, except for a rope from God and a rope from the people. And they stayed in the wrath of God and were struck with humiliation; that is because they were disbelieving in the revelations of God and killing the prophets without right; that is for what they disobeyed and were transgressing.

3:113   They are not all the same, from the people of the Book are a nation that is upright; they recite the revelations of God during the night hours and they prostrate.

3:114   They believe in God and the Last Day, and they advocate for good and prohibit vice, and they hasten in goodness; these are of the good doers.

3:115   And what they do of good will not be turned back, and God is aware of the righteous.

3:116   As for those who rejected, neither their money nor their children will avail them anything from God. These are the people of the Fire, in it they abide.

3:117   The example of what they spend in this world is like a wind in which there is a frost; it afflicts the field of the people who wronged themselves, and thus destroys it. God did not wrong them, but it was their souls that they wronged.

3:118   O you who believe do not take as an inner circle any from besides yourselves; they will only disrupt you greatly. They wish that you deviate; the hatred is apparent out of their mouths and what their chests conceal is even greater! We have made clear for you the signs if you comprehend.

3:119   Here you love them while they do not love you, and you believe in the entire Book. And if they meet you they say: "We believe," and if they are alone they bite their fingers out of frustration at you. Say: "Die in your frustration, God is aware of what is in the chests."

3:120   If any good befalls you it disturbs them, and if any bad befalls you they rejoice with it. And if you are patient and righteous their planning will not harm you at all. God is Encompassing all they do.

3:121   And as you departed from your family to prepare for the believers their stations for battle—and God is Hearer, Knowledgeable.

3:122 When two parties from among you were obsessed that they would fail; while God was their supporter. In God the believers should trust.

3:123 God had granted you victory at Badr, while you had been the lesser, so reverence God that you may be thankful.

3:124 When you said to the believers: "Is it not enough for you that your Lord would supply you with three thousand of the angels sent down?"

3:125 Indeed, if you are patient and are righteous and they come and attack you, He will supply you with five thousand of the angels battle trained.

3:126 And God did not give this except as good news to you, and so that your hearts may be assured with it. Victory is only from God, the Noble, the Wise.

3:127 Thus He will sever a group of those who reject, or disgrace them; then they will turn back frustrated.

3:128 You will have no say in the matter, for He may pardon them, or punish them; for they are wicked.

3:129 And to God is what is in the heavens and in the earth, He forgives whom He pleases, and He punishes whom He pleases; and God is Forgiving, Merciful.

3:130 O you who believe, do not consume usury, compounding over and over; and reverence God that you may succeed.

3:131 And be aware of the Fire that has been prepared for the rejecters.

3:132 And obey God and the messenger so that you may obtain mercy.

3:133 And race towards forgiveness from your Lord and a Paradise whose width encompasses the width of the heavens and of the earth; it has been prepared for the righteous.

3:134 The ones who spend in prosperity and hardship, and who repress anger, and who pardon the people; God loves the good doers.

3:135 And those who, if they commit immorality, or wrong themselves, they remember God and seek forgiveness for their sins. And who can forgive the sins except God? And they do not persist in what they have done while they know.

3:136 To these the recompense will be forgiveness from their Lord and estates with rivers flowing beneath them; abiding therein. Excellent is the recompense of the workers.

3:137 Many nations have come before you, so roam the earth and see how the punishment was for the deniers.

3:138 This is a clarification for the people and a reminder for the righteous.

3:139 Do not be weak, and do not grieve, for you will have the upper hand, if you are believers.

3:140 If you are wounded, then know that the other group is also wounded. And such are the days, We alternate them between the people, so that God will distinguish those who believe, and so He may make witnesses from among you; and God does not love the wicked.

3:141 And God will prove those who believe and He will condemn the rejecters.

3:142 Or did you think that you would enter Paradise without God distinguishing those who would strive among you and distinguishing those who are patient?

3:143 And you used to long for death before you came upon it; so now you see it right in front of you!

3:144 And Mohammed is but a messenger, like many messengers who have passed before him. If he dies or is killed will you turn back on your heels? And whoever turns back on his heels, he will not harm God in the least. And God will recompense the thankful.

3:145 It is not permitted for a person to die except by the permission of God in an appointed record. And whoever wants the reward of this world We give him of it, and whoever wants the reward of the Hereafter, We give him of it. And We will reward the thankful.

3:146 And many a prophet had a large number of devotees fighting with him. They did not waver by what afflicted them in the cause of God, nor did they become weak, nor did they become discouraged; and God loves the patient ones.

3:147 And they did not say except: "Our Lord, forgive us our sins and our shortcomings in our responsibility, and make firm our foothold, and grant us victory over the rejecting people."

3:148 So God gave them the reward of this world and the best reward of the Hereafter; and God loves the good doers.

3:149 O you who believe, if you obey those who have rejected, then they will turn you back on your heels and you will turn back as losers.

3:150 It is God who is your Patron, and He is the best victor.

3:151 We will cast terror in the hearts of those who have rejected, because of what they have set up besides God while He never sent down any authority to do so, and their destiny is the Fire. Miserable is the abode of the wicked.

3:152 And God has fulfilled His promise to you, that you would overwhelm them with His permission; but then you failed and disputed in the matter and disobeyed after He showed you what you had sought. Some of you want this world, and some of you want the Hereafter. Then He let you retreat from them that He may test you; and He has pardoned you. God is with great grace over the believers.

3:153 For you were ascending to the high ground and would not even glance towards anyone, and the messenger was calling to you from behind. Therefore He gave you worry to replace your worry, so that you would not have sadness by what has passed you, or for what afflicted you, and God is Expert over what you do.

3:154 Then He sent down to you after the worry a tranquility in sleepiness, it overtook a group of you; and another group was obsessed with themselves, they were thinking about God other than the truth, the thoughts of the days of ignorance. They say: "Why are we involved in this affair?" Say: "The entire affair is for God." They hide in their souls what they do not show to you, they say: "If we had a say in this affair then none of us would have been killed here." Say: "If you were inside your own homes, then the ones who had been marked for death would have come out to their resting place." God will test what is in your chests and bring out what is in your hearts. God is Knowledgeable as to what is in the chests.

3:155 Those of you who turned away the day the two hosts met, it was the devil who made them slip due to some of what they had earned. And God has pardoned them, for God is Forgiver, Compassionate.

3:156 O you who believe do not be like those who rejected and said to their brothers when they had gone forth in the land or on the offensive: "If they were here with us they would not have died nor been killed." God will make this a source of grief in their hearts, and God grants life and death, and God is watching over what you do.

3:157   And if you are killed in the cause of God or die, then forgiveness from God and mercy are far greater than all they can put together.

3:158   And if you die or are killed, then to God you will be gathered.

3:159   It was a mercy from God that you were soft towards them; had you been harsh and mean hearted, they would have dispersed from you; so pardon them and ask forgiveness for them, and consult them in the matter; but when you are convinced, then put your trust in God; for God loves those who put their trust.

3:160   If God grants you victory then none can defeat you, and if He abandons you then who can grant you victory after Him? And towards God the believers should put their trust.

3:161   It was not for any prophet to embezzle, and he who embezzles will be brought with what he has embezzled on the Day of Resurrection, then every soul will be given what it has earned without being wronged.

3:162   Is he who follows the pleasure of God as he who draws the wrath of God and his abode is Hell and a miserable destiny?

3:163   They are in grades with God, and God is Seer of what they do.

3:164   God has bestowed grace upon the believers by sending them a messenger from among themselves reciting His revelations and purifying them and teaching them the Book and the wisdom, and they were before in manifest darkness.

3:165   And so it was when you suffered setback; even though you afflicted them with twice as much setback; you said: "Where is this coming from?" Say: "It is from yourselves." God is capable of all things.

3:166   And what you suffered on the day the two hosts met was with the permission of God, and to let the believers know.

3:167   And to let those who are hypocrites know, that they were told: "Come fight in the cause of God or defend," they said: "If we knew how to fight we would have followed you." They are closer to rejection than they are to belief. They say with their mouths what is not in their hearts, and God is aware of what they conceal.

3:168   Those who remained and said to their brothers: "If they obeyed us they would not have been killed." Say: "Then avert death away from yourselves if you are truthful!"

3:169   And do not think that those who are killed in the cause of God are dead. No, they are alive at their Lord receiving a bounty.

3:170   Happy with what God has granted them from His grace, and they rejoice in those who have yet to follow after them. There is no fear upon them nor do they grieve.

3:171   They rejoice with the bounty of God and grace; God will not waste the recompense of the believers.

3:172   Those who have answered God and the messenger after they were afflicted with wounds. For those of them who did good and were righteous is a great recompense.

3:173   The ones who the people said to them: "The people have gathered against you, so be concerned by them," but it only increased their faith and they said: "God is sufficient for us, and He is the best to put our trust in."

3:174   So they came back with a recompense from God and a bounty, no harm would touch them. And they had followed the pleasure of God, and God is the One with great pleasure.

3:175   It is only the devil trying to create fear for his allies, so do not fear them, but fear Me if you are believers.

3:176   And do not be saddened by those who rush into disbelief. They will not harm God in the least. God does not wish to make for them any share in the Hereafter, and they will have a painful retribution.

3:177   Those who have purchased rejection with belief will not harm God in the least, and they will have a painful retribution.

3:178   And let not those who reject think that We are providing for them out of the goodness of themselves. We are only providing for them so that they may increase in sin, and they will have a humiliating retribution.

3:179   God was not to leave the believers as they were without distinguishing the rotten from the good. And God was not to let you know the future, but God chooses from His messengers whom He wishes; so believe in God and His messengers. And if you believe and are righteous, then you will have a great recompense.

3:180   And let not those who are stingy with what God has given them of His bounty think that it is good for them, no, it is evil for them. They will be surrounded by what they were stingy with on the

Day of Resurrection. And to God will be the inheritance of the heavens and the earth; and God is Expert over what you do.

3:181 God has heard the words of those who said: "God is poor and we are rich!" We will record what they have said and their killing of the prophets without right; and We will say: "Taste the retribution of the Fire!"

3:182 This is for what their hands have delivered, and God does not wrong the servants.

3:183 Those who said: "God has pledged to us that we should not believe in a messenger unless he brings us an offering which the fire will devour." Say: "Messengers have come to you before me with clarity and with what you have said, so why did you kill them if you were truthful?"

3:184 If they deny you, then messengers before you were also denied; they came with the proofs and the scriptures and the Book of Enlightenment.

3:185 Every person will taste death, and you will be recompensed your dues on the Day of Resurrection. Whoever is swayed from the Fire and entered into Paradise, he has indeed won. This worldly life is nothing more than the enjoyment of vanity.

3:186 We will test you in your wealth and in yourselves, and you will hear from those who have been given the Book from before you and from the polytheists much annoyance. And if you are patient and righteous, then that is from a strength of conviction.

3:187 And God took the covenant of those who were given the Book: "You will make it clear to the people and not conceal it." But they placed it behind their backs and purchased with it a cheap price. Miserable indeed is what they have purchased.

3:188 Do not think that those who are happy with what they have been given, and they love to be praised for what they did not do; do not think they are saved from the punishment. For them is a painful retribution.

3:189 And to God is the sovereignty of the heavens and the earth, and God is capable of all things.

3:190 In the creation of the heavens and the earth, and the difference between the night and the day, are signs for those who possess intelligence.

45

3:191   Those who remember God while standing, and sitting, and on their sides, and they ponder over the creation of the heavens and the earth: "Our Lord you have not created this without purpose, glory to You, spare us the retribution of the Fire!"

3:192   "Our Lord, whoever You admit to the Fire has been disgraced. The wicked will have no supporters."

3:193   "Our Lord, we have heard a caller inviting to the faith: "Believe in your Lord," so we have believed. Our Lord forgive us our bad deeds, and forgive our sins, and let us die in the company of the righteous."

3:194   "Our Lord, and grant us what You have promised through Your messengers, and do not embarrass us on the Day of Resurrection. You do not break the promise."

3:195   Their Lord answered them: "I do not waste the work of any worker from among you, whether male or female, you are all as each other. For those who emigrated and were driven out from their homes and were harmed in My cause, and they fought and were killed, I will forgive for them their sins and admit them to estates with rivers flowing beneath them." A recompense from God; and God has the best recompense.

3:196   Do not be deceived by the success of those who have rejected in the land.

3:197   A brief enjoyment, then their abode is Hell. What a miserable abode!

3:198   As for those who reverence their Lord, they will have estates with rivers flowing beneath them; abiding therein as a dwelling from God. What is with God is better for the obedient.

3:199   And from the people of the Book are those who believe in God and what was sent down to you and what was sent down to them; fearful to God, they do not purchase with the revelations of God a cheap price. These will have their recompense with their Lord. For God is swift in reckoning.

3:200   O you who believe, be patient and call for patience, and stand firm, and reverence God that you may succeed.

CHAPTER 4

4:0 In the name of God, the Almighty, the Merciful.

4:1 O people, be aware of your Lord who has created you from one person and He created from it its mate and sent forth from it many men and many women; and be aware of God whom you ask about, and the relatives. God is Watcher over you.

4:2 And give the orphans their money; and do not substitute the rotten for the good, and do not consume their money to your money; for truly it is a great sin!

4:3 And if you fear that you cannot be equitable to the orphans, then you may marry those who are agreeable to you of the women: two, and three, and four. But if you fear you will not be fair, then only one, or whom you are committed to by your oath. This is best that you do not face financial hardship.

4:4 And give the women their charities willingly, and if they remit any of it to you of their own will, then you may take it with good feelings.

4:5 And do not give the immature ones your money for which God has made you overseers, and spend on them from it and clothe them, and speak to them in goodness.

4:6 And test the orphans when they reach puberty, then, if you have determined from them comprehension, then give them their money, and do not deliberately consume it wastefully or quickly before they grow up. And whoever is rich, then let him not claim anything, and if he is poor then let him consume in kindness. If you give to them their money, then make a witness for them, and God is enough for Reckoning.

4:7 For the men is a portion from what the parents and the relatives left behind, and for the women is a portion from what the parents and relatives left behind, be it little or much; a forced portion.

4:8 And if the distribution is attended by the relatives and the orphans and the needy, then you shall give them part of it and say to them a kind saying.

4:9 And let them be concerned, that if it was they who had left behind them a weak progeny, would they not fear for them? Let them reverence God and let them say what is appropriate.

4:10   Those who consume the money of the orphans illicitly, in fact they are consuming fire in their bellies, and they will endure the Blaze.

4:11   God directs you regarding your children: "To the male shall be as that given to two females; however, if the women are more than two, then they will have two thirds of what is left behind; and if she is only one, then she will have one half. And to his parents, each one of them shall have one sixth of what is left behind, if he has a child. If he has no child, and his parents are the heirs, then to his mother is one third; and if he has siblings then to his mother is one sixth. All after a will is carried through or a debt. Your parents and your children, you do not know which are closer to you in benefit—an edict from God, for God is Knowledgeable, Wise."

4:12   And for you is half from your wives of what is left behind, if they have no child; however, if they have a child, then to you is one quarter of what is left behind. All after a will is carried through or a debt. And to them is one quarter of what is left behind, if you have no child; however, if you have a child, then to them is one eighth of what is left behind. All after a will is carried through or a debt. And if a man or a woman who is being inherited has no dependents, but has a brother or a sister, then to each one of them is one sixth, but if they are more than this then they are to share in one third. All after a will is carried through or a debt, to avoid causing harm. A dispensation from God, and God is Knowledgeable, Compassionate.

4:13   These are the boundaries of God, and whoever obeys God and His messenger, He will admit him to estates with rivers flowing beneath them, abiding therein. This is the great triumph.

4:14   And whoever disobeys God and His messenger, and transgresses His boundaries, He will admit him to a Fire, abiding therein, and he will have a humiliating retribution.

4:15   And those of your women who commit immorality, you shall bring four witnesses over them from among you; if they bear witness, then you shall restrict them in the homes until death terminates their lives, or God makes for them a way out.

4:16   And the two men who commit it from among you, you shall trouble them. If they repent and reform, then leave them alone. God is Redeemer, Merciful.

4:17   Repentance is only for those who commit a sin out of ignorance and then repent soon after; these will be forgiven by God, for God is Knowledgeable, Wise.

4:18 And there will be no repentance for those who commit sin then when death comes upon any one of them he says: "I repent now!" Nor for those who die while they are rejecters. For those We have prepared a painful retribution.

4:19 O you who believe, it is not permissible for you to inherit from the women by force. And do not make difficulty for them so that you may take away some of what you have given them, unless they commit a clear immorality. And live with them in kindness. If you dislike them, then perhaps you dislike something while God makes in it much good.

4:20 And if you wish to replace one wife with another, and you have given one of them a large amount, then do not take anything from it. Will you take it by falsehood while it is clearly a sin?

4:21 And how can you take it when you have become intimate with each other, and they have taken from you a solemn covenant?

4:22 And do not marry who your fathers had married from the women, except what has already been done. It is an immorality, and an abhorrence, and an evil path.

4:23 Forbidden for you are your mothers, and your daughters, and your sisters, and the sisters of your father, and the sisters of your mother, and the daughters of your brother, and the daughters of your sister, and your foster mothers who suckled you, and your sisters from suckling, and the mothers of your women, and your step-daughters who are in your lodgings from your women with whom you have already consummated the marriage; if you have not consummated the marriage then there is no sin upon you; and those who were in wedlock with your sons who are from your seed, and that you join between two sisters except what has already been done. God is Forgiving, Merciful.

4:24 And the emancipated from the women—except those committed to by your oath—is God's decree over you. And it is permitted for you to seek beyond this category that you employ your wealth, to be emancipated, not for illicit sex. So, for those of them you find pleasing, then you shall give them their dowries as an obligation; and there is no sin upon you for what you agree on after the obligation. God is Knowledgeable, Wise.

4:25 And whoever of you cannot afford to marry the emancipated female believers, then from those committed to by your oath of the believing young women. And God is more aware of your faith, some of you to each other. You shall marry them with the permission of their parents, and give them their dowries in kindness. To be emancipated—not for illicit sex or taking lovers. Once they are emancipated, then any of them who comes with an immorality shall have half of what is upon those already emancipated of the punishment. This is for those who fear a hardship from among you, but if you are patient it is better for you. And God is Forgiver, Merciful.

4:26   God wants to clarify for you and guide you to the paths of those before you, and pardon you, and God is Knowledgeable, Wise.

4:27   And God wants to pardon you, but those who follow desires want that you would be diverted into a great diversion.

4:28   God wants to alleviate for you; and mankind was created weak.

4:29   O you who believe, do not consume your money between you unjustly, unless it is through a trade which is mutually agreed by you. And do not kill yourselves; God is Merciful towards you.

4:30   And whoever does so out of animosity and transgression, We will cast him into a fire; and this for God is easy to do.

4:31   If you avoid the major sins that you are prohibited against, then We will cancel your existing sins and admit you to a generous entrance.

4:32   And do not envy that which God has graced some of you over others with. For the men is a portion of what they earned, and for the women is a portion of what they earned. And ask God from His grace; God is knowledgeable in all things.

4:33   And for each We have made inheritors for what was left behind by the parents and the relatives. And those bound by your oath, you shall give them their portion. God is witness over all things.

4:34   The men are to support the women with what God has bestowed upon them over one another and for what they spend of their money. The upright females are dutiful; keeping private the personal matters for what God keeps watch over. As for those females from whom you fear rebellion, then you shall advise them, and abandon them in the bedchambers, and withdraw from them; if they obey you, then do not seek a way over them; God is Most High, Great.

4:35   And if you fear a permanent rift between them, then send a judge from his family and a judge from her family. If they want to reconcile, then God will bring them together. God is Knowledgeable, Expert.

4:36   And serve God and do not set up anything with Him, and do good to the parents, and the relatives, and the orphans, and the needy, and the neighbor who is a relative, and the neighbor nearby, and the friend nearby, and the wayfarer, and those committed to by your oath. God does not love the arrogant, the boastful.

4:37   Those who are stingy and order the people to stinginess, and they conceal what God has given them from His bounty. And We have prepared for the rejecters a humiliating retribution.

4:38   And those who spend their money to show off to the people, and they do not believe in God or the Last Day. And whoever has the devil as his associate, then what a miserable associate!

4:39   What would bother them if they believed in God and the Last Day and spent from the provisions of God? God is aware of them.

4:40   Indeed, God does not wrong the weight of an atom; and if it is good He will double it. And He grants from Himself a great recompense.

4:41   How is it then when We bring forth from every nation a witness, and bring you as a witness over these?

4:42   On that Day those who rejected and disobeyed the messenger will wish that the earth would swallow them; but they cannot hide any narrative from God.

4:43   O you who believe, do not come near the Connection while you are intoxicated, until you know what you are saying. Nor if you have had intercourse, unless a wayfarer, until you wash. And if you are ill, or traveling, or one of you has excreted feces, or you had sexual contact with the women, and could not find water, then you shall select from the clean soil; you shall wipe your faces and hands. God is Pardoning, Forgiving.

4:44   Did you not note those who have been given a portion of the Book? They purchased straying, and they want you to stray from the path.

4:45   And God is fully aware of your enemies; and God is enough as a supporter, and God is enough as a victor.

4:46   From among those who are Jewish are some who take the words out of context, and they say: "We hear and disobey, and listen but let not any listen, and shepherd us," in a twisting of their tongues and as a mockery of the system! And had they said: "We hear and obey, and listen, and watch over us," it would have been better for them and more upright; but God has cursed them for their disbelief, they do not believe except very little.

4:47 O you who have received the Book, believe in what We have sent down affirming what is with you, before We cast down faces and turn them on their backs or curse them as the people of the Sabbath were cursed. And the will of God is always done.

4:48 God does not forgive that partners be set up with Him, and He forgives other than that for whom He pleases. Whoever sets up partners with God has indeed invented a great sin.

4:49 Did you not note those who ascribe purity to themselves? No, it is God who purifies whom He wills, and they will not be wronged in the least.

4:50 See how they invent lies about God! And that is enough as a clear sin.

4:51 Did you not note those who were given a portion of the Book, they believe in sorcery and evil, and they say to those who rejected: "You are better guided than those who believed the path."

4:52 These are the ones whom God has cursed, and whoever God curses, you will not find for him a victor.

4:53 Or would they have a portion of the sovereignty? If so, then they would not give the people a speck.

4:54 Or do they envy the people for what God has given them of His bounty? We have given the descendants of Abraham the Book and the wisdom; We have given them a great kingship.

4:55 Some of them believed in it, and some of them turned away from it. In Hell will be enough flames.

4:56 Those who have rejected Our revelations, We will admit them to a Fire. Every time their skins are cooked, We replace them with other skins that they may taste the retribution. God is Noble, Wise.

4:57 And those who believe and do good, We will admit them to estates with rivers flowing beneath them; abiding therein eternally, in it they will have pure mates, and We will admit them to a vast shade.

4:58　God orders you to deliver anything you have been entrusted with to its owners. And if you judge between the people, then you shall judge with justice. It is always the best that God prescribes for you. God is Hearer, Seer.

4:59　O you who believe, obey God and obey the messenger and those in authority among you. But if you dispute in any matter, then you shall refer it to God and His messenger if you believe in God and the Last Day. That is better and more suitable for knowing.

4:60　Did you not note those who claimed they believed in what was sent down to you and what was sent before you? They wanted to seek judgment using evil, while they were ordered to reject it. It is the devil who wants to lead them far astray.

4:61　And if they are told: "Come to what God has sent down and to the messenger," you see the hypocrites turning away from you strongly.

4:62　Why then, when disaster befalls them for what their hands have delivered, do they come to you swearing by God that they only wanted to do good and reconcile?

4:63　These are a people whom God knows what is in their hearts, so turn away from them and advise them, and say to them in their souls a clear saying.

4:64　We do not send a messenger except to be obeyed with the permission of God. And had they come to you when they had wronged themselves and sought the forgiveness of God, and the messenger sought forgiveness for them, they would have then found God to be Pardoning, Merciful.

4:65　No, by your Lord, they will not believe until they make you judge in what they dispute with each other, then they will not find in their souls any animosity for what you have decided, and they will comply completely.

4:66　And had We decreed for them: "Kill yourselves," or "Leave your land," they would not have done so except for a few of them. And if they had done what they were advised with, it would have been better for them and helped to strengthen them.

4:67　Then We would have given them from Us a great recompense.

4:68　And We would have guided them to a straight path.

4:69　And whoever obeys God and the messenger will be among those whom God has graced from the prophets and the truthful and the martyrs and the upright. What an excellent companionship!

4:70   That is the bounty from God; and God knows what is best.

4:71   O you who believe, take your precaution by going out in clusters, or going out all together.

4:72   And from among you are those who would slow behind, so that if disaster befalls you he would say: "God has graced me that I was not a martyr with them!"

4:73   And if grace from God benefits you, he will speak as if there had not been affection between you and him: "Oh, I wish I had been with them so I would have triumphed a great triumph."

4:74   Let those who seek to purchase the Hereafter rather than this world fight in the cause of God. And whoever fights in the cause of God and is killed or attains victory, then We will grant him a great recompense.

4:75   And why do you not fight in the cause of God, when the weak among the men and women and children say: "Our Lord, bring us out of this town whose people are wicked, and grant us from Yourself a supporter, and grant us from Yourself a victor!"

4:76   Those who believe fight in the cause of God, while those who reject fight in the cause of evil; so fight the supporters of the devil, for the planning of the devil is weak.

4:77   Did you not note those who were told: "Cease your aggression, and hold the Connection, and contribute towards purification." But when fighting was decreed for them, a group of them were concerned towards the people as they would have been concerned towards God or even more so. And they said: "Our Lord, why did You decree fighting for us? If only You would delay for us until another time." Say: "The enjoyment of this world is little, and the Hereafter is far better for those who are aware; you will not be wronged in the least."

4:78   Wherever you may be, death will find you, even if you are in fortified towers. If any good befalls them, they say: "This is from God," and if any evil befalls them, they say: "This is from you!" Say: "All is from God;" what is wrong with these people, they barely understand any narrative!

4:79   Any good that befalls you is due to God, and any evil that befalls you is due to yourself. We have sent you as a messenger to the people and God is enough as a witness.

4:80   Whoever obeys the messenger has obeyed God; and whoever turns away, We have not sent you as a guardian over them.

4:81   And they say: "Obedience," but when they come out from being with you, a group of them prepares for other than what you have said, and God records what they planned. So turn away from them and put your trust in God. God is enough for your trust.

4:82   Do they not reflect on the Qur'an? If it was from any other than God they would have found in it many a discrepancy.

4:83   And if any matter regarding security, or fear, comes to them they make it publicly known, but if they had referred it to the messenger and to those entrusted from them then it would have been known by those who studied it from them. And had it not been for the grace of God upon you and His mercy, you would have followed the devil, except for a few.

4:84   So fight in the cause of God; you are not responsible except for yourself. And enjoin the believers: "Perhaps God will put a stop to the might of those who disbelieved." And God is far Mightier and far more Punishing.

4:85   Whoever intercedes with a good intercession, he will have a reward of it; and whoever intercedes with an evil intercession, he will receive a share of it. And God has control over all things.

4:86   And if you are greeted with a greeting, then return an even better greeting or return the same. God is Reckoning over all things.

4:87   God, there is no god except He. He will gather you for the Day of Resurrection in which there is no doubt. Who is more truthful a narrative than God?

4:88   What is the matter with you that you are divided into two groups over the hypocrites, while God has regressed them for what they have earned? Do you want to guide those whom God misguides? Whoever God causes to be misguided, you will never find for him a path.

4:89   They hope that you will reject as they have rejected, then you will be the same. Do not take any of them as allies until they emigrate in the cause of God. If they turn away, then take them and kill them wherever you find them; and do not take from them any ally or supporter.

4:90 Except for those who reach a people with whom you have a covenant, or if they come to you with a reluctance in their chests to fight you or to fight their own people. Had God willed He would have given them strength and they would have fought you. But if they retire from you, and do not fight you, and they offer you peace; then God does not make for you a path against them.

4:91 You will find others who want to be safe among you and safe among their own people. Every time they are returned to the test, they fall back in it. If they do not withdraw from you, and offer you peace, and restrain their hands; then you may take them, and you may kill them wherever you engage them. For these We have given you a clear authority.

4:92 And it is not for a believer to kill another believer except by accident. And whoever kills a believer by accident, then he shall free a believing slave, and give compensation to the family; except if they remit it. If he was from a people who are enemies to you, and he was a believer, then you shall free a believing slave. And if he was from a people with whom you have a covenant, then a compensation to his family, and free a believing slave. Whoever does not find, then the fasting of two consecutive months as a repentance from God; for God is Knowledgeable, Wise.

4:93 And whoever kills a believer intentionally, then his recompense shall be Hell, abiding therein, and God will be angry with him, and curse him, and for him is prepared a great retribution.

4:94 O you who believe, if you strike in the cause of God, you shall investigate carefully. And do not say to he who greets you with peace: "You are not a believer!" You are seeking the vanity of this world; but with God are many riches. That is how you were before, but God graced you, so investigate carefully. God is expert over what you do.

4:95 Not equal are those who stayed behind from the believers; except those disabled; with those who strived in the cause of God with their money and lives. God has preferred those who strive with their money and lives over those who stayed behind by a grade; and to both God has promised goodness; and God has preferred those who strived over those who stayed behind by a great reward.

4:96 Grades from Him and forgiveness and a mercy. God is Forgiving, Merciful.

4:97 Those whose lives are terminated by the angels, while they had wronged themselves; they said: "What situation were you in?"

They said: "We were oppressed on the earth." They said: "Was the earth of God not wide enough that you could emigrate in it?" To these their abode will be Hell; what a miserable destiny!

4:98 Except for those who were oppressed from the men, women, and children who could not devise a plan nor could be guided to a way.

4:99 For these, perhaps God will pardon them. God is Pardoner, Forgiving.

4:100 Whoever emigrates in the cause of God will find in the earth many spoils and a bounty. And whoever leaves his home emigrating to God and His messenger, then is overcome by death; his recompense has fallen to God, and God is Forgiving, Merciful.

4:101 And if you go forth in the land, then there is no harm that you shorten from the Connection, if you fear that the rejecters will try you. The rejecters are to you a clear enemy.

4:102 And if you are with them and you hold the Connection for them, then let a group from among them stand with you and let them bring their weapons; and when they have prostrated then let them be behind you; and let a group who has not yet connected come and connect with you, and let them be wary and let them bring their weapons with them. The rejecters hope that you would neglect your weapons and goods so they can come upon you in one blow. There is no sin upon you if you are impeded by rainfall, or if you are ill, that you place down your weapons. And be wary. God has prepared for the rejecters a humiliating retribution.

4:103 Once you are done with the Connection, then remember God while standing, or sitting, or on your sides. Then, when you are secure, hold the Connection. Indeed, the Connection for the believers is a book that is scheduled.

4:104 And do not falter in the pursuit of the remaining group. If you are feeling pain, then they are also feeling pain as you are; and you seek from God what they do not seek. God is Knowledgeable, Wise.

4:105 We have revealed to you the Book with the truth that you may judge between the people by that which God has shown you, and do not be an advocate for the treacherous.

4:106 And seek forgiveness from God; for God is Forgiver, Merciful.

4:107 And do not argue on behalf of those who betray themselves. God does not love those who are betrayers, sinners.

4:108   They may conceal this from the people, but they do not conceal it from God, and He was with them when they schemed what He does not approve of to be said. God is Encompassing what they do.

4:109   Here you are arguing on their behalf in this world, but who will argue on their behalf with God on the Day of Resurrection? Or, who will be their sponsor?

4:110   And whoever does any evil, or wrongs himself, then seeks the forgiveness of God; he will find God is Forgiver, Merciful.

4:111   And whoever earns any sin, then he has brought it on himself. And God is Knowledgeable, Wise.

4:112   And whoever earns a wrongdoing or sin, then blames it on an innocent person; he has incurred falsehood and a clear sin.

4:113   And had it not been for the grace of God upon you and His mercy, a group of them would have obsessed on misguiding you; they would not have misguided except themselves, nor would they harm you in anything. And God has sent down to you the Book and the wisdom, and He has taught you what you did not know. And the grace of God upon you is great.

4:114   There is no good in most of what they privately confer, except whoever orders a charity or kindness or reconciliation between the people. And whoever does this seeking the grace of God, We will give him a great recompense.

4:115   And whoever is hostile to the messenger after the guidance has been clarified to him, and he follows other than the path of the believers; We will grant him what he has sought and deliver him to Hell; what a miserable destination.

4:116   God does not forgive that partners be set up with Him, and He forgives other than that for whom He pleases. Whoever sets up partners with God has indeed strayed a far straying.

4:117   They are calling on females besides Him. Indeed, they are only calling on a persistent devil.

4:118   God has cursed him; and he said: "I will take from Your servants a sizeable portion."

4:119   "And I will misguide them and make them desire, and I will command them so that they will mark the ears of the hoofed animals, and I will command them so they will make change to the creation of God." Whoever takes the devil as a supporter other than God, then he has indeed lost a great loss.

4:120   He promises them and makes them desire, but what the devil promises them is only vanity.

4:121   For these, their abode shall be Hell, and they will find no escape from it.

4:122   As for those who believe and do good works, We will admit them to estates with rivers flowing beneath them, abiding therein eternally. The promise of God is truth; and who is more truthful in saying than God?

4:123   It will not be by what you desire, nor by what the people of the Book desire. Whoever works evil, he will be paid for it; and he will not find for himself besides God any supporter or victor.

4:124   And whoever does good works, whether male or female, and is a believer, then these will be admitted to Paradise, and they will not be wronged in the least.

4:125   And who is better in the system than the one who submits himself to God, and he is a good doer, and he follows the creed of Abraham in monotheism? And God took Abraham as a friend.

4:126   And to God is what is in the heavens and the earth; and God is Encompassing all things.

4:127   And they seek a ruling regarding the women, say: "God will give you a ruling regarding them and what is being recited to you in the Book regarding the orphans' mothers whom you wish to marry but have not given them what was decreed for them, and the oppressed from the children: That you stand for the orphans in equality." Whatever good you do, then God is aware of it.

4:128   And if a woman fears from her husband rebellion or disregard, then there is no sin upon them to find a solution of reconciliation between themselves; and reconciliation is best. And the souls are brought by need; and if you are kind and do right, then God is expert over what you do.

4:129   And you will not be able to be fair regarding the women even if you make every effort; so do not sway too greatly and leave her as one hanging in a void. And if you reconcile and do right, then God is Forgiver, Merciful.

4:130 And if they separate, then God will provide for each of them from His bounty. God is Vast, Wise.

4:131 And to God is what is in the heavens and the earth; and We have instructed those who were given the Book before you, and you, to be aware of God. And if you reject, then to God is all that is in the heavens and the earth; God is Rich, Praiseworthy.

4:132 And to God is all that is in the heavens and the earth; and God is enough as a Caretaker.

4:133 O you people, if He wills, He can make all of you cease to exist; then He will bring others in your place. God is most capable to do this.

4:134 Whoever seeks the reward of this world, then with God is the reward of this world and the Hereafter. God is Hearing, Watchful.

4:135 O you who believe, stand with justice as witnesses to God, even if against yourselves, or the parents or the relatives. Even if he be rich or poor, God is more worthy of them, so do not follow desire into being unjust. And if you twist or turn away, then God is Expert over what you do.

4:136 O you who believe; believe in God and His messenger, and the Book which was sent down to His messenger, and the Book which was sent before. And whoever rejects God, and His angels, and His Books, and His messengers, and the Last Day; then he has strayed a far straying.

4:137 Those who believed, then rejected, then believed, then rejected, then they increased in rejection; God was not to forgive them nor to guide them to the path.

4:138 Give news to the hypocrites that they will have a painful retribution.

4:139 Those who take the rejecters as allies instead of the believers: "Do they seek glory with them?" All glory belongs to God.

4:140 And it has been sent down to you in the Book, that if you hear the revelations of God being rejected and mocked, then do not sit with them until they move on to a different narrative; if not, then you are like them. God will gather the hypocrites and the disbelievers in Hell all together.

4:141 Those who linger and observe you, if you have a victory from God they say: "Were we not with you?" And if the rejecters have success, they say: "Did we not side with you and deter the believers from you?" God will judge between you on the Day of Resurrection, and God will not grant the rejecters any success over the believers.

4:142 The hypocrites seek to deceive God, while He is deceiving them; and if they attend to the Connection, they do so lazily, only to show the people; they do not remember God except very little.

4:143 They are swaying in-between, neither with this group nor with that group. Whoever God will misguide, you will not find for him a way.

4:144 O you who believe, do not take the rejecters as allies instead of the believers. Do you want God to have a reason against you?

4:145 The hypocrites will be in the lowest pit of the Fire; and you will not find for them a victor.

4:146 Except those who repent, and amend, and hold fast to God, and are loyal in their system to God; then these will be with the believers. And God will give the believers a great recompense.

4:147 What would God want with your punishment if you were only thankful and believed? God is Thankful, Knowledgeable.

4:148 God does not love that any negative sayings be publicized, except if one is wronged. God is Hearer, Knowledgeable.

4:149 If you reveal what is good or hide it, or forgive what is bad, then God is Pardoner, Capable.

4:150 Those who rejected God and His messengers, and they want to make a separation between God and His messengers, and they say: "We believe in some and reject some!" And they desire to take a path in-between.

4:151 These are the true rejecters; and We have prepared for the rejecters a humiliating retribution.

4:152 And those who believe in God and His messengers and do not make a distinction between any of them, We will give them their recompense. And God is Forgiving, Merciful.

4:153 The people of the Book ask you to bring down to them a book from the heaven. They had asked Moses for even more than that, for they said: "Show us God openly!" So the thunderbolt took them for their wickedness. Then they took the calf after the clarity had come to them, and We pardoned them for this; We gave Moses a clear authority.

4:154 And We raised the mount above them by the covenant they took, and We said to them: "Enter the passageway by crouching." And We said to them: "Do not transgress the Sabbath;" and We took from them a solemn covenant.

4:155 So, for the breaking of their covenant, and their rejection of the revelations of God, and their killing of the prophets without right, and their saying: "Our hearts are shielded." Indeed, God has stamped upon their hearts because of their rejection; they do not believe, except for a few.

4:156 And for their rejection and their saying about Mary a great falsehood.

4:157 And their saying: "We have killed the Messiah, Jesus, son of Mary, messenger of God!" And they had not killed him, nor crucified him, but it appeared to them as if they had. And those who dispute are in doubt regarding him, they have no knowledge except to follow conjecture; they did not kill him for a certainty.

4:158 Instead, God had raised him to Himself; and God is Noble, Wise.

4:159 And from the people of the Book are those who refused to believe in him before his death, and on the Day of Resurrection he will be witness against them.

4:160 Because of wickedness from among those who are Jewish, We made forbidden to them the good things that were always permissible to them; and for their deterring many from the path of God.

4:161 And for their taking of usury, while they were prohibited from doing so, and for their consuming the money of the people unjustly. We have prepared for the disbelievers among them a painful retribution.

4:162 But those of them who are well founded in knowledge, and the believers, they believe in what was sent down to you and what was sent down before you; and those who hold the Connection, and those who contribute towards purification, and those who believe in God and the Last Day; to these We will give them their recompense greatly.

4:163 We have inspired you as We had inspired Noah and the prophets after him. And We had inspired Abraham, and Ishmael, and Isaac, and Jacob, and the Patriarchs, and Jesus, and Job, and Jonah, and Aaron, and Solomon; and We gave David the Psalms.

4:164 And messengers whom We have narrated to you from before, and messengers whom We have not narrated to you; and God spoke to Moses directly.

4:165 Messengers who were bearers of good news and warners, so that there will be no excuse for the people with God after the messengers. God is Noble, Wise.

4:166 But God bears witness for what He has sent down to you with His knowledge, and the angels bear witness; and God is enough as a witness.

4:167 Those who have rejected and turned away from the path of God, they have strayed a far straying.

4:168 Those who have rejected and did wrong, God was not to forgive them, nor guide them to a path.

4:169 Except to the path of Hell, they will abide therein eternally. For God this is very easy.

4:170 O people, a messenger has come to you with the truth from your Lord, so believe; that is better for you. And if you reject, then to God is what is in the heavens and the earth. And God is Knowledgeable, Wise.

4:171 O people of the Book, do not overstep in your system, nor say about God except the truth. Jesus, son of Mary, was no more than a messenger of God and His word, which He cast to Mary, and a Spirit from Him. So believe in God and His messengers, and do not say: "Three." Cease, for it is better for you. God is only One god, be He glorified that He should have a son! To Him is all that is in the heavens and the earth; and God is enough as a Caretaker.

4:172 The Messiah is not too proud to be a servant to God, nor are the angels who are close to Him. Whoever is too proud from His service, and is arrogant, then He will gather them all towards Him together.

4:173 As for those who believe and do good works, He will give them their recompense and increase for them from His bounty. And as for those who are too proud and arrogant, He will punish them a painful retribution, and they will not find besides God any supporter or victor.

4:174 O people, proof has come to you from your Lord, and We have sent down to you a guiding light.

4:175 As for those who believe in God and hold fast to Him, He will admit them in a mercy from Him and a bounty, and He will guide them to Himself, a straight path.

4:176   They seek a ruling from you, say: "God gives you the ruling for those who have no dependants. If a person passes away and has no child, but has a sister, then she shall receive half of what is left behind; and he will inherit from her if she has no child. However, if he has two sisters, then they will receive two thirds of what is left behind; and if he has siblings, men and women, then to the male shall be as that given to two females." God makes clear to you that you do not stray; God is aware of all things.

Chapter 5

5:0   In the name of God, the Almighty, the Merciful.

5:1   O you who believe, fulfill the contracts. Permitted for you are the animal livestock, except that which is being recited to you—while maintaining the ban on hunting while you are under restriction. God decrees as He pleases.

5:2   O you who believe, do not violate the symbols of God, nor the restricted Month, nor the offerings, nor the regulations, nor the safety of the restricted House; for they are seeking a bounty from their Lord and a blessing. And when it is permitted for you, then you may hunt. And let not the hatred of another people; because they had barred you from the restricted Temple; make you aggress. And help each other in piety and righteousness, and do not help each other in sin and transgression. And be aware of God, for the retribution of God is severe.

5:3   Forbidden for you is that which is already dead, and blood, and the meat of pig, and what was sacrificed with to other than God. And that which has been strangled, and that which has been bludgeoned, and that which has fallen from a height, and that which has been gored, and that which a wild animal has savaged— unless it was slaughtered while it still lived—and what has been slaughtered on altars, and what you divide through arrows of chance. This is all nasty. Today the rejecters have given up from your system, so do not be concerned by them, but be concerned by Me. Today I have perfected your system for you, and completed My blessings upon you, and I have approved submission as the system for you. So, whoever is forced by severe hunger and not seeking sin, then God is Forgiving, Merciful.

5:4   They ask you what was made permissible to them, say: "All the good things have been made permissible for you, and what the birds of prey and trained dogs catch, you teach them from what God teaches you." So eat from what they have captured for you and mention the name of God upon it, and be aware of God. God is swift in reckoning.

5:5   Today, the good things have been made permissible to you, and the food of those who have been given the Book is permissible for you, and your food is permissible for them. And the emancipated females from those who are believers, and the emancipated females from those who have been given the Book before you; on condition that you give them their dowries. To be emancipated— not for illicit sex or taking lovers. And whoever rejects belief, then his work has fallen, and in the Hereafter he is of the losers.

5:6   O you who believe, when you attend to the Connection, then wash your faces and your hands up to the elbows, and wipe your heads and your feet to the ankles; and if you have had intercourse, then you shall purify. And if you are ill, or traveling, or you have excreted feces, or you have had sexual contact with the women, and you cannot find water, then you shall select from the clean soil; you shall wipe your faces and your hands with it. God does not want to place any hardship on you, but He wants to purify you and to complete His blessings upon you that you may be thankful.

5:7   And remember the blessings of God over you and His covenant that He has bound you with, for which you have said: "We hear and obey," and be aware of God; for God knows what is in the chests.

5:8   O you who believe, stand for God and be witnesses for justice, and let not the hatred towards a people make you avoid being just. Be just, for it is closer to righteousness, and be aware of God. God is expert over what you do.

5:9   God has promised those who believe and do good works that they will have forgiveness and a great recompense.

5:10   And those who reject and deny Our revelations, they are the dwellers of Hell.

5:11   O you who believe, remember the blessings of God upon you when a group desired to aggress against you, and He restrained their hands from you. And reverence God. And in God the believers should put their trust.

5:12   And God has taken the covenant of the Children of Israel, and We raised from them twelve representatives. And God said: "I am with you if you hold the Connection, and contribute towards purification, and believe in My messengers, and support them, and lend God a loan of righteousness; then I will cancel your sins and admit you into estates with rivers flowing beneath them. Whoever rejects after this from you, then he has strayed from the path."

5:13   Because of them breaking their covenant, We have cursed them, and made their hearts become hardened; they take the words out of context; and they forgot much of what they were reminded of. And you will still discover betrayal in them except for a few; so pardon them and overlook; God loves the good doers.

5:14   And from those who have said: "We are Nazarenes," We have taken their covenant and they have forgotten much of what they were reminded of; so We planted between them animosity and hatred until the Day of Resurrection; and God will inform them of what they had done.

5:15   O people of the Book, Our messenger has come to you to clarify for you much of what you were hiding from the Book, and to pardon over much. A light has come to you from God and a clarifying Book.

5:16   God guides with it whoever follows His acceptance, to the ways of peace; and it brings them out of the darkness and into the light with His permission; and it guides them to a straight path.

5:17   Rejecters indeed are those who have said: "God is the Messiah, son of Mary." Say: "Who has any power against God if He had wanted to destroy the Messiah, son of Mary, and his mother, and all who are on the earth!" And to God is the sovereignty of the heavens and the earth and all that is in-between; He creates what He pleases. God is capable of all things.

5:18   And the Jews and the Nazarenes said: "We are the children of God, and His loved ones." Say: "Then why does He punish you for your sins?" No, you are merely mortals which He has created. He forgives whom He pleases, and He punishes whom He pleases. And to God is the sovereignty of the heavens and the earth and all that is in-between, and to Him is the destiny.

5:19   O people of the Book, Our messenger has come to clarify for you after a lack of messengers; so that you cannot say: "No bearer of good news or warner has come to us;" for a bearer of good news and a warner has come to you; and God is capable of all things.

5:20 And Moses said to his people: "My people, remember the grace of God upon you that He made among you prophets, and made you sovereigns, and He gave you what He had not given any from the worlds."

5:21 "O my people, enter the holy land as God has decreed for you, and do not turn your backs, or you will become losers."

5:22 They said: "O Moses, in it are a mighty people, and we will not enter it until they leave from it. So when they leave from it, then we will enter."

5:23 Two men from among those who were reverent—being blessed by God—said: "Enter upon them by storming the gate; if you can enter it, then you will be the victors; and put your trust in God if you are believers."

5:24 They said: "O Moses, we will never enter it as long as they are in it, so go you and your Lord and fight, we will stay right here!"

5:25 He said: "My Lord, I do not possess except myself and my brother, so separate between us and between the wicked people."

5:26 He said: "Then it has become forbidden for them for forty years, and they will be lost in the land." Do not be sorrowful over the wicked people.

5:27 And recite to them the news of the two sons of Adam with truth. They had both made an offering, and it was accepted from one of them, and not accepted from the other. He said: "I will kill you!" He said: "God only accepts from the righteous."

5:28 "If you stretch your hand to kill me, I will not stretch my hand to kill you, for I fear God, Lord of the worlds."

5:29 "I want you to have both my sin and your own sin, and you will then be among the dwellers of the Fire. Such is the recompense of the wicked."

5:30 So he found it in himself to kill his brother; so he killed him. He thus became one of the losers.

5:31 So God sent forth a raven to scratch the land and show him how to deal with the body of his brother. He said: "Woe to me! Am I not even able to be like this raven and deal with the body of my brother?" So he became of those who regretted.

5:32 It is because of this that We have decreed for the Children of

Israel: "Anyone who kills a person for other than murder, or corruption in the land; then it is as if he has killed all the people! And whoever spares a life, then it is as if he has given life to all the people." Our messengers had come to them with clarities, but many of them are, after this, still corrupting on the earth.

5:33 The recompense of those who fight God and His messenger, and seek to make corruption in the land, is that they will be killed or crucified or that their hands and feet be cut off from alternate sides or that they be banished from the land; that is a disgrace for them in this world and in the Hereafter they will have a great retribution.

5:34 Except for those who repent before you overpower them, then know that God is Forgiving, Merciful.

5:35 O you who believe, be aware of God and seek a way to Him, and strive in His cause; that you may succeed.

5:36 Those who have rejected, if they had all that is on the earth and the same again with it to ransom against the retribution of the Day of Resurrection, it will not be accepted from them; and they will have a painful retribution.

5:37 They want to exit from the Fire, but they can never exit from it; and they will have a permanent retribution.

5:38 And the male thief, and the female thief, you shall cut their resources—as a penalty for what they have earned—to be made an example of from God. God is Noble, Wise.

5:39 Whoever repents after his wrongdoing and amends, then God will accept his repentance. God is Forgiving, Merciful.

5:40 Did you not know that God possesses the sovereignty of the heavens and the earth. He punishes whom He wills and He forgives whom He wills; and God is capable of all things.

5:41 O messenger, do not be saddened by those who increase in disbelief from among those who said: "We believe" with their mouths while their hearts did not believe. And from among those who are Jewish, there are those who listened to lies; they listened to people who never came to you; they distort the words from their context, and they say: "If you are given this, then take it, but if you are given anything different, then beware!" And whoever God wants to test, then you will not possess anything for him against God. These are the ones whose hearts God did not want to purify; in this world they will have humiliation, and in the Hereafter they will have a great retribution.

5:42   They listen to lies, and consume money illicitly. If they come to you, then you may judge between them or turn away from them; and if you turn away from them then they cannot harm you in the least; and if you judge then judge between them with justice. God loves those who are just.

5:43   And how can they make you their judge when they have the Torah, in which there is the judgment of God; then they turn away after that. Those are not believers.

5:44   We have sent down the Torah, in it is a guidance and a light; the prophets who have submitted judged with it for those who are Jewish, and the Rabbis, and the Priests, for what they were entrusted of the Book of God, and they were witness over. So do not be concerned with the people but be concerned with Me; and do not purchase with My revelations a cheap price. And whoever does not judge with what God has sent down, then these are the rejecters.

5:45   And We have decreed for them in it that a life for a life, and an eye for an eye, and a nose for a nose, and an ear for an ear, and a tooth for a tooth, and the wounds to be impartial; and whoever remits anything of it, then it will cancel sins for him. And whoever does not judge with what God has sent down, then these are the wicked.

5:46   And We sent in their footsteps Jesus, son of Mary, affirming what was between his hands of the Torah. And We gave him the Gospel, in it is a guidance and a light, and affirming what was between his hands of the Torah, and a guidance and a lesson for the righteous.

5:47   And let the people of the Gospel judge with what God has sent down in it. And whoever does not judge with what God has sent down, then these are the wicked.

5:48   And We have sent down to you the Book with the truth, affirming what is between your hands of the Book and superseding it. So judge between them by what God has sent down, and do not follow their desires from what has come to you of the truth. For each of you We have made decrees, and a structure; and if God had willed, He would have made you all one nation, but He tests you with what He has given you; so race to do good. To God you will return all of you, and He will inform you regarding that in which you dispute.

5:49 And judge between them by what God has sent down, and do not follow their desires, and beware lest they divert you away from some of what God has sent down to you. If they turn away, then know that God wants to inflict them with some of their sins; and many of the people are wicked.

5:50 Is it the judgment of the days of ignorance that they seek? And who is better than God as a judge for a people who comprehend?

5:51 O you who believe, do not take the Jews and the Nazarenes as allies, for they are allies to one another; and whoever takes them as such from among you is one of them. God does not guide the wicked people.

5:52 You will see those who have a disease in their hearts hurrying to them, saying: "We are concerned that a disaster will befall us!" Perhaps God will bring a victory or a decree from Himself, then they will become regretful over what they had kept hidden within themselves.

5:53 And those who believe said: "Were these the ones who swore oaths by God that they are with you?" Their works have collapsed, and they have become losers.

5:54 O you who believe, whoever from among you turns away from His system, then God will bring a people whom He loves and they love Him; humble towards the believers, dignified towards the rejecters; they strive in the cause of God and do not fear to be blamed by those who blame. This is the grace of God, He bestows it upon whom He wills; God is Encompassing, Knowledgeable.

5:55 For your supporter are God and His messenger and those who believe; they hold the Connection and contribute towards purification, and they kneel.

5:56 And whoever allies God and His messenger and those who believe; then the party of God are the ones who will be victorious.

5:57 O you who believe, do not take as allies those who have taken your system for mockery and play from among those who have been given the Book before you and the rejecters. And be aware of God if you are believers.

5:58 And if you call to the Connection, they take it for mockery and play. That is because they are a people who do not comprehend.

5:59 Say: "O people of the Book, do you hate us simply because we believe in God and in what was sent down to us and what was sent down before?" Alas, the majority of them are wicked.

5:60 Say: "Shall I inform you of worse than this as a punishment from God? Those whom God cursed and became angry at them, and He made from them apes and pigs and servants of evil. Those have a worse place and are more astray from the right path."

5:61 And if they come to you they say: "We believe," while they had entered in with rejection and went out with the same. God is aware of what they were hiding.

5:62 And you see many of them hasten to sin and transgression and consuming money illicitly. Miserable indeed is what they were doing.

5:63 If only the Rabbis and Priests had prohibited them for speaking in sin and consuming money illicitly. Miserable indeed is what they have done.

5:64 And the Jews said: "The hand of God is tied down!" Their hands will be tied down, and they will be cursed for what they have said. No, His hands are wide open spending as He wills. And for many of them, what has been sent down to you will increase them in rebellion and rejection; and We have cast between them animosity and hatred until the Day of Resurrection. Every time they ignite the fire of war, God puts it out; and they seek to make corruption in the land; and God does not love the corrupters.

5:65 And if the people of the Book only had believed and been aware, We would have cancelled for them their sins and admitted them to gardens of bliss.

5:66 And if they had upheld the Torah and the Gospel, and what was sent down to them from their Lord, they would have been rewarded from above them and from beneath their feet. From among them is a pious nation, but most of them only do evil.

5:67 O messenger, deliver what was sent down to you from your Lord, and if you do not then you have not delivered His message; and God will protect you from the people. And God does not guide the rejecting people.

5:68 Say: "O people of the Book, you are not upon anything until you uphold the Torah and the Gospel and what was sent down to you from your Lord." And for many of them, what was sent down to you from your Lord will only increase them in transgression and rejection. So do not feel sorry for the rejecting people.

5:69 Surely those who believe, and those who are Jewish, and the Sabians, and the Nazarenes, whoever of them believes in God and the Last Day and does good works; then they will have nothing to fear nor will they grieve.

5:70 We have taken the covenant of the Children of Israel and We sent to them Our messengers. Every time a messenger came to them with what their souls did not desire, a group of them they would reject, and a group of them they would kill.

5:71 And they did not consider it might be a test, so they were blind and deaf. But God would have accepted the repentance from them; but many of them were still blind and deaf. God is Seer over what they do.

5:72 Rejecters indeed are those who have said: "God is the Messiah, son of Mary." And the Messiah said: "O Children of Israel, serve God, my Lord and your Lord. Whoever sets up partners with God, then God will restrict Paradise from him, and his destiny will be the Fire; and the wicked will have no supporters."

5:73 Rejecters indeed are those who have said: "God is third of three!" There is no god except One god. If they do not cease from what they are saying, then those who reject from among them will be afflicted with a painful retribution.

5:74 Would they not repent to God and seek His forgiveness? God is Forgiving, Merciful.

5:75 The Messiah, son of Mary, is no more than a messenger; like whom messengers have passed away; and his mother was trustworthy, they used to eat the food. See how We clarify the signs for them, then see how they deviate.

5:76 Say: "Do you serve other than God what cannot harm you or benefit you?" God is the Hearer, the Knower.

5:77 Say: "O people of the Book, do not overstep in your system other than the truth, and do not follow the desires of a people who have been misguided before, and they misguide many; and they strayed from the right path."

5:78 Cursed are those who have rejected from among the Children of Israel by the tongue of David and Jesus, son of Mary. That is for what they have disobeyed, and for what they transgressed.

5:79 They would not stop each other from doing vice. Wickedness is what they used to do.

5:80   You see many of them allying the rejecters. Wicked is what their souls have provided for them, for the wrath of God is upon them, and in the retribution they will abide.

5:81   And if they had believed in God and the prophet, and what was sent down to him, then they would not have taken them as allies; but many of them are wicked.

5:82   You will find the people with the greatest animosity towards those who believe are the Jews and those who are polytheists; and you will find the closest in affection to those who believe are those who said: "We are Nazarenes;" that is because among them are Priests and Monks, and they are not arrogant.

5:83   And if they hear what was sent down to the messenger you see their eyes flooding with tears, for what they have known as the truth, they say: "Our Lord, we believe, so record us with the witnesses."

5:84   "And why should we not believe in God and what has come to us of the truth? And we yearn that our Lord admits us with the righteous people."

5:85   So God recompensed them for what they have said with estates with rivers flowing beneath them, abiding therein; such is the recompense of the good doers.

5:86   And those who rejected and denied Our revelations; they are the dwellers of Hell.

5:87   O you who believe, do not make forbidden the good things that God has made permissible to you, and do not aggress; God does not love the aggressors.

5:88   And eat from what God has provided for you, good and permissible; and be aware of God in whom you believe.

5:89   God will not hold you for your casual oaths, but He will hold you for what oaths you have made binding; its cancellation shall be the feeding of ten poor from the average of what you feed your family, or that you clothe them, or that you free a slave; whoever cannot find such shall fast for three days; this is a cancellation for making your oaths when you swear. And be careful from making oaths. It is such that God clarifies for you His revelations that you may be thankful.

5:90   O you who believe, intoxicants, and gambling, and altars, and arrows of chance are made foul by the work of the devil. You shall avoid him so that you may be successful.

5:91 The devil only wants to cause strife between you through intoxicants and gambling, and to turn you away from remembering God and from the Connection. Will you be deterred?

5:92 And obey God and obey the messenger, and be aware. If you turn away then know that it is the duty of Our messenger to deliver clearly.

5:93 There is no sin upon those who believe and do good works for what they eat if they are aware and believe and do good works, then they are aware and believe, then they are aware and do good; God loves the good doers.

5:94 O you who believe, God will test you with some game coming within reach of your hands and your spears, so that God will know who reverences Him while unseen. Whoever transgresses from now on, then he will have a painful retribution.

5:95 O you who believe, do not kill any game while you are under restriction; and whoever of you kills it deliberately, then the recompense is to value that hoofed animal which was killed, which shall be judged by two equitable persons from you, and to make it as a donation to reach the Ka'bah. Or, its expiation shall be in using it to feed the needy ones, while he abstains from it; that is to suffer the results of his deed; God forgives what has past. And whoever returns, then God will seek vengeance on him. God is Noble, capable of vengeance.

5:96 Permitted for you is the catch of the sea, to eat it as enjoyment for you and for those who travel; and forbidden for you is the catch of the land as long as you are under restriction; and be aware of God to whom you will be gathered.

5:97 God has made the Ka'bah—the restricted House—to be a symbol for the people, and for the restricted Month, and the offerings, and the regulations; that is so you may know that God knows what is in the heavens and what is in the earth, and that God is aware of all things.

5:98 Know that God is powerful in retribution, and that God is Forgiving, Merciful.

5:99 The messenger is only to deliver. And God knows what you reveal and what you conceal.

5:100 Say: "The rotten and the good are not equal, even if the abundance of the rotten impresses you." So be aware of God, O you who possess intelligence, that you may succeed.

5:101 O you who believe, do not ask about things which, if clarified, would harm you—and if you ask about them with the Qur'an being revealed, then they will become clear to you. God pardons for them, and God is Forgiving, Compassionate.

5:102 A people before you had asked the same, then they became rejecters in it.

5:103 God did not decree any restrictions for those that produced litters, or those set free by oath to roam, or those that that give twin female births, or the bulls who fathered two generations; but the people who rejected invented lies to God, and most of them do not comprehend.

5:104 And if they are told: "Come to what God has sent down, and to the messenger;" they say: "We are content with what we found our fathers doing." What if their fathers did not know anything nor were they guided?

5:105 O you who believe, you are responsible for yourselves; none who are misguided can harm you if you are guided. To God is your return, all of you, and then He will inform you of what you have done.

5:106 O you who believe, witnessing shall be done if death is approaching one of you and a will is being made—by two who are equitable amongst you. Or, by two who are unknown to you if you have gone forth in the land and death is approaching. If you have doubt regarding them, then you will hold them after the Connection, and let them swear by God: "We will not purchase with it any price, even if it was from a near relative, and we will not conceal the testimony of God, else we are of the sinners."

5:107 If it is then found that they had indeed incurred the sin, then two others, from those who have been named as beneficiaries, will take their place; and they will swear by God: "Our testimony is more truthful than their testimony, and if we aggress, then we are of the wicked."

5:108 This is the least that can bring the testimony at its face value, for fear that their oaths would be disregarded as the previous oaths. And be aware of God, and listen; God does not guide the wicked people.

5:109 The Day God will gather the messengers and He will say:

"What was the response you received?" They said: "We have no knowledge, you are the Knower of all the unseen."

5:110   God said: "O Jesus, son of Mary, recall My blessings upon you and your mother, that I supported you with the Holy Spirit; you spoke to the people in the cradle and middle age; and I taught you the Book and the wisdom, and the Torah, and the Gospel; and you would create from clay the shape of a bird, then blow into it and it becomes a bird with My permission; and you would heal the blind and the leaper with My permission; and you would bring out the dead with My permission. And I have restrained the Children of Israel from you, that you came to them with proofs; but those who rejected among them said: 'This is clearly magic!'"

5:111   "And I inspired the disciples: 'You shall believe in Me and My messenger;' they said: 'We believe, and bear witness that we have submitted.'"

5:112   And the disciples said: "O Jesus, son of Mary, can your Lord send down for us a feast from the heaven?" He said: "Be aware of God if you are believers."

5:113   They said: "We want to eat from it and so our hearts become relieved, and so we know that you are truthful, and so that we can become a witness over it."

5:114   Jesus, son of Mary, said: "Our god, our Lord, send down to us a feast from the heaven, that it becomes a joy to us from the first to the last, and a sign from You, and provide for us, You are the best provider."

5:115   God said: "I will send it down to you, but whoever rejects after this from among you, I will punish him a punishment like no one else from the worlds will be punished!"

5:116   And God will say: "O Jesus, son of Mary, did you tell the people to take you and your mother as gods other than God?" He said: "Glory to You, I cannot say what I have no right of. If I had said it then You know it, You know what is in my self while I do not know what is in Your self. You are the Knower of the unseen."

5:117   "I only said to them what You commanded me to, that: 'You shall serve God, my Lord and your Lord.' And I was witness over them as long as I was with them, but when You terminated my life, You were watcher over them. You are witness over all things."

5:118   "If You punish them, then they are Your servants, and if You forgive them, then You are the Noble, the Wise."

5:119   God will say: "This is a Day when the truth will benefit the truthful; they will have estates with rivers flowing beneath them, abiding therein eternally; God has become pleased with them and they are pleased with Him. Such is the greatest victory."

5:120   To God is the sovereignty of the heavens and the earth and all that is in them; and He is capable of all things.

CHAPTER 6

6:0   In the name of God, the Almighty, the Merciful.

6:1   Praise be to God who has created the heavens and the earth, and who made the darkness and the light; yet those who have rejected their Lord continue to deviate.

6:2   He is the One who created you from clay, then He decreed a period of time for you; a time only known by Him. Yet you still deny.

6:3   And He is God in the heavens and the earth. He knows your secrets and what you reveal; and He knows what you earn.

6:4   And every sign that came to them from their Lord, they turned away from it.

6:5   They have denied the truth when it came to them. The news will ultimately come to them of what they were mocking.

6:6   Did they not see how many generations We have destroyed before them? We granted them dominance over the land more than what We granted you, and We sent the sky to them abundantly, and We made rivers flow beneath them; then, We destroyed them for their sins, and established after them a new generation.

6:7   And if We had sent down to you a book already written on paper, and they touched it with their own hands, then those who have rejected would say: "This is but clear magic!"

6:8   And they said: "If only an angel were sent down to him?" But if We had sent down an angel, the matter would be settled, then they would no longer be respited.

6:9   And had We sent an angel, We would have made him appear as a man, and We would have confounded them in what they already are confounded.

6:10   Messengers before you were mocked, but those who ridiculed suffered the consequences of that which they mocked.

6:11   Say: "Roam the earth, then see what the punishment of the rejecters was!"

6:12   Say: "To whom is all that is in the heavens and the earth?" Say: "To God." He has decreed mercy on Himself, that He will gather you to the Day of Resurrection in which there is no doubt. Those who have lost their souls, they do not believe.

6:13   And for Him is what resides in the night and in the day; and He is the Hearer, the Knower.

6:14   Say: "Shall I take other than God as an ally; the Initiator of the heavens and the earth; while He feeds and is not fed!" Say: "I have been commanded to be the first who submits." And do not be of the polytheists.

6:15   Say: "I fear if I disobey my Lord, the retribution of a great Day!"

6:16   Whoever He spares from it, then He has had mercy on him; and that is the clear triumph.

6:17   And if God were to inflict you with harm, then none can remove it except He; and if He were to bless you with good, then He is capable of all things.

6:18   And He is the Supreme over His servants; and He is the Wise, the Expert.

6:19   Say: "Which is the greatest testimony?" Say: "God is witness between me and you, and He has inspired to me this Qur'an that I may warn you with it and whoever it reaches, that you are bearing witness that with God are other gods!" Say: "I do not bear witness!" Say: "He is only One god, and I am innocent of what you have set up!"

6:20   Those to whom We have given the Book know it as they know their children. Those who lost their souls, they do not believe.

6:21   And who is more wicked than he who invents lies about God, or denies His revelations! The wicked will never succeed.

6:22   And the Day We gather them all, then We say to the polytheists: "Where are your partners whom you used to claim?"

6:23   Then, their only excuse was to say: "By God, our Lord, we were not polytheists!"

6:24   See how they lied to themselves, and that which they invented was lost to them.

6:25   And from them are those who listen to you; and We have made covers over their hearts to prevent them from understanding it, and a deafness in their ears; and if they see every sign they will not believe; even when they come to you they argue, those who reject say: "This is nothing except tales of old!"

6:26   And they prohibit others from it, and keep away themselves from it; but they will only destroy themselves, yet they do not notice.

6:27   And if you could see when they are standing over the Fire, they say: "If only we could be sent back, we would not deny the revelations of our Lord, and we would be believers!"

6:28   Indeed, it is now apparent to them what they had been concealing before; and if they were sent back they would return again to what they were prohibited from doing, they are but liars!

6:29   And they had said: "There is only this worldly life, and we will not be resurrected!"

6:30   And if you could see them when they are standing at their Lord; He said: "Is this not the truth?" They said: "Yes, by our Lord," He said: "Then taste the retribution for what you have rejected."

6:31   Losers are those who have denied their meeting with God; until the Hour comes to them suddenly, then they say: "We deeply regret that which we have wasted in it," and they will carry their burdens on their backs; miserable indeed is their burden.

6:32   And the worldly life is nothing more than play and distraction, and the abode of the Hereafter is far better for those who are righteous. Do you not comprehend?

6:33   We know that you are saddened by what they say; they are not rejecting you, but it is the revelations of God which the wicked disregard.

6:34   Messengers before you were denied, but they were patient for what they were denied, and they were harmed until Our victory came to them; there is no changing the words of God. News of the messengers has come to you.

6:35   And if their aversion has become too much for you, then perhaps you could make a tunnel in the earth, or a ladder to the heavens, and bring them a sign. Had God willed, He would have gathered them to the guidance; so do not be of the ignorant ones.

6:36   Only those who listen will respond. As for the dead, God will resurrect them, then to Him they will return.

6:37   And they said: "If only a sign was sent to him from his Lord!" Say: "God is able to send a sign, but most of them would not know."

6:38   And there is not a creature on the earth, nor a bird that flies with its wings, except they belong to nations like you belong. We did not leave anything out of the record; then to their Lord they will be gathered.

6:39   And those who deny Our revelations, they are deaf and dumb, in darkness. Whoever God wishes He misguides, and whoever He wishes He puts him on a straight path.

6:40   Say: "We will see when the retribution of God comes to you, or the Hour comes to you, if you will still call on any other than God. If you are being truthful."

6:41   "No, it is Him alone you will call on; and He will remove that which you called Him for, if He wills; and you will forget what you set up."

6:42   And We have sent others to nations before you. We then took them with adversity and hardship, perhaps they would implore.

6:43   If only they had implored when Our punishment came to them; but their hearts hardened, and the devil adorned for them what they used to do.

6:44   So when they forgot what they had been reminded of, We opened for them the gates of all opportunities; and when they were happy with what they were given, We took them suddenly! They were confounded.

6:45   It was thus that the remainder of the wicked people were wiped out; and praise be to God, Lord of the worlds.

6:46   Say: "Do you see that if God were to take away your hearing and your eyesight, and He seals your hearts; which god besides God can bring it to you?" See how We dispatch the signs, but then they turn away.

6:47   Say: "Do you see if the retribution of God comes to you suddenly, or gradually, will anyone be destroyed except the wicked people?"

6:48   And We do not send the messengers except as bearers of good news and warners; whoever believes, and does good, then there is no fear for them nor will they grieve.

6:49   And those who deny Our revelations, the retribution will inflict them for what wickedness they were in.

6:50   Say: "I do not say to you that I possess the treasures of God, nor do I know the future, nor do I say to you that I am an angel. I merely follow what is inspired to me." Say: "Are the blind and the seer the same? Do you not think?"

6:51   And warn with it those who realize that they will be gathered to their Lord; they do not have besides Him any ally nor intercessor; perhaps they will be righteous.

6:52   And do not turn away those who call on their Lord at dawn and dusk seeking His face; you are not responsible for their judgment, nor are they responsible for your judgment; if you turn them away, then you will be of the wicked.

6:53   And it is such that We test them with one another, so that they may say: "Are these the ones whom God has graced from among us?" Is God not aware of the thankful?

6:54   And if those who believe in Our revelations come to you, then say: "Peace be upon you, our Lord has decreed mercy upon Himself, that any of you who commits sin out of ignorance and then repents afterwards and amends, then He is Forgiving, Merciful."

6:55   And it is such that We explain the revelations, and point out the way of the criminals.

6:56   Say: "I am prohibited from serving those you call upon other than God" Say: "I will not follow your desires, otherwise I would go astray and I would not be of those guided."

6:57   Say: "I am on a clarity from my Lord and you have denied it. I do not have what you hasten towards; the judgment is with God only; He narrates the truth, and He is the best decider."

6:58   Say: "If I had what you were hastening towards, then the matter between us would have been resolved. And God is fully aware of the wicked."

6:59　　And with Him are the keys of the unseen, none know them except He. And He knows what is in the land and in the sea; and not a leaf falls except He knows of it; nor a seed in the darkness of the earth; nor anything moist or anything dry; all in a clear record.

6:60　　And He is the One who seizes you during the night, and He knows what you have done during the day, then He sends you back again to complete an appointed term; then to Him is your return and He will inform you of what you used to do.

6:61　　And He is the Supreme over His servants, and He sends over you guardians. So that when the time of death comes to one of you, Our messengers terminate his life, and they do not neglect any.

6:62　　Then they are returned to God, their true Patron; to Him is the judgment and He is the swiftest of reckoners.

6:63　　Say: "Who rescues you from the darkness of the land and the sea?" You call on Him in humility and in secret: "If You save us from this, we will be of the thankful!"

6:64　　Say: "God will save you from it and from all distresses, yet you will still set up partners!"

6:65　　Say: "He is able to send retribution from above you or from below your feet, or He will make you belong to opposing factions, then He will let you taste the might of each other." See how We dispatch the signs, perhaps they may understand.

6:66　　And your people denied it, while it is the truth. Say: "I am not a guardian over you!"

6:67　　"For every news there is a time, and you will come to know."

6:68　　And if you encounter those who make fun of Our revelations, then turn away from them until they move on to a different narrative; and if the devil makes you forget, then do not sit after remembering with the wicked people.

6:69　　And those who are righteous are not responsible for their judgment, but to remind; perhaps they will be aware.

6:70　　And leave alone those who have taken their system for play and distraction, and the worldly life has tempted them. And remind with it that a soul will suffer for what it has earned, it will not have besides God any ally nor intercessor; and even if it brings all justice, none will be accepted from it. These are the ones who have suffered with what they have earned; for them will be a boiling drink, and a painful retribution for what they had rejected.

6:71 Say: "Shall we call upon other than God what cannot benefit us or harm us, and we turn back on our heels after God has guided us?" This is like the one whom the devils have managed to mislead on the earth, he is confused, having friends who call him to the guidance: "Come to us!" Say: "The guidance is the guidance of God, and we have been ordered to submit to the Lord of the worlds."

6:72 And you shall hold the Connection, and be aware; and to Him you will be gathered.

6:73 And He is the One who has created the heavens and the earth with the truth, and the day He says: "Be," then it is! His saying is truth; and to Him is the sovereignty the Day the horn is blown. Knower of the unseen and the seen; He is the Wise, the Expert.

6:74 And Abraham said to his father, Azar: "Will you take statues as gods? I see you and your people are clearly misguided."

6:75 And it is such that We showed Abraham the kingdom of the heavens and the earth, so that he will be of those who have certainty.

6:76 When the night covered him, he saw a planet, and he said: "This is my Lord." But when it disappeared he said: "I do not like those who disappear."

6:77 So when he saw the moon rising, he said: "This is my Lord." But when it disappeared he said: "If my Lord does not guide me, then I will be among the wicked people!"

6:78 So when he saw the sun rising, he said: "This is my Lord, this is bigger." But when it disappeared he said: "My people, I am innocent of what you have set up."

6:79 "I shall turn my face to the One who initiated the heavens and the earth, in monotheism, and I am not of the polytheists."

6:80 And his people debated with him. He said: "Do you debate with me regarding God, when He has guided me? I do not fear that which you have set up except if my Lord wills; my Lord encompasses all things in knowledge; will you not remember?"

6:81 "And how can I possibly fear what you have set up; yet you do not fear that you have set up partners with God, for which He has not sent down upon you any authority! So which of our two groups is more worthy of security if you know?"

6:82   Those who believe and do not confound their belief with wrongdoing; they will have security, and they are guided.

6:83   And such was Our argument that We gave Abraham over his people; We raise the degree of whom We please. Your Lord is Wise, Knowledgeable.

6:84   And We granted him Isaac and Jacob, both of whom We guided; and Noah We guided from before; and from his progeny is David, and Solomon, and Job, and Joseph, and Moses, and Aaron. It is such that We recompense the good doers.

6:85   And Zechariah and John, and Jesus, and Elias; all were from the upright.

6:86   And Ishmael and Elisha and Jonah and Lot; and each We have preferred over the worlds.

6:87   And from their fathers and their progeny and their brothers We have also chosen; and We guided them to a straight path.

6:88   Such is the guidance of God, He guides with it whom He pleases of His servants. And if they set up partners, then all that they had worked would fall away from them.

6:89   Those to whom We have given the Book, and the judgement, and the prophethood, if they reject it, then We will entrust it to a people who will not reject it.

6:90   These are the ones guided by God; so let their guidance be an example. Say: "I do not ask you for any wage; this is but a reminder for the worlds."

6:91   And they did not appreciate God as He deserves to be appreciated, for they said: "God has never sent down anything to any mortal." Say: "Who then has sent down the Book which Moses had come with, a light and a guidance for the people? You treat it simply as paper for display, and you conceal much; and you were taught what neither you nor your fathers knew." Say: "God has." Then leave them playing in their folly.

6:92   And this is a Book which We have sent down, blessed, affirming what is between his hands, and that you may warn the mother of towns and those around it. And those who believe in the Hereafter believe in it, and they maintain their connecting.

6:93   And who is more wicked than he who invents lies about God, or says: "It has been inspired to me," when We did not inspire anything to him; or who says: "I will bring down the same as what God has sent down." And if you could only see the wicked at the moments of death when the angels have their arms opened: "Bring yourselves out, today you will be given the severest punishment for what you used to say about God without truth, and you used to be arrogant towards His revelations."

6:94   "And you have come to Us individually, just as We had created you the first time; and you have left behind you all that We have provided for you; and We do not see your intercessors with you that you used to claim were with you in partnership; all is severed between you, and what you have claimed has abandoned you."

6:95   God is the splitter of the seeds and the grains; He brings the living out from the dead and He brings the dead out from the living. Such is God; so why are you deluded?

6:96   Initiator of the morning and Maker of the night to reside in; and the sun and the moon for counting. Such is the measure of the Noble, the Knowledgeable.

6:97   And He is the One who made for you the stars, to guide you by them in the darkness of the land and the sea. We have explained the signs to a people who know.

6:98   And He is the One who initiated you from one person; with a place for stability and development. We have explained the signs to a people who understand.

6:99   And He is the One who sent down water from the heaven, and We brought out with it plants of every kind. We brought out from it a green from which We bring out complex seeds; and what is from the palm trees, from its sheaths hanging low and near; and gardens of grapes; and olives and pomegranates, comparable and not comparable. Look at its fruit when it blossoms and its ripeness. In this are signs for a people who believe.

6:100 And they set up partners with God from among the Jinn, while He had created them. And they invented for Him sons and daughters without them having any knowledge! Be He glorified and exalted above what they describe.

6:101 Originator of the heavens and the earth, how can He have a son when He did not take a wife? And He created all things and He is knowledgeable in all things.

6:102 Such is God, your Lord, there is no god except He; creator of all things, so serve Him. And He is Caretaker over all things.

6:103 The eyesight cannot reach Him, yet He can reach all eyesight; and He is the Subtle, the Expert.

6:104 "Visible proofs have come to you from your Lord; so whoever can see, does so for himself, and whoever is blinded, will be such. I am not a watcher over you."

6:105 It is thus that We dispatch the signs and that they may say: "You have studied," and We will make it clear for a people who know.

6:106 Follow what is inspired to you from your Lord; there is no god except He, and turn away from the polytheists.

6:107 And if God had willed, they would not have set up partners. And We did not place you over them as a guardian, nor are you over them as a sponsor.

6:108 And do not insult those who call on other than God, lest they insult God out of ignorance. And We have similarly adorned for every nation their works; then to their Lord is their return and He will inform them of what they had done.

6:109 And they swore by God using their strongest oaths; that if a sign came to them they would believe in it. Say: "The signs are from God; and how do you know that once it comes, that they will not disbelieve?"

6:110 And We divert their minds and eyesight, as they did not believe in it the first time; and We leave them in their transgression, blundering.

6:111 And if We had sent down to them the angels, and the dead spoke to them, and We had gathered before them everything, they still would not believe except if God wills. Alas, most of them are ignorant.

6:112 And as such, We have permitted the enemies of every prophet— human and Jinn devils—to inspire each other with fancy words in order to deceive. Had your Lord willed, they would not have done it. You shall disregard them and their fabrications.

6:113 And that will be listened to by the minds of those who do not believe in the Hereafter, and they will accept it, and they will take of it what they will.

6:114 "Shall I seek other than God as a judge when He has sent down to you the Book fully detailed?" Those to whom We have given the Book know it is sent down from your Lord with the truth; so do not be of those who have doubt.

6:115 And the word of your Lord is completed with truth and justice; there is no changing His words. He is the Hearer, the Knower.

6:116 And if you obey most of those on the earth they will lead you away from the path of God; that is because they follow conjecture, and that is because they only guess.

6:117 Your Lord is fully aware of who strays from His path, and He is fully aware of the guided ones.

6:118 So eat from that on which the name of God has been remembered, if you indeed believe in His revelations.

6:119 And why should you not eat that on which the name of God has been mentioned, when He has fully detailed to you what has been made forbidden; except what you are forced to? Many misguide by their desires without knowledge; your Lord is fully aware of the transgressors.

6:120 And leave alone, publicly and privately, that which is a sin; those who earn sin will be punished for what they have taken.

6:121 And do not eat from that which the name of God has not been mentioned, for it is wickedness. And the devils they inspire their supporters to argue with you; and if you obey them, then you are polytheists.

6:122 Is he who was dead and to whom We gave life, and We made for him a light to walk with among the people, as he whose example is in darkness and he will not exit from it? It is such that the work of the rejecters has been adorned for them.

6:123 And as such, We have permitted in every town the influential from its criminals, to scheme in it. They only scheme their own souls without perceiving.

6:124 And if a sign comes to them they say: "We will not believe until we are given the same as what the messengers of God were given!" God is fully aware of where He makes His message; those criminals will have debasement with God and a painful retribution for what they had schemed.

6:125 Whoever God wishes to guide, He will comfort his chest to submission; and whoever He wishes to misguide, He will make his chest tight and constricted, as one who is ascending towards the heaven. It is such that God makes foulness upon those who do not believe.

6:126   And this is the straight path of your Lord. We have fully detailed the revelations to a people who remember.

6:127   They will have the abode of peace with their Lord; He is their supporter because of what they used to do.

6:128   And the Day We gather them all: "O assembly of Jinn, you have managed to take many from mankind." Their supporters from mankind said: "Our Lord, we have indeed enjoyed one another, and we have reached our destiny to which You delayed us." He said: "The Fire is your dwelling, abiding therein, except as your Lord wishes." Your Lord is Wise, Knowledgeable.

6:129   It is such that We make the wicked as supporters to one another for what they have earned.

6:130   "O assembly of Jinn and mankind, did not messengers come to you from amongst you and narrate to you My revelations, and warn you of the meeting of this Day?" They said: "Yes, we bear witness upon ourselves;" and the worldly life deceived them, and they bore witness upon themselves that they were rejecters.

6:131   That is because your Lord was not to destroy any town because of its wickedness while its people were unaware.

6:132   But there are degrees for what they had done; and your Lord is not unaware of what they do.

6:133   And your Lord is the Rich, possessor of Mercy. If He wished, He could remove all of you and bring after you whom He pleases, just as He established you from the seed of another people.

6:134   What you have been promised will come, you cannot escape it.

6:135   Say: "My people, work as you see fit, for I too am working. You will then know to whom will be the punishment of the Hereafter. The wicked will not succeed."

6:136   And they made for God a portion of what He provided them from the crops and the hoofed animals; they said: "This is for God," by their claims, "And this is for our partners." So what was for their partners did not reach God, and what was for God, it reached their partners! Miserable is how they judged.

6:137 And it was adorned for the polytheists, by their partners, to kill their children in order to turn them and to confound their system for them. Had God willed they would not have done this, so ignore them and what they invent.

6:138 And they said: "These hoofed animals and crops are reserved, and none shall eat from them except as we please," by their claims; and hoofed animals whose backs are forbidden, and hoofed animals over which they do not mention the name of God as an innovation against Him. He will recompense them for what they invented.

6:139 And they said: "What is in the bellies of these hoofed animals is exclusive for our males and forbidden for our wives, and if comes out dead, then they will be partners in it." God will recompense them for what they describe. He is Wise, Knowledgeable.

6:140 Losers are those who have killed their children foolishly, without knowledge, and they forbade what God had granted them by lying about God. They have strayed and they were not guided.

6:141 And He is the One who initiated gardens; both trellised and untrellised; and palm trees, and plants, all with different taste; and olives and pomegranates, comparable and not comparable. Eat from its fruit when it blossoms and give its due on the day of its harvest; and do not waste. He does not like the wasteful.

6:142 And from the hoofed animals are those for burden, and also for clothing. Eat from what God has provided you and do not follow the footsteps of the devil; he is to you a clear enemy.

6:143 Eight, in pairs: from the sheep two, and from the goats two. Say: "Is it the two males that He forbade or the two females, or what the wombs of the two females bore? Inform me if you are truthful!"

6:144 And from the camels two, and from the cattle two. Say: "Is it the two males that He forbade or the two females, or what the wombs of the two females bore? Or were you witnesses when God ordered you with this?" Who is more wicked than he who invents lies about God to misguide the people without knowledge. God does not guide the wicked people.

6:145 Say: "I do not find in what is inspired to me to be forbidden for any eater to eat, except: that it be already dead, or running blood, or the meat of pig—for it is foul—or what has become nasty by being sacrificed to other than God." But whoever is forced to, without seeking disobedience or transgression, then your Lord is

Forgiving, Merciful.

6:146   And for those who are Jewish We have made forbidden all that have undivided hoofs; and from the cattle and the sheep We made forbidden their fat except what is attached to the back, or entrails, or mixed with bone. That is a punishment for their rebellion, and We are truthful.

6:147   If they deny you, then say: "Your Lord has vast mercy, but His might will not be turned away from the criminal people."

6:148   Those who are polytheists will say: "If God wished, we would not have set up partners, nor would have our fathers, nor would we have made anything forbidden." Those before them lied in the same way, until they tasted Our might. Say: "Do you have any knowledge to bring out to us? You only follow conjecture, you only guess."

6:149   Say: "With God is the greatest argument. If He wished He would have guided you all."

6:150   Say: "Bring forth your witnesses who bear witness that God has made this forbidden." If they bear witness, then do not bear witness with them, nor follow the desires of those who deny Our revelations, and those who do not believe in the Hereafter; and they make equals with their Lord!

6:151   Say: "Come let me recite what your Lord has forbidden for you: that you should not set up anything with Him; and do good to your parents; and do not kill your children for fear of poverty, We provide for you and for them; and do not come near immorality, what is public of it and private; and do not kill the life, as God has forbidden this, except in justice. That is what He enjoined you that you may comprehend."

6:152   "And do not come near the money of the orphan, except for what is best, until he reaches his independence; and give honestly full measure and weight equitably. We do not burden a soul except with what it can bear, and if you speak then be just even if against a relative; and regarding the pledges made to God, you shall observe them. This He has enjoined you that you may remember."

6:153   And this is My path, a straight one. "So follow it, and do not follow the other paths lest they divert you from His path. That is what He has enjoined you to that you may be righteous."

6:154   Then We gave Moses the Book, to complete for those who do right, and to fully detail all things, and a guide and mercy that they may believe in the meeting of their Lord.

6:155   And this is a Book that We have sent down which is blessed, so follow it and be aware, that you may receive mercy.

6:156   Lest you say: "The Book was only sent down to two groups before us, and we were unaware of their study!"

6:157   Or you say: "If the Book was sent to us we would have been more guided than they!" Clarity has come to you from your Lord, and a guidance and a mercy. Who is more wicked than he who denies the revelations of God and turns away from them? We will punish those who turn away from Our revelations with the pain of retribution for what they turned away.

6:158   Do they wait until the angels come to them, or your Lord comes, or certain signs come from your Lord? The Day certain signs come from your Lord, it will do no good for any soul to believe if it did not believe before, or it gained good through its belief. Say: "Wait, for we are waiting."

6:159   Those who have divided their system and become sects, you are not with them in anything. Their matter will be with God, then He will inform them of what they had done.

6:160   Whoever comes with a good deed, he will receive ten times its worth, and whoever comes with a sin, he will only be recompensed its like; they will not be wronged.

6:161   Say: "My Lord has guided me to a straight path, an upright system, the creed of Abraham the monotheist; he was not of the polytheists."

6:162   Say: "My connecting, and my rites, and my life, and my death, are all to God—Lord of the worlds."

6:163   "He has no partner, and it is to this that I was commanded, and I am the first of those who have submitted."

6:164   Say: "Shall I seek other than God as a Lord when He is the Lord of everything?" And every soul earns what is for it; and no bearer may carry the burden of another. Then to your Lord is your return and He will inform you of what you disputed in.

6:165   And He is the One who made you inheritors on the earth, and He raised some of you over others in grades, to test you with what He had given you. Your Lord is swift to punishment, and He is Forgiving, Merciful.

CHAPTER 7

7:0   In the name of God, the Almighty, the Merciful.

7:1   ALMS'

7:2   A Book that has been sent down to you, so let there not be any burden in your chest from it, that you may warn with it; and a reminder to the believers.

7:3   Follow what was sent down to you from your Lord, and do not follow besides Him any supporters. Little do you remember!

7:4   And how many a town have We destroyed; for Our punishment came to them while sleeping, or while resting.

7:5   Then their only saying when Our punishment came to them was: "We were wicked!"

7:6   We will question those to whom the message was sent, and We will question the messengers.

7:7   We will narrate to them with knowledge, for We were not absent.

7:8   And the balance on that Day will be the truth. So, those whose weights are heavy on the balance, those are the successful ones.

7:9   And whoever has light weights, then these are the ones who lost their souls for what they transgressed of Our revelations.

7:10   And We granted you dominion on the earth, and made for you in it a habitat; little do you give thanks!

7:11   And We created you, then We shaped you, then We said to the angels: "Yield to Adam;" so they yielded except for Satan, he was not of those who yielded.

7:12   He said: "What has prevented you from yielding when I have ordered you?" He said: "I am far better than him, You created me from fire and created him from clay!"

7:13   He said: "Descend from it, for it is not for you to be arrogant here; depart, for you are disgraced."

7:14   He said: "Grant me respite until the Day they are resurrected?"

7:15   He said: "You are granted."

7:16   He said: "For that which You have caused me to be misled, I will stalk for them on Your straight path."

7:17 "Then I will come to them from between their hands, and from behind them, and from their right, and from their left; and You will find most of them unthankful."

7:18 He said: "Get out from this, you are despised and banished. As for those of them who follow you, I will fill Hell with you all!"

7:19 "And O Adam, reside you and your mate in the paradise, and eat from it as you both wish, and do not come near this tree, else you will be of those who have wronged."

7:20 But the devil whispered to them, to reveal to them what was not apparent to them of their bodies; and he said: "Your Lord did not prohibit you from this tree except that you would become angels, or you would be immortal."

7:21 And he swore to them: "I am giving good advice."

7:22 So he misled them with deception; and when they tasted the tree, their bodies became apparent to them, and they rushed to cover themselves with the leaves of the paradise; and their Lord called to them: "Did I not prohibit you from that tree, and tell you that the devil is your clear enemy?"

7:23 They said: "Our Lord, we have wronged ourselves and if You do not forgive us and have mercy on us, then we will be of the losers!"

7:24 He said: "Descend; for you are enemies to one another; and on the earth you will have residence and provisions until the appointed time."

7:25 He said: "In it you will live and in it you will die, and from it you will be brought forth."

7:26 O Children of Adam, We have sent down for you garments to cover your bodies, and to adorn; and the garment of righteousness is the best. That is from the signs of God, perhaps they will remember.

7:27 O Children of Adam, do not let the devil afflict you as he evicted your parents from the paradise; he removes from them their garments to show them their bodies. He and his tribe see you from where you do not see them. We have made the devils as allies for those who do not believe.

7:28 And if they commit immorality, they say: "We found our fathers doing such, and God ordered us to it." Say: "God does not order immorality! Do you say about God what you do not know?"

7:29   Say: "My Lord orders justice, and that you set your faces at every temple, and that you call on Him, while being faithful to Him in the system; as He initiated you, so you will return."

7:30   A group He has guided and a group have deserved misguidance; that is because they have taken the devils as allies besides God; and they think they are guided!

7:31   O Children of Adam, dress nicely at every temple, and eat and drink and do not indulge; He does not like the indulgers.

7:32   Say: "Who has made forbidden the nice things that God has brought forth for His servants and the good provisions?" Say: "They are meant for those who believe during this worldly life, and they will be exclusive for them on the Day of Resurrection." It is such that We explain the revelations for those who know.

7:33   Say: "My Lord has made forbidden immorality; what is public of it and private; and sin, and aggression without cause, and that you set up partners with God that which He has never authorized, and that you say about God what you do not know."

7:34   And for every nation will be an appointed time; when their time is reached, they will not delay by one hour nor advance.

7:35   O Children of Adam, when messengers come to you from amongst yourselves and narrate to you My revelations; then for those who are aware, and upright, there will be no fear over them nor will they grieve.

7:36   As for those who reject Our revelations, and become arrogant towards them; then these are the dwellers of the Fire, in it they will abide.

7:37   Who is more wicked than he who invents lies about God, or denies His revelations? These will receive their recompense from the record; so that when Our messengers come to terminate their lives, they will say: "Where are those whom you used to call on besides God?" They said: "They have abandoned us!" And they bore witness upon themselves that they were rejecters.

7:38   He said: "Enter with the multitude of nations before you from mankind and Jinn to the Fire!" Every time a nation entered, it cursed its sister nation, until they are all gathered inside it; then the last of them says to the first: "Our Lord, these are the ones who have misguided us, so give them double the retribution of the Fire!" He replied: "Each will receive double, but you do not know."

7:39 And the first of them said to the last: "You have no preference over us, so taste the retribution for what you have earned!"

7:40 Those who have denied Our revelations, and became arrogant towards them, the gates of the heavens will not open for them, nor will they enter Paradise until the camel passes through the eye of a needle. It is such that We recompense the criminals.

7:41 They will have Hell as an abode, and from above them will be covers. It is thus We recompense the wicked.

7:42 As for those who believe and do good; We do not burden a soul except with what it can bear; those are the dwellers of Paradise, in it they will abide.

7:43 And We removed what was in their chests of hate; rivers will flow beneath them; and they will say: "Praise be to God who has guided us to this, and we would not have been guided unless God guided us. The messengers of our Lord had come with the truth." And it was called to them: "This is Paradise; you have inherited it for what you have done."

7:44 And the dwellers of Paradise called the dwellers of the Fire: "We have found what our Lord promised us to be true; did you find what your Lord promised to be true?" They said: "Indeed!" Then a caller announced between them: "The curse of God is on the wicked."

7:45 "The ones who repel from the path of God, and sought to make it crooked; and regarding the Hereafter they were rejecters."

7:46 And between them is a veil, and on the elevated platform are men who recognized others by their features. And they called out to the dwellers of Paradise: "Peace be upon you!" They have not yet entered it, but they are hoping.

7:47 And when their eyes are turned towards the dwellers of the Fire, they say: "Our Lord, do not place us with the wicked people!"

7:48 And the people standing on the elevated platform called on men they recognized by their features, they said: "What good did your large number do for you, or what you were arrogant for?"

7:49 "Were these not the ones whom you swore God would not grant them of His mercy?" Enter Paradise, there is no fear for you nor will you grieve.

7:50 And the dwellers of the Fire called on the dwellers of Paradise: "Give us some water, or what God has provided for you?" They said: "God has forbidden them for the rejecters."

7:51 The ones who took their system for distraction and play, and were preoccupied with this worldly life. Today We forget them as they forgot their meeting on this Day, and they did not heed Our revelations.

7:52 And We have come to them with a Book which We have detailed with knowledge; a guidance and a mercy to those who believe.

7:53 Are they waiting for what it says to come true? On the Day it comes true, those who previously forgot it will say: "The messengers of our Lord have come with the truth! Are there any intercessors to intercede for us? Or can we be sent back and we will work differently than what we did?" They have lost their souls and what they have invented has abandoned them.

7:54 Your Lord is God who has created the heavens and the earth in six days, then He settled upon the Throne. The night runs away from the day, which seeks it continually; and the sun and the moon and the stars are commissioned by His command; to Him is the creation and the command. Glory to God, Lord of the worlds.

7:55 Call on your Lord in humility and in secret. He does not like the aggressors.

7:56 And do not corrupt the earth after it has been made right; and call on Him fearing and hoping. Surely the mercy of God is near the righteous.

7:57 He is the One who sends the winds to be dispersed between His hands of mercy; so when it carries a heavy cloud, We drive it to a dead land, and We send down the water with it and We bring forth fruits of all kind. It is thus that We will bring out the dead, perhaps you will remember.

7:58 And the good land, its plants are brought forth with the permission of its Lord. And for the one that is rotten, it does not bring forth except very little. It is such that We dispatch the signs for a people who are thankful.

7:59 We had sent Noah to his people, so he said: "My people, serve

God, you have no god besides Him. I fear for you the retribution of a great Day!"

7:60 The leaders from his people said: "We see that you are clearly misguided."

7:61 He said: "My people, I am not misguided, but I am a messenger from the Lord of the worlds."

7:62 "To deliver to you the messages of my Lord, and I advise you, and I know from God what you do not know."

7:63 "Are you surprised that a reminder has come to you from your Lord through a man from among you to warn you, that you may be righteous, and that you may receive mercy?"

7:64 They denied him, so We saved him and those with him in the ship, and We drowned those who denied Our revelations; they were a blind people.

7:65 And to 'Aad We sent their brother Hud, he said: "My people, serve God, you have no god besides Him. Will you not be righteous?"

7:66 The leaders who rejected from among his people said: "We see you in foolishness, and we think you are one of the liars."

7:67 He said: "My people, there is no foolishness in me, but I am a messenger from the Lord of the worlds."

7:68 "To deliver to you the messages of my Lord, and to you I am a trustworthy advisor."

7:69 "Are you surprised that a reminder has come to you from your Lord through a man from among you to warn you? And remember that He made you successors after the people of Noah, and He increased you in status. So remember the grace of God, that you may succeed."

7:70 They said: "Have you come to us to serve God alone and abandon what our fathers had served? Bring us what you promise if you are of the truthful ones!"

7:71 He said: "You have incurred from your Lord foulness and wrath. Do you argue with me over names which you and your fathers have created with no authority being sent down by God? Wait then, and I will wait with you."

7:72 We saved him and those with him by a mercy from Us, and We destroyed the remnant of those who rejected Our revelations,

97

they were never believers.

7:73 And to Thamud, We sent their brother Saleh, he said: "My people, serve God, you have no god besides Him; clarity has come to you from your Lord, this is the camel of God, in her you have a sign, so leave her to eat in God's earth, and do not harm her, else the painful retribution will take you."

7:74 "And remember that He made you successors after 'Aad, and He established you in the land so that you make palaces on its plains, and you carve homes in the mountains. So remember the grace of God, and do not roam the earth as corrupters."

7:75 The leaders who were arrogant from among his people said to those who were weak and believed from among them: "How do you know that Saleh was sent from his Lord?" They said: "It is in that which he has been sent that we believe."

7:76 Those who were arrogant said: "In that which you believe, we reject!"

7:77 They thus killed the camel and defied the command of their Lord, and they said: "O Saleh, bring us what you promised us if you are of the messengers!"

7:78 The earthquake took them, thus they became lifeless in their home.

7:79 Thus he turned away from them, and said: "My people, I have delivered to you the message of my Lord and advised you; but you do not like the advisers."

7:80 And Lot, he said to his people: "Do you commit immorality such as none of those of the worlds had done before?"

7:81 "You are approaching the men out of desire instead of the women! Indeed, you are a transgressing people."

7:82 The only response of his people was: "Drive them out of your town, for they are a people who make out to be pure!"

7:83 We saved him and his family, except for his wife; she was of those who were destroyed.

7:84 And We rained down upon them a rain, so see how was the punishment for the criminals.

7:85 And to Midyan, their brother Shu'ayb, he said: "My people, serve God, you have no god besides Him. Clarity has come to you from your Lord, so give full weight and measure, and do not hold back from the people what belongs to them, and do not make corruption on the earth after it has been set right. That is better for you if you believe."

7:86 "And do not stand on every path, robbing, and turning away from the path of God those who believe in Him, and you seek to make it crooked. And remember that you were few and He multiplied you; and see how is the retribution of the corrupters."

7:87 "And if a group of you believes in what I have been sent with, and a group disbelieves, then wait until God judges between us. He is the best of judges."

7:88 And the leaders who became arrogant from among his people said: "We will drive you out of our town Shu'ayb, along with those who have believed with you, or you shall return to our creed!" He said: "Will you force us?"

7:89 "We will then be inventing lies about God if we return to your creed after God has saved us from it; and we will not return to it except if God our Lord wills, our Lord encompasses everything with knowledge, in God we put our trust. Our Lord, make an opening between us and between our people with the truth, you are the best of openers."

7:90 And the leaders who rejected from among his people said: "If you follow Shu'ayb, then you are losers."

7:91 The earthquake took them, thus they became lifeless in their home.

7:92 Those who denied Shu'ayb, it is as if they had never prospered therein. Those who denied Shu'ayb, they were the losers.

7:93 Thus he turned away from them, and said: "My people, I have delivered to you the messages of my Lord and advised you. How can I feel sorry over a rejecting people?"

7:94 And We do not send a prophet to any town, except afterwards We afflict its people with adversity and hardship that they may implore.

7:95 Then We replaced the bad with good, until they neglected and said: "Our fathers were touched by both hardship and prosperity." We then take them suddenly, while they are unaware.

7:96 And if only the people of the towns had believed and been aware, then We would have opened for them blessings from the heavens and the earth; but they denied, so We took them for what they had earned.

7:97 Are the people of the towns sure that Our punishment will not come to them at night while they are sleeping?

7:98 Or are the people of the towns sure that Our punishment will not come to them during the late morning while they are playing?

7:99 Have they become secure about the scheming of God? None are secure about the scheming of God except the people who are the losers.

7:100 Is it not a guide for those who inherited the land after them, that if We wished We could have punished them immediately for their sins? And We stamp on their hearts, so they do not hear.

7:101 These are the towns whose news We narrate to you; their messengers had come to them with proofs, but they would not believe in what they had denied before. It is such that God stamps on the hearts of the rejecters.

7:102 And We did not find most of them up to their pledge, rather, We found most of them wicked.

7:103 Then after them We sent Moses with Our signs to Pharaoh and his commanders. But they did wrong in them, so see how is the end of the corrupters.

7:104 And Moses said: "O Pharaoh, I am a messenger from the Lord of the worlds."

7:105 "It is not proper for me to say about God except the truth; I have come to you with a proof from your Lord. So send with me the Children of Israel."

7:106 He said: "If you have come with a sign then bring it, if you are of the truthful?"

7:107 He cast down his staff and it manifested into a serpent.

7:108 And he drew out his hand, and it became pure white for the onlookers.

7:109 The commanders from among the people of Pharaoh said: "This is a knowledgeable magician!"

7:110 "He wishes to drive you out of your land; what is your command?"

7:111 They said: "Delay him and his brother, and send gatherers to the cities."

7:112   "They will come to you with every knowledgeable magician."

7:113   And the magicians came to Pharaoh, they said: "We require a reward if we are the victors."

7:114   He said: "Yes, and you will be made close to me."

7:115   They said: "O Moses, either you cast, or we will cast?"

7:116   He said: "You cast." So when they cast, they bewitched the eyes of the people, and instilled terror in them, and they came with a great magic.

7:117   And We inspired Moses: "Cast down your staff;" then it was eating up what they fabricated!

7:118   Thus the truth was set, and what they did was made of no effect.

7:119   They were thus defeated there and then, and they turned in disgrace.

7:120   And the magicians went down prostrating.

7:121   They said: "We believe in the Lord of the worlds."

7:122   "The Lord of Moses and Aaron."

7:123   Pharaoh said: "Have you become believers before I have given you permission? This is surely some scheme which you have schemed in the city to drive its people out; you will reveal what you know."

7:124   "I will cut off your hands and feet from alternate sides, then I will crucify you all."

7:125   They said: "It is to our Lord that we will return."

7:126   "And you are only seeking revenge on us because we believed in the signs of our Lord when they came to us. Our Lord, provide us with patience, and let us die as submitters."

7:127   And the commanders from among the people of Pharaoh said: "Will you let Moses and his people corrupt the land, and abandon you and your gods?" He said: "We will kill their children and rape their women; we will be supreme over them."

7:128   Moses said to his people: "Seek help with God, and be patient; the earth is for God, He will inherit it to whom He pleases of His servants; and the ending will be for the righteous."

7:129 They said: "We were being harmed before you came to us and since you have come to us." He said: "Perhaps your Lord will destroy your enemy, and make you successors in the land, so He sees how you work?"

7:130 And We afflicted the people of Pharaoh for years with a shortage in crops, perhaps they would remember.

7:131 When any good came to them, they said: "This is ours," and when any bad afflicted them, they blamed it on Moses and those with him. Their blame is with God, but most of them do not know.

7:132 And they said: "No matter what you bring us of a sign to bewitch us with, we will never believe in you."

7:133 So We sent them the flood, and the locust, and the lice, and the frogs, and the blood; all detailed signs; but they turned arrogant, they were a criminal people.

7:134 And when the affliction befell them, they said: "O Moses, call on your Lord for what He has pledged with you, that if you remove this affliction from us, then we will believe in you and we will send with you the Children of Israel."

7:135 So when We removed from them the affliction, until a future time, they broke their pledge.

7:136 We thus took vengeance upon them and drowned them in the running water; for their denial of Our signs, and their disregard of them.

7:137 And We let the people who were weak inherit the east of the land and the west of it which We have blessed. And the good word of your Lord was completed towards the Children of Israel for their patience; and We destroyed what Pharaoh and his people were doing, and what they contrived.

7:138 And We let the Children of Israel cross the sea, then they came upon a people who were devoted to statues made for them; they said: "O Moses, make for us a god like they have gods?" He said: "You are an ignorant people!"

7:139 "These people are ruined for what they are in, and evil is what they do."

7:140 He said: "Shall I seek other than God as a god for you when He has preferred you over the worlds?"

7:141 And We had saved you from the people of Pharaoh, they were afflicting you with the worst punishment; they used to kill your children and rape your women; and in that was a great test from your Lord.

7:142 And We set a meeting for Moses in thirty nights, and We complemented them with ten, so the designated time of his Lord was set at forty nights. And Moses said to his brother Aaron: "Be my successor with my people and be upright, and do not follow the path of the corrupters."

7:143 So when Moses came to Our designated time, and his Lord spoke to him, he said: "My Lord, let me look upon you." He said: "You will not see Me, but look upon the mountain, if it stays in its place then you will see Me." So when his Lord revealed Himself to the mountain, He caused it to crumble; thus Moses fell unconscious. When he awoke, he said: "Glory to You, I repent to You and I am the first of those who believe."

7:144 He said: "O Moses, I have chosen you over the people with My message and My words; so take what I have given you and be of the thankful."

7:145 And We wrote for him on the tablets from all things a lesson, and detailing all things. Take it with strength and order your people to take the best from it. I will show you the abode of the wicked.

7:146 I will turn away from My revelations those who are arrogant on the earth without right, and if they see every sign they do not believe in it, and if they see the path of guidance they do not take it as a path; and if they see the path of mischief, they take it as a path. That is because they have denied Our revelations and were heedless of them.

7:147 And those who deny Our revelations and the meeting of the Hereafter, their works have collapsed. Are they not being recompensed except for what they used to do?

7:148 And the people of Moses, in his absence, made from their jewelry the form of a calf that emitted a cry. Did they not see that it could not speak to them, nor guide them to any way? They took it and they were wicked.

7:149 And when they realized what their hands had done, and they saw that they had gone astray, they said: "If our Lord will not have mercy on us and forgive us, then we will be of the losers!"

7:150 And when Moses returned to his people, angry and grieved, he said: "Miserable is what you have done after I was gone; do you wish to hasten the action of your Lord?" And he cast down the tablets, and took his brother by his head dragging him towards him. He said: "Son of my mother, the people overpowered me and nearly killed me, so do not make the enemies rejoice over me, and do not make me with the wicked people."

7:151 He said: "My Lord, forgive me and my brother, and admit us in Your mercy; and You are the Most Merciful of those who show mercy."

7:152 Those who took the calf will be dealt with a wrath from their Lord and a humiliation in this worldly life. It is such that We punish the fabricators.

7:153 As for those who commit sin but then repent afterwards and believe; your Lord after that is Forgiving, Merciful.

7:154 And when the anger subsided from Moses, he took the tablets; and in its inscription was a guidance and a mercy for those who reverence their Lord.

7:155 And Moses selected from his people seventy men for Our designated time; so when the earthquake seized them, he said: "My Lord, if You wished You could have destroyed them before this, and me as well. Will you destroy us for what the foolish among us have done? It is all Your test, You misguide with it whom You please and You guide with it whom You please. You are our Supporter, so forgive us and have mercy on us; You are the Best Forgiver."

7:156 "And decree for us good in this world, and in the Hereafter; we have been guided towards You." He said: "My punishment, I afflict with it whom I choose, and My mercy encompasses all things. I will thus decree it for those who are aware and contribute towards purification, and those who believe in Our revelations."

7:157 Those who follow the messenger, the gentile prophet, whom they find written for them in the Torah and the Gospel; he advocates them for good and prohibits them from vice, and he makes permissible for them the good things, and he makes forbidden for them the vile things, and he removes their burden and the shackles that are upon them. So those who believe in him, and support him, and help him persevere, and follow the light that was sent down with him; these are the successful ones.

7:158 Say: "O people, I am a messenger of God to you all. The One who has the sovereignty of the heavens and the earth, there is no god except He; He gives life and causes death." So believe in God and His messenger, the gentile prophet, who believes in God and His words; and follow him that you may be guided.

7:159 And from among the people of Moses are a nation who guide with the truth and with it they become just.

7:160 And We separated them into twelve patriarch nations; and We inspired Moses when his people wanted to drink: "Strike the rock with your staff," thus twelve springs burst out of it. Each people then knew from where to drink. And We shaded them with clouds and We sent down to them manna and quail: "Eat from the good things that We have provided for you." They did not wrong Us, but it was their souls that they wronged.

7:161 And they were told: "Reside in this town and eat from it as you please, and say: "Our load is removed," and enter the passageway by crouching, We will forgive for you your wrongdoings, and We will increase for the good doers."

7:162 Those who were transgressors among them altered what was said to them with something different; so We sent to them an affliction from the heaven for what transgression they were in.

7:163 And ask them about the town which was by the sea, after they had transgressed the Sabbath; their fish would come to them openly on the day of their Sabbath, and when they are not in Sabbath, they do not come to them! It is such that We afflicted them for what wickedness they were in.

7:164 And a nation from among them said: "Why do you preach to a people whom God will destroy or punish a painful retribution?" They said: "A plea to your Lord, and perhaps they may be aware."

7:165 So when they forgot that which they were reminded of, We saved those who prohibited wickedness, and We took those who transgressed with a grievous retribution for what wickedness they were in.

7:166 So when they persisted in that which they had been prohibited from, We said to them: "Be despicable apes!"

7:167 And your Lord has sworn that He will send upon them, until the Day of Resurrection, people who would inflict severe punishments on them. Your Lord is swift to punish, and He is Forgiving, Merciful.

7:168 And We divided them through the land as nations. From them are the upright, and from them are other than that. And We tested them with good things and bad, perhaps they will return.

7:169 Then, a generation came after them who inherited the Book, but they opted for the materialism of that which is lower; and they say: "It will be forgiven for us." And they continue to opt for the materialism if it comes to them; was not the covenant of the Book taken on them that they would only say the truth about God, and they studied what was in it? And the abode of the Hereafter is better for those who are aware. Do you not comprehend?

7:170 As for those who hold fast to the Book, and they hold the Connection; We will not waste the reward of the righteous.

7:171 And We raised the mountain above them as if it were a cloud, and they thought it would fall on them: "Take what We have given you with strength and remember what is in it that you may be righteous."

7:172 And your Lord took for the children of Adam from their backs, their progeny; and He made them witness over themselves: "Am I not your Lord?" They said: "Yes, we bear witness." Thus you cannot say on the Day of Resurrection that you were unaware of this.

7:173 Nor can you say: "It was our fathers who set up partners before and we were simply a progeny who came after them. Would You destroy us for what the innovators did?"

7:174 It is such that We explain the revelations, perhaps they will return.

7:175 And recite to them the news of the person whom Our revelations were given to him, but he removed himself from them, and thus the devil followed him, and he became of those who went astray.

7:176 And if We had wished, We could have raised him with it, but he stuck to the earth and he followed his desire. His example is like the dog, if you scold him he pants, and if you leave him he pants; such is the example of the people who deny Our revelations. So narrate the stories, perhaps they will think.

7:177 Miserable is the example of the people who denied Our revelations, and it was their souls that they had wronged.

7:178 Whoever God guides, then he is the guided one; and whoever He misguides, then these are the losers.

7:179   And We have given to Hell many of the Jinn and mankind; they had hearts with which they did not understand, and they had eyes with which they did not see, and they had ears with which they did not hear. They are like hoofed animals; no, they are even more astray. These are the unaware ones.

7:180   And to God belongs the most beautiful names, so call Him by them; and leave alone those who deviate His names. They will be punished for what they used to do.

7:181   And from among those We created is a nation who guides with the truth, and with it they are just.

7:182   As for those who deny Our revelations, We will entice them from where they do not know.

7:183   And I will encourage them, for My planning is formidable.

7:184   Do they not reflect? Their companion has no madness; but he is a clear warner.

7:185   Have they not looked at the dominion of the heavens and the earth, and all that God has created? Perhaps their time is drawing near; so in which narrative after this one will they believe?

7:186   Whoever God misguides, then there is none to guide him; and He leaves them blindly wandering in their transgression.

7:187   They ask you regarding the Hour: "When will be its time?" Say: "Its knowledge is with my Lord, none can reveal its coming except He. It is heavy through the heavens and the earth; it will not come to you except suddenly." They ask you, as if you are responsible for it! Say: "Its knowledge is with God, but most of the people do not know."

7:188   Say: "I do not possess for myself any benefit or harm, except what God wills. And if I could know the future, then I would have increased my good fortune, and no harm would have come to me. I am but a warner and a bearer of good news to a people who believe."

7:189   He is the One who has created you from one person, and He made from it its mate to reside with. When he dwelled with her, she became pregnant with a light load, and she continued with it; then when it became heavy, they called on God, their Lord: "If You give us an upright child, then we will be among the thankful."

7:190   But when He gave them an upright child, they set up partners

107

with Him in what He had given them. God be exalted above what they set up as partners.

7:191   Do they set up those who do not create anything, while they are created?

7:192   And they cannot give them aid, nor can they aid themselves?

7:193   And if you invite them to the guidance they will not follow you. It is the same whether you invite them or simply keep quiet.

7:194   Those whom you call on besides God are servants like you; so let them answer for you if you are truthful.

7:195   Do they have feet with which to walk? Or, do they have hands with which to strike? Or, do they have eyes with which to see? Or, do they have ears with which to hear? Say: "Call on your partners, then plan against me. You will not be given respite."

7:196   "My supporter is God who sent down the Book; and He takes care of the righteous."

7:197   As for those whom you call on besides Him, they cannot aid you, nor can they aid themselves.

7:198   And when you invite them to the guidance, they do not listen. And you see them looking at you, while they do not see.

7:199   Take to pardoning, and order what is good, and turn away from the ignorant ones.

7:200   And if bitterness from the devil afflicts you, then seek refuge with God. He is the Hearer, the Knower.

7:201   Those who are pious, when any evil from the devil touches them, they remember, then they can see.

7:202   And their brethren attempt to drive them towards error, they do not cease.

7:203   And because you do not bring them a sign, they say: "If only you had brought one." Say: "I only follow what is inspired to me from my Lord. This is an evidence from your Lord, and a guide and mercy to a people who believe."

7:204   And if the Qur'an is being read, then listen to it and pay attention, that you may receive mercy.

7:205   And remember your Lord within yourself, in humility and in reverence; and without loudness in words, during the morning and the evening. And do not be of the careless ones.

7:206 Those who are at your Lord, they are never too proud to serve Him, and they glorify Him, and to Him they yield.

CHAPTER 8

8:0 In the name of God, the Almighty, the Merciful.

8:1 They ask you regarding the spoils, say: "The spoils are for God and the messenger." So be aware of God, and be upright in matters between you; and obey God and His messenger if you are believers.

8:2 The believers are those whom, when God is mentioned, their hearts reverence; and when His revelations are recited to them, it increases their faith; and they put their trust in their Lord.

8:3 They hold the Connection, and from Our provisions to them they spend.

8:4 These are the true believers; they will have grades with their Lord and a forgiveness and a generous provision.

8:5 As your Lord made you go out from your home with the truth, but a party from among the believers disliked this.

8:6 They argue with you about the truth when it has been made clear to them; as if they were being herded towards death while they are watching!

8:7 And God promises you that one of the two parties will be defeated by you; and you wish that the one least armed be the one. But God wishes that the truth be manifest with His words, and that He eliminates the remnant of the rejecters.

8:8 So that the truth will be manifest, and the falsehood will be finished; even if the criminals hate it.

8:9 You called on help from your Lord and He answered you: "I will provide you with one thousand angels in succession."

8:10 And God did not do this except to give you good news, and that your hearts may be assured by it. And victory is only from God; for God is Noble, Wise.

8:11   Sleep overcame you to give you tranquility from Him; and He sent down to you water from the sky to purify you with it and cause the affliction of the devil to leave you; and so that He may strengthen your hearts and set firm your feet.

8:12   Your Lord inspired to the angels: "I am with you so keep firm those who believe. I will cast terror into the hearts of those who have rejected; so strike above the necks, and strike from them every one standing."

8:13   That is because they have transgressed against God and His messenger. And whoever transgresses against God and His messenger, then God is severe in retribution.

8:14   This is for you to sample, and for the rejecters will be a retribution of Fire.

8:15   O you who believe; when you encounter those who have rejected on the battlefield, do not flee from them.

8:16   And whoever on that day flees from them; unless it is part of the battle strategy or if he is retreating back to his group; then he has drawn the wrath of God upon him, and his abode will be Hell. What a miserable destiny.

8:17   It was not you who killed them, but it was God who killed them. And it was not you who launched when you did, but it was God who launched. And so that the believers would be tested well by Him. God is Hearer, Knowledgeable.

8:18   That, and God weakens the plans of the rejecters.

8:19   If you sought conquest, then conquest has come to you, but if you cease, then it is better for you. And if you return again, then We will also return, and your group will avail you nothing even if it is many. God is with the believers.

8:20   O you who believe, obey God and His messenger, and do not turn away from him while you have heard.

8:21   And do not be like those who said: "We hear," but they do not hear.

8:22   The worst creatures with God are the deaf and dumb who do not comprehend.

8:23   And if God had found any good in them, then He would have made them listen. And if He had made them listen, they would have turned away while they are in aversion.

8:24   O you who believe, answer the call of God and His messenger when he calls you to what will grant you life. And know that God comes between a person and his heart, and that to Him you will be gathered.

8:25   And be aware of a test that will not only afflict those of you who were wicked; and know that God is severe in retribution.

8:26   And remember when you were but a few who were weak in the land, you were fearful that the people might capture you. But He sheltered you, and He supported you with His victory, and He provided you with good provisions, so that you may be thankful.

8:27   O you who believe, do not betray God and the messenger, nor betray your trust, while you know.

8:28   And know that your money and your children are a test, and that God has the greatest reward.

8:29   O you who believe, if you are aware of God, He will make a criterion for you, and He will cancel your sins and forgive you. God is possessor of great grace.

8:30   And the rejecters plot against you to arrest you, or to kill you, or to expel you. And they plot, and God plots, and God is the best of plotters.

8:31   And if Our revelations are recited to them, they say: "We have listened, and if we wish, we could have said the same thing. This is nothing except tales of old!"

8:32   And they said: "Our god, if this is the truth from You, then send down upon us a rain of rocks from the heaven or bring upon us a painful retribution."

8:33   And God will not punish them while you are with them, nor will God punish them while they continue to seek forgiveness.

8:34   And why should God not punish them when they are turning others away from the restricted Temple, and they were never its protectors! Its protectors are the righteous; but most of them do not know.

8:35   And their connecting at the House was nothing but noise and aversion. Taste the retribution for what you have rejected.

8:36   Those who have rejected, they spend their money to turn others away from the path of God. They will spend it, then it will become an anguish for them, then they will be defeated. Those who have rejected will be gathered to Hell.

8:37 This is so that God will distinguish the rotten from the good, and so that the rotten will be gathered together into one heap then He will cast it all into Hell. These are the losers.

8:38 Say to the rejecters, if they cease, then what has passed before will be forgiven to them, and if they return to it, then the example of the previous generations has already been given.

8:39 And fight them all until there is no more oppression, and the entire system is for God. But if they cease, then God is Seer over what they do.

8:40 And if they turn away, then know that God is your Patron. What an excellent Patron, and what an excellent Victor.

8:41 And know that anything you profit, one-fifth shall go to God and the messenger, and the relatives, and the orphans, and the poor, and the wayfarer. You will do this if you believe in God and in what We revealed to Our servant on the Day of the Criterion, the day the two armies clashed; and God is capable of all things.

8:42 When you were on the near side, and they were on the far side, then the supply line became directly beneath you. And if you had planned for this meeting, you would have disagreed on its timing, but God was to enforce a command that was already done. So that He would destroy those to be destroyed with proof, and to let those who will live be alive with proof; and God is Hearer, Knowledgeable.

8:43 God showed them to you as being few in your dream, and if He had shown them to you to be many, then you would have failed and you would have disputed in the matter, but God saved you. He is the Knower of what is in the chests.

8:44 And He showed them to you when you met as being few to your eyes, and He made you appear as being fewer to their eyes. That was so the decree of God would come to be; and to God all matters are returned.

8:45 O you who believe, when you encounter a force, stand firm and mention God excessively, that you may succeed.

8:46 And obey God and His messenger, and do not dispute else you will fail and your momentum will depart, and be patient. God is with the patient.

8:47   And do not be like those who came out from their homes to boast and to be seen by the people, and they repel others from the path of God; and God is aware of what they do.

8:48   And the devil adorned their work for them, and he said: "No people can defeat you today, and I am by your side." But when the two forces came together, he turned back on his heels and he said: "I am innocent from you! I see what you do not see. I fear God, and God is severe in punishment."

8:49   The hypocrites and those who have a disease in their hearts said: "These people have been deceived by their system." But whoever puts his trust in God, then God is Noble, Wise.

8:50   And if you could only see as the angels terminate the lives of those who have rejected, they strike their faces and their backs: "Taste the punishment of the blazing Fire!"

8:51   "This is for what your hands have delivered, and God does not wrong the servants."

8:52   Like the behavior of the people of Pharaoh, and those before them; they rejected the signs of God, so God took them by their sins. God is Strong, severe in punishment.

8:53   That is because God was not to change any blessing He bestowed upon a people, unless they change what is in themselves. God is Hearer, Knowledgeable.

8:54   Like the behavior of the people of Pharaoh, and those before them; they denied the signs of their Lord, so We destroyed them by their sins, and We drowned the people of Pharaoh; all of them were wicked.

8:55   The worst creatures to God are those who reject, for they do not believe.

8:56   Those of them with whom you made a pledge, then they break their pledge every time, and they do not take heed.

8:57   So, when you engage them in battle, set them as an example for those who will come after them; perhaps they may remember.

8:58   And if you are being betrayed by a people, then you shall likewise move against them. God does not love the betrayers.

8:59   And let not those who have rejected think that they have escaped; they will never avail themselves.

8:60 And prepare for them all that you can of might, and from the steeds of war, that you may instill terror with it towards the enemy of God and your enemy, and others besides them whom you do not know but God knows them. And whatever you spend in the cause of God will be returned to you, and you will not be wronged.

8:61 And if they seek peace, then you also seek it, and put your trust in God. He is the Hearer, the Knowledgeable.

8:62 And if they wish to deceive you, then God is sufficient for you. He is the One who supported you with His victory and with the believers.

8:63 And He made unity between their hearts. And if you had spent all that is on the earth, you would not have united between their hearts, but God united between them. He is Noble, Wise.

8:64 O prophet, God is sufficient for you, and whoever followed you from the believers.

8:65 O prophet, urge the believers to fight. If there are twenty of you who are patient, they will defeat two hundred. And if there are one hundred of you, they will defeat one thousand from among those who reject; that is because they are a people who do not understand.

8:66 Now, God has alleviated for you, for He knows that there is weakness in you. If there are one hundred of you who are patient, they will defeat two hundred. And if there are one thousand of you, they will defeat two thousand with the permission of God. God is with the patient.

8:67 It was not for any prophet to take prisoners unless it was in a battle engagement. You desire the materials of this world, while God wants the Hereafter for you. God is Noble, Wise.

8:68 Had it not been previously ordained from God, then a severe punishment would have afflicted you for what you took.

8:69 So consume what you have gained, permissible and good, and be aware of God. God is Forgiving, Merciful.

8:70 O prophet, say to those prisoners whom you hold: "If God finds in your hearts any good, He will grant you better than what He took from you, and He will forgive you. God is Forgiving, Merciful."

8:71 And if they want to betray you, then they had already betrayed

God before, but He has overpowered them; and God is Knowledgeable, Wise.

8:72   Those who have believed and emigrated and strived with their money and lives in the cause of God, and those who have sheltered and supported; these are the allies of one another. And those who believed but did not emigrate, you do not owe them any obligation until they emigrate. But if they seek your help in the system, then you must support them, except if it is against a people with whom there is a covenant between you and them. And God is Seer over what you do.

8:73   As for those who reject, they are allies to one another. If you do not do this, then there will be oppression on the earth and great corruption.

8:74   And those who have believed and emigrated and strived in the cause of God, and those who have sheltered and supported, these are truly the believers. They will have a forgiveness and a generous provision.

8:75   And those who believed afterwards and emigrated and strived with you, then they are from you. And the relatives by birth are also supportive of one another in the Book of God. God is aware of all things.

CHAPTER 9

9:1   A revocation is made by God and His messenger to those with whom you have made a pledge from among the polytheists.

9:2   "Therefore, roam the land for four months and know that you will not escape God, and that God will humiliate the rejecters."

9:3   And an announcement from God and His messenger to the people, on the day of the greater Pilgrimage: "That God and His messenger are innocent from the polytheists." If you repent, then it is better for you, and if you turn away, then know that you will not escape God. And give news to those who have rejected of a painful retribution.

9:4   Except for those with whom you had made a pledge from among the polytheists if they did not reduce anything from it nor did they support anyone against you; you shall continue the pledge with them until its expiry. God loves the righteous.

9:5   So when the restricted Months have passed, then you may kill the polytheists wherever you find them, and take them, and surround them, and stand against them at every point. If they repent, and they hold the Connection, and they contribute towards purification, then you shall leave them alone. God is Forgiving, Merciful.

9:6   And if any of the polytheists seeks your protection, then you may protect him so that he may hear the words of God, then let him reach his sanctity. This is because they are a people who do not know.

9:7   How can the polytheists have a pledge with God and with His messenger? Except for those with whom you made a pledge near the restricted Temple, as long as they are upright with you, then you are upright with them. God loves the righteous.

9:8   How is it that when they come upon you they disregard all ties, either those of kinship or of pledge. They seek to please you with their words, but their hearts deny, and the majority of them are wicked.

9:9   They purchased with the revelations of God a cheap price, so they repel others from His path. Evil indeed is what they used to do.

9:10   They do not respect those who are believers, nor a kinship, nor a pledge. These are the transgressors.

9:11   If they repent, and they hold the Connection, and they contribute towards purification, then they are your brothers in the system. We explain the revelations for a people who know.

9:12   And if they break their oaths after making their pledge, and they challenge the authority of your system; then you may kill the leaders of rejection. Their oaths are nothing to them, perhaps they will then cease.

9:13   Would you not fight a people who broke their oaths, and obsessed to expel the messenger, especially while they were the ones who attacked you first? Are you concerned about them? It is God who is more deserving that you be concerned with if you are believers.

9:14   Fight them; perhaps God will punish them by your hands and humiliate them and grant you victory over them and heal the chests of the believing people.

9:15   And to remove the anger from their hearts; God pardons whom he pleases. God is Knowledgeable, Wise.

9:16   Or did you think that you would be left alone? God will come to distinguish those of you who strived and did not take other than God and His messenger and the believers as helpers. God is Expert in what you do.

9:17   It was not for the polytheists to build the temples of God while they bear witness over their own rejection. For these, their works have fallen, and in the Fire they will abide.

9:18   Rather, the temples of God are built by he who believes in God and the Last Day, and he holds the Connection, and he contributes towards purification, and is only concerned by God. It is these that will be of the guided ones.

9:19   Have you made the watering of the pilgrim and the building of the restricted Temple the same as one who believes in God and the Last Day and he strives in the cause of God? They are not the same with God. And God does not guide the wicked people.

9:20   Those who believed and emigrated and strived in the cause of God with their money and their lives are in a greater degree with God. These are the winners.

9:21   Their Lord gives them good news: a mercy from Him, and approval, and gardens for them in which there is everlasting bliss.

9:22   They will abide in it eternally. With God there is a great reward.

9:23   O you who believe, do not take your fathers nor brothers as allies if they prefer rejection to belief. And whoever of you takes them as such, then these are the wicked.

9:24   Say: "If your fathers, and your sons, and your brothers, and your wives, and your kin, and money which you have gathered, and a trade which you would be concerned over its decline, and homes which you find pleasing; if these are dearer to you than God and His messenger and striving in His cause, then wait until God brings His decision. And God does not guide the wicked people."

9:25   God has granted you victory in many battlefields. And on the day of Hunayn when you were pleased with your great numbers but it did not help you at all, and the land became tight around you for what it held, then you turned to flee.

9:26   Then God sent down His tranquility upon His messenger and the believers, and He sent down soldiers which you did not see, and He punished those who rejected. Such is the recompense of the rejecters.

9:27   Then God will accept the repentance of whom He pleases after that. God is Forgiving, Merciful.

9:28   O you who believe, the polytheists are impure, so let them not come near the restricted Temple after this calendar year of theirs; and if you fear poverty, then God will enrich you from His blessings if He wills. God is Knowledgeable, Wise.

9:29   Fight those who do not believe in God or the Last Day, nor do they forbid what God and His messenger have forbidden, nor do they uphold the system of truth; from among the people who have been given the Book; until they pay the reparation, willingly or unwillingly, and they are subdued.

9:30   The Jews said: "Ezra is the son of God," and the Nazarenes said: "The Messiah is the son of God." Such is their utterances with their mouths, they imitate the sayings of those who rejected before them. God will fight them. They are deluded from the truth!

9:31   They have taken their Priests and Monks to be patrons besides God, and the Messiah, son of Mary, while they were only commanded to serve One god, there is no god except He, be He glorified against what they set up.

9:32   They want to extinguish the light of God with their mouths, but God refuses such and lets His light continue, even if the rejecters hate it.

9:33   He is the One who has sent His messenger with the guidance and the system of truth, so that it will expose all other systems, even if the polytheists hate it.

9:34   O you who believe, many of the Priests and Monks consume the money of the people in falsehood, and they repel from the path of God. And those who hoard gold and silver, and do not spend it in the cause of God, give them news of a painful retribution.

9:35   On the Day when it will be heated in the fire of Hell, and their foreheads and sides and backs will be branded with it: "This is what you have hoarded for yourselves, so taste what you have hoarded!"

9:36   The count of the months with God is twelve months in the book of God the day He created the heavens and the earth; four of them are restricted. This is the correct system; so do not wrong yourselves in them; and fight the polytheists collectively as they fight you collectively. And know that God is with the righteous.

9:37　In the use of the intercalary exists an increase in rejection; that those who have rejected may misguide with it. They make it permissible one calendar year, and forbid it one calendar year, so as to circumvent the count of what God has made forbidden; thus they make permissible what God has made forbidden. Their evil works have been adorned for them, and God does not guide the rejecting people.

9:38　O you who believe, what is wrong with you when you are told: "Mobilize in the cause of God," you become heavy on the earth. Have you become content with this worldly life over the Hereafter? The enjoyment of this worldly life compared to the Hereafter is nothing.

9:39　If you do not mobilize, then He will punish you with a painful retribution, and He will replace you with another people, and you do not bother Him in the least. God is capable of all things.

9:40　If you do not help him, then God has helped him. When those who rejected expelled him, he was one of only two, and when they were in the cave, he said to his friend: "Do not grieve, for God is with us." So God sent down His tranquility over him and He supported him with soldiers that you did not see, and He made the word of those who rejected be the lowest, and the word of God be the highest. God is Noble, Wise.

9:41　Mobilize in light gear or heavy gear, and strive with your money and lives in the cause of God. That is best if only you knew.

9:42　If it were a near gain, or an easy journey, they would have followed you; but the distance was too much for them. And they will swear by God: "If we could have, we would have gone with you." They destroy themselves, and God knows they are liars.

9:43　God pardons you; why did you give them leave before it became clear to you who are truthful, and who are lying?

9:44　Those who believe in God and the Last Day will not ask leave. They strive with their money and their lives. And God is aware of the righteous.

9:45　Those who ask leave are the ones who do not believe in God and the Last Day, and their hearts are in doubt. In their doubts they are wavering.

9:46　And if they had wanted to go then they would have taken all precautions for it, but God disliked them coming forth, so He made them lag behind, and they were told: "Stay with those who have stayed."

9:47　Had they gone with you they would have added nothing except disruption, and they would have hurried about seeking to cause for you an ordeal; and there are some among you who listen to them. God is aware of the wicked.

9:48　They wanted to cause an ordeal from before, and they turned matters upside down for you until the truth came and the command of God was revealed, while they hated it.

9:49　And from them are those who say: "Grant me leave, and do not test me." But it is in the test that they have indeed fallen, and Hell is surrounding the rejecters.

9:50　When any good befalls you, it upsets them, and if any bad befalls you, they say: "We have taken our precaution beforehand," and they turn away happy.

9:51　Say: "Nothing will befall us except what God has decreed for us, He is our Patron." And in God the believers shall put their trust.

9:52　Say: "You can only expect for us one of two good things; while we wait for you to be afflicted by God with a retribution from Him, or by our hands. So wait, we are with you waiting."

9:53　Say: "Spend willingly or unwillingly, it will not be accepted from you. You are a wicked people."

9:54　And what prevented what they would spend from being accepted from them except that they rejected God and His messenger, and they do not attend to the Connection except lazily, and they do not spend except unwillingly.

9:55　So do not be impressed by their wealth or children; God only wishes to punish them with it in the worldly life, and so that their souls will be taken while they are rejecters.

9:56　And they swear by God that they are with you, while they are not with you; but they are a people who are indecisive.

9:57　If they find a refuge, or cave, or any place to enter, they will run to it while they are in haste.

9:58　And from them are those who criticize you regarding the charities. If they are given from it, they are content; and if they are not given from it, they become enraged!

9:59　And if they had only been content with what God and His messenger had given them, and they had said: "God suffices; God will give us from His bounty, and His messenger; it is towards God that we desire."

9:60   Indeed, the charities are for the poor, and the needy, and those who work to collect them, and those whose hearts have been united, and to free the slaves, and those in debt, and in the cause of God, and the wayfarer. A duty from God, and God is Knowledgeable, Wise.

9:61   And from them are those who harm the prophet, and they say: "He only listens!" Say: "What he listens to is best for you. He believes in God, and he has trust for the believers, and he is a mercy to those who believe among you." And those who harm the messenger of God will have a painful retribution.

9:62   They swear to you by God in order to please you; while God and His messenger are more worthy to be pleased if they are believers.

9:63   Did they not know that whoever is hostile towards God and His messenger, he will have the fire of Hell, abiding therein. Such is the greatest humiliation.

9:64   The hypocrites fear that a chapter will be sent down which will expose what is in their hearts. Say: "Mock, for God will bring out what you fear."

9:65   And if you ask them they say: "We were only jesting and playing." Say: "In God and His revelations and His messenger you were mocking?"

9:66   Do not apologize, for you have rejected after your belief. If We pardon one group from you, We will punish another group. That is because they were criminals.

9:67   The hypocrite males and the hypocrite females, they are to each other. They advocate for vice and prohibit good, and they close their hands. They forgot God, so He will forget them; indeed, the hypocrites are the wicked.

9:68   God has promised the hypocrite males and the hypocrite females and the rejecters a Fire in Hell, in it they will abide; it will be enough for them. And God has cursed them and they will have a lasting retribution.

9:69   Like those before them, they were more powerful than you, and with more wealth and children. They enjoyed their lives, and you enjoyed your lives as those before you enjoyed their lives; and you jested as they jested. They had their works crumble in this world and the next, and they were the losers.

9:70   Did the news not come to them of those before them, the people of Noah and 'Aad and Thamud. And the people of Abraham, and the dwellers of Midyan, and those overthrown. Their messengers came to them with clarity; it was not God who wronged them, but it was themselves that they wronged.

9:71   And the believing males and the believing females, they are allies to one another. They advocate for good and prohibit vice, and they hold the Connection, and they contribute towards purification and they obey God and His messenger. God will have mercy on them; God is Noble, Wise.

9:72   God has promised the believing males and the believing females estates with rivers flowing beneath them, abiding therein, and pleasing homes in gardens of delight. And the acceptance from God is the most important; such is the great triumph.

9:73   O prophet, strive against the rejecters and the hypocrites and be firm against them. Their dwelling is Hell, what a miserable destiny!

9:74   They swear by God that they did not say it, while they had said the word of rejection, and they rejected after they had submitted, and they were obsessed with what they could not possess; and they could not find any fault except that God and His messenger had enriched them from His bounty. If they repent it is better for them, and if they turn away, then God will punish them severely in this world and the next. They will not have on the earth any ally or supporter.

9:75   And from them are those who pledged to God: "If He gives us from His bounty, then we will believe and we will be among the upright."

9:76   So when He gave them from His bounty, they became stingy with it, and they turned away while they were averse.

9:77   Thus, hypocrisy follows in their hearts until the Day they meet Him; that is for breaking what they promised God, and for what they were lying.

9:78   Did they not know that God knows their secrets, and their private counsel, and that God is the Knower of all the unseen?

9:79   Those who criticize the volunteers among the believers in charities; that they only have their efforts to give; so they mock them. God mocks them, and they will have a painful retribution.

9:80 Whether you seek forgiveness for them, or do not seek forgiveness for them. If you seek forgiveness for them seventy times, God will not forgive them. That is because they have rejected God and His messenger; and God does not guide the wicked people.

9:81 Those who have remained are happy with their position of lagging behind the messenger of God, and they disliked striving with their money and lives in the cause of God; and they say: "Do not mobilize in the heat." Say: "The fire of Hell is much hotter," if they could only understand.

9:82 Let them laugh a little, and cry a lot, a recompense for what they have earned.

9:83 So, if God sends you back to a group of them, and they ask your permission to come with you, then say: "You will not come with me ever; nor will you fight any enemy with me. You had accepted staying behind the first time, so stay with those who remain behind."

9:84 And do not connect upon any of them that has died—ever; nor stand at his grave. They have rejected God and His messenger and died while they were wicked.

9:85 And do not be impressed by their wealth and their children; God only wishes to punish them with it in this world, and so their souls will be taken while they are rejecters.

9:86 And if a chapter is sent down: "That you shall believe in God and strive with His messenger," those with wealth and influence ask your leave and they say: "Let us be with those who remain behind."

9:87 They were content to stay with those who remained behind, and it was imprinted on their hearts, for they do not understand.

9:88 But the messenger and those who believe with him have strived with their money and their lives. For them will be the good things, and they are the successful ones.

9:89 God has prepared for them estates with rivers flowing beneath them, abiding therein. Such is the great gain.

9:90 And those who had an excuse from among the Nomads came so leave would be given to them, and those who denied God and His messenger simply stayed behind. Those who rejected from them will be inflicted with a painful retribution.

9:91 There is no blame to be placed upon the weak, or the sick, or those who do not find anything to spend on, if they are sincere towards God and His messenger. There is no argument against the good doers; and God is Forgiving, Merciful.

9:92 Nor upon those who came to ride out with you, while you said: "I do not have any mounts for you;" they turned away while their eyes were flooded with tears out of sadness, for they could not find anything to contribute.

9:93 Indeed, the argument is against those who sought your leave while they were rich. They accepted to be with those who remained behind, and God stamps their hearts, for they do not know.

9:94 They will apologize to you when you return to them, say: "Do not apologize, we will not believe you, for God has told us of your news." And God will see your work, as will His messenger, then you will be returned to Knower of the unseen and the seen, He will inform you of what you did.

9:95 They will swear by God to you, when you return to them, so that you would let them be. So let them be, for they are foul, and their destiny is Hell as a recompense for what they earned.

9:96 They swear to you so that you would accept them. Even if you accept them, God does not accept the wicked people.

9:97 The Nomads are the worst in rejection and hypocrisy, and more likely not to know the boundaries of what God has sent down upon His messenger. God is Knower, Wise.

9:98 And from the Nomads are those who look upon what they spend as a fine, and wait for misfortune upon you. They will have the misfortune of evil, and God is Hearer, Knowledgeable.

9:99 And from the Nomads are those who believe in God and the Last Day, and looks to what he spends to make him closer to God—and the connections with the messenger. It indeed makes them closer. God will admit them in His mercy; God is Forgiving, Merciful.

9:100 And the first forerunners from among the emigrants and the supporters, and those who followed them in goodness; God has accepted them, and they have accepted Him; and He has prepared for them estates with rivers flowing beneath them, abiding therein eternally. Such is the great triumph.

9:101 And from among the Nomads around you are hypocrites, and from among the people of the city, they persist in hypocrisy. You do not know them, but We know them. We will punish them twice, then they will be returned to a great punishment.

9:102 And others who have acknowledged their sins, they have mixed a good work with another that was bad. Perhaps God will pardon them. God is Forgiving, Merciful.

9:103 Take from their money a charity to sanctify them and purify them with it, and connect upon them; for your connection is a tranquility for them; and God is Hearer, Knowledgeable.

9:104 Did they not know that it is God who accepts repentance from His servants, and He takes the charities, and that God is the Pardoner, the Merciful.

9:105 And say: "Work, and God will see your work and His messenger and the believers. And you will be sent back to Knower of the unseen and the seen, and He will inform you of what you did."

9:106 And others are waiting for the decision of God; either He will punish them, or He will pardon them. God is Knowledgeable, Wise.

9:107 And there are those who have taken a temple to do harm and cause rejection, and to divide between the believers, and as an outpost for those who fought God and His messenger before. They will swear that they only wanted to do good, and God bears witness that they are liars.

9:108 Do not stand in it ever. A temple that is founded on righteousness from the first day is more worthy that you stand in it; in it are men who love to purify themselves. And God loves the purified.

9:109 Is he who founds his building on obtaining righteousness from God and His acceptance better, or he who founds his building on the edge of a cliff which is about to crumble, so that it crumbled with him into the fires of Hell? And God does not guide the wicked people.

9:110 Their buildings that they built continue to cause doubt in their hearts, until their hearts are severed. And God is Knowledgeable, Wise.

9:111 God has purchased from the believers their very lives and their wealth, that they will have Paradise; they fight in the cause of God—so they kill and are killed—a promise that is true upon Him in the Torah and the Gospel and the Qur'an. And whoever fulfills this pledge with God, then have good news of the pledge which you are concluded with. Such is the great triumph.

9:112　The repenters, the servers, the appreciative, the activists, the kneeling, the prostrating, the advocates for good and the prohibiters of vice, and the adherents to God's boundaries—and give good news to the believers.

9:113　It is not for the prophet and those who believe that they should seek forgiveness for the polytheists, even if they are relatives, after it has been made clear to them that they are the dwellers of Hell.

9:114　And Abraham seeking forgiveness for his father was only because of a promise he had made to him. But when it became clear that he was the enemy of God, he disowned him. Abraham was kind, compassionate.

9:115　And it is not for God to misguide a people after He guided them, until He makes clear to them what they should avoid. God is aware of all things.

9:116　To God is the sovereignty of the heavens and the earth, He brings life and death. You have none besides God as a supporter or victor.

9:117　God has pardoned the prophet and the emigrants and the supporters who had followed him in the darkest hour, even though the hearts of some of them nearly deviated, but then He pardoned them. He is towards them Compassionate, Merciful.

9:118　And also the three who were left behind, until the land, as vast as it is, became strained to them, and their very souls became strained, and they thought there was no shelter from God except to Him. Then He pardoned them that they may repent. God is the Redeemer, the Merciful.

9:119　O you who believe, be aware of God and be with the truthful.

9:120　It is not advisable for the dwellers of the city and those around them of the Nomads that they should lag behind after the messenger of God, nor should they yearn for themselves above him. That is because any thirst that will come to them, or fatigue, or hunger in the cause of God, or any step that they take which will annoy the rejecters, or any gain they have over any enemy; it will be recorded as a good deed for them. God does not waste the reward of the good doers.

9:121　And anything small or large they spend, or any valley they cross, it will be recorded for them. God will recompense them with the best of what they did.

9:122 And it is not advisable for the believers to mobilize in their entirety. For every battalion that marches out, let a group remain to study the system, and warn their people when they return to them, perhaps they will be aware.

9:123 O you who believe, fight those who are around you of the rejecters, and let them find strength in you; and know that God is with the righteous.

9:124 And when a chapter is sent down, some of them say: "Who has been increased in faith by this?" For those who believe, it has increased their faith, and they rejoice.

9:125 As for those who have a disease in their hearts, it only increased foulness to their foulness, and they died as rejecters.

9:126 Do they not see they are tested every calendar year once or twice? But then they do not repent, nor do they remember.

9:127 And when a chapter is sent down, they look at one another: "Does anyone see you?" Then they turn away. God turns away their hearts, for they are a people who do not understand.

9:128 A messenger has come to you from yourselves, troubled over your deviation, anxious over you, towards the believers he is compassionate, merciful.

9:129 If they turn away, then say: "God is sufficient for me, there is no god except He, in Him I place my trust and He is the Lord of the great Throne."

CHAPTER 10

10:0 In the name of God, the Almighty, the Merciful.

10:1 ALR, these are the signs of the Book of Wisdom.

10:2 Is it a surprise for the people who We inspired a man from among them: "Warn the people and give good news to those who believe, that they will have a footing of truth with their Lord." The rejecters said: "This is clearly magic!"

10:3 Your Lord is God who has created the heavens and the earth in six days, then He settled upon the Throne; He manages all affairs. There is no intercessor except after His permission. Such is God your Lord, so serve Him. Would you not remember?

10:4 To Him is your return, all of you, for the promise of God is true. He initiates the creation then He returns it; to recompense with justice those who have believed and have done good works. As for those who have rejected, they will have a boiling drink, and a painful retribution for what they had rejected.

10:5 He is the One who has made the sun a radiance, and the moon a light, and He has measured its phases; that you may know the number of the years and the count. God has not created this except with the truth. He clarifies the revelations for a people who know.

10:6 In the difference between the night and the day and what God has created in the heavens and the earth are signs for a people who are aware.

10:7 As for those who do not wish to meet Us, and they are content with the worldly life, and they feel secure by it, and they are unaware of Our signs.

10:8 To these will be the destiny of the Fire for what they earned.

10:9 Those who believe and do good works, their Lord will guide them by their faith. Rivers will flow beneath them in gardens of bliss.

10:10 Their saying in it is: "Be You glorified, our god!" And their greeting in it is: "Peace," and the end of their saying is: "Praise be to God, Lord of the worlds!"

10:11 And if God hastened for the people the evil as He hastens for them the good, then they would have been ruined. We thus leave those who do not wish to meet Us wandering in their transgression.

10:12 And when hardship touches man, he calls upon Us on his side or sitting or standing. But when We remove his hardship from him, he carries on as if he never called upon Us for a hardship which touched him! Thus it was made to appear good to the transgressors what they had done.

10:13 And We have destroyed the generations before you when they transgressed; and their messengers had come to them with clear proofs, but they would not believe. It is such that We recompense the criminal people.

10:14 Then We made you successors on the earth after them to see how you would perform.

10:15 And when Our clear revelations were recited to them, those who do not wish to meet Us said: "Bring a Qur'an other than this, or change it!" Say: "It is not for me to change it of my own accord, I merely follow what is inspired to me. I fear, if I disobeyed my Lord, the retribution of a great Day!"

10:16 Say: "If God had willed, I would not have recited it to you, nor would you have known about it. I have been residing among you for nearly a lifetime before this; do you not comprehend?"

10:17 Who is more wicked than he who invents lies about God or denies His revelations? The criminals will never succeed.

10:18 And they serve besides God what does not harm them or benefit them, and they say: "These are our intercessors with God." Say: "Are you informing God of what He does not know in the heavens or the earth?" Be He glorified and exalted above what they set up.

10:19 The people were but one nation, then they differed. And had it not been for a previous command from your Lord, the matter would have been immediately judged between them for what they differed.

10:20 And they say: "If only a sign was sent down to him from his Lord." Say: "The future is with God, so wait, and I will wait with you."

10:21 And if We let the people taste a mercy after some hardship had afflicted them, they take to scheming against Our revelations! Say: "God is faster in scheming;" Our messengers record what you scheme.

10:22 He is the One who carries you on land and on the sea. And when you are on the ships and We drive them with a good wind which they rejoice with, a strong gust comes to them and the waves come to them from all sides, and they think that they are finished, they implore God with loyalty and devotion to His system: "If You save us from this, we will be of the thankful."

10:23 But when He saves them, they then traverse through the land with injustice. "O people, what you seek out is only the luxury of this worldly life, then to Us is your return and We will inform you of all that you had done."

10:24 The example of the worldly life is like a water which has come down from the sky, so it mixed with the plants of the earth from what the people and the hoofed animals eat. Then the earth takes its shape and becomes beautiful and its inhabitants think that they have mastered it; then Our judgment comes by night or by day, so We make it a wasteland as if it never prospered by the yesterday! It is such that We clarify the revelations for a people who think.

10:25   God calls to the abode of peace, and He guides those whom He wishes to a straight path.

10:26   For those who do good will be good and more, and their faces will not be darkened or humiliated. These are the people of Paradise, in it they will abide.

10:27   As for those who earn evil, the recompense of evil will be evil like it, and they will be humiliated. They do not have anyone to help them from God. It is as if their faces have been covered by a piece of darkness from the night. These are the people of the Fire, in it they will abide.

10:28   And on the Day We gather them all, then We will say to those who were polytheists: "Stop where you are, you and your partners," then We will separate between them, and their partners will say: "It was not us that you served!"

10:29   "God is enough as a witness between us and you, that we were unaware of you serving us."

10:30   It is then that every soul will know what it has done, and they will be returned to God their true patron, and they have been abandoned by that which they had invented.

10:31   Say: "Who provides for you from the heavens and the earth? Who possesses the hearing and the eyesight? And who brings the living out from the dead and brings the dead out from the living? And who manages all affairs?" They will say: "God." Say: "Will you not be righteous!"

10:32   Such is God, your true Lord. So what is after the truth except straying! Why then do you turn away?

10:33   It was thus that the command of your Lord came against those who were wicked, for they did not believe.

10:34   Say: "Are there any from those whom you have set up as partners who can initiate the creation and then return it?" Say: "God initiates the creation and then returns it." How are you deluded!

10:35 Say: "Are there any of those whom you set up as partners who can guide to the truth?" Say: "God guides to the truth. Is He who guides to the truth more worthy of being followed, or he who does not guide except after he is guided? What is wrong with you, how do you judge?"

10:36 Most of them only follow conjecture. While conjecture does not avail against the truth in anything. God is aware of what they do.

10:37 This Qur'an could not have been produced without God; it is to affirm what is between his hands, and to give details of the Book in which there is no doubt, from the Lord of the worlds.

10:38 Or do they say: "He has invented it!" Say: "Then bring a chapter like it, and call on whom you can besides God if you are truthful."

10:39 No, they have lied about that which they had no knowledge, nor has its explanation come to them. It is also how those before them denied, so see how was the retribution of the wicked!

10:40 And there are some of them who believe in it, and some of them do not believe in it. Your Lord is better aware of the transgressors.

10:41 And if they deny you, then say: "I have my deeds, and you have your deeds. You are innocent from what I do, and I am innocent from what you do."

10:42 And there are some of them who listen to you; but can you make the deaf hear, if they do not comprehend?

10:43 And there are some of them who look at you; but can you guide the blind, if they do not see?

10:44 God does not wrong the people in the least, but it is the people who wrong themselves.

10:45 And the Day He gathers them, it will be as if they had stayed but an hour of a day. They will get to know one another. Losers will be those who have denied meeting God, and they have not been guided.

10:46 And if We show you some of what We promise them, or We terminate your life, to Us is their return. Then God is a witness over what they do.

10:47 And for every nation is a messenger; so when their messenger comes, the matter is decreed between them with justice, and they are not wronged.

10:48 And they say: "When is this promise if you are truthful?"

10:49 Say: "I do not possess for myself any harm or benefit except what God wills. For every nation is a time. When their time comes, they cannot delay it one hour nor advance it."

10:50 Say: "Do you see if His retribution will come to you by night or by day, then which portion would the criminals hasten in?"

10:51 "Will you then, when it occurs, believe in it? While now you are hastening it on!"

10:52 Then it will be said to those who were wicked: "Taste the everlasting retribution. You are only recompensed for what you have earned!"

10:53 And they seek news from you: "Is it true?" Say: "Yes, by my Lord it is true, and you cannot escape from it."

10:54 And if every soul who wronged had possessed all that is on the earth, it would have attempted to ransom it. And they declared their regret when they saw the retribution, and it was judged between them with fairness. They were not wronged.

10:55 To God is what is in the heavens and the earth. The promise of God is true, but most of them do not know.

10:56 He gives life, and He brings death, and to Him you will return.

10:57 O people, advice has come to you from your Lord and a healing for what is in the chests, and a guidance and a mercy for the believers.

10:58 Say: "By the grace of God and His mercy." For that let them rejoice, that is better than all that they gather.

10:59 Say: "Have you seen what God has sent down to you from provisions, then you have made some of it forbidden and some permissible?" Say: "Did God authorize you, or do you invent lies about God?"

10:60 And what will those who invent lies about God think on the Day of Resurrection? God is with great bounty to the people, but most of them are not thankful.

10:61 And any matter you are in, or any reciting you do of the Qur'an, or any work you do; We are witnesses over you when you undertake it. Nothing is hidden from your Lord, not even the weight of an atom on the earth or in the heavens, nor smaller than that nor larger, except it is in a clear record.

10:62 For the allies of God, there is no fear over them nor will they grieve.

10:63 Those who have believed and are aware.

10:64 For them are glad tidings in the worldly life and in the Hereafter. There is no changing the words of God. Such is the great triumph.

10:65 And do not be saddened by their speech, for all glory is to God. He is the Hearer, the Knowledgeable.

10:66 Certainly, to God belongs all who are in the heavens and those who are on the earth. As for those who call on partners besides God, they only follow conjecture, and they only guess.

10:67 He is the One who made the night for you to reside in, and the day to see. In that are signs for a people who listen.

10:68 They said: "God has taken a son." Glory be to Him! He is the Rich. To Him is what is in the heavens and the earth. Do you have proof for this? Or do you say about God what you do not know?

10:69 Say: "Those who invent lies about God, they will not be successful."

10:70 A short pleasure in this world, then to Us is their return and We will make them taste the severe retribution for what they were rejecting.

10:71 And recite to them the news of Noah, as he said to his people: "My people, if my station has become too troublesome for you, and my reminding you of the signs of God, then in God I place my trust. So gather your evidence and your partners, then make certain your evidence does not become against you, then come to judge me, and do not hold back."

10:72 "But if you turn away, then I have not asked you for any wage, for my wage is with God. And I have been commanded to be of those who have submitted."

10:73 They denied him, so We saved him and those with him in the ship, and We made them successors, and We drowned those who denied Our revelations. So see how was the punishment of those who were warned!

10:74 Then, after him, We sent messengers to their own people, so they

133

came to them with proofs. But they did not want to believe in what they had already denied beforehand. Thus it is We stamp upon the hearts of the transgressors.

10:75 Then, after them, We sent Moses and Aaron with Our signs to Pharaoh and his leaders, but they turned arrogant, they were a criminal people.

10:76 So when the truth came to them from Us, they said: "This is clearly magic!"

10:77 Moses said: "Would you say this about the truth when it came to you? Is this magic? The magicians will not be successful."

10:78 They said: "Have you come to us to turn us away from that which we found our fathers upon, and so that you two would have greatness in the land? We will not believe in you."

10:79 And Pharaoh said: "Bring me every knowledgeable magician."

10:80 So, when the magicians came, Moses said to them: "Cast what you will cast."

10:81 So when they cast, Moses said: "What you have brought is magic, God will disable it. God does not set right the works of the corrupters."

10:82 "And so that God will set the truth with His words, even if the criminals hate it."

10:83 But none believed in Moses from his people except some from their descendants, because of their fear from Pharaoh and his commanders that he would persecute them. Pharaoh was high in the land, and he was of the tyrants.

10:84 And Moses said: "O my people, if you believe in God, then put your trust in Him if you have submitted."

10:85 They said: "In God we put our trust. Our Lord, do not make us a test for the wicked people."

10:86 "And save us by Your mercy from the rejecting people."

10:87 And We inspired to Moses and his brother: "You shall seek out homes for your people in Egypt; and leave your homes to be a focal point, and hold the Connection. And give good news to the believers."

10:88 And Moses said: "Our Lord, you have given Pharaoh and his commanders adornments and wealth in this worldly life so that they will misguide from Your path. Our Lord, wipe out their wealth and bring grief to their hearts; for they will not believe until they see the painful retribution."

10:89 He said: "Your call has been responded to, so keep straight and do not follow the path of those who do not know."

10:90 And We helped the Children of Israel cross the sea, and Pharaoh and his soldiers followed them out of hatred and animosity. But when he was certain to drown, he said: "I believe that there is no god except the One in whom the Children of Israel believe, and I am of those who have submitted."

10:91 Now you say this? While before you disobeyed and were of the corrupters!

10:92 This day, We will preserve your body, so that you become a sign for those after you. But most of the people are unaware of Our signs!

10:93 And We had directed the Children of Israel to a place of truth, and We provided them from the good things, and they did not differ until the knowledge came to them. Your Lord will judge between them on the Day of Resurrection for what they differed in.

10:94 If you are in doubt regarding what We have sent down to you, then ask those who have been reading the Book from before you. The truth has come to you from your Lord, so do not be of those who doubt.

10:95 And do not be of those who have denied the revelations of God, for you will be of the losers.

10:96 Those who have deserved the retribution of your Lord do not believe.

10:97 Even if every sign were to come to them; until they see the painful retribution.

10:98 If there was any town that benefited from its belief, then that was the people of Jonah. When they believed, We removed from them the retribution of disgrace in this worldly life, and We let them enjoy until a time.

10:99 And had your Lord willed, all the people on the earth in their entirety would have believed. Would you force the people to make them believe?

10:100 And it is not for a soul to believe except with the permission of God. And He lets foulness be upon those who do not comprehend.

10:101 Say: "Look at all that is in the heavens and the earth." But what good are the signs and warnings to a people who do not believe?

10:102 Are they waiting for the days like those who have passed away before them? Say: "Wait, for I am with you waiting."

10:103 Then We will save Our messengers and those who believe. It is thus binding upon Us that We save the believers.

10:104 Say: "O people, if you are in doubt of my system, then I do not serve those whom you serve besides God. But I serve God; the One who will terminate your lives; and I have been commanded to be of the believers."

10:105 And set your face to the system of monotheism, and do not be of the polytheists.

10:106 And do not call upon other than God what does not benefit you or harm you; if you do, then you are of the wicked.

10:107 And if God afflicts you with any harm, then none can remove it except He; and if He wanted good for you, then none can turn away His grace, He brings it to whom He wishes of His servants. And He is the Forgiver, the Merciful.

10:108 Say: "O people, the truth has come to you from your Lord, so whoever is guided is being guided for himself, and whoever is misguided will remain so, and I am not a caretaker over you."

10:109 And follow what is being inspired to you and be patient until God judges. And He is the best of judges.

CHAPTER 11

11:0 In the name of God, the Almighty, the Merciful.

11:1 ALR, a Book whose verses have been made fixed, then detailed, from One who is Wise, Expert.

11:2 "That you shall serve none other than God. I am to you from Him a warner and a bearer of good news."

11:3 "And seek forgiveness from your Lord, then repent to Him; He will provide you with good provisions to an appointed term. And He bestows His grace upon those who are of grace." And if they turn away: "Indeed, I fear for you the retribution of a great day!"

11:4   "To God is your return, and He is capable of all things."

11:5   Alas, they have folded their chests to hide from it. Even when they cover themselves under their garments, He knows what they keep secret and what they declare. He is Knower of all that is in the chests.

11:6   And there is not a creature on the earth but on God is its provision. And He knows where it dwells and where it hides. All is in a clear record.

11:7   He is the One who has created the heavens and the earth in six days, and His Throne was upon the water; so as to test who from among you works the best. And when you say: "You will be resurrected after the death," those who have rejected say: "This is but clear magic!"

11:8   And if We delay for them the retribution to a near period, they will say: "What has kept it?" Alas, on the Day it comes to them, nothing will turn it away from them, and they will be surrounded by that which they used to mock.

11:9   And if We give the human being a taste of a mercy from Us, then We withdraw it from him; he becomes despairing, rejecting.

11:10   And if We give him the taste of a blessing after hardship has afflicted him, he says: "Evil has gone from me!" He becomes happy, boastful.

11:11   Except for those who are patient and do good works; these will have a pardon, and a great reward.

11:12   So perhaps you wish to ignore some of what has been inspired to you, and you are depressed by it, because they say: "If only a treasure was sent down with him, or an angel had come with him!" You are but a warner, and God is Caretaker over all things.

11:13   Or do they say: "He has invented it!" Say: "Then bring ten invented chapters like it, and call on whom you can besides God if you are truthful."

11:14   So, if they do not respond to you, then know that it has been sent down with the knowledge of God, and that there is no god except He. Will you then submit?

11:15 Whoever wants the worldly life and its adornments, then We will grant them their works in it, and they will not be short changed in it.

11:16 These will have nothing but fire in the Hereafter, and what they have done will be in vain, and evil is what they have worked.

11:17 For those who are on a clarity from their Lord, and are followed by a testimony from Him; and before it was the Book of Moses, a beacon and a mercy; they will believe in it. And whoever rejects it from among the Confederates, then the Fire is his meeting place. So do not be in any doubt about it. It is the truth from your Lord, but most of the people do not believe.

11:18 And who is more wicked than he who invents lies about God? They will be displayed before their Lord, and the witnesses will say: "These are the ones who have lied about their Lord." Alas, the curse of God will be upon the wicked.

11:19 Those who repel others from the path of God and they seek to twist it; and regarding the Hereafter they are in denial.

11:20 These are the ones who will not escape on the earth, nor do they have besides God any allies. The retribution will be doubled for them. They were not able to hear, nor could they see.

11:21 They are the ones who have lost their souls, and what they had invented has abandoned them.

11:22 There is no doubt, that in the Hereafter they are the greatest losers.

11:23 Those who believe and do good works, and are humble towards their Lord; they are the dwellers of Paradise, in it they will remain.

11:24 The example of the two groups is like the blind and deaf, and the seer and hearer. Are they the same when compared? Do you not take heed?

11:25 And We had sent Noah to his people: "I am to you a clear warner!"

11:26 "That you serve none except God. I fear for you the retribution of a painful day."

11:27 The leaders who rejected from among his people said: "We do not see you except as a mortal like us, and we see that only the lowest among our people who have no opinion have followed you. And we do not see a thing that makes you better than us; in fact, we think you are liars."

11:28 He said: "O my people, do you see that should I be upon a clarity from my Lord, and He has given me a mercy from Himself, that you may be blinded to it? Shall we compel you to it while in fact you hate it?"

11:29 "And my people, I do not ask you for money, my wage is from God. Nor will I turn away those who believe, for they will meet their Lord. But I see that you are a people who are ignorant."

11:30 "And my people, who will give me victory against God if I turn them away? Will you not remember!"

11:31 "Nor do I say to you that I have the treasures of God, nor do I know the future, nor do I say that I am an angel, nor do I say to those whom your eyes look down upon that God will not grant them any good. God is more aware of what is in their souls; in such case I would be among the wicked."

11:32 They said: "O Noah, you have argued with us, and continued arguing with us, so bring us what you promise us if you are of the truthful ones."

11:33 He said: "It is God who will bring it to you if He wishes; you will not have any escape."

11:34 "And my advice will not benefit you if I wanted to advise you and God wanted that you should go astray. He is your Lord, and to Him you will return."

11:35 Or do they say: "He has invented it?" Say: "If I have invented it, then I am responsible for my crime, and I am innocent from your crimes."

11:36 And it was inspired to Noah: "No more of your people will believe except those who have already believed. So do not be saddened by what they have done."

11:37 "And construct the ship under Our eyes and Our inspiration, and do not speak to Me regarding those who are wicked. They will be drowned."

11:38 And as he was constructing the ship, every time any cluster from his people passed by, they mocked him. He said: "If you mock us, then we also mock you as you mock."

11:39 "You will know to whom the retribution will come to disgrace him, and upon him will be a lasting punishment."

11:40 So, when Our command came and the chamber erupted. We said: "Carry in it a pair from each kind, and your family; except those against whom the word has been issued; and whoever has believed." But those who believed with him were few.

11:41 And he said: "Ride in it, in the name of God shall be its running and its anchorage. My Lord is Forgiving, Merciful."

11:42 And while it was running with them in waves like mountains, Noah called to his son, who was in an isolated place: "My son, ride with us, and do not be with the rejecters!"

11:43 He said: "I will take refuge to the mountain which will protect me from the water." He said: "There is no protection from the decree of God except for those He has granted mercy." And the wave came between them, so he was one of those who drowned.

11:44 And it was said: "O land, swallow your water, and O sky, cease." And the water was diminished, and the matter concluded. And it came to rest on the Judi, and it was said: "Away with the wicked people."

11:45 And Noah called on his Lord, and he said: "My Lord, my son is from my family, and your promise is the truth, and you are the Wisest of all Judges."

11:46 He said: "O Noah, he is not from your family, he was of an unrighteous deed, so do not ask what you have no knowledge of. I advise you not to be of the ignorant."

11:47 He said: "My Lord, I seek refuge with You from asking You what I do not have knowledge of. And if You do not forgive me and have mercy on me, I will be of the losers!"

11:48 It was said: "O Noah, descend in peace from Us and blessings upon you and upon nations to come from those with you. And nations whom We will give enjoyment, then a painful retribution will reach them from Us."

11:49 This is from the news of the unseen that We inspire to you. Neither did you nor your people know this, so be patient; the ending will be for the righteous.

11:50 And to 'Aad was sent their brother Hud. He said: "My people, serve God, you have no god besides Him; you are simply conjecturing."

11:51 "My people, I do not ask you for any wage, my wage is from the One who has initiated me. Will you not comprehend?"

11:52 "And my people, seek forgiveness from your Lord, then repent to Him; He will send the sky to you abundantly, and He will add might to your might. So do not turn away as criminals."

11:53 They said: "O Hud, you have not come to us with any proof, nor will we leave our gods based on what you say. We will not believe in you."

11:54 "All we can say is that perhaps some of our gods have seized you with evil." He said: "I make God my witness, and all of you witness, that I am innocent of what you have set up."

11:55 "Besides Him, so plan against me all of you, then do not give me respite."

11:56 "I have placed my trust in God, my Lord and your Lord. There is not a creature except He will seize it by its forelock. My Lord is on a straight path."

11:57 "So, if you turn away, then I have delivered what I have been sent to you with, and my Lord will bring after you a people who are not like you; and you cannot harm Him the least. My Lord is Guardian over all things."

11:58 And when Our command came, We saved Hud and those who had believed with him by a mercy from Us, and We saved them from a mighty retribution.

11:59 Such was the case of 'Aad. They disregarded the revelations of their Lord, and they disobeyed His messengers, and they followed the command of every stubborn tyrant.

11:60 And they were followed by a curse in this world and on the Day of Resurrection, for 'Aad rejected their Lord. So away with 'Aad, the people of Hud.

11:61 And to Thamud was their brother Saleh. He said: "O my people, serve God, you have no god besides Him. He has established you from the earth, and has made you settle in it; so seek His forgiveness, then repent to Him. My Lord is Near, Responsive."

11:62 They said: "O Saleh, you were well liked among us before this. Do you prohibit us from serving what our fathers served? We are in serious doubt as to what you are inviting us."

11:63 He said: "O my people, do you see that should I be upon a clarity from my Lord, and He has given me a mercy from Himself. Who would then support me against God if I disobey Him? You would only increase me in loss!"

11:64 "And O my people, this is the camel of God, in her you have a sign. So leave her to eat from God's earth freely, and do not harm her, or else a close retribution will take you."

11:65 But they slaughtered her. So he said: "Take enjoyment in your dwellings for three days. This is a promise not to be denied."

11:66 So, when Our command came, We saved Saleh and those who had believed with him by a mercy from Us and against the disgrace of that day. Your Lord is the Powerful, the Noble.

11:67 And those who had wronged were taken by the scream, thus they became lifeless in their homes.

11:68 It is as if they had never lived there. For Thamud rejected their Lord. So away with Thamud.

11:69 And Our messengers came to Abraham with good news, they said: "Peace" He said: "Peace," and he made no delay in bringing a roasted calf.

11:70 But when he saw that their hands did not go towards it, he mistrusted them, and he began to have fear of them. They said: "Have no fear, we have been sent to the people of Lot."

11:71 And his wife was standing, so she laughed when We gave her the good news of Isaac, and after Isaac, Jacob.

11:72 She said: "O my! Shall I give birth when I am an old woman, and here is my husband an old man? This is indeed a strange thing!"

11:73 They said: "Do you wonder at the decree of God? The mercy of God and blessings are upon you O people of the House. He is Praiseworthy, Glorious."

11:74 So when the shock had left Abraham, and the good news had been fathomed, he began to argue with Us for the people of Lot.

11:75 Abraham was compassionate, kind, obedient.

11:76 "O Abraham, turn away from this. The command of your Lord has been passed, and a retribution that will not be turned back is coming for them."

11:77   And when Our messengers came to Lot, he was grieved by them and he felt discomfort for them and he said: "This is a distressful day."

11:78   And his people came rushing towards him, and before it they were committing sin, he said: "My people, these are my daughters, they are purer for you, so be aware of God and do not disgrace me regarding my guests. Is there no wise man among you?"

11:79   They said: "You know we have no interest in your daughters, and you are aware of what we want!"

11:80   He said: "If only I had strength against you, or I could find for myself some powerful support."

11:81   They said: "O Lot, we are messengers of your Lord; they will not be able to harm you, so travel with your family during the cover of the night and let not any of you look back except for your wife, she will be afflicted with what they will be afflicted. Their scheduled time will be the morning. Is the morning not near?"

11:82   So when Our command came, We made its highest part become its lowest, and We rained on it with hardened fiery projectiles.

11:83   Prepared by your Lord, and they are never far from the wicked.

11:84   And to Midyan was their brother Shu'ayb, he said: "My people, serve God, you have no god besides Him, and do not give short in the measure and the weight. I see you in prosperity, and I fear for you the retribution of a day that is surrounding."

11:85   "And my people, give full in the measure and the weight equitably, and do not hold back from the people what is theirs, and do not roam the land corrupting."

11:86   "What will remain for you with God is far better if you are believers. And I am not a guardian over you."

11:87   They said: "O Shu'ayb, does your connecting order you that we leave what our fathers served, or that we do not do with our money as we please? It seems only you are the compassionate, the wise!"

11:88   He said: "O my people, do you see that if I am on clear evidence from my Lord, and He has provided me with good provision from Him, then I would not want to contradict by doing what I am prohibiting you from. I only want to make right what I can, and my guidance is only with God. To Him I place my trust, and to Him I repent."

11:89 "And my people, let not your hatred towards me incriminate you that you suffer the fate of what afflicted the people of Noah, or the people of Hud, or the people of Saleh; and the people of Lot were not far off from you."

11:90 "And seek forgiveness from your Lord then repent to Him. My Lord is Merciful, Loving."

11:91 They said: "O Shu'ayb, we do not understand most of what you say, and we see you as weak among us. And, if it were not for your clan, we would have stoned you, and you have no power over us."

11:92 He said: "My people, is my clan more important to you than God, while you have cast Him away behind your backs? My Lord is encompassing what you do."

11:93 "And my people, continue to act as you do, and I will act. You will then come to know to whom the retribution will come to humiliate him and who is the liar. Watch then, and I will watch with you."

11:94 And when Our command came, We saved Shu'ayb and those who believed with him by a mercy from Us; and the scream took those who had wronged, thus they became lifeless in their homes.

11:95 It is as if they had never lived there. Away with Midyan as it was away with Thamud.

11:96 And We sent Moses with Our signs and a clear authority.

11:97 To Pharaoh and his commanders; but they followed the order of Pharaoh; and the order of Pharaoh was not wise.

11:98 He will be at the head of his people on the Day of Resurrection, and he will lead them to the Fire. What a miserable place they will be brought in!

11:99 And they were followed by a curse in this one, and on the Day of Resurrection. What a miserable path to follow!

11:100 That is from the news of the towns which We narrate to you; some are still standing and some have been wiped out.

11:101 And We had not wronged them, but they had wronged themselves; their gods that they called on besides God did not rescue them at all when the command of your Lord came, and they only added to their destruction.

11:102 And such is the seizing of your Lord when He seizes the towns while they are wicked. His taking is painful, severe.

11:103 In this is a sign for he who fears the retribution of the Hereafter. That is a Day towards which all the people will be gathered, and that is a Day which will be witnessed.

11:104 And We do not delay it except to a term already prepared for.

11:105 On the Day it comes, no person will speak except with His permission. Some of them will be distraught, some will be happy.

11:106 As for those who are distraught, they will be in the Fire; in it for them is a sighing and a wailing.

11:107 Abiding therein as long as the heavens and the earth exist, except for what your Lord wishes. Your Lord does as He pleases.

11:108 As for those who are happy, they will be in Paradise; abiding therein as long as the heavens and the earth exist, except for what your Lord wishes, a giving without end.

11:109 So do not be in doubt as to what these people serve. They serve nothing except what their fathers before them served. We will give them their recompense in full.

11:110 And We gave Moses the Book, yet they disputed in it; and had it not been for a word which was already given by your Lord, their case would have been judged immediately. They are in grave doubt concerning it.

11:111 And to each your Lord will recompense their works. He is Expert in what they do.

11:112 So be upright, as you have been commanded, and those who have repented with you; and do not transgress. He is Seer over what you do.

11:113 And do not side with those who are wicked, else you will incur the Fire; and you will not have besides God any allies, and you will not be victorious.

11:114 And hold the Connection at two parts of the day, and the near side of the night. The good deeds take away the bad. This is a reminder to those who remember.

11:115 And be patient, for God does not waste the reward of the good doers.

11:116 If only there was from the previous generations a people with wisdom who prohibited corruption on the earth, except the few that We saved of them. And those who were wicked followed the enjoyment they were in, and they were criminal.

11:117 And your Lord will not destroy the towns unjustly, while its people are good doers.

11:118 And if your Lord had wished, He could have made all the people one nation, but they still would have continued to disagree.

11:119 Except whom your Lord has mercy upon; and for that He has created them. And the word of your Lord came true: "I will fill Hell with the Jinn and the people together!"

11:120 And all We narrate to you from the news of the messengers is to calm your mind. And in this has come to you the truth and a lesson and a reminder for the believers.

11:121 And say to those who do not believe: "Continue to do what you will, we will also do."

11:122 "And wait, for we are also waiting."

11:123 And to God is the unseen of the heavens and the earth, and to Him all matters return. So serve Him and put your trust in Him. Your Lord is not unaware of what you all do.

CHAPTER 12

12:0 In the name of God, the Almighty, the Merciful.

12:1 ALR, these are the signs of the Book of Clarity.

12:2 We have sent it down a Qur'an in Arabic, perhaps you will comprehend.

12:3 We narrate to you the best stories through what We have inspired to you in this Qur'an; and before it you were of those who were unaware.

12:4 When Joseph said to his father: "My father, I have seen eleven planets and the sun and the moon, I saw them prostrating to me."

12:5 He said: "O my son, do not narrate your vision to your brothers, or they will plan against you. The devil is to the human being a clear enemy."

12:6　And as such, your Lord has chosen you, and He teaches you the interpretation of the narrations, and He completes His blessings upon you and upon the descendants of Jacob, as He completed it for your fathers before that, Abraham and Isaac. Your Lord is Knowledgeable, Wise.

12:7　In Joseph and his brothers are signs for those who seek.

12:8　For they said: "Joseph and his brother are more loved by our father than us, while we are a numerous group. Our father is clearly misguided."

12:9　"Kill Joseph or cast him in the land, so that the face of your father will be only for you, and after that you can be an upright people."

12:10　One among them said: "Do not kill Joseph, but if you are going to do a thing, then cast him into the bottom of the well, so that anyone traveling by will pick him up."

12:11　They said: "Our father, why do you not trust us with Joseph? And we will be giving him advice."

12:12　"Send him with us tomorrow to enjoy himself and play, and we will take care of him."

12:13　He said: "It saddens me that you should take him, and I fear that the wolf will eat him if you will be absent of him."

12:14　They said: "If the wolf eats him, while we are a numerous group, then we are the losers."

12:15　So, when they went with him they had agreed to place him into the bottom of the well. And We inspired to him: "You will inform them of this act of theirs while they will not expect it."

12:16　And they came to their father in the evening, crying.

12:17　They said: "Our father, we went to race and left Joseph by our things, and the wolf ate him! But you would not believe us even if we were truthful."

12:18　And they came with his shirt stained in false blood. He said: "You have invented this tale yourselves. So sweet patience, and God is sought for help against what you describe."

12:19　And a traveling caravan came and they sent their man to draw water, but when he drew he said: "Good news, there is a boy!" So they hid him as merchandise. And God is aware of what they did.

12:20   And they sold him for a low price, a few coins of silver, and they regarded him as insignificant.

12:21   And he from Egypt who had bought him said to his wife: "Make his stay generous, perhaps he will benefit us or we may take him as a son." And it was thus that We established Joseph in the land and to teach him the interpretation of the narrations. And God has full control over his situation, but most of the people do not know.

12:22   And when he reached his independence, We gave him judgment and knowledge. It is thus that We reward the good doers.

12:23   And the woman, in whose house he was staying, attempted to seduce him away from himself. And she closed the doors and said: "I have prepared myself for you." He said: "I seek refuge with God, He is my Lord, He has made good my stay; the wicked do not succeed."

12:24   And she was obsessed with him, and he did obsess with her—had it not been that he saw the proof of his Lord—it was thus that We turned evil and immorality away from him; he is of Our loyal servants.

12:25   And as they rushed towards the door, she tore his shirt from behind; and they found her master at the door. She said: "What is the punishment for he who wanted evil for your family? Is it not that he be imprisoned or punished painfully?"

12:26   He said: "She is the one who seduced me from myself," and a witness from her family gave testimony: "If his shirt was torn from the front, then she is truthful, and he is the liar."

12:27   "And if his shirt is torn from behind, then she is lying, and he is truthful."

12:28   So when he saw that his shirt was torn from behind, he said: "This is from your female planning, your female planning is indeed great!"

12:29   "Joseph, turn away from this. And you woman, seek forgiveness for your sin; you were of the wrongdoers."

12:30   And some women in the city said: "The wife of the governor is trying to seduce her young man from himself; she is taken by love. We see her clearly misguided."

12:31   So when she heard of their scheming, she sent for them and prepared a banquet for them, and she gave each one of them a knife. And she said: "Come out to them," so when they saw him they exalted him and cut their hands, and they said: "Praise be to God, this is not a mortal, but an honorable angel!"

12:32 She said: "This is the one whom you blamed me for, and I have seduced him from himself but he refused. And if he does not do as I command him, he will be imprisoned, and he will be one of those disgraced."

12:33 He said: "My Lord, prison is better to me than what they are inviting me to do. And if You do not turn their plans away from me, I will fall for them and be of the ignorant."

12:34 So his Lord responded to him, and He turned away their plans from him. He is the Hearer, the Knowledgeable.

12:35 But it appealed to them, even after they had seen the signs, to imprison him for a time.

12:36 And with him in the prison entered two young men. One of them said: "I dreamt that I was pressing wine," and the other said: "I dreamt that I was carrying bread on top of my head, and that the birds were eating from it." "Tell us its interpretation, for we see that you are of the good doers."

12:37 He said: "No provision of food will come to you, except that I would have informed you both about its interpretation before it comes to you. That is from what my Lord has taught me. I have just left the creed of a people who do not believe in God, and they are rejecting the Hereafter."

12:38 "And I have followed the creed of my fathers Abraham, and Isaac, and Jacob. It was not for us to set up partners with God at all. That is the blessings of God over us and over the people, but most of the people are not thankful."

12:39 "O my fellow inmates, are various lords better, or God, the One, the Supreme?"

12:40 "What you serve besides Him are nothing except names which you have created, both you and your fathers, God has not sent down any authority for such. The judgment is for none except God. He has ordered that none be served except He. That is the true system, but most of the people do not know."

12:41 "My fellow inmates, one of you will be serving wine for his lord, while the other will be crucified so that the birds will eat from his head. The matter which you have sought is now concluded."

12:42 And he said to the one of them whom he thought would be saved: "Mention me to your lord." But the devil made him forget to mention to his lord, so he remained in prison for a few years.

12:43 And the king said: "I continue to dream of seven fat cows being eaten by seven thin ones, and seven green pods and others which are dry. O you commanders, tell me what my vision means if you are able to interpret the visions."

12:44 They said: "It is nothing except bad dreams; and we are not knowledgeable in the interpretation of dreams."

12:45 And the one who had been saved of the two, and remembered after all this time said: "I will tell you of its interpretation, so let me be sent."

12:46 "Joseph, O man of truth, explain to us the matter regarding seven fat cows being eaten by seven thin ones, and seven green pods and others which are dry? Then perhaps I may go back to the people so they will know."

12:47 He said: "You will plant regularly for seven years, and whatever you harvest you must leave it in its pods, except for the little that you will eat."

12:48 "Then there will come seven after that which are severe and which will consume all that you plant except for what you have stored."

12:49 "Then after that will come a calendar year in which the people will have abundant rain and which they will be able to produce once again."

12:50 And the king said: "Bring him to me." So when the messenger came to him, he said: "Go back to your lord and ask him what was the matter regarding the women who cut their hands? Indeed, my Lord is aware of their plans."

12:51 He said: "What is your plea that you tried to seduce Joseph from himself?" They said: "God be sought! We know of no evil on his part." The wife of the governor said: "Now the truth must be known, I did seek to seduce Joseph from himself and he is of the truthful ones."

12:52 "That is so he knows that I will not betray him while he is not present and that God does not guide the planning of the betrayers."

12:53 "And I do not make myself free of blame, for the soul is inclined to sin, except that which my Lord has mercy upon. My Lord is Forgiving, Merciful."

12:54 And the king said: "Bring him to me so that I may employ him to my person." So when he spoke to him, he said: "Today you are with us in a high standing and trusted."

12:55 He said: "Appoint me over the granaries of the land, for I know how to keep records and I am knowledgeable."

12:56 And it was such that We gave Joseph authority in the land, to travel in it as he pleases. We bestow Our mercy upon whom We please, and We do not waste the reward of the good doers.

12:57 And the reward of the Hereafter is better for those who believe and are aware.

12:58 And the brothers of Joseph came and entered upon him, and he recognized them, but they did not recognize him.

12:59 So, when he furnished them with their provisions, he said: "Bring me a brother of yours who is from your father. Do you not see that I give full measure of grain and that I am the best of hosts?"

12:60 "But if you do not bring him to me, then there shall be no measure of grain for you with me, and do not come near me."

12:61 They said: "We will try to get him away from his father, and we shall be successful."

12:62 And he said to his servants: "Return their goods into their saddlebags, so that they may recognize it when they return to their family so that they may come back."

12:63 So when they returned to their father, they said: "Our father, we have been banned from getting anymore measure of grain, so send our brother with us so we may be given a measure of grain, and we will be his guardians."

12:64 He said: "Shall I trust him with you as I trusted you with Joseph before that? God is the best guardian, and He is the Most Merciful of those who show mercy."

12:65 So when they opened their baggage, they found their goods had been returned to them, and they said: "Our father, what more can we desire, these are our goods returned to us, so we can get more for our family, and be guardians over our brother, and increase a measure of grain to load a camel. That is truly an easy measure!"

12:66 He said: "I will not send him with you until you come to me with a covenant to God that you will bring him back unless you are completely overtaken." So when they brought him their covenant, he said: "God is placed in trust over what we say."

12:67 And he said: "My sons, do not enter from one gate, but enter from separate gates; and I cannot avail you anything against God, for the judgment is to God. In Him I place my trust, and in Him those who place their trust should trust."

12:68 And when they entered from where their father had commanded them, it would not have availed them in the least against God, but it was out of a concern in the soul of Jacob that he brought out. And he is with knowledge for what We taught him, but most of the people do not know.

12:69 And when they entered upon Joseph, he called his brother to himself and said: "I am your brother, so do not be saddened by what they have done."

12:70 So when he furnished them with their provisions, he placed the measuring bowl in the saddlebag of his brother, then a caller cried out: "O you in the caravan, you are thieves!"

12:71 They said, while coming towards them: "What is it you are missing?"

12:72 They said: "We are missing the measuring bowl of the king, and whoever can produce it, will be given the load of a camel; and I will be bound by this."

12:73 They said: "By God, you know we have not come to cause corruption in the land, and we are not thieves!"

12:74 They said: "What shall be the punishment, if you are liars?"

12:75 They said: "The punishment is that he in whose saddlebag it is found will himself serve as the punishment. It is so that we punish the wicked."

12:76 So he began with their bags before the bag of his brother. Then he brought it out of the bag of his brother. It was such that We planned for Joseph, for he would not have been able to take his brother under the system of the king, except that God wished it so. We raise the degrees of whom We please, and over every one of knowledge is the All Knowledgeable.

12:77 They said: "If he has stolen, there was a brother of his before who also had stolen." Joseph kept this all inside himself, and did not reveal anything to them. He said: "You are in an awkward position, and God best knows what you describe."

12:78 They said: "O governor, he has an elderly father, so take one of us in his place. Indeed we see you as one of the good doers."

12:79 He said: "Refuge is sought with God that we would take anyone except he whom we found our belongings with. Indeed, we would then be wrong doers."

12:80 So when they gave up from him, they held a conference in private. The eldest of them said: "Did you not know that your father has taken a covenant over you with God, and before this you also failed in your duty with Joseph? I will not leave this land until my father permits me to do so or that God will judge for me. He is the best of judges."

12:81 "Return to your father, and tell him: 'Our father, your son has stolen, and we did not witness except what we learned, and we could not know the unseen!"

12:82 "And ask the people of the town which we were in, and the caravan which we have returned with. We are being truthful!'"

12:83 He said: "No, for it is your own souls that have conspired you to this. So patience is most fitting, perhaps God will bring them all to me. He is the Knowledgeable, the Wise."

12:84 And he turned away from them and said: "Oh, my sorrow over Joseph." And his eyes turned white from sadness, and he became blind.

12:85 They said: "By God, you will never cease to remember Joseph until you become senile or become dead!"

12:86 He said: "I merely complain my grief and sorrow to God, and I know from God what you do not know."

12:87 "My sons, go and inquire about Joseph and his brother, and do not despair from the spirit of God. The only ones who would despair from the spirit of God are the people who are rejecters."

12:88 So when they entered upon him, they said: "O governor, we have been afflicted with harm, us and our family, and we have come with poor goods to trade, so give us a measure of grain, and be charitable towards us, for God rewards the charitable."

12:89 He said: "Do you know what you have done with Joseph and his brother, while you were ignorant?"

12:90 They said: "Are you indeed Joseph?" He said: "I am Joseph, and this is my brother. God has been gracious to us. For anyone who reverences and is patient, God will not waste the reward of the good doers."

12:91 They said: "By God, God has indeed preferred you over us and we have been wrongdoers."

12:92 He said: "There is no blame on you this day, may God forgive you, and He is the Most Merciful of those who show mercy."

12:93 "Take this shirt of mine and cast it over the face of my father, and he will have sight; and bring to me all your family."

12:94 And when the caravan departed, their father said: "I do indeed feel the scent of Joseph, except that you may think me senile."

12:95 They said: "By God, you are back to your old misguidance."

12:96 Then, when the bearer of good news came, he cast it over his face and he regained sight. He said: "Did I not tell you that I know from God what you do not know?"

12:97 They said: "Our father, ask forgiveness for our sins, indeed we were wrongdoers."

12:98 He said: "I will ask forgiveness for you from my Lord, He is the Forgiving, the Merciful."

12:99 So when they entered upon Joseph, he took his parents to him and he said: "Enter Egypt, God willing, in security."

12:100 And he raised his parents upon the throne, and they fell in prostration to Him. And he said: "My father, this is the interpretation of my vision from before. My Lord has made it true, and He has been good to me that He took me out of prison and brought you out of the wilderness after the devil had made bitterness between me and my brothers. My Lord is Kind to whom He wills. He is the Knowledgeable, the Wise."

12:101 "My Lord, You have given me sovereignty and taught me the interpretation of the narrations. Initiator of the heavens and the earth, You are my Protector in this world and the Hereafter. Let me die as one who has submitted, and join me with the good doers."

12:102 That is from the news of the unseen that We inspire to you. You were not among them when they arranged their plan and were scheming.

12:103 And most of the people, even if you are diligent, will not believe.

12:104 And you are not asking them for any wage, it is but a reminder to the worlds.

12:105 And how many a sign in the heavens and the earth do they pass by, while they are turning away from it.

12:106 And most of them will not believe in God except while setting up partners.

12:107 Are they secure against the coming of an enveloping retribution from God, or that the Hour will come to them suddenly while they do not perceive?

12:108 Say: "This is my way, I invite to God in full disclosure, myself and whoever follows me. And glory be to God; and I am not of the polytheists."

12:109 And We have not sent before you except men, to whom We gave inspiration, from the people of the towns. Will they not roam the earth and see how was the punishment of those before them? And the abode of the Hereafter is far better for those who are aware. Do you not comprehend?

12:110 Then, when the messengers gave up, and they thought that they have been denied, Our victory came to them. We then save whom We wish, and Our punishment cannot be swayed from the wicked people.

12:111 In their stories is a lesson for those who possess intelligence. It is not a narrative that has been invented, but to affirm what is between his hands and a detailing of all things, and a guidance and a mercy for a people who believe.

CHAPTER 13

13:0 In the name of God, the Almighty, the Merciful.

13:1 ALMR, these are the signs of the Book. And what has been sent down to you from your Lord is the truth; but most of the people do not believe.

13:2 God, who raised the heavens without any pillars that you can see, then He settled upon the Throne, and He commissioned the sun and the moon, each running for an appointed term. He manages all affairs, and He details the signs so that you will be aware of the meeting with your Lord.

13:3 And He is the One who has spread out the land, and made in it stabilizers and rivers, and all the fruits He made in pairs. The night covers the day. In that are signs for a people who think.

13:4 And on the earth are neighboring pieces of land with gardens of grapes and plants and palm trees, some of which may be twin sharing the same root, or single, even though they are being watered with the same water source; and We make preference for some of them over others in what they consume. In that are signs for a people who comprehend.

13:5 And if you are surprised, then what is more surprising is their saying: "Can it be that when we are dust, we will be created anew!" These are the ones who have rejected their Lord, and they will have shackles around their necks, and they are the dwellers of the Fire, in it they will abide.

13:6 And they hasten towards you with evil before good, and the examples of those before them have already been given. And your Lord is with forgiveness towards the people for their transgression, and your Lord is severe in retribution.

13:7 And those who reject say: "If only a sign was sent down to him from his Lord." You are but a warner, and to every people is a guide.

13:8 God knows what every female carries, and how short her pregnancy is or how long. And everything with Him is measured.

13:9 The Knower of the unseen and the seen, the Great, the Most High.

13:10 It is the same whether any of you conceals what is said or openly declares it; whether he hides in the night, or goes openly in the day.

13:11 Present with him and behind him are retainers, they preserve him from the command of God. God does not change the condition of a people until they change the condition of their souls. And if God wanted to harm a people, then there is no turning Him back, nor will they have any protector against Him.

13:12 He is the One who shows you the lightning, giving you fear and hope. And He establishes the heavy clouds.

13:13   And the thunder glorifies His praise, and the angels are in awe of Him, and He sends the thunderbolts to strike with them whom He wills. Yet they are still arguing regarding God, while He is severe in punishment.

13:14   To Him is the call of truth. And those who are called on besides Him, they will not respond to them in anything; like one who places his hands openly in the water to drink, except it never reaches his mouth. The call of the rejecters is nothing but in misguidance.

13:15   And to God will prostrate all who are in the heavens and the earth, willingly and unwillingly, as do their shadows in the morning and the evening.

13:16   Say: "Who is the Lord of the heavens and the earth?" Say: "God." Say: "Have you taken besides Him allies who do not possess for themselves any benefit or harm?" Say: "Is the blind and the seer the same? Or do the darkness and the light equate? Or have they set up partners with God who have created like His creation, so the creations all seemed the same to them?" Say: "God has created all things, and He is the One, the Supreme."

13:17   He sends down water from the sky, so valleys flow according to their capacity, and the flood produces foam. And from what they burn to smelt jewelry or goods is produced a similar foam. It is in such a manner that God strikes the falsehood with the truth. As for the foam, it passes away, and as for what benefits the people, it remains in the earth. It is such that God puts forth the examples.

13:18   For those who have responded to their Lord is goodness. As for those who have not responded to Him, if they had all that is on the earth twice over, they would ransom it to be saved. For these will be a terrible reckoning, and their abode is Hell; what a miserable abode.

13:19   Is he who knows that the truth has been sent down to you from your Lord like he who is blind? Only those who possess intelligence will remember.

13:20   Those who fulfill the pledge of God, and they do not break the covenant.

13:21   And those who deliver what God has ordered to be delivered, and they are concerned towards their Lord and they fear a terrible reckoning.

13:22   And those who are patient seeking the face of their Lord; and they hold the Connection, and they spend from what We have bestowed upon them secretly and openly, and they counter evil with good; these will have an excellent abode.

13:23 The gardens of delight; which they will enter with those who are good doers from their fathers and their mates and their progeny. And the angels will enter upon them from every gate.

13:24 "Peace be upon you for what you have been patient for. Excellent indeed is the final abode."

13:25 As for those who break their pledge with God after having made its covenant, and they withhold what God has ordered to be delivered, and they cause corruption on the earth; upon those is a curse and they will have a miserable abode.

13:26 God gives the provisions for whom He wishes, and He is Capable. And they were happy with the worldly life, but the worldly life compared to the Hereafter is nothing except a brief enjoyment.

13:27 And those who have rejected say: "If only a sign were sent down to him from his Lord!" Say: "God misguides whom He wishes and guides to Him whoever is repenting."

13:28 The ones who have believed, and their hearts are relieved by the remembrance of God; for in the remembrance of God the hearts are relieved.

13:29 The ones who have believed, and have done good works, there will be happiness for them and a wonderful abode.

13:30 Thus, We have sent you to a nation, as with other nations before it, so that you may recite to them that which has been inspired to you; while they are still rejecting the Almighty. Say: "He is my Lord, there is no god except He, in Him I place my trust and to Him is my repentance."

13:31 And if a Qur'an were to be used to move mountains, or to slice the earth, or the dead were spoken to with it! Indeed, to God are all matters. Did not those who have believed know that if God had wished He would have guided all the people? As for those who reject, they continue to be stricken with disaster or it comes near to their homes, until the promise of God comes true. God does not break the appointment.

13:32 And messengers before you were mocked, but I gave time to those who had rejected, then I took them; so how was My punishment?

13:33 It is He who is standing upon every soul for what it has earned;

yet they set up partners with God. Say: "Name them? Or are you informing Him of what He does not know on the earth or is it just a show of words?" Indeed, to the rejecters, their scheming is made to appear pleasing, and they are repelled from the path. And whoever God misguides will have no guide.

13:34 They will have a punishment in the worldly life, and the punishment of the Hereafter is more difficult. And they will have no defender against God.

13:35 The example of Paradise which the righteous are promised, is that rivers flow beneath it, and its provisions are continuous as is its shade. Such is the abode of those who were righteous, while the abode of the rejecters is the Fire.

13:36 And those to whom We have previously given the Book rejoice at what has been sent down to you, but there are some from the Confederates who reject parts of it. Say: "I am only ordered to serve God and not set up any partner with Him. Towards Him I implore and towards Him is the return."

13:37 And thus We sent it down—a judgment in Arabic. And if you follow their desires after what has come to you of the knowledge, then you will not have any ally or defender against God.

13:38 And We have sent messengers before you and We have made for them mates and offspring. It was not for a messenger to come with any sign except with the permission of God; for each period there is a Book.

13:39 God erases and confirms what He wishes, and with Him is the Mother of the Book.

13:40 And if We show you some of what We promise them, or We terminate your life, then you are only to deliver while for Us is the reckoning.

13:41 Do they not see that We come to the land and reduce it from its edges? And God gives judgment and there is none to override His judgment. And He is swift in reckoning.

13:42 And those before them had schemed, but to God is all scheming. He knows what every soul earns and the rejecters will come to know to whom is the better abode.

13:43 And those who reject say: "You are not a messenger." Say: "God is enough as a witness between me and you; the One who has the knowledge of the Book."

CHAPTER 14

14:0 In the name of God, the Almighty, the Merciful.

14:1 ALR, a Book which We have sent down to you so that you may bring the people out of the darkness and into the light with the permission of their Lord, to the path of the Noble, the Praiseworthy.

14:2 God, to whom belongs all that is in the heavens and the earth. And woe to the rejecters from a severe retribution.

14:3 The ones who have preferred the worldly life over the Hereafter, and they repel from the path of God, and they seek to make it crooked. Those are the ones who are in misguidance.

14:4 And We have not sent any messenger except in the language of his people, so he may clarify for them. But God misguides whom He wills, and He guides whom He wills. And He is the Noble, the Wise.

14:5 And We sent Moses with Our signs: "You shall bring your people out of the darkness and into the light, and remind them of the days of God." In this are signs for everyone patient and thankful.

14:6 And Moses said to his people: "Remember the blessings of God upon you that He saved you from the people of Pharaoh; they were afflicting you with the worst punishment, and they used to slaughter your children, and rape your women. And in that was a great test from your Lord."

14:7 And your Lord proclaimed: "If you give thanks, I will increase for you, but if you are rejecting, then My retribution is severe."

14:8 And Moses said: "If you reject, you and all who are on the earth together, then know that God is Rich, Praiseworthy."

14:9 Did not news come to you of those before you: the people of Noah, and 'Aad, and Thamud, and those after them whom none know except God? Their messengers came to them with clarity, but they placed their hands onto their mouths and said: "We are rejecting what you have been sent with, and we are in doubt as to what you are inviting us to."

14:10 Their messengers said: "Is there doubt regarding God, the initiator of the heavens and the earth? He invites you so that He may forgive some of your sins, and delay you to an appointed term." They said: "You are merely mortals like us; you wish to turn us away from what our fathers used to serve. So come to us with a clear proof."

14:11 Their messengers said: "We are indeed mortals like you, but God will bestow His grace upon whom He pleases from His servants. And it is not up to us to bring you proof except with the permission of God. And in God the believers should place their trust."

14:12 "And why should we not place our trust in God, when He has guided us in our paths. And we will be patient to the harm you inflict upon us. And in God those who trust should place their trust."

14:13 And those who rejected said to their messengers: "We will expel you from our land, or you will return to our creed." It was then that their Lord inspired to them: "We will destroy the wicked."

14:14 "And We will let you reside in the land after them. That is for those who fear My station and fear My warning."

14:15 And they sought victory, and every arrogant tyrant was then made to lose.

14:16 From behind him is Hell, and he will be poured from a putrid water.

14:17 He tries to drink it, but it cannot be swallowed, and death comes to him from everywhere, but he will not die; and from behind him is a powerful retribution.

14:18 The example of those who reject their Lord is that their works are like ashes, upon which the wind blows strongly on a stormy day, they cannot get anything of what they earned; such is the straying far away.

14:19 Did you not see that God created the heavens and the earth with the truth? If He wished, He would remove you and bring a new creation.

14:20 And that for God is not difficult to do.

14:21 And they appeared before God, all of them. And the weak ones said to those who were arrogant: "We were following you, so will you avail us anything from the retribution of God?" They said: "If God had guided us, then we would have guided you. It makes no difference if we cry out or are patient, for we have no refuge."

14:22 And the devil said when the matter was complete: "God had promised you the promise of truth, and I promised you and broke my promise. And I had no power over you except that I invited you and you responded to me. So do not blame me, but blame yourselves; I cannot help you nor can you help me. I reject that you have set me up as a partner before this; the wicked will have a painful retribution."

14:23 And those who believed and did good works were admitted to estates with rivers flowing beneath them. In them they will abide with the permission of their Lord. Their greeting therein is "Peace."

14:24 Did you not note how God puts forth the example that a good word is like a good tree, whose root is firm and whose branches are in the sky.

14:25 It bears its fruit every so often with the permission of its Lord; and God puts forth the examples for the people, perhaps they will remember.

14:26 And the example of a vile word is like a vile tree which has been uprooted from the surface of the earth, it has nowhere to settle.

14:27 God makes firm those who believe with firm sayings in the worldly life, and in the Hereafter. And God misguides the wicked, and God does what He wishes.

14:28 Did you not see those who replaced the blessings of God with rejection, and they caused their people to dwell in the abode of destruction?

14:29 Hell is where they will burn, what a miserable place to settle.

14:30 And they made to God equals in order that they may misguide from His path. Say: "Enjoy, for your destiny is to the Fire."

14:31 Say to My servants who believe, that they should hold the Connection, and spend from what provisions We granted them secretly and openly, before a Day comes when there is no trade therein, nor will there be any friends.

14:32 God is the One who has created the heavens and the earth, and He has sent down water from the sky thus bringing out with it fruits as provisions for you, and He has commissioned for you the ships to run in the sea by His command, and He has commissioned for you the rivers.

14:33 And He has commissioned for you the sun and the moon, in continuity; and He has commissioned for you the night and the day.

14:34 And He has given you from all that you have asked Him. And if you count the blessings of God, you will not be able to number them. The human being is indeed transgressing, disbelieving.

14:35 And so it was, that Abraham said: "My Lord, make this a land of peace, and keep me and my sons away from serving statues."

14:36 "My Lord, they have misguided many from among the people. So, whoever follows me, then he is of me, and whoever disobeys me, then You are Forgiving, Merciful."

14:37 "Our Lord, I have resided part of my progeny in a valley without vegetation, near Your restricted House. Our Lord, that they may hold the Connection, so let the minds of the people incline towards them and give provisions to them of the fruits that they may give thanks."

14:38 "Our Lord, you know what we hide and what we declare. And nothing at all is hidden from God on the earth or in the heavens."

14:39 "Praise be to God who has granted me to my old age Ishmael and Isaac; my Lord is Hearer of the prayer."

14:40 "My Lord, let me hold the Connection, and also from my progeny. Our Lord, and accept my prayer."

14:41 "Our Lord, forgive me and my parents, and the believers on the Day the reckoning is called."

14:42 And do not think that God is unaware of what the wicked do. He is merely delaying them to a Day when all eyes are watching.

14:43 They will approach with their heads bowed, and their eyes will not blink, and their minds will be void.

14:44 And warn the people of the Day when the retribution will come to them, and those who have been wicked will say: "Our Lord, delay this for us until a short time, and we will heed your call and follow the messengers!" Did you not swear before this that you would last forever?

14:45 And you resided in the dwellings of those who had wronged themselves, and it was made clear to you what We did to them; and We had put forth the examples for you.

14:46 And they schemed their scheming, and their scheming is known to God; and their scheming was enough to make the mountains cease to exist.

14:47 So do not think that God will fail to keep His promise to His messengers. God is Noble, capable of seeking revenge.

14:48 The Day the earth is replaced with another earth, as are the heavens, and they will appear before God, the One, the Supreme.

14:49 And you will see the criminals on that Day chained in shackles.

14:50 Their clothes will be of tar, and the fire will overwhelm their faces.

14:51 Thus God will recompense every soul for what it had earned. God is swift in reckoning.

14:52 This is a directive for the people and so that they are warned with it, and so that they know that there is but One god, and so that those who possess intelligence will remember.

CHAPTER 15

15:0 In the name of God, the Almighty, the Merciful.

15:1 ALR, these are the signs of the Book, and a clear Qur'an.

15:2 Ultimately, those who have rejected will wish they had submitted!

15:3 Leave them to eat and enjoy, and let them be preoccupied with wishful thinking. They will come to know.

15:4 We have not destroyed any town except that it had an appointed time.

15:5 No nation can quicken its fate, nor can they delay it.

15:6 And they said: "O you upon whom the reminder has been sent down, you are crazy."

15:7 "Why not bring us the angels if you are of the truthful ones?"

15:8 We do not send down the angels except with the truth, and then they would have no more delay.

15:9 Indeed it is We who have sent down the reminder, and indeed it is We who will preserve it.

15:10   And We had sent before you, among the groups of old.

15:11   And no messenger would come to them, except that they would mock him.

15:12   It is such that We let it seep into the hearts of the criminals.

15:13   They do not believe in it, while the way of the earlier generations has gone before.

15:14   And if We opened for them a gate in the heaven and they were to continue ascending into it,

15:15   They would have said: "Our sight has been fogged. No, we are a people being bewitched!"

15:16   And We have placed towers in the heaven and We have made them pleasant to the onlookers.

15:17   And We have guarded it from every outcast devil.

15:18   Except he who manages to eavesdrop, he will be pursued by a visible flame.

15:19   And the land We have stretched, and placed stabilizers in it, and We have planted in it from everything in balance.

15:20   And We have made for you in it a habitat, and for those to whom you are not providers.

15:21   And there is not a thing, except that We have treasuries of it, yet We do not send it down except in a precise measure.

15:22   And We send the winds to pollinate, so We cause the water to descend from the sky, so We give to you to drink—and it is not you who store it up.

15:23   And it is indeed We who bring to life and make to die, and We are the inheritors.

15:24   And We know those who have advanced among you, and We know those who have lagged.

15:25   And it is your Lord who will gather them. He is Wise, Knowledgeable.

15:26   And We have created the human being from a sludge from hot sediment.

15:27   And the Jinn, We created him before that from the fire of the fierce hot winds.

15:28 And your Lord said to the angels: "I am creating a mortal from a sludge from hot sediment."

15:29 "So when I evolve him, and blow from My Spirit in him, you shall yield to him."

15:30 Thus, all of the angels yielded.

15:31 Except for Satan, he refused to be of those who yielded.

15:32 He said: "O Satan, what is the matter that you are not of those who yielded?"

15:33 He said: "I am not to yield to a mortal whom You have created from a sludge from hot sediment."

15:34 He said: "Exit from here, you are cast out."

15:35 "And a curse shall be upon you until the Day of Judgment."

15:36 He said: "My Lord, respite me until the Day they are resurrected."

15:37 He said: "You are given respite."

15:38 "Until the Day of the time appointed."

15:39 He said: "My Lord, for that by which You have caused me to be misled, I will beautify for them what is on the earth, and I will mislead them all."

15:40 "Except Your servants from among them, the loyal ones."

15:41 He said: "This shall be a straight path to Me."

15:42 "For My servants, you shall have no authority over them, except those who are misled and follow you."

15:43 "And that Hell shall be their appointment, all of them."

15:44 "It has seven gates, for every gate will be an assigned segment from them."

15:45 The righteous will be in gardens and springs.

15:46 "Enter it in peace and security."

15:47 And We removed what animosity was in their chests, they are brothers in quarters facing one another.

15:48 No fatigue shall touch them, nor will they be evicted from it.

15:49 Inform My servants that I am the Forgiver, the Merciful.

15:50 And that My punishment is a painful retribution.

15:51 And inform them of the guests of Abraham.

15:52 When they entered upon him, they said: "Peace." He said: "We are worrisome of you."

15:53 They said: "Do not worry, we bring you glad tidings of a knowledgeable boy."

15:54 He said: "You would give me such glad tidings when old age has come upon me? How can that be?"

15:55 They said: "We have brought you glad tidings that are true, so do not be of those in denial."

15:56 He said: "And who would deny the mercy of his Lord except the misguided ones!"

15:57 He said: "What then is your affair, O messengers?"

15:58 They said: "We have been sent to a people who are criminals."

15:59 "Except for the family of Lot, we will save them all."

15:60 "Except for his wife, we have evaluated that she will be with those destroyed."

15:61 So when the messengers came to the family of Lot.

15:62 He said: "You are an unknown people."

15:63 They said: "Alas, we have come to you with that which they are doubting."

15:64 "And we have come to you with the truth, and we are forthcoming."

15:65 "So let your family leave during the late hours of the night, and you follow just behind them, and do not let any of you look back, and go to where you are commanded."

15:66 And We made the matter known to him, that the remainder of these people would be wiped out by the morning.

15:67 And the people of the city came seeking good news.

15:68 He said: "These are my guests, so do not embarrass me!"

15:69   "And be aware of God, and do not disgrace me!"

15:70   They said: "Did we not prohibit you from the world?"

15:71   He said: "Here are my daughters if it is your intention."

15:72   By your life, they are in their intoxication, blundering.

15:73   So the scream took them at sunrise.

15:74   Thus We made its highest part become its lowest, and We rained upon them fiery projectiles.

15:75   In this are signs for those who see.

15:76   And it was on an established path.

15:77   In that is a sign for the believers.

15:78   And the people of the Sycamore were wicked.

15:79   So, We sought revenge from them. And they are in a clear ledger.

15:80   And the dwellers of the enclosure disbelieved the messengers.

15:81   And We gave them Our signs, but they turned away from them.

15:82   And they used to carve from the mountains homes, to be secure.

15:83   So the scream took them in the morning.

15:84   What benefit did what they earn make for them?

15:85   And We have not created the heavens and the earth and what is in between except with the truth. And the Hour is coming, so overlook their faults gracefully.

15:86   Your Lord is the Creator, the Knower.

15:87   And We have given you seven that are dual, and the great Qur'an.

15:88   Do not crave with your eyes what We have bestowed upon some couples from them, and do not grieve for them, and lower your wing for the believers.

15:89   And say: "I am the clarifying warner."

15:90   As for the dividers in what We sent down.

15:91   The ones who have made the Qur'an partial.

15:92   By your Lord, We will ask them all.

15:93 Regarding what they used to do.

15:94 So proclaim what you have been commanded and turn away from the polytheists.

15:95 We will relieve you from those who mocked.

15:96 Those who place with God another god. They will come to know.

15:97 And We know that your chest is strained by what they say.

15:98 So glorify the praise of your Lord, and be of those who prostrate.

15:99 And serve your Lord until certainty comes to you.

CHAPTER 16

16:0 In the name of God, the Almighty, the Merciful.

16:1 The command of God has come; so do not hasten it. Be He glorified and exalted above the partners they set up.

16:2 He sends down the angels with the Spirit by His command upon whom He wishes of His servants: "That you shall warn that there is no god except I, so be aware of Me."

16:3 He has created the heavens and the earth with the truth. Be He exalted above the partners they set up.

16:4 He has created the human being from a seed, but then he becomes clearly in opposition.

16:5 And the hoofed animals He has created them for you, in them is warmth and benefits, and from them you eat.

16:6 And for you in them is beauty, when you relax and when you travel.

16:7 And they carry your loads to a land that you would not have been able to reach except with great strain. Your Lord is Compassionate, Merciful.

16:8 And the horses and the mules and the donkeys, that you may ride them and as an adornment; and He creates what you do not know.

16:9 And upon God the path is sought; and from it are deviations. And if He had wished, He could have guided you all.

16:10   He is the One who has sent down water from the sky for you, from it you drink, and from it are woods in which you pasture.

16:11   He brings forth with it the vegetation and the olives and the palm trees and the grapes, and of all the fruits; in that are signs for a people who think.

16:12   And He has commissioned for you the night and the day, and the sun and the moon, and the stars are commissioned by His command. In that are signs for a people who comprehend.

16:13   And what He has placed for you on the earth in various colors. In that are signs for a people who remember.

16:14   And He is the One who has commissioned the sea, that you may eat from it a tender meat, and that you may extract from it pearls that you wear. And you see the ships flowing through it, so that you may seek from His bounty, and that you may be thankful.

16:15   And He has cast onto the earth stabilizers so that it would not tumble with you, and rivers, and paths, perhaps you will be guided.

16:16   And landmarks, and by the star they are guided.

16:17   Is He who creates the same as he who does not create? Will you not remember?

16:18   And if you count the blessings of God, you will not be able to number them. God is Forgiving, Merciful.

16:19   And God knows what you conceal and what you reveal.

16:20   As for those they call on besides God, they do not create a thing, but are themselves created!

16:21   They are dead, not alive, and they do not perceive when they will be resurrected.

16:22   Your god is One god. Those who do not believe in the Hereafter, their hearts are denying, and they are arrogant.

16:23   Certainly, God knows what they hide and what they reveal. He does not like the arrogant.

16:24   And if they are told: "What has your Lord sent down?" They say: "Fictional tales of old!"

16:25   They will carry their burdens in full on the Day of Resurrection, and also from the burdens of those whom they misguided without knowledge. Miserable indeed is their burden.

16:26   Those before them had schemed, so God came to their buildings from the foundation, thus the roof fell on top of them; and the retribution came to them from where they did not know.

16:27   Then, on the Day of Resurrection He will humiliate them, and say: "Where are My partners regarding whom you used to dispute?" Those who have received the knowledge said: "The humiliation today and the misery are upon the rejecters."

16:28   Those whom their lives are terminated by the angels, while they had wronged themselves: "Amnesty, we have not done any evil!" "Alas, God is aware of what you have done."

16:29   "So enter the gates of Hell, in it you shall reside; such is the abode of the arrogant."

16:30   And it was said to those who were righteous: "What has your Lord sent down?" They said: "All goodness." For those who have done good in this world there is good; and the Hereafter is goodness. Excellent indeed is the home of the righteous.

16:31   Gardens of delight; which they will enter, with rivers flowing beneath them, in it they will have what they wish. It is such that God rewards the righteous.

16:32   Those whom their lives are terminated by the angels, while they had been good, they will say: "Peace be upon you, enter Paradise because of that which you have done."

16:33   Are they waiting for the angels to come for them, or a command from your Lord? It was exactly the same as what those before them did. God did not wrong them, but it was their own souls that they wronged.

16:34   Thus it was, that the evil of their work has afflicted them, and they will be surrounded by that which they used to mock.

16:35   And those who were polytheists said: "If God had wished, we would not have served a thing other than Him; neither us nor our fathers; nor would we have made forbidden anything other than from Him." Those before them did exactly the same thing; so are the messengers required to do anything except deliver with clarity?

16:36   And We have sent a messenger to every nation: "You shall serve

171

God and avoid evil." Some of them were guided by God, and some of them deserved to be misguided. So travel the earth, and see how the punishment was of those who denied.

16:37 If you are concerned for their guidance, God does not guide whom He misguides; and they will have no supporters.

16:38 And they swore by God, in their strongest oaths, that God will not resurrect he who dies. No, it is a promise of truth upon Him, but most of the people do not know.

16:39 So that He will clarify for them that in which they have disputed, and so that those who have rejected will know that they were liars.

16:40 Indeed, Our saying to a thing, if We wanted it, is that We say to it: 'Be,' and it is.

16:41 And those who have emigrated for God, after they were oppressed, We will grant them good in the world, and the reward of the Hereafter will be greater, if only they knew.

16:42 Those who are patient, and put their trust in their Lord.

16:43 And We did not send any except men before you whom We inspired, so ask the people who have received the reminder if you do not know.

16:44 With proofs and the scriptures. And We sent down to you the reminder to reveal to the people what was sent to them, and perhaps they will think.

16:45 Have those who schemed evil guaranteed that God will not make the earth swallow them, or the retribution come to them from where they do not expect?

16:46 Or that He will take them in their sleep? For they cannot stop it.

16:47 Or that He will take them while they are in a state of fear? Your Lord is Compassionate, Merciful.

16:48 Have they not seen that what God has created of a thing, its shadow inclines to the right and the left in prostration to God; and they are humbled!

16:49 And to God prostrate all those in the heavens and all those on the earth, from the creatures and the angels, and they are not arrogant.

16:50   They fear their Lord from above them, and they do what they are commanded.

16:51   And God said: "Do not take two gods, there is only One god, so it is Me that you shall reverence."

16:52   And to Him is what is in the heavens and the earth, and the system shall be to Him. Is it other than God that you shall be aware of?

16:53   And any blessing that is with you is from God. Then, when harm afflicts you, to Him you cry out.

16:54   Then, when He removes the harm from you, a group of you set up partners with their Lord!

16:55   So they reject what We have given them. Enjoy, for you will come to know.

16:56   And they allocate a portion from what We provide for them to that which they have no knowledge of. By God, you will be asked about the lies you have invented!

16:57   And they assign daughters to God; be He glorified; and to them is what they desire.

16:58   And when one of them is given news of a female, his face becomes darkened and he is in grief!

16:59   He hides from his people because of the bad news he has received. Shall he keep her with dishonor, or bury her in the sand? Miserable indeed is how they judge!

16:60   To those who do not believe in the Hereafter is the worst example, and to God is the highest example, and He is the Noble, the Wise.

16:61   And if God were to call the people to account for their transgression, He would not have left on it a single creature. But He delays them to a determined time; so when their time comes, they do not delay by one hour and they do not advance.

16:62   And they assign to God what they hate, and their tongues describe with lies that they will have what is good. No doubt they will have the Fire, for they have rebelled.

16:63   By God, We had sent to nations before you, but the devil adorned their work for them. So he is their ally today, and they will have a painful retribution.

16:64 And We have not sent down the Book to you except that you may clarify for them that in which they have disputed, and as a guidance and a mercy for a people who believe.

16:65 And God has sent down water from the sky, so He revives the land with it after its death. In that is a sign for a people who listen.

16:66 And for you there is a lesson in the hoofed animals; We give you to drink from what is in its belly between the digested food and the blood, pure milk which is relieving for the drinkers.

16:67 And from the fruits of the palm trees and the grapes you produce intoxicants and good provision. In that is a sign for a people who comprehend.

16:68 And your Lord inspired to the bees: "You shall take homes of the mountains and of the trees and of what they erect."

16:69 "Then you shall eat from every fruit, so seek the path your Lord has made easy." From its belly will emerge a liquid that has different colors, in it is a healing for the people. In that is a sign for a people who will think.

16:70 And God has created you, then He will end your lives. And some of you will continue to old age so that he will not know anything more after his knowledge. God is Knowledgeable, Capable.

16:71 And God has preferred some of you over others in provision. Yet, those who have been preferred will not relinquish their provision to those who are committed to by their oath, that they may become equal in it. Is it the favor of God that they deny?

16:72 And God has made for you mates from among yourselves, and He has made from your mates sons and grandchildren, and He has provided you from the good provisions. Is it the falsehood that they believe in, while the favor of God they reject?

16:73 And they serve besides God that which does not and cannot possess anything of the provisions from the heaven or the earth.

16:74 So do not give examples to God. God knows while you do not know.

16:75 God puts forth the example of a slave who is owned and cannot achieve anything, against one whom We have provided a good provision which he spends of it secretly and openly. Are they the same? Praise be to God, but most of them do not know.

16:76 And God puts forth the example of two men, one of them is mute and he cannot achieve anything, and he is a burden to his guardian. Wherever he points him, he does not come with any good. Is he the same as one who orders good and he is upon a straight path?

16:77 And to God is the unseen of the heavens and the earth, and the matter of the Hour is like the blink of the eye or nearer. God is capable of all things.

16:78 And God brought you out of the wombs of your mothers while you knew nothing. And He has made for you the hearing and the eyesight and the minds, perhaps you would be thankful.

16:79 Have they not looked at the birds held in the atmosphere of the sky? No one holds them up except God. In that are signs for a people who believe.

16:80 And God has made your homes a habitat, and He has made for you from the hides of the hoofed animals homes which you find light when you travel and when you camp; and from its wool, fur, and hair you make furnishings and goods, until a time.

16:81 And God has made for you shade from what He has created, and He has made from the mountains a refuge for you, and He has made for you garments which protect you from the heat, and garments which protect you from attack. It is such that He completes His blessings upon you, that perhaps you may submit.

16:82 So if they turn away, then you are only required to deliver clearly.

16:83 They recognize the blessings of God, then they deny them. And most of them are rejecters.

16:84 And the Day We send from every nation a witness, then those who have rejected will not be given leave, nor will they be allowed to repent.

16:85 And then those who were wicked will see the retribution; it will not be lightened for them, nor will they be given respite.

16:86 And when those who were polytheists saw their partners, they said: "Our Lord, these are our partners that we used to call upon besides You." But they returned in answer to them: "You are liars!"

16:87 And they offered submission to God on that Day; and what they had invented abandoned them!

16:88　Those who rejected, and repelled others from the path of God, We have added them retribution over the retribution, for what they had corrupted.

16:89　And the Day We send to every nation a witness against them from themselves, and We have brought you as a witness against these. And We have sent down to you the Book as a clarification for all things, and a guidance and a mercy and good tidings to those who have submitted.

16:90　God orders justice and goodness and that you shall help your relatives, and He prohibits immorality and vice and transgression. He warns you that you may remember.

16:91　And fulfill your pledge to God when you pledge so, and do not break your oath after making it, for you have made God a sponsor over you. God is aware of what you do.

16:92　And do not be like she who unraveled her knitting after it had become strong, by breaking your oaths as a means of deception between you. That a nation shall be more numerous than another nation, for God puts you to the test by it. And He will show you on the Day of Resurrection that which you were disputing in.

16:93　And if God had wished, He would have made you one nation, but He misguides whom He wishes, and He guides whom He wishes. And you will be asked about what you used to do.

16:94　And do not use your oaths as a means of deception between you, that a foot will slip after it has been made firm, and you will taste the evil of turning away from the path of God, and you will have a great retribution.

16:95　And do not purchase with the pledge of God a cheap price. What is with God is far better for you if you know.

16:96　What you have will run out, while what God has will remain. And We will deliver to those who are patient their reward for the best of what they used to do.

16:97　Whoever does good works, whether male or female, and is a believer, We will give him a good life and We will reward them their dues with the best of what they used to do.

16:98　When you read the Qur'an, you shall seek refuge with God from the outcast devil.

16:99　He has no authority over those who believe, and who put their trust in their Lord.

16:100 His authority is over those who follow him, and set him up as a partner.

16:101 And if We exchange a revelation in place of another revelation; and God is more aware of what He is revealing; they say: "You are making this up!" Alas, most of them do not know.

16:102 Say: "The Holy Spirit has brought it down from your Lord with the truth, so that those who believe will be strengthened, and as a guidance and good news for those who have submitted."

16:103 And We are aware that they say: "A mortal is teaching him." The tongue of the one they refer to is non-Arabic, while this is a clear Arabic tongue.

16:104 Those who do not believe in the revelations of God, God will not guide them, and they will have a painful retribution.

16:105 Inventing fabrications is only done by those who do not believe in the revelations of God; and these are the liars.

16:106 Whoever rejects God after having believed—except for he who is forced while his heart is still content with belief—and has comforted his chest towards rejection, then these will have a wrath from God and they will have a great retribution.

16:107 That is because they have preferred the worldly life over the Hereafter, and God does not guide the rejecting people.

16:108 Those are the ones whom God has stamped on their hearts, and their hearing, and their sight, and these are the unaware ones.

16:109 Without doubt, in the Hereafter they are the losers.

16:110 Then your Lord is; for those who emigrated after they were persecuted, then they strived and were patient; your Lord is, after that, Forgiver, Merciful.

16:111 The Day every soul will come to argue for itself, and every soul will be paid in full for what it did, and they will not be wronged.

16:112 And God puts forth the example of a town which was peaceful and content, its provisions were coming to it bountifully from all places, but then it rebelled against the blessings of God, and God made it taste hunger and fear for what they used to do.

16:113 And a messenger came to them from themselves, but they denied him, so the punishment took them while they were wicked.

16:114 So eat from what God has provided you, that which is good and permissible, and be thankful for the blessing of God, if it is indeed He whom you serve.

16:115 He has only forbidden for you that which is already dead, and blood, and the meat of pig, and what was sacrificed with to other than God. But whoever is forced to, without seeking disobedience or transgression, then God is Forgiver, Merciful.

16:116 And do not say, as to what your tongues falsely describe: "This is permissible, and that is forbidden;" that you seek to invent lies about God. Those who invent lies about God will not succeed.

16:117 A small enjoyment, and they will have a painful retribution.

16:118 And for those who are Jewish, We forbade what We narrated to you before. And We did not wrong them, but they were wronging themselves.

16:119 Then your Lord to those who do evil out of ignorance, then they repent after that and they make good, your Lord after that is Forgiver, Merciful.

16:120 Abraham was a nation, dutiful to God, a monotheist, and he was not of the polytheists.

16:121 Thankful for His blessings. He chose him and guided him to a straight path.

16:122 And We gave him good in this world, and in the Hereafter he is of the upright ones.

16:123 Then We inspired to you: "You shall follow the creed of Abraham, monotheism, and he was not of the polytheists."

16:124 Indeed, the Sabbath was only decreed for those who had disputed in it, and your Lord will judge between them for that in which they had disputed.

16:125 Invite to the path of your Lord with wisdom and good advice, and argue with them in that which is better. Your Lord is fully aware of who is misguided from His path, and He is fully aware of the guided ones.

16:126 And if you punish, then punish with equivalence to that which you were punished. And if you are patient then it is better for the patient ones.

16:127 And be patient, for your patience is on none except God. And do not grieve for them, and do not be depressed by what they scheme.

16:128 God is with those who are aware and are good doers.

CHAPTER 17

17:0 In the name of God, the Almighty, the Merciful.

17:1 Glory be to the One who took His servant by night from the restricted Temple to the farthest Temple—which We had blessed around—so that We may show him of Our signs. Indeed, He is the Hearer, the Seer.

17:2 And We gave Moses the Book and We made it a guidance for the Children of Israel: "Do not believe in any besides Me."

17:3 The progeny of those whom We carried with Noah, he was a thankful servant.

17:4 And We decreed to the Children of Israel in the Book, that you will make corruption twice on the earth, and that you will become very high and mighty.

17:5 So, when the promise of the first one comes to pass, We would send against you servants of Ours who are very powerful, thus they managed to breach your very homes, and this was a promise which has come to pass.

17:6 Then We gave back to you your independence from them, and We supplied you with wealth and sons, and We made you more influential.

17:7 If you do good, then it will be good for you, and if you do bad, then so be it. But when the promise of the second time comes, they will make your faces filled with sorrow and they will enter the Temple as they did the first time, and they will strike down all that was raised up.

17:8 Perhaps your Lord will have mercy on you, and if you revert then We will also revert. And We made Hell a gathering place for the rejecters.

17:9 This Qur'an guides to that which is more upright, and it gives glad tidings to the believers who do good works that they will have a bountiful reward.

17:10　And for those who do not believe in the Hereafter, We have prepared for them a painful retribution.

17:11　And the human being calls to evil as much as he calls to good, and the human being was always hasty.

17:12　And We made the night and the day as two signs, so We erased the sign of night and We made the sign of day to see in, that you may seek bounty from your Lord, and that you may know the number of the years and the count. And everything We have detailed completely.

17:13　And We have attached to the neck of every human being his deeds, and We bring forth for him a record on the Day of Resurrection which he will find on display.

17:14　Read your record! It is sufficient for you that you are aware of yourself today.

17:15　Whoever is guided is guided for himself, and whoever is misguided is for his own loss. And no bearer may carry the burden of another; and We were not to punish until We send a messenger.

17:16　And if We wish to annihilate a town, We leave its reckless to rule it, then they commit wickedness in it, then the word is given, then We destroy it completely.

17:17　And how many a generation have We destroyed after Noah? And it is enough for your Lord to have knowledge and sight over the sins of His servants.

17:18　Whoever seeks the life of haste, We will hasten for him what he wishes, then We will make Hell for him a place which he will reach disgraced and rejected.

17:19　And whoever seeks the Hereafter and struggles for it as it deserves, and is a believing person, then their struggle is appreciated.

17:20　For both groups, We will bestow from the bounty of your Lord; and the bounty of your Lord was not confined.

17:21　See how We have preferred some of them over the others; and in the Hereafter are greater levels, and greater preference.

17:22　Do not make with God another god, or you will find yourself disgraced, abandoned.

17:23 And your Lord decreed that you shall not serve except He, and do good to your parents. Should one of them or both of them reach old age, do not say to them a word of disrespect nor shout at them, but say to them a kind saying.

17:24 And lower for them the wing of humility through mercy, and say: "My Lord, have mercy upon them as they have raised me since I was small."

17:25 Your Lord is fully aware of what is in your souls. If you are good, then He is to the obedient a Forgiver.

17:26 And give the relative his due, and the poor, and the wayfarer; and do not waste excessively.

17:27 Those who waste excessively are brothers to the devils, and the devil was to his Lord a rejecter.

17:28 And if you turn away from them to seek a mercy from your Lord which you desire, then say to them a gentle saying.

17:29 And do not make your hand stingy by holding it to your neck, nor shall you lay it fully open so you become in despair and regret.

17:30 Your Lord lays out openly the provision for whom He wishes, and He is able to do so. He is Expert and Seer over His servants.

17:31 And do not kill your children out of concern of poverty; We shall provide for you and them. The killing of them was a big mistake.

17:32 And do not come near adultery, for it is immoral and an evil path.

17:33 And do not take a life, for God has made this forbidden, except in the course of justice. And whoever is killed innocently, then We have given his heir authority, so let him not transgress in the taking of a life, for He will be given victory.

17:34 And do not come near the money of the orphan, except for that which is best, until he reaches his independence. And fulfill the pledge, for the pledge brings great responsibility.

17:35 And give full measure when you deal, and weigh with a balance that is straight. That is good and better in the end.

17:36 And do not uphold what you have no knowledge of; for the hearing, and eyesight, and mind—all these you are responsible for.

17:37 And do not walk in the land arrogantly, for you will not penetrate

181

the earth, nor will you reach the mountains in height.

17:38   All of this is bad, and disliked by your Lord.

17:39   That is from what your Lord has inspired to you of the wisdom. And do not make with God another god, or you will be cast into Hell, blameworthy and regretting.

17:40   Has your Lord preferred for you the males, while He takes the females as angels? You are indeed saying a grave thing!

17:41   And We have dispatched in this Qur'an that they may remember, but it only increases their aversion!

17:42   Say: "If there had been gods with Him as they say, then they would have tried to gain a way to the Throne."

17:43   Be He glorified and exalted above what they say, a great falsehood.

17:44   He is glorified by the seven heavens and the earth and that which is in them, and there is not a thing except it glorifies His praise, but you do not comprehend their glorification. He is Compassionate, Forgiving.

17:45   And when you read the Qur'an, We place between you and those who do not believe in the Hereafter an unseen veil.

17:46   And we place shields over their hearts, that they should not understand it, and a deafness in their ears. And if you mention your Lord in the Qur'an alone, they run away turning their backs in aversion.

17:47   We are fully aware of what they are listening to, for they are listening to you but while they are in private counsel the wicked say: "You are following a man who is bewitched!"

17:48   See how they put forth the examples for you. They have gone astray, and cannot come to the path.

17:49   And they said: "When we are bones and fragments, will we then be resurrected to a new creation?"

17:50   Say: "Even if you become rocks or metal."

17:51   "Or a creation that is held dear in your chests." They will say: "Who will return us?" Say: "The One who initiated you the first time." They will shake their heads to you and say: "When is this?" Say: "Perhaps it is near."

17:52 The Day He calls you and you respond by His grace, and you think that you only stayed a little while.

17:53 And say to My servants to speak that which is best. The devil makes bitterness between them. The devil is to the human being a clear enemy.

17:54 Your Lord is fully aware of you, if He wishes He will have mercy on you, or if He wishes He will punish you. And We have not sent you as a guardian over them.

17:55 And your Lord is fully aware of who is in the heavens and the earth. And We have preferred some prophets over others, and We gave David the Psalms.

17:56 Say: "Call on those you have claimed besides Him. For they have no power to remove harm from you or shift it."

17:57 The ones you call on, they are themselves seeking a path to their Lord which is nearer, and they desire His mercy, and they fear His retribution. The retribution of your Lord is to be feared!

17:58 And there is not a town before the Day of Resurrection that We will not destroy it, or punish it with a severe punishment. This has been written in the record.

17:59 And what stopped Us from sending the signs except that the previous people disbelieved in them. And We sent to Thamud the camel with foresight, but they did her wrong. And We do not send the signs except to make them fearful.

17:60 And when We said to you: "Your Lord has encompassed the people." And We did not make the vision that We showed you except as a test for the people, and the tree that was cursed in the Qur'an. And We are making them fearful, but it only increases their transgression.

17:61 And We said to the angels: "Yield to Adam." So they yielded except for Satan, he said: "Shall I yield to one you have created from clay!"

17:62 He said: "Shall I show You this one whom You have preferred over me, that if You respite me until the Day of Resurrection, I will seize his progeny, except for a few."

17:63 He said: "Go, and whoever follows you from them. Hell shall be the reward to you all, a reward well deserved."

17:64 "And entice whoever you can of them with your voice, and mobilize all your forces and men against them, and you may share with them in their money and children, and promise them." But the devil promises nothing but deceit.

17:65 "As for My servants, you will have no power over them." And your Lord is enough as a Caretaker.

17:66 Your Lord is the One who drives the ships for you in the sea so that you may seek of His bounty. He is Merciful towards you.

17:67 And if harm should afflict you at sea, then all those whom you called on besides Him suddenly vanish from you except for Him. So when He saves you to dry land, you turn away. The human being is ever rejecting.

17:68 Are you confident that He will not cause this side of the land to swallow you up, or that He would not send a violent storm against you? Then you will find no caretaker for yourselves.

17:69 Or are you confident that He would not send you back again in it, then He would send against you a violent wind and cause you to drown for your rejection? Then you will not find a second chance with Us.

17:70 And We have honored the Children of Adam and carried them in the land and the sea, and We have provided for them of the good things, and We have preferred them over many of those We created in a marked preference.

17:71 The Day We call every people by their beacon. Then, whoever are given their book by their right, they will read their book, and they will not be wronged in the least.

17:72 And whoever is blind in this, then he will be blind in the Hereafter and more astray from the path.

17:73 And they nearly diverted you from what We inspired to you so that you would fabricate something different against Us, and then they would have taken you as a friend!

17:74 And if We had not made you stand firm, you were about to side with them a little bit.

17:75 Then, We would have made you taste double the retribution in this life and double the retribution in death. And then you would not find for yourself any victor against Us.

17:76 And they nearly intimidated you so they could drive you out of the land. But then they would have been destroyed shortly after you were gone.

17:77 Such was the way of those whom We had sent before you of Our messengers. And you will not find any change in Our way.

17:78 Hold the Connection at the rubbing of the sun to the murkiness of the night; and the Qur'an at dawn—the Qur'an at dawn is witnessed.

17:79 And from the night, as an addition, you shall reflect upon it for yourself, perhaps your Lord would grant you a station that is praiseworthy.

17:80 And say: "My Lord, admit me an entrance of truth and let me exit an exit of truth, and grant me from Yourself a support to victory."

17:81 And say: "The truth has come and falsehood has perished. False-hood is always bound to perish!"

17:82 And We send down from the Qur'an what is a healing and mercy to the believers. And it only increases the wicked in their loss.

17:83 And if We bless man, he turns away and turns his side. But when adversity touches him, he is despairing!

17:84 Say: "Let each work according to his own. Your Lord is fully aware of who is best guided to the path."

17:85 And they ask you concerning the Spirit. Say: "The Spirit is from the authority of my Lord; and the knowledge you were given was but very little."

17:86 And if We wished, We would take away that which We have inspired to you. Then you would not find for yourself with it against Us a caretaker.

17:87 Except for a mercy of your Lord. His grace upon you has been great.

17:88 Say: "If all mankind and the Jinn were to gather to bring a Qur'an like this, they could not come with its like, even if they were helping one another."

17:89 And We have dispatched to the people in this Qur'an from every example, but most of the people refuse to be anything but rejecters!

17:90 And they said: "We will not believe unto you until you cause a spring of water to burst out of the ground."

17:91 "Or that you have an estate of palm trees and grapes, and you cause gushing rivers to burst through it."

17:92 "Or that you make the heaven fall upon us in pieces as you claimed, or that you bring God and the angels before us."

17:93 "Or that you have a luxurious home, or that you can ascend into the heavens. And we will not believe in your ascension unless you bring for us a book that we can read." Say: "Glory be to my Lord. Am I anything other than a mortal messenger!"

17:94 And what stopped the people from believing when the guidance came to them, except that they said: "Has God sent a mortal messenger?"

17:95 Say: "If the earth had angels walking about in security, We would have sent down to them from the heaven an angel as a messenger."

17:96 Say: "God suffices as a witness between me and you. He is Expert and Seer over His servants."

17:97 Whoever God guides is the truly guided one. And whoever He misguides then you will not find for them any allies except for Him. And We gather them on the Day of Resurrection on their faces, blind, mute, and deaf; their abode will be Hell. Every time it dies down, We increase for them the fire.

17:98 Such is their recompense that they rejected Our revelations, and they said: "If we are bones and fragments, will we be sent into a new creation?"

17:99 Did they not see that God who has created the heavens and the earth is able to create their like? And He has made an appointed time for them in which there is no doubt. But the wicked refuse anything except rejection.

17:100 Say: "If you were the ones possessing the vaults of the mercy of my Lord, you would have held back for concern of spending. And the human being was always stingy!"

17:101 And We had given Moses nine clear signs. So ask the Children of Israel, when he came to them, then Pharaoh said: "I think that you Moses are bewitched!"

17:102 He said: "You know that no one has sent these down except for the Lord of the heavens and the earth as visible proofs. And I think that you Pharaoh are doomed!"

17:103 So he wanted to entice them out of the land. But We drowned him and all those with him.

17:104 And We said after him to the Children of Israel: "Dwell on the earth, then, when the time of the second promise comes, We will bring you all together as a mixed crowd."

17:105 And it is with the truth that We have sent it down, and with the truth it came down. And We have not sent you except as a bearer of good news and a warner.

17:106 And a Qur'an that We have divided, so that you may read it to the people over time; and We have brought it down gradually.

17:107 Say: "Believe in it or do not believe in it. Those who have been given the knowledge before it, when it is recited to them, they fall to their chins prostrating."

17:108 And they say: "Praise be to our Lord. Truly, the promise of our Lord was fulfilled."

17:109 And they fall upon their chins crying, and it increases them in humility.

17:110 Say: "Call on God or call on the Almighty; by whichever you call on, to Him are the best names." And do not be too loud in your connecting, nor too quiet; but seek a path in between.

17:111 And say: "Praise be to God who has not taken a son, nor does He have a partner in sovereignty, nor does He have an ally out of weakness." And glorify Him greatly.

CHAPTER 18

18:0 In the name of God, the Almighty, the Merciful.

18:1 Praise be to God who has sent down the Book to His servant, and He has not made in it any crookedness.

18:2 It is valuable, giving warning of the severe punishment from Him; and it gives glad tidings to the believers who do good works, that they will have an excellent reward.

18:3 In which they will remain eternally.

18:4 And to warn those who said: "God has taken a son."

18:5 They have no knowledge of this, nor do their fathers. Tremendous indeed is the word coming out of their mouths. They are but saying a lie!

18:6 Perhaps you will torment yourself in grief over them, because they will not believe in this narrative at all.

18:7 We have made what is on the earth an adornment for them, so that We will test them as to which of them is best in works.

18:8 And We will surely make what is on it completely barren.

18:9 Have you perceived that the dwellers of the cave and the numerals were of Our wondrous signs?

18:10 When the youths hid in the cave, and they said: "Our Lord, bring us a mercy from Yourself, and help us in our affair!"

18:11 So We sealed their ears in the cave for many years.

18:12 Then We sent them to know which of the two groups had remained for as long as they stayed.

18:13 We narrate to you their news with the truth. They were youths who believed in their Lord, and We increased them in guidance.

18:14 And We made firm their hearts when they stood and said: "Our Lord, the Lord of the heavens and the earth, we will not call besides Him any god. If we have done so then it was in error."

18:15 "Here are our people, they have taken gods besides Him, while they do not come with any clear authority. Who then is more wicked than he who invents lies about God?"

18:16 So when you withdraw from them and what they serve besides God, seek refuge in the cave, and your Lord will spread His mercy upon you and prepare for your problem a solution.

18:17 And you see the sun when it rises, it visits their cave from the right, and when it sets, it touches them from the left, while they are in an enclosure from it. That is from the signs of God. Whoever God guides is the guided one, and whoever He misguides, you will not find for him any ally to give direction.

18:18 And you would think they are awake while they are asleep. And We turn them on the right-side and on the left-side, and their dog has his arms outstretched at the threshold. If you looked upon them you would have run away from them and you would have been filled with terror from them!

18:19 And it was thus that We delivered them so they would ask themselves. A speaker from among them said: "How long have you stayed?" They said: "We stayed a day or part of a day." He said: "Your Lord is surely aware how long you stayed, so send one of you with these stamped coins of yours to the city, and let him see which is the tastiest food, and let him come with a provision of it. And let him be careful and let no one notice you."

18:20 "If they discover you, they will stone you or return you to their creed. Then you will never be successful."

18:21 And it was thus that We let them be found, that they would know that the promise of God is true and that there is no doubt regarding the Hour. They argued among themselves regarding them, so they said: "Erect a monument upon them, for their Lord is most aware of them!" Those whose argument was lost said: "We should construct a temple over them."

18:22 They will say: "Three, the fourth is their dog." And they say: "Five, the sixth is their dog," guessing at what they do not know. And they say: "Seven, and the eighth is their dog." Say: "My Lord is fully aware of their number, none know them except for a few." So do not argue regarding them except with proof, and do not seek information regarding them from anyone.

18:23 And do not say of anything: "I will do this tomorrow,"

18:24 Lest, "God willing." And remember your Lord if you forget and say: "Perhaps my Lord will guide me to what is nearer than this in wisdom."

18:25 And they remained in their cave for three hundred years, and increased nine.

18:26 Say: "God is fully aware how long they remained, to Him is the unseen of the heavens and the earth, He sees and hears. They do not have besides Him any ally, and He does not share in His judgment with anyone."

18:27 And recite what has been inspired to you from the Book of your Lord, there is no changing His words, and you will not find besides Him any refuge.

18:28 And hold yourself with those who call on their Lord at dawn and dusk seeking His face, and let not your eyes overlook them that you seek the beauty of this worldly life. And do not obey he whom We have made his heart heedless of Our remembrance and he followed his desire, and his fate was lost.

18:29 And say: "The truth is from your Lord, so let whoever desires believe, and whoever desires reject." We have prepared for the wicked a Fire whose walls will be surrounding them. And if they cry out, they are given a water like boiling oil which burns their faces. What a dreadful drink and what a miserable place!

18:30 Those who believe and do good works, We do not waste the reward of those who have done good works.

18:31 They will have gardens of delight with rivers flowing beneath them, and they will be adorned with bracelets of gold and they will wear green garments of fine silk. They will sit in it on raised thrones. Beautiful is the reward, and beautiful is the dwelling.

18:32 And give them the example of two men: We made for one of them two gardens of grapes, and We surrounded them with palm trees, and We made crops in their midst.

18:33 Each of the two gardens brought forth its produce, and none failed in the least. And We caused a river to gush through them.

18:34 And he had fruit, so he said to his friend while discussing with him: "I am better off than you financially, and of great influence."

18:35 And he went back into his garden while he had wronged himself. He said: "I do not think that this will ever perish."

18:36 "And I do not think that the Hour is coming. And if I am returned to my Lord, then I will surely find even better things for me."

18:37 His friend said to him while discussing with him: "Have you disbelieved in the One who has created you from dust, then from a seed, then He evolved you into a man?"

18:38 "But He is God, my Lord, and I do not set up any partners at all with my Lord."

18:39 "And if you enter your garden, you should say: 'This is what God has given, there is no power except by God.' You see me as being less than you in wealth and in children?"

18:40 "Perhaps my Lord will give me better than your garden, and He will send upon it a tornado from the sky, so it becomes completely barren."

18:41 "Or that its water becomes deep underground, so you will not be capable of seeking it."

18:42 So his fruits were ruined, and he began turning his hands at that which he had spent on it while it remained destroyed upon its branches. And he said: "I wish I had not set up any partner with my Lord!"

18:43 And he had no group which could help against God, and he would not have had victory.

18:44 Such is the true authority of God. He is best to reward, and best to end.

18:45 And give them the example of this worldly life is like a water which We have sent down from the sky, so that the plants of the earth mix with it and it becomes murky being moved by the wind. And God is capable of all things.

18:46 Money and children are the beauty of this worldly life. But the good deeds that remain behind are better with your Lord for a reward, and better for hope.

18:47 And the Day We move the mountains, and you see the earth level, and We gather them; so We will not leave out anyone of them.

18:48 And they are displayed before your Lord as a column: "You have come to Us as We had created you the first time. No, you claimed We would not make for you an appointed time!"

18:49 And the record was displayed, so you see the criminals fearful of what is in it. And they say: "Woe to us! What is with this record that it does not leave out anything small or large but has counted it." And they found what they had done present. And your Lord does not wrong anyone.

18:50 And We said to the angels: "Yield to Adam." So they all yielded except for Satan. He was of the Jinn, he disobeyed the order of his Lord. Will you take him and his progeny as allies besides Me, while they are your enemy? Miserable for the transgressors is the substitute!

18:51 I did not make them witness the creation of the heavens and the earth, nor the creation of themselves. Nor do I take the misleaders as helpers.

18:52 The Day when He says: "Call on your partners that you had claimed." So they called them, but they did not respond to them.

And We made between them a place of annihilation.

18:53 And the criminals saw the Fire, and they realized they will be placed in it, and they did not find any way to avert it.

18:54 And We have dispatched in this Qur'an for the people from every example; but the human being has always been most argumentative.

18:55 And what prevented the people from believing when the guidance came to them, and to seek forgiveness from their Lord? Are they waiting for what happened to the people of old to come to them, or that the retribution be brought to them face to face?

18:56 And We do not send the messengers except as bearers of good news and warners. But those who reject will argue using falsehood to overshadow the truth with it. And they took My revelations and what they have been warned by for mockery!

18:57 And who is more wicked than he who was reminded of the revelations of his Lord but he turned away from them, and he forgot what his hands had done. We have made veils upon their hearts from understanding it, and a deafness in their ears. And if you invite them to the guidance, they will never be guided.

18:58 And your Lord is forgiving, with mercy. If He were to evaluate the people for what they had already earned, He would hasten for them the retribution. No, they have an appointment, beyond which they will find no escape.

18:59 And those towns, We destroyed them when they transgressed. And We made for their destruction an appointed time.

18:60 And Moses said to his youth: "I will not stop until I reach the junction of the two seas, or I spend a lifetime trying."

18:61 But when they reached the junction that was in-between, they forgot their fish, and it was able to make its way back to the sea in a stream.

18:62 And when they passed further on, he said to his youth: "Bring us our lunch; we have found much fatigue in this journey of ours."

18:63 He said: "Do you remember when we rested upon the rock? I forgot the fish, and it was the devil who made me forget to remember it. It made its way back to the sea amazingly!"

18:64 He said: "That is what we have been seeking!" So they went back retracing their steps.

18:65   So they came upon a servant of Ours whom We had given him mercy from Us and We had taught him knowledge from Us.

18:66   Moses said to him: "Can I follow you so that you will teach me from the guidance you have been taught?"

18:67   He said: "You will not be able to have patience with me."

18:68   "And how can you be patient about that which you have not been given any news?"

18:69   He said: "You will find me, God willing, to be patient. And I will not disobey any command of yours."

18:70   He said: "If you follow me, then do not ask about anything until I mention it to you."

18:71   So they ventured forth until they rode in a boat and he made a hole in it. He said: "Have you made a hole in it to drown its people? You have done something dreadful!"

18:72   He said: "Did I not tell you that you will not be able to have patience with me?"

18:73   He said: "Forgive me for what I forgot, and do not be hard upon my request with you."

18:74   So they ventured forth until they came upon a boy, and he killed him. He said: "Have you killed an innocent person without justice? You have done something awful!"

18:75   He said: "Did I not tell you that you will not be able to have patience with me?"

18:76   He said: "If I ask you about anything after this, then do not keep me in your company. You will then have a reason over me."

18:77   So they ventured forth until they came to the people of a town. They requested food from its people but they refused to host them. Then they found a wall which was close to collapsing, so he built it. He said: "If you had wished, you could have asked a wage for it!"

18:78   He said: "For this, we will now part ways. I will inform you of the meanings of those things that you could not have patience over."

18:79   "As for the boat, it belonged to some poor people who were working the sea, so I wanted to damage it as there was a king coming who takes every boat by force."

18:80 "And as for the boy, his parents were believers, so we were concerned that he would oppress them by his transgression and disbelief."

18:81 "So we wanted their Lord to replace for them with one who is better than him in purity and closer to mercy."

18:82 "And as for the wall, it belonged to two orphaned boys in the city, and underneath it was a treasure for them, and their father was a good man, so your Lord wanted that they reach their independence and bring out their treasure as a mercy from your Lord. And none of what I have done was of my own accord. That is the meaning of what you could not have patience for."

18:83 And they ask you about the Two Horned One, say: "I will recite to you a remembrance of him."

18:84 We had facilitated for him in the land, and We had given him the means to all things.

18:85 So he followed the means.

18:86 Until he reached the setting of the sun; he found it setting at a hot spring, and he found a people near it. We said: "O Two Horned One, either you shall punish, or you shall do them good."

18:87 He said: "As for he who has done wrong, we will punish him then he will be returned to his Lord and He will punish him an awful punishment."

18:88 "And as for he who believes and does good, then he will have the reward of goodness, and we will speak to him simply of our plan."

18:89 Then he followed the means.

18:90 So when he reached the emergence of the sun, he found it emerging on a people whom We did not make for them any cover against it.

18:91 So it was, and We have encompassed what news he found.

18:92 Then he followed the means.

18:93 Until he reached an area that was between two barriers, he found within it a people who could barely understand anything said.

18:94 They said: "O Two Horned One, Gog and Magog are corrupters of the land, so shall we make a tribute for you that you will make between us and them a barrier?"

18:95 He said: "What my Lord has given me is far better. So help me with strength and I will make between you and them a landfill."

18:96 "Bring me dense metal," until he leveled between the two sides. He said: "Blow," until he made it into fire. He said: "Bring me tar so I can pour it over."

18:97 So they could not penetrate it, and they could not advance in it.

18:98 He said: "This is a mercy from my Lord. But when the promise of my Lord comes, He will make it crumble. And the promise of my Lord is truth."

18:99 And We leave them that day, to surge into one another. And the horn was blown, so We gathered them together.

18:100 And We displayed Hell on that Day to the rejecters openly.

18:101 Those whose eyes were covered against My remembrance, and they were unable to hear.

18:102 Did those who reject think that they could take My servants as allies besides Me? We have prepared Hell for the rejecters as a dwelling.

18:103 Say: "Shall we inform you of the greatest losers?"

18:104 "Those whose efforts in the worldly life were wasted while they thought they were doing good!"

18:105 These are the ones who rejected the revelations of their Lord and His meeting. So their works were in vain, and We will not give them any value on the Day of Resurrection.

18:106 That is their recompense, Hell; for what they rejected and for taking My revelations and My messengers for mockery!

18:107 Those who believe and do good works, they will have the gardens of Paradise as a dwelling.

18:108 Abiding therein. They will not want to be moved from it.

18:109 Say: "If the sea were an inkwell for the words of my Lord, then the sea would run out before the words of my Lord run out;" even if We were to bring another like it as an extension.

18:110 Say: "I am but a mortal like you, being inspired that your god is One god. So whoever looks forward to meeting his Lord, then let him do good works, and not serve anyone besides his Lord."

CHAPTER 19

19:0 In the name of God, the Almighty, the Merciful.

19:1 KH'YA'S'

19:2 A reminder of the mercy of your Lord to His servant Zechariah.

19:3 When he called out to his Lord secretly.

19:4 He said: "My Lord, my bones have gone frail, and my hair has turned white, and I have never been mischievous in imploring You my Lord."

19:5 "And I fear the kinfolk after I am gone, and my wife is infertile, so grant me from Yourself an ally."

19:6 "To inherit from me, and inherit from the descendants of Jacob. And make him, my Lord, well pleasing."

19:7 "O Zechariah, We give you glad tidings of a boy whose name is John. We have not given that name before to anyone."

19:8 He said: "My Lord, how can I have a boy when my wife is infertile, and I have reached a very old age?"

19:9 He said: "It is such that your Lord has said. It is an easy thing for Me. And I had created you before, when you were not a thing."

19:10 He said: "My Lord, make for me a sign." He said: "Your sign is that you will not speak to the people for three nights consecutively."

19:11 So he went out among his people from the enclosure, and indicated to them that they should glorify Him at dawn and dusk.

19:12 "O John, take the Book with confidence." And We gave him authority while in his youth.

19:13 And tenderness from Us, and purity, and he was ever righteous.

19:14 And dutiful to his parents, and never was he a disobedient tyrant.

19:15 And peace be upon him the day he was born, and the day he dies, and the Day he is resurrected alive.

19:16 And recall in the Book Mary, when she withdrew herself from her family to a place which was to the east.

19:17 So she took a veil to separate her from them, so We sent Our Spirit to her, and he took on the shape of a mortal in all similarity.

19:18 She said: "I seek refuge with the Almighty from you if you are righteous."

19:19 He said: "I am the messenger of your Lord, to grant you the gift of a boy who is pure."

19:20 She said: "How can I have a boy when no mortal has been with me; and I have never been unchaste?"

19:21 He said: "It is such that your Lord has said, it is easy for Me. And We shall make him a sign for the people and a mercy from Us. It is a matter already ordained."

19:22 So she was pregnant with him, and she went to deliver in a far place.

19:23 Then the birth pains came to her, by the trunk of a palm tree. She said: "I wish I had died before this, and became totally forgotten!"

19:24 But then he called to her from beneath her: "Do not be sad, your Lord has made below you a stream."

19:25 "And using the trunk of the palm tree, shake towards you; it will cause ripe dates to fall upon you."

19:26 "So eat and drink and be content. If you see any mortal, then say: 'I have vowed an abstinence for the Almighty, so I will not talk today to any of mankind.'"

19:27 Then she came to her people carrying him. They said: "O Mary, you have come with a thing totally unexpected!"

19:28 "O sister of Aaron, your father was not a wicked man, and your mother was never unchaste!"

19:29 So she pointed to him. They said: "How can we talk to someone who is a child in a cradle?"

19:30 He said: "I am a servant of God, He has given me the Book and made me a prophet."

19:31 "And He made me blessed wherever I am, and He has charged me with the Connection and purification as long as I am alive."

19:32 "And to be dutiful to my mother, and He has not made me a mischievous tyrant."

19:33 "And peace be upon me the day I was born, and the day I die, and the Day I am resurrected alive."

19:34 Such was Jesus, son of Mary, and this is the truth of the matter in which they doubt.

19:35 God was never to take a son, be He glorified. If He decrees a matter, then He simply says to it: 'Be,' and it is.

19:36 And God is my Lord and your Lord, so serve Him. This is a straight path.

19:37 Thus the Confederates disputed between them. Therefore, woe to those who have rejected from the scene of a terrible Day.

19:38 Listen to what they say and watch on the Day they come to Us. But the wicked today are in a clear misguidance.

19:39 And warn them of the Day of Remorse. When the matter is decided while they are oblivious, and they do not believe.

19:40 It is We who will inherit the earth and all that is on it. And to Us they will return.

19:41 And recall in the Book, Abraham; he was a man of truth, a prophet.

19:42 When he said to his father: "O father, why do you serve what does not hear or see, nor help you in anything?"

19:43 "My father, knowledge has come to me which did not come to you. So follow me that I will guide you to a level path."

19:44 "My father, do not serve the devil. For the devil was ever disobedient to the Almighty."

19:45 "My father, I fear that a retribution will inflict you from the Almighty and that you will become an ally to the devil."

19:46 He said: "Have you forsaken my gods O Abraham? If you do not stop this, I will stone you. You should let me be."

19:47 He said: "Peace be upon you, I will ask forgiveness for you from my Lord. He has been most kind to me."

19:48 "And I will abandon you and what you call on besides God. And I will implore my Lord, hoping that I will not be mischievous in imploring my Lord."

19:49 So when he abandoned them and what they served besides God, We granted him Isaac and Jacob, and each of them We made a prophet.

19:50 And We granted them from Our mercy, and We made for them a tongue of truthfulness to be heard.

19:51 And recall in the Book, Moses; he was loyal, and he was a messenger prophet.

19:52 And We called him from the right side of the mount, and We brought him close to talk with.

19:53 And We granted him from Our mercy his brother Aaron as a prophet.

19:54 And recall in the Book, Ishmael; he was truthful to his promise, and he was a messenger prophet.

19:55 And he used to instruct his family with the Connection and purification, and his Lord was pleased with him.

19:56 And recall in the Book, Enoch; he was a man of truth, a prophet.

19:57 And We raised him to a high place.

19:58 Those are the ones whom God has graced from the prophets from the progeny of Adam, and those We carried with Noah, and from the progeny of Abraham and Israel, and from whom We have guided and chosen. When the revelations of the Almighty are recited to them, they fall down prostrating, and in tears.

19:59 Then, generations came after them who lost the Connection, and followed desires. They will find their consequences.

19:60 Except for whoever repents and believes and does good works; they will be admitted to Paradise, and they will not be wronged in the least.

19:61 Gardens of delight; that the Almighty had promised His servants in the unseen. His promise must come to pass.

19:62 They will not hear in it any nonsense, only peace. And they will have their provision in it morning and evening.

19:63 Such is Paradise that We inherit to any of Our servants who are righteous.

19:64 "And we are not sent except by the authority of your Lord. To

Him are our present and our future, and all that is in-between. And your Lord was never to forget."

19:65 "The Lord of the heavens and the earth and what is between them. So serve Him and be patient in His service. Do you know anything that is like Him?"

19:66 And the human being says: "Can it be that when I am dead, I will be brought out alive?"

19:67 Does the human being not remember that We created him before, when he was not a thing?

19:68 By your Lord, We will gather them and the devils, then We will place them around Hell on their knees.

19:69 Then We will drag out from every clan the ones which were most in opposition to the Almighty.

19:70 Then, it is We who are best aware of those who deserve to be burnt therein.

19:71 And every single one of you will encounter it. This for your Lord is a certainty that will come to pass.

19:72 Then We will save those who were righteous, and We will leave the wicked in it on their knees.

19:73 And when Our clear revelations were recited to them, those who rejected said to those who believed: "Which of our two groups is in a better station and more prosperous?"

19:74 And how many a generation have We destroyed before them? They had more wealth and more influence.

19:75 Say: "Whoever is in misguidance, then the Almighty will lead them on." Until they see what they have been promised, either the retribution or the Hour. Then they will know who is in a worse place and weaker in power.

19:76 And God increases the guidance of those who are guided. And the goodness that endures is better with your Lord as a reward and a far better return.

19:77 Did you see the one who rejected Our revelations and said: "I will be given wealth and children."

19:78 Did he look into the future? Or has he taken a pledge with the Almighty?

19:79 No, We will record what he says, and We will increase for him the retribution significantly.

19:80 Then We inherit from him all that he said, and he shall come to Us all alone.

19:81 And they have taken gods besides God to be for them their glory.

19:82 On the contrary, they will reject their service of them and they will be standing against them.

19:83 Did you not note that We send the devils upon the rejecters to push them with incitement?

19:84 So do not be in haste towards them; We are preparing for them a preparation.

19:85 The Day We gather the righteous to the Almighty as a delegation.

19:86 And We drive the criminals to Hell as a herd.

19:87 None will possess intercession, except for he who has taken a pledge with the Almighty.

19:88 And they said the Almighty has taken a son!

19:89 You have come with a gross blasphemy.

19:90 The heavens are about to shatter from it, and the earth crack open, and the mountains fall and crumble.

19:91 That they claimed that the Almighty had a son!

19:92 And what need does the Almighty have to take a son?

19:93 When all there is in the heavens and the earth will come to the Almighty as servants.

19:94 He has encompassed them, and counted them one by one.

19:95 And all of them will come to Him on the Day of Resurrection, all alone.

19:96 As for those who believe and do good works, the Almighty will bestow upon them goodwill.

19:97 Thus We have made this easy in your tongue so that you may give good news with it to the righteous and that you may warn with it the quarrelsome people.

19:98 And how many a generation have We destroyed before them? Do you perceive any of them or hear from them a sound?

CHAPTER 20

20:0 In the name of God, the Almighty, the Merciful.

20:1 T'H'

20:2 We did not send down to you the Qur'an so you may suffer.

20:3 It is but a reminder for he who is concerned.

20:4 Sent down from the One who has created the earth and the heavens above.

20:5 The Almighty, upon the Throne He settled.

20:6 To Him is what is in the heavens and what is on the earth, and what is between them, and what is beneath the ground.

20:7 And if you will declare openly what you say, then surely He knows the secret and what is hidden.

20:8 God, there is no god except He, to Him are the beautiful names.

20:9 And did the narrative of Moses come to you?

20:10 When he saw a fire, he said to his family: "Stay here, I have seen a fire, perhaps I can bring a piece from it, or find at the fire some guidance."

20:11 So when he came to it he was called: "O Moses."

20:12 "I am your Lord, so take off your slippers; you are in the holy valley Tuwa."

20:13 "And I have chosen you, so listen to what is being inspired."

20:14 "I am God, there is no god except Me, so serve Me and hold the Connection for My remembrance."

20:15 "The Hour is coming, I am almost keeping it hidden, so that every soul will be recompensed with what it struggled."

20:16 "So do not be deterred from it by he who does not believe in it and followed his desire and perished."

20:17 "And what is in your right hand O Moses?"

20:18 He said: "It is my staff, I lean on it, and I guide my sheep with it, and I have other uses in it."

20:19 He said: "Cast it down O Moses."

20:20 So he cast it down, and it became a moving serpent!

20:21 He said: "Take it and do not be fearful, We will turn it back to its previous form."

20:22 "And place your hand under your arm, it will come out white without blemish, as another sign."

20:23 "This is to show you Our great signs."

20:24 "Go to Pharaoh, for he has transgressed."

20:25 He said: "My Lord, comfort for me my chest."

20:26 "And make my mission easy."

20:27 "And remove the knot in my tongue."

20:28 "So they can understand what I say."

20:29 "And allow for me an advisor from my family."

20:30 "Aaron, my brother."

20:31 "So that I may strengthen my resolve through him."

20:32 "And share with him my mission."

20:33 "So that we may glorify You plenty."

20:34 "And remember You plenty."

20:35 "You have been seer over us."

20:36 He said: "You have been given what you asked O Moses."

20:37 "And We have graced you another time."

20:38 "When We inspired to your mother what was inspired."

20:39 "That she should cast him in the basket, and cast it in the running water, so the running water will place him on the shore, where an enemy of Mine and his will take him. And I placed upon you love from Me. And that you shall be raised under My eye."

20:40 "That your sister should follow, and say: 'Shall I guide you to a person who will nurse him.' Thus We returned you to your mother, so that she may be pleased and not be sad. And you killed a person, but We saved you from harm and We tested you greatly.

So it was that you stayed with the people of Midyan for many years, then you came here by fate O Moses."

20:41   "And I have raised you for Myself."

20:42   "Go, you and your brother with Our signs, and do not linger from My remembrance."

20:43   "Go, both of you, to Pharaoh, for he has transgressed."

20:44   "So say to him soft words, perhaps he will remember or be concerned."

20:45   They said: "Our Lord, we fear that he would let loose upon us, or transgress."

20:46   He said: "Do not fear, I am with you, I hear and I see."

20:47   So come to him and say: "We are messengers from your Lord, so send with us the Children of Israel, and do not punish them. We have come to you with a sign from your Lord, and peace be upon those who follow the guidance."

20:48   "It has been inspired to us that the retribution will be upon he who denies and turns away."

20:49   He said: "So who is the lord of you both O Moses?"

20:50   He said: "Our Lord is the One who gave everything its creation, then guided."

20:51   He said: "What then has happened to the previous generations?"

20:52   He said: "The knowledge of it is with my Lord, in a record. My Lord does not err or forget."

20:53   The One who made for you the earth habitable and He traced out paths for you in it, and He brought down water from the sky, so We brought out with it pairs of vegetation of all types.

20:54   Eat and raise your hoofed animals. In that are signs for those with thought.

20:55   From it We created you and in it We return you, and from it We bring you out another time.

20:56   And We showed him Our signs, all of them, but he denied and refused.

20:57   He said: "Have you come to us to take us out of our land with your magic O Moses?"

20:58 "We will bring you a magic like it, so let us make an appointment between us and you which neither of us will break, a place where we both agree."

20:59 He said: "Your appointment is the day of festival, and when the people start crowding during the late morning."

20:60 So Pharaoh went away, and he gathered his plan then he came.

20:61 Moses said to them: "Woe to you, do not invent lies about God, else the retribution will take you, and miserable is the one who invents."

20:62 So they disputed in their matter between themselves, and they kept private their counsel.

20:63 They said: "These are but two magicians who want to take you out of your land with their magic, and they want to do away with your ideal way."

20:64 "So agree your plan, then come as one front. Whoever wins today will succeed."

20:65 They said: "O Moses, either you cast down or we will be the first to cast down."

20:66 He said: "You cast down." So their ropes and staffs appeared from their magic as if they were moving.

20:67 And Moses held some fear in himself.

20:68 We said: "Do not fear, you will best them."

20:69 "And cast down what is in your right hand it will consume what they have made. They have only made the plans of a magician, and the magician will not succeed no matter what he does."

20:70 So the magicians went down in prostration. They said: "We believe in the Lord of Aaron and Moses."

20:71 He said: "Have you believed to him before taking my permission? He is surely your great one who has taught you magic. So, I will cut off your hands and feet from alternate sides, and I will crucify you on the trunks of the palm trees, and you will come to know which of us is greater in retribution and more lasting!"

20:72 They said: "We will not prefer you over the proofs that have come to us, and over He who initiated us. So issue whatever judgment you have, for you only issue judgment in this worldly life."

20:73 "We have believed in our Lord that He may forgive us our wrong-doings, and what you had forced us into doing of magic; and God is better and more lasting."

20:74 He who comes to his Lord as a criminal, he will have Hell, where he will neither die in it nor live.

20:75 And he who comes to Him as a believer doing good works, for those will be the highest ranks.

20:76 Gardens of delight, with rivers flowing beneath them, abiding therein. Such is the reward of he who is developed.

20:77 And We inspired to Moses: "Take My servants out, and strike for them a path through the sea that is dry. You shall not fear being overtaken, nor be concerned."

20:78 So Pharaoh followed them with his soldiers, but the running water came-over and covered them.

20:79 Thus, Pharaoh misled his people and he did not guide.

20:80 O Children of Israel, We have saved you from your enemy, and We summoned you at the right side of the mount, and We sent down to you manna and quail.

20:81 Eat from the good things that We have provided for you and do not transgress in this else My wrath will be upon you. Whoever has incurred My wrath is lost.

20:82 And I am forgiving for whoever repents and does good works, then is guided.

20:83 "And what has caused you to rush ahead of your people O Moses?"

20:84 He said: "They are coming in my tracks, and I came quickly to you my Lord so you would be pleased."

20:85 He said: "We have tested your people after you left, and the Sumerian misguided them."

20:86 So Moses returned to his people angry and disappointed. He said: "My people, did not your Lord promise you a good promise? Has the waiting for the pledge been too long, or did you want that the wrath of your Lord be upon you? Thus you broke the promise with me."

20:87 They said: "We did not break the promise by our own will, but we were loaded with the burden of the ornaments of the people so we cast them down, and it was such that the Sumerian suggested."

20:88   He thus produced for them the form of a calf that emitted a cry. So they said: "This is your god and the god of Moses, but he had forgotten!"

20:89   Did they not see that it did not respond to them? Nor did it possess for them any harm or benefit?

20:90   And Aaron said to them before: "My people, you are being tested with it. Your Lord is the Almighty, so follow me and obey my command!"

20:91   They said: "We will remain devoted to it until Moses comes back to us."

20:92   He said: "O Aaron, what prevented you when you saw them being astray?"

20:93   "Do you not follow me? Have you disobeyed my command?"

20:94   He said: "O son of my mother, do not grab me by my beard nor by my head. I was concerned that you would say that I separated between the Children of Israel, and that I did not follow your orders."

20:95   He said: "So what do you have to say O Sumerian?"

20:96   He said: "I noticed what they did not notice, so I took a handful from where the messenger was standing, and I cast it in. This is what my soul inspired me to do."

20:97   He said: "Then be gone, for you will have it in this life to say: "I am not to be touched" And you will have an appointed time which you will not forsake. And look to your god that you remained devoted to, we will burn it, then we will obliterate it in the running waters completely."

20:98   Surely your god is God; for which there is no god except He. His knowledge encompasses all things.

20:99   And it is such that We narrate to you the news of what has passed. And We have given you from Us a remembrance.

20:100 Whoever turns away from it, then he will carry a burden on the Day of Resurrection.

20:101 They will remain therein; and the load will be miserable for them on the Day of Resurrection.

20:102 The Day the horn is blown, and We gather the criminals on that Day blue.

20:103 They whisper among themselves: "You have only been away for a period of ten."

20:104 We are fully aware of what they say, for the best among them will say: "No, you have only been away for a day."

20:105 And they ask you about the mountains, so say: "My Lord will obliterate them completely."

20:106 "Then He will leave it as a smooth plain."

20:107 "You will not see in it any crookedness or curves."

20:108 On that Day, they will follow the caller, there is no crookedness to him. And all voices will be humbled for the Almighty, you will not be able to hear except whispers.

20:109 On that Day, no intercession will be of help, except for he whom the Almighty allows and accepts what he has to say.

20:110 He knows their present and their future, and they do not have any of His knowledge.

20:111 And the faces shall be humbled for the Living, the Eternal. And whoever carried wickedness with him has failed.

20:112 And whoever does any good works, while he is a believer, then he should not fear injustice nor being given less than his due.

20:113 And thus We sent it down—a Qur'an in Arabic. And We dispatched in it the warnings, perhaps they will become aware or it will cause them to remember.

20:114 Then High above all is God, the King, the True. And do not be hasty with the Qur'an before its inspiration is completed to you, and say: "My Lord, increase my knowledge."

20:115 And We had made a pledge to Adam from before, but he forgot, and We did not find in him the will power.

20:116 And We said to the angels: "Yield to Adam." They all yielded except for Satan, he refused.

20:117 So We said: "O Adam, this is an enemy to you and your mate. So do not let him take you out from the paradise, else you will have hardship."

20:118 "You will have in it that you will not go hungry nor need clothes."

20:119 "And you will have in it that you will not go thirsty nor suffer from heat."

20:120 But the devil whispered to him, he said: "O Adam, shall I lead you to the tree of immortality and a kingdom which will not waste away?"

20:121 So they both ate from it, and their bodies became apparent to them, and they began to place leaves on themselves from the paradise. Adam had disobeyed his Lord, and had gone astray.

20:122 Then his Lord recalled him, and He forgave him, and gave guidance to him.

20:123 He said: "Descend from this, all of you, for you are enemies to one another. So, when My guidance comes to you, then, whoever follows My guidance, he will not go astray nor suffer."

20:124 "And whoever turns away from My remembrance, then he will have a miserable life, and We will raise him blind on the Day of Resurrection."

20:125 He said: "My Lord, you have raised me blind while I used to be able to see?"

20:126 He said: "It was the same when Our revelations came to you, you forgot them, and similarly today you will be forgotten."

20:127 And it is such that We recompense he who transgresses, and did not believe in the revelations of his Lord. And the retribution of the Hereafter is more severe and more lasting.

20:128 Is it not a guide to them how many generations We had destroyed before them, which they are walking now in their homes? In that are signs for the people of understanding.

20:129 And had it not been for a word already given by your Lord, they would have been held to account immediately.

20:130 So be patient to what they are saying and glorify the grace of your Lord before the rising of the sun, and before its setting, and at the approach of the night you shall glorify—and at the edges of the day, perhaps you may be content.

20:131 And do not crave with your eyes what We have bestowed upon some couples from them; the flower of the worldly life; so as to test them in it; and the provision of your Lord is better and more lasting.

20:132 And instruct your family with the Connection, and be patient for it. We do not ask you for provision, for We provide for you. And the ending will be for righteousness.

20:133 And they said: "If only he would bring us a sign from his Lord!" Did not proof come to them from what is in the previous scripts?

20:134 And if We had destroyed them with a retribution before this, they would have said: "Our Lord, if only You had sent us a messenger so we could follow Your revelations before we are humiliated and shamed!"

20:135 Say: "All are waiting, so wait, and you will come to know who are the people upon the even path and who are guided."

CHAPTER 21

21:0 In the name of God, the Almighty, the Merciful.

21:1 The judgment for the people has come near, while they are turning away unaware.

21:2 When a reminder comes to them from their Lord that is recent, they listen to it while playing.

21:3 Their hearts are preoccupied, and those who are wicked confer privately: "Is he not but a mortal like you? Would you accept this magic while you know?"

21:4 Say: "My Lord knows what is said in the heavens and on the earth, and He is the Hearer, the Knower."

21:5 They said: "No, these are just bad dreams; no, he made it up; no, he is a poet. So let him bring us a sign like those who were sent before."

21:6 None of the towns which We destroyed before them had believed. Will they be the ones who believe?

21:7 And We did not send before you except men whom We inspired to. So ask the people of the reminder if you do not know.

21:8 And We did not make for them forms that do not need to eat, nor were they immortal.

21:9   Then We fulfilled the promise to them, so We saved them and whom We pleased, and We destroyed those who transgressed.

21:10   We have sent down to you a Book in which is your remembrance. Do you not comprehend?

21:11   And how many a town have We destroyed because it was wicked, and We established after them a different people?

21:12   So it was that when they perceived Our power, they were running from it.

21:13   "Do not run, and come back to that which you were living lavishly in and your homes; so that you will be questioned."

21:14   They said: "Woe to us, we have been wicked!"

21:15   So that remained as their cry, until We made them into a silent harvest.

21:16   And We did not create the heavens and the earth and what is between them for entertainment.

21:17   If We wanted to be amused, We could have done so from what is already with Us, if that is what We wished to do.

21:18   No, We cast with the truth upon the falsehood, so it disrupts it, and then it retreats. And woe to you for what you have described.

21:19   And to Him is whoever is in the heavens and on the earth. And those who are near Him are not too proud to serve Him, nor do they complain.

21:20   They glorify in the night and the day, they do not cease.

21:21   Or have they taken earthly gods who can resurrect?

21:22   If there were gods in them except for God, then they would have been ruined. Glory be to God, the Lord of the Throne from what they describe.

21:23   He is not questioned about what He does, while they will be questioned.

21:24   Or have they taken gods besides Him? Say: "Bring your proof. This is a reminder of those with me and a reminder of those before me." But, most of them do not know the truth, so they turn away.

21:25   And We did not send any messenger before you except that We inspired him that: "There is no god except Me, so serve Me."

21:26 And they said: "The Almighty has taken a son!" Be He glorified, they are all but honored servants.

21:27 They do not speak ahead of Him, and on His command they act.

21:28 He knows their present and their future, and they cannot intercede unless it is for those whom He is pleased with. And, from His concern, they are worried.

21:29 And whoever of them says: "I am a god besides Him," then that person We will punish with Hell. It is such that We punish the wicked.

21:30 Have those who rejected not seen that the heavens and the earth were one piece, so We split them apart? And that We have made from the water everything that lives. Will they not believe?

21:31 And We made on the earth stabilizers so that it would not tumble with them, and We made in it wide paths that they may be guided.

21:32 And We made the sky a protective ceiling; and yet, from its signs they are turning away!

21:33 And He is the One who has created the night and the day, and the sun and the moon, each swimming in an orbit.

21:34 And We did not grant to any mortal that came before you immortality. If you are going to die, would they be immortal?

21:35 Every soul will taste death. And We burden you with evil and good as a test, and it is to Us that you will return.

21:36 And when those who reject see you, they take you for mockery: "Is this the one who speaks about your gods!" While in the remembrance of the Almighty they are rejecters!

21:37 Man has been created from haste. I will show you My signs, so do not be hasty.

21:38 And they say: "When will this promise come to pass if you are truthful?"

21:39 If only those who reject knew, that they will not be able to ward off the fire from their faces, nor from their backs, nor will they be helped.

21:40 No, it will come to them suddenly. And they will not be able to turn it away, nor will they be delayed.

21:41 And messengers before you were mocked, but those who ridiculed were then surrounded by that which they mocked!

21:42 Say: "Who can protect you during the night and the day from the Almighty?" No, they are turning away from the remembrance of their Lord.

21:43 Or do they have gods that will protect them from Us? They cannot help themselves, nor can they be protected from Us.

21:44 It was Us who gave luxury to these and their fathers, until they grew old with age. Do they not see that We come to the land and reduce it from its edges? Will they be able to win?

21:45 Say: "I am merely warning you with the inspiration." But the deaf do not hear the call when they are being warned.

21:46 And if a trace of the torment of your Lord touches them, they will say: "Woe to us, we have been wicked!"

21:47 And We place the balances of justice for the Day of Resurrection, so that no soul will be wronged in the least. Even if it was the weight of a mustard seed, We will bring it. And We are enough as a Reckoner.

21:48 And We had given Moses and Aaron the Criterion, a shining light, and reminder for the righteous.

21:49 Those who are concerned towards their Lord in the unseen, and they are weary of the Hour.

21:50 And this is a blessed reminder which We have sent down. Will you be deniers of it?

21:51 And before that We gave Abraham his understanding, and We were aware of him.

21:52 As he said to his father and people: "What are these images to which you are devoted?"

21:53 They said: "We found our fathers worshipping them."

21:54 He said: "You and your fathers have been clearly misguided."

21:55 They said: "Have you come to us with the truth, or are you simply playing?"

21:56 He said: "No, your lord is the Lord of the heavens and the earth, the One who initiated them. And I bear witness to such."

21:57 "And by God, I will plan against your statues after you have gone away and given your backs."

21:58 So he broke them into pieces except for the biggest of them, so that they may turn to him.

21:59 They said: "Who has done this to our gods? He is surely one of the wicked."

21:60 They said: "We heard a young man mentioning them. He was called Abraham."

21:61 They said: "Bring him before the eyes of the people so that they may be witness."

21:62 They said: "Did you do this to our gods O Abraham?"

21:63 He said: "It was the biggest one of them here who did it, so ask them, if they do speak!"

21:64 So they turned and said to themselves: "It is indeed ourselves who have been wicked!"

21:65 Then they returned to their old ideas: "You know that they do not speak!"

21:66 He said: "Do you serve besides God that which does not benefit you at all nor harm you?"

21:67 "I am fed up of you and to what you serve besides God! Do you not comprehend?"

21:68 They said: "If you are to do anything, then burn him, and give victory to your gods."

21:69 We said: "O fire, be cool and safe upon Abraham."

21:70 And they wanted to plan against him, but We made them the losers.

21:71 And We saved him and Lot to the land which We have blessed in for the worlds.

21:72 And We granted him Isaac and, as an addition, Jacob. And each of them We made a good doer.

21:73 And We made them leaders who guide by Our command, and We inspired them to do good works and hold the Connection and contribute towards purification, and they were in service to Us.

21:74 And Lot, We gave him judgment and knowledge, and We saved him from the town that used to do vile things. They were a people of evil, wicked.

21:75 And We admitted him into Our mercy. He was of the good doers.

21:76 And Noah when he called out before that, thus We responded to him, and We saved him and his family from the great distress.

21:77 And We granted him victory against the people who denied Our revelations. They were a people of evil, so We drowned them all.

21:78 And David and Solomon, when they gave judgment in the case of the crop that was damaged by the sheep of the people, and We were witness to their judgment.

21:79 So We gave Solomon the correct understanding, and both of them We have given judgment and knowledge. And We commissioned the mountains with David to praise, and the birds. This is what We did.

21:80 And We taught him the making of armor for you to protect you from your enemy. Are you then thankful?

21:81 And to Solomon the gusting winds run by his command all the way to the land which We have blessed in. And We were aware of everything.

21:82 And from the devils are those who dive for him, and they perform other tasks, and We were guardian over them.

21:83 And Job when he called his Lord: "I have been afflicted with harm, and You are the Most Merciful of those who show mercy!"

21:84 So We answered him, and We removed what was afflicting him, and We brought him back his family and others with them as a mercy from Us and a reminder to those who serve.

21:85 And Ishmael and Enoch and Isaiah, all of them were patient.

21:86 And We admitted them in Our mercy, they were of the good doers.

21:87 And the one with 'N,' when he went off in anger, and he thought that We would not be able to take him. Then he called out in the darkness: "There is no god except You! Glory be to You, I was of the wicked!"

21:88 So We responded to him and We saved him from distress. And it is such that We save the faithful.

21:89 And Zechariah when he called out to his Lord: "My Lord, do not leave me without an heir, and You are the best inheritor."

21:90 So We responded to him, and We granted him John, and We cured his wife. They used to hasten to do good, and they would call to Us in joy and in fear. And of Us they were reverent.

21:91 And the one who safeguarded her chastity, so We blew into her from Our Spirit, and We made her and her son a sign for the worlds.

21:92 This is your nation, one nation, and I am your Lord so serve Me.

21:93 And they disputed in the matter among themselves. Each of them will be returned to Us.

21:94 So whoever does good works and he is a believer, then his efforts will not be rejected and We will record it for him.

21:95 And it is forbidden for a town that We destroy, that they return!

21:96 Until Gog and Magog is opened, and from every angle they will come forth.

21:97 And the promise of truth draws near. Then, when it is seen by the eyes of those who rejected: "Woe to us, we have been oblivious to this. Indeed, we were wicked!"

21:98 Both you and what you serve besides God shall be fuel for Hell; you will enter it.

21:99 If these had been gods, then they would not have entered it! And all will abide therein.

21:100 They will be breathing heavily in it, and they will not be heard therein.

21:101 As for those who deserved good from Us, they will be removed far away from it.

21:102 They shall not hear the slightest sound from it, and they will be in what their souls desires abiding therein.

21:103 The great horror will not sadden them, and the angels will receive them: "This is your Day which you have been promised."

21:104 On the Day when We roll up the heavens like the scroll of a book is rolled up. As We initiated the first creation, so shall We return it. It is a promise of Ours that We will do this.

21:105 And We have written in the Psalms: "After the remembrance, that the earth will be inherited by My servants who do good."

21:106 In this is a directive for a people who serve.

21:107 And We have not sent you except as a mercy to the worlds.

21:108 Say: "It is inspired to me that your god is but One god, so will you submit to Him?"

21:109 So if they turn away, then say: "I have given you notice sufficiently, and I do not know if what you are promised is near or far."

21:110 "He knows that which is spoken publicly and He knows that which you keep secret."

21:111 "And for all I know, it may be a test for you and an enjoyment for a while."

21:112 He said: "My Lord, judge with the truth. And our Lord, the Almighty, is sought for what you describe."

CHAPTER 22

22:0 In the name of God, the Almighty, the Merciful.

22:1 O people, be aware of your Lord, for the quaking of the Hour is a terrible thing.

22:2 The moment you see it, every nursing mother will leave her suckling child, and every pregnant one will miscarry, and you will see the people intoxicated while they are not intoxicated, but the retribution of God is most severe.

22:3 And from the people is he who argues regarding God without knowledge, and he follows every rebellious devil.

22:4 It was decreed that anyone who allies him, he will mislead him, and guide him to the retribution of Fire.

22:5 O people, if you are in doubt as to the resurrection, then We have created you from dust, then from a seed, then from an embryo, then from a fetus developed and undeveloped so that We make it clear to you. And We settle in the wombs what We wish to an

217

appointed time, then We bring you out a child, then you reach your maturity, and of you are those who will pass away, and of you are those who are sent to an old age where he will not be able to learn any new knowledge after what he already has. And you see the land still, but when We send down the water to it, it vibrates and grows, and it brings forth of every lovely pair.

22:6   That is because God is the truth, and He gives life to the dead, and He is capable of all things.

22:7   And the Hour is coming, there is no doubt in it, and God will resurrect those who are in the graves.

22:8   And from the people are those who argue regarding God with no knowledge nor guidance nor enlightening Book.

22:9   Bending his side to misguide from the path of God. He will have humiliation in this world and We will make him taste on the Day of Resurrection the retribution of burning.

22:10   That is for what your hands have delivered, and God does not wrong the servants.

22:11   And from the people there is he who serves God nervously. So if good comes to him, he is content with it; and if an ordeal comes to him, he makes an about-face. He has lost this world and the Hereafter. Such is the clear loss.

22:12   He calls upon besides God what will not harm him and what will not benefit him. Such is the far straying.

22:13   He calls on those who harm him more than they benefit him. What a miserable patron, and what a miserable companion.

22:14   God admits those who believe and do good works to estates with rivers flowing beneath them. God does as He wishes.

22:15   Whoever thinks that God will not grant him victory in this world and the Hereafter, then let him extend his reasons to the heavens, then let him cease and see whether this action has removed the cause of his anger.

22:16   And as such, We have sent down clear revelations, and God guides whoever He wishes.

22:17   Surely those who believe; and those who are Jewish, and the Sabians, and the Nazarenes, and the Zoroastrians; and those who were polytheists; God will separate between them on the Day of

Resurrection. For God is witness over all things.

22:18 Did you not see that to God yields what is in the heavens and what is on the earth, and the sun and the moon and the stars and the mountains and the trees and what moves, and many of the people, and many who have deserved the retribution. And whoever God disgraces, then none can honor him. God does what He pleases.

22:19 Here are two opponents who have disputed regarding their Lord; as for those who rejected, outer garments made from fire are cut out for them, and boiling water is poured from above their heads.

22:20 It melts the inside of their bellies and their skin.

22:21 And they will have hooked rods of iron.

22:22 Every time they want to escape the anguish, they are returned to it. Taste the retribution of the burning!

22:23 God will admit those who believe and do good works to estates with rivers flowing beneath them, wherein they will be adorned with bracelets of gold and pearls, and their garments will be of silk.

22:24 And they are guided to the good sayings, and guided to the path of the Praiseworthy.

22:25 Surely, those who have rejected and repel from the path of God, and from the restricted Temple that We have made for the people—for the one devoted therein and the one who visits it—and whoever inclines to evil action in it, We will let them taste a painful retribution.

22:26 And We have directed Abraham to the location of the House: "Do not set up anyone with Me, and purify My House for those who visit, and those who are standing, and the kneeling, the prostrating."

22:27 And call out to the people with the Pilgrimage, they will come to you walking and on every transport, they will come from every deep enclosure.

22:28 So that they may witness benefits for themselves, and mention the name of God in the appointed days for what He has provided for them of the animal livestock. So eat from it and feed the needy and the poor.

22:29 Then let them complete their duties and fulfill their vows, and let them traverse at the ancient House.

22:30 Thus, and whoever honors the prohibitions of God, then it is better for him with his Lord. And permitted for you are the hoofed animals; except what is being recited to you; so avoid the foulness of idols and avoid saying false statements.

22:31 Monotheists to God, not setting up anything with Him. And whoever sets up partners with God, then it is as if he has fallen from the sky and the birds snatch him or the wind takes him to a place far off.

22:32 Thus, and whoever honors the symbols of God, then it is from the piety of the hearts.

22:33 In them are benefits to an appointed time, then their place is to the ancient House.

22:34 And for every nation We have established rites that they may mention the name of God for what He has provided for them of the animal livestock. Your god is One god; submit to Him and give good tidings to those who obey.

22:35 Those who, when God is mentioned, their hearts reverence, and they are patient to what befalls them, and they hold the Connection, and from what We provide them they spend.

22:36 And the sacrifice of cattle, We have made it for you to be among the symbols of God; you will have goodness in it. So remember the name of God upon them as they are lined up; then, once their bodies have become still, you may eat from them and feed with them the poor and the needy. It was thus that We have commissioned them for you, that you may be thankful.

22:37 Neither their meat nor their blood reaches God, but what reaches Him is the righteousness from you. It was thus that He has commissioned them for you, so that you may magnify God for what He has guided you to, and give news to the good doers.

22:38 God defends those who believe. God does not love any betrayer, rejecter.

22:39 Permission has been given to those who are being fought—for they have been wronged. And God is able to give them victory.

22:40 The ones who were driven out of their homes without justice, except that they said: "Our Lord is God!" And if it were not for God defending the people against themselves, then many assemblies, and markets, and connectings, and temples where the name of God is frequently mentioned, would have been destroyed. God will give victory to those who support Him. God is Powerful, Noble.

22:41   Those whom, if We allow them to have authority in the land, they hold the Connection, and they contribute towards purification, and they advocate for good and prohibit vice. And to God is the conclusion of all matters.

22:42   And if they deny you, then before them the people of Noah and 'Aad and Thamud had also denied.

22:43   And the people of Abraham and the people of Lot.

22:44   And the dwellers of Midyan; and Moses was denied. So I granted respite to the rejecters then I took them, how then was My punishment?

22:45   So how many a town have We destroyed while it was doing wrong, so that it is lying in ruins with its wells abandoned, and empty palaces.

22:46   Have they not roamed the earth and had hearts with which to comprehend and ears with which to hear? No, it is not the sight which is blind, but it is the hearts that are in the chests that are blind.

22:47   And they seek you to hasten the retribution; and God will not break His promise. And a day with your Lord is like one thousand of the years which you count.

22:48   And many a town I have given it respite while it was doing wrong, then I seized it! And to Me is the destiny.

22:49   Say: "O people, I am but a clear warner to you!"

22:50   As for those who believe and do good works, for them is a forgiveness and a great provision.

22:51   And those who seek to obstruct Our revelations, those are the dwellers of Hell.

22:52   And We did not send before you any messenger or prophet, without having the devil interfere with his wishes. God then duplicates what the devil has cast, and God secures His revelations. And God is Knower, Wise.

22:53 That He may make what the devil has cast as a test for those who have a disease in their hearts and those whose hearts are hardened. And the wicked are far away in opposition.

22:54 And to let those who have been given knowledge know that it is the truth from your Lord, and they will believe in it, and their hearts will soften to it. And God will guide those who believe to a straight path.

22:55 And those who have rejected will remain to be in doubt from it until the Hour comes to them suddenly, or the retribution of a barren Day comes to them.

22:56 The sovereignty on that Day is to God, He will judge between them. So as for those who have believed and did good works, they are in gardens of bliss.

22:57 And those who rejected and disbelieved Our revelations, those will have a humiliating retribution.

22:58 And those who emigrated in the cause of God, then they were killed or died, God will provide them with a good provision, and God is the best of providers.

22:59 He will admit them an entrance that they will be pleased with, and God is Knowledgeable, Compassionate.

22:60 It is decreed that whoever retaliates with equal measure as was retaliated against him, then he was persecuted for this, God will give him victory. God is Pardoning, Forgiving.

22:61 That is because God merges the night into the day, and He merges the day into the night. And God is Hearer, Seer.

22:62 That is because God is the truth, and what they call on besides Him is falsehood. And God is the Most High, the Great.

22:63 Did you not see that God sends down water from the sky, and then the land becomes green? God is Compassionate, Expert.

22:64 To Him is what is in the heavens and what is on the earth. And God is the Rich, the Praiseworthy.

22:65 Did you not see that God has commissioned for you what is on the earth? And the ships sail in the sea with His permission. And He holds the sky so that it would not collapse upon the earth, except by His permission. Indeed, God is Kind towards the people, Merciful.

22:66 He is the One who gave you life, then He makes you die, then He gives you life. But the human being is always rejecting!

22:67 For every nation We have established rites which they are to fulfill. So do not let the matter fall into dispute. And call upon your Lord, for you are on a guidance which is straight.

22:68 And if they argue with you, then say: "God is fully aware of what you do."

22:69 "God will judge between you on the Day of Resurrection in what you dispute therein."

22:70 Did you not know that God knows what is in the heavens and the earth? All is in a record. All that for God is easy.

22:71 And they serve besides God what He did not send any authority upon, and what they have no knowledge of. And the wicked will not have any helper.

22:72 And if Our clear revelations are recited to them, you see denial in the faces of those who have rejected. They are nearly close to attacking those who are reciting to them Our revelations! Say: "Shall I inform you of what is worse than this? The Fire, which God has promised to those who have rejected. What a miserable destiny!"

22:73 O people, an example is being put forth so listen to it: those you call upon besides God will not create a fly even if they all gathered to do so. And if the fly takes anything from them, they will not be able to return anything from it. Weak is both the seeker and the sought!

22:74 They have truly underestimated the power of God; for God is Powerful, Noble.

22:75 God chooses messengers from among the angels and from among the people. God is Hearer, Seer.

22:76 He knows their present and their future. And to God all matters are returned.

22:77 O you who believe, kneel and prostrate and serve your Lord and do good that you may succeed.

22:78 And strive for God a genuine striving. He is the One who has chosen you, and He has made no hardship for you in the system— the creed of your father Abraham. He is the One who named you

223

'those who have submitted' from before and in this; so let the messenger be witness over you and you be witness over the people. So hold the Connection and contribute towards purification and hold tight to God, He is your patron. What an excellent Patron, and what an excellent Supporter.

CHAPTER 23

23:0 In the name of God, the Almighty, the Merciful.

23:1 The believers are indeed successful.

23:2 Those who, in their connecting, have humility.

23:3 And they abstain from vain talk.

23:4 And they are active towards purification.

23:5 And they maintain their chastity.

23:6 Except around their mates, or those who are committed to by their oath, they are free from blame.

23:7 But whoever seeks anything beyond this, then these are the transgressors.

23:8 And those who look after what they have been entrusted to and to their pledges.

23:9 And those who maintain their connectings.

23:10 These are the inheritors.

23:11 The ones who shall inherit Paradise, in it they will abide.

23:12 And We have created the human being from an extract from clay.

23:13 Then We made him a seed in a safe lodging.

23:14 Then We created the seed into an embryo, then We created the embryo into a fetus, then We created the fetus into bone, then We covered the bone with flesh, then We brought forth a new creation. Blessed is God, the best of creators.

23:15 Then after that, you will die.

23:16 Then you will be resurrected on the Day of Resurrection.

23:17   And We have created above you seven paths; and We were never, with regards to the creation, unaware.

23:18   And We sent down from the sky water in due measure, then We let it reside in the land, and We are capable of taking it away.

23:19   So We brought forth for you gardens of palm trees and grapes, for which you will find many fruits and from it you will eat.

23:20   And a tree which emerges from the mount of Sinai, it grows oil and is a relish for those who eat.

23:21   And in the hoofed animals are lessons for you. We give you to drink from what is in its bellies, and you have many other benefits from them, and of them you eat.

23:22   And on them and on the ships you are carried.

23:23   And We have sent Noah to his people, so he said: "O my people, serve God, you have no other god besides Him. Will you not take heed?"

23:24   But the leaders who rejected from among his people said: "What is this but a mortal like you? He wants to make himself better than you! And if it was indeed the will of God, He would have sent down angels. We did not hear such a thing among our fathers of old."

23:25   "He is no more than a man who has madness in him. So keep watch on him for a while."

23:26   He said: "My Lord, grant me victory for what they denied me."

23:27   So We inspired him: "Construct the ship under Our eyes and Our inspiration. Then, when Our command comes and the chamber erupts, then you shall take in it a pair from each kind, and your family; except those of them upon whom the word has been issued. And do not address Me regarding those who have done wrong, for they will be drowned."

23:28   So when you and those who are with you have embarked on the ship, then say: "All praise is due to God who has saved us from the wicked people."

23:29   And say: "My Lord, cause me to embark upon a blessed place, for You are the best for those who embark."

23:30   In this are signs, and We will always test.

23:31 Then We raised after them a different generation.

23:32 So We sent a messenger to them from among them: "Serve God, you have no other god besides Him. Will you not take heed?"

23:33 And the leaders from among his people who rejected and denied the meeting of the Hereafter; and We indulged them in this worldly life; said: "What is this but a mortal like you? He eats from what you eat and he drinks from what you drink."

23:34 "And if you obey a mortal like you, then you will indeed be losers."

23:35 "Does he promise you that if you die and become dust and bones that you will be brought out?"

23:36 "Far fetched is what you are being promised."

23:37 "There is nothing but our worldly life, we die and we live, and we will not be resurrected."

23:38 "He is but a man who has invented a lie against God, and we will not believe in him."

23:39 He said: "My Lord, grant me victory for what they denied me."

23:40 He said: "In a little while they will be in regret."

23:41 So the scream took them with justice, and We made them as dead plants. So away with the wicked people.

23:42 Then We raised after them different generations.

23:43 No nation can hasten its appointed time, nor can it delay.

23:44 Then We sent Our messengers in succession. Every time there came to a nation their messenger, they denied him. So We made them follow one another, and We let them become narrations. So away with a people who do not believe!

23:45 Then We sent Moses and his brother Aaron with Our signs and a clear authority.

23:46 To Pharaoh and his commanders. But they became arrogant, for they were a high and mighty people.

23:47 So they said: "Shall we believe two mortals like us, while their people are servants to us?"

23:48 So they denied them, and they became of those who were destroyed.

23:49 And We have given Moses the Book, so that they may be guided.

23:50 And We made the son of Mary and his mother a sign, and We gave them refuge on high ground, a place for resting and with a flowing stream.

23:51 "O messengers, eat from what is good, and do good work. I am aware of what you do."

23:52 "And this is your nation, one nation, and I am your Lord so be aware."

23:53 But the affair was disputed between them into segments. Every group happy with what it had.

23:54 So leave them in their error until a time.

23:55 Do they not think why We are extending them with wealth and sons?

23:56 We are quick to give them the good things. But they do not perceive.

23:57 As for those who are, from the concern of their Lord, worried.

23:58 And they believe in the revelations of their Lord.

23:59 And they do not set up anything with their Lord.

23:60 And they give of what they were given, and their hearts are full of reverence that they will return to their Lord.

23:61 These are the ones who race in doing good, and they are the forerunners to it.

23:62 And We do not burden a soul except with what it can bear. And We have a record that speaks with the truth, they will not be wronged.

23:63 No, their hearts are unaware of this! And they have deeds besides this which they are doing.

23:64 Until We take their carefree people with the retribution, then they will shout for help.

23:65 Do not shout for help today, for you will not be helped against Us.

23:66 My revelations were recited to you, but you used to turn back on your heels.

23:67 You were too proud from it, talking evil about it; and you defiantly disregarded it.

23:68 Did they not ponder the words, or has there come to them that which had not come to their fathers of old?

23:69 Or did they not know their messenger? So they are in denial of him.

23:70 Or do they say that there is a madness in him? No, he has come to them with the truth, but most of them are hateful of the truth.

23:71 And if the truth were to follow their desires, then the heavens and the earth and all who are in them would have been corrupted. No, We have come to them with their reminder, but from their reminder they are turning away.

23:72 Or do you ask them for a wage? The wage of your Lord is best, and He is the best of providers.

23:73 And you are inviting them to a straight path.

23:74 And those who do not believe in the Hereafter, they are deviating away from the path.

23:75 And if We were to have mercy on them and remove what distress was upon them, they would still return to persist in their transgression, blundering.

23:76 And when We seized them with the punishment, they did not humble themselves to their Lord nor did they invoke Him.

23:77 Until We open for them a door of immense retribution, then they become in sorrow and despair.

23:78 And He is the One who established for you the hearing, and the sight, and the minds. Little do you give thanks.

23:79 And He is the One who multiplied you on the earth, and to Him you will be returned.

23:80 And He is the One who gives life and brings death, and to Him is the alteration of the night and the day. Do you not comprehend?

23:81 No, they have said the same as what the people of old had said.

23:82 They said: "If we are dead and become dust and bones, will we then be resurrected?"

23:83   "We, as well as our fathers, have been promised this from before. This is nothing except tales of old!"

23:84   Say: "To whom is the earth and whoever is in it if you know?"

23:85   They will say: "God." Say: "Will you then not remember!"

23:86   Say: "Who is the Lord of the seven heavens and the Lord of the great Throne?"

23:87   They will say: "God." Say: "Will you then not take heed?"

23:88   Say: "In whose hand is the sovereignty of all things, and He protects while there is no protector against Him, if you know?"

23:89   They will say: "God." Say: "Then why are you deceived?"

23:90   No, We have come to them with the truth, and they are truly liars.

23:91   God has not taken a son, nor is there with Him any god. If it were so, then every god would have taken what he created and they would have tried to overtake each other. God be glorified against what they describe!

23:92   The Knower of the unseen and the seen. Be He exalted above what they set up.

23:93   Say: "My Lord, if You show me what they are promised."

23:94   "My Lord, then do not leave me among the wicked people."

23:95   And We are able to show you what We promise them.

23:96   Push away evil with that which is better. We are better aware of what they describe.

23:97   And say: "My Lord, I seek refuge with You from the whispers of the devils."

23:98   "And I seek refuge with you, my Lord, lest they be present with me."

23:99   Until death comes to one of them, he says: "My Lord, send me back."

23:100   "So that I may do good in that which I have left behind." No, it is but a word he is speaking. And there is a screen to prevent them from going back until the Day they are all resurrected.

23:101   So when the horn is blown, then there will be no kinship between them on that Day, nor will they ask for one another.

23:102 So, those whose weights are heavy on the balance, those are the successful ones.

23:103 And those whose weights are light on the balance, those are the ones who lost their souls, in Hell they will abide.

23:104 The Fire will scorch their faces, and in it their grin will be with displaced lips.

23:105 "Were My revelations not recited to you, then you denied them?"

23:106 They said: "Our Lord, our wickedness overcame us, and we were a misguided people."

23:107 "Our Lord, bring us out of it, and if we return to such, then we are indeed wicked."

23:108 He said: "Be humiliated therein and do not speak to Me."

23:109 There was a group from among My servants who used to say: "Our Lord, we have believed, so forgive us, and have mercy upon us, for You are the best of those who show mercy."

23:110 But you mocked them, so much so that they made you forget My remembrance, and you used to laugh at them.

23:111 I have rewarded them today for their patience, they are indeed the winners.

23:112 He said: "How long have you stayed in the earth in terms of years?"

23:113 They said: "We remained for a day, or for part of a day. So ask those who kept count."

23:114 He said: "You have remained for very little, if only you knew."

23:115 "Did you think that We have created you without purpose, and that you would not return to Us?"

23:116 So, Exalted is God, the true King, there is no god except He, the Lord of the noble Throne.

23:117 And whoever calls on another god with God when he has no proof for such, then his judgment is with his Lord. The rejecters will never succeed.

23:118 And say: "My Lord, forgive and have mercy, and you are the best of those who are merciful."

CHAPTER 24

24:0   In the name of God, the Almighty, the Merciful.

24:1   A chapter which We have sent down and imposed, and We have sent down in it clear revelations that you may remember.

24:2   The adulteress and the adulterer, you shall lash each of them with one hundred lashes, and do not let any pity overtake you regarding the system of God if you believe in God and the Last Day. And let a group of the believers witness their punishment.

24:3   The adulterer will only marry an adulteress or she who is a polytheist. And the adulteress, she will only be married to an adulterer or he who is a polytheist. And such has been made forbidden for the believers.

24:4   And those who accuse the emancipated females, then they do not bring forth four witnesses, you shall lash them with eighty lashes, and do not accept their testimony ever; and those are the wicked.

24:5   Except for those who repent after this and do good, then God is Forgiving, Merciful.

24:6   And those who accuse their spouses, but they have no witnesses except for themselves, then the testimony of one of them is to be equivalent to that of four witnesses if it is sworn by God that he is being truthful.

24:7   And the fifth shall be the curse of God upon him if he is of the liars.

24:8   And the punishment will be averted from her if she bears witness four times by God that he is of the liars.

24:9   And the fifth shall be the curse of God upon her if he is speaking the truth.

24:10   All this is from the grace of God upon you and His mercy. And God is Forgiving, Wise.

24:11   Those who have brought forth the false accusation were a group from among you. Do not think it is bad for you, for it is good for you. Every person among them will have what he deserves of the sin. And as for he who had the greatest portion of it, he will have a great retribution.

24:12   If only when you heard it the believing males and the believing females should have thought good of their own selves and said: "This is an obvious lie!"

24:13   If only they had brought four witnesses to it. If they did not have the witnesses, then these with God are the liars.

24:14   And had it not been for the grace of God upon you, and His mercy in this world and the Hereafter, a great retribution would have touched you for what you have spoken.

24:15   For you have cast it with your tongues, and you say with your mouths what you have no knowledge of, and you think it is a minor issue, while with God it was great.

24:16   And when you heard it you should have said: "It was not right for us to speak of this. Glory be to You, this is a great lie."

24:17   God warns you not to repeat something similar to this ever, if you are believers.

24:18   And God clarifies for you the revelations; and God is Knower, Wise.

24:19   As for those who enjoy that immorality spreads among those who have believed, they will have a painful retribution in this world and the Hereafter. And God knows while you do not know.

24:20   And all this is from the favor of God upon you and His mercy. And God is Compassionate, Merciful.

24:21   O you who believe, do not follow the footsteps of the devil. And whoever follows the footsteps of the devil should know that he advocates immorality and vice. And had it not been for the grace of God upon you and His mercy, not one of you would have ever been purified, but God purifies whom He wishes, and God is Hearer, Knower.

24:22   And let not those among you who have been given provision and abundance refuse to give to the relatives, and the needy, and those who have immigrated in the cause of God. Let them pardon and forgive. Would you not like God to forgive you? And God is Forgiving, Merciful.

24:23   Surely, those who accuse the emancipated innocent believing females, they will be cursed in this world and the Hereafter, and they will have a painful retribution.

24:24   On the Day when their tongues, and their hands, and their feet will bear witness against them for what they used to do.

24:25 On that Day, God will pay them what they are owed in full, and they will know that God is the Truth Manifested.

24:26 The vile females are for the vile males, and the vile males are for the vile females. And the good females are for the good males, and the good males are for the good females; these are innocent from what statements have been made, and for them is forgiveness and a generous provision.

24:27 O you who believe, do not enter any homes except your own unless you perceive a welcome and you greet the people in them. This is best for you, perhaps you will remember.

24:28 But, if you do not find anyone in them then do not enter until you are given permission. And if you are told: "Go back," then go back for it is better for you. And God is aware of what you do.

24:29 There is no sin upon you that you enter homes which are abandoned if in them there are belongings of yours. And God knows what you reveal and what you hold back.

24:30 Tell the believing men to lower their gaze and maintain their chastity. This is purer for them. God is fully aware of what you do.

24:31 And tell the believing females to lower their gaze and maintain their chastity; and they should not reveal their attractiveness except what is apparent. And they should put forth their shawls over their cleavage, and they should not reveal their attraction except to their husbands, or their fathers, or fathers of their husbands, or their sons, or the sons of their husbands, or their brothers, or the sons of their brothers, or the sons of their sisters, or their women, or those committed to by their oath, or the male servants who are without need, or the child who has not yet understood the nakedness of women. And they should not strike with their feet in a manner that reveals what they are keeping hidden of their beauty. And repent to God, all of you believers, that you may succeed.

24:32 And marry off those among you that are single, and the good from among your male and female servants. If they are poor, then God will grant them from His grace. And God is Encompassing, Knowledgeable.

24:33 And let those who are not able to marry continue to be chaste until God enriches them of His bounty. And if those who are committed to by your oath seek to consummate the marriage,

233

then document it with them if you find that they are ready, and give them from the wealth of God which He has bestowed upon you. And do not force your young women to be unchaste if they have desired to be emancipated, in order that you may make a gain in the goods of this worldly life. And if anyone has compelled them, then for their compulsion, God is Forgiving, Merciful.

24:34   And We have sent down to you clarifying revelations and an example of those who came before you and a lesson for the righteous.

24:35   God is the Light of the heavens and the earth. The example of His light is like a niche within which there is a lamp, the lamp is encased in a glass, the glass is like a radiant planet, which is lit from a blessed olive tree that is neither of the east nor of the west, its oil nearly gives off light even if not touched by fire. Light upon light, God guides to His light whom He pleases. And God sets forth examples for the people, and God is aware of all things.

24:36   In houses that God has permitted to be raised, and His name mentioned in them. He is glorified therein in the mornings and the evenings.

24:37   By men not distracted by trade or sale from the remembrance of God and holding the Connection, and contributing towards purification. They fear a Day when the hearts and sight will be overturned.

24:38   God will reward them for the best of what they did, and He will increase them from His grace. And God provides for whom He wishes without reckoning.

24:39   As for those who reject, their works are like a mirage in the desert. A thirsty person thinks it is water, until he reaches it, he finds it is nothing; and he finds God there and He pays him his due, and God is swift in reckoning.

24:40   Or like the darkness out in a deep ocean in the midst of violent waves, with waves upon waves and dark clouds. Darkness upon darkness, if he brings out his own hand, he could barely see it. And for whoever God does not make a light, he will have no light.

24:41   Do you not see that everything in the heavens and the earth glorifies God? Even the birds in formation, each knows its connection and its glorification. And God is fully aware of everything they do.

24:42   And to God is the sovereignty of the heavens and the earth, and to God is the final destiny.

24:43 Do you not see that God drives the clouds, then He joins them together, then He makes them into a stack; so you see the soft rain coming out of them? And He sends down hail from the sky from mountains, so He strikes with it whoever He wills, and He diverts it from whoever He wills; the vivid flash of its lightning almost blinds the eyes.

24:44 God rotates the night and the day. In that is a lesson for those who have insight.

24:45 And God created every moving creature from water. So some of them move on their bellies, and some walk on two legs, and some walk on four. God creates whatever He wills. God is capable of all things.

24:46 We have sent down to you clarifying revelations, and God guides whoever He wills to a straight path.

24:47 And they say: "We believe in God and in the messenger, and we obey," but a group of them turn away after that. These are not believers.

24:48 And if they are invited to God and His messenger to judge between them, a party of them turn away.

24:49 But, if the judgment is in their favor, they come to him readily!

24:50 Is there a disease in their hearts, or are they doubtful? Or do they fear that God and His messenger would wrong them in the judgment? In fact, they are the wrong doers.

24:51 The utterance of the believers when they are invited to God and His messenger to judge in their affairs is to say: "We hear and obey." These are the winners.

24:52 And whoever obeys God and His messenger, and is concerned by God, and aware of Him, then these are the winners.

24:53 And they swear by God with their strongest oaths that if you would only order them they would mobilize. Say: "Do not swear, for obedience is an obligation. God is Expert over what you do."

24:54 Say: "Obey God, and obey the messenger." But if they turn away, then he is only responsible for his obligation, and you are responsible for your obligations. And if you obey him, you will be guided. The messenger is only required to deliver clearly.

24:55　God promises those among you who believe and do good works, that He will make them successors on the earth, as He made successors of those before them, and He will enable for them their system which He has approved for them, and He will substitute security for them in place of fear: "That they serve Me, not setting up anything with Me." And as for those who reject after that, these are the wicked.

24:56　And hold the Connection and contribute towards purification, and obey the messenger, that you may attain mercy.

24:57　Do not think that those who disbelieve will remain in the land. Their abode is Hell. What a miserable destiny!

24:58　O you who believe, let those among you who are committed to by your oath, and those who have not attained puberty, request your permission regarding three times: before the dawn Connection, and when you put off your garments from the noon time, and after the evening Connection. These are three private times for you. Other than these times, it is not wrong for you or them to intermingle with one another. God thus clarifies the revelations for you. And God is Knowledgeable, Wise.

24:59　And when your children reach puberty, then let them seek your permission like it was sought by those before them. God thus clarifies His revelations for you. And God is Knowledgeable, Wise.

24:60　And the women who are past child bearing, who no longer seek to get married, have no sin upon them if they put off their garments, provided they are not adorned for beauty. And if they remain as they were, then it is better for them. God is Hearer, Knower.

24:61　There is no blame upon the blind, nor is there any blame upon the crippled, nor is there any blame upon the ill, nor is there any blame upon yourselves, if you eat at your homes, or the homes of your fathers, or the homes of your mothers, or the homes of your brothers, or the homes of your sisters, or the homes of your paternal uncles, or the homes of your paternal aunts, or the homes of your maternal uncles, or the homes of your maternal aunts, or that which you possess their keys, or that of your friends. You commit nothing wrong by eating together or as individuals. When you enter any home, you shall greet each other a greeting from God that is blessed and good. God thus explains the revelations for you that you may comprehend.

24:62　The believers are those who believe in God and His messenger, and when they are with him in a meeting, they do not leave him without permission. Those who ask permission are the ones who do believe in God and His messenger. If they ask your permission, in order to attend to some of their affairs, you may grant permission to whoever you wish, and ask God to forgive them. God is Forgiver, Merciful.

24:63　Do not let the calling of the messenger between you be as if you are calling each other. God is fully aware of those among you who slip away under flimsy excuses. Let those who oppose his command beware, for an ordeal may strike them, or a painful retribution.

24:64　Certainly, to God belongs all that is in the heavens and the earth. Surely, He knows what your condition is; and on the Day when they are returned to Him, He will inform them of everything they had done. God is aware of all things.

CHAPTER 25

25:0　In the name of God, the Almighty, the Merciful.

25:1　Blessed is the One who sent down the Criterion to His servant, so it can be a warner to the world.

25:2　The One to whom belongs the sovereignty of the heavens and the earth, and He did not take a son, and He does not have any partner in kingship. And He created everything and measured it precisely.

25:3　And they took besides Him gods that do not create anything and are themselves created! And they do not possess for themselves any harm or benefit, nor do they possess death or life, nor resurrection.

25:4　And those who rejected said: "This is but a falsehood that he invented and other people have helped him with it." Certainly, they have come with what is unjust and fabricated.

25:5　And they said: "Fictional tales of old! He wrote them down while they were being dictated to him morning and evening."

25:6　Say: "It was sent down by the One who knows the secrets in the heavens and the earth. He is always Forgiving, Merciful."

25:7　And they said: "What is with this messenger that he eats the food and walks in the market places? If only an angel were sent down to him so that he would jointly be a warner."

25:8 "Or that a treasure is given to him, or that he has a paradise that he eats from." And the wicked said: "You are but following a man bewitched!"

25:9 See how they put forth the examples for you; they have strayed, and they cannot find a path.

25:10 Blessed is the One who if He wishes can make for you better than that. Gardens with rivers flowing beneath them, and He will make for you palaces.

25:11 But they have denied the Hour, and We have prepared for those who deny the Hour a flaming fire.

25:12 When it sees them from afar, they hear its raging and roaring.

25:13 And when they are cast into it from a tight crevice, in chains, they call out their remorse.

25:14 Do not call out one remorse today, but call out many a remorse.

25:15 Say: "Is that better or the garden of eternity that the righteous have been promised?" It is their reward and destiny.

25:16 In it they will have what they wish eternally. It is upon your Lord an obligated promise.

25:17 And on the Day when We gather them together with what they served besides God; then He will say: "Did you misguide My servants here, or did they stray from the path?"

25:18 They said: "Glory be to You, it was not for us to take besides You any allies; indeed You gave them and their fathers luxury until they forgot the remembrance, and they were a lost people."

25:19 They have refuted what you claimed, so you will not find any excuse nor any victor. And whoever has done wrong among you, We will let him taste a great retribution.

25:20 And We have not sent before you any messengers except that they ate the food and walked in the market places. And We have made some of you as a test for others to see if you will have patience. And your Lord was ever seeing.

25:21 And those who do not expect to meet Us said: "If only the angels were sent down upon us, or that we see our Lord." They have become arrogant in their souls, and they have produced a great blasphemy!

25:22 On the Day they see the angels, that is not good news for the criminals. And they will be saying: "An inviolable enclosure!"

25:23 And We turned to the work that they did, so We made it into scattered dust.

25:24 The dwellers of Paradise on that Day are in the best abode and the best destiny.

25:25 And the Day when the heaven will be filled with clouds, and the angels will be sent down in succession.

25:26 The true kingship on that Day will be to the Almighty. And it is a Day which will be very hard on the rejecters.

25:27 And that Day the wrongdoer will bite on his hand and say: "I wish I had taken the path with the messenger!"

25:28 "Woe to me, I wish I did not take so and so as a friend!"

25:29 "He has misguided me from the remembrance after it came to me, and the devil was always a betrayer of mankind!"

25:30 And the messenger said: "My Lord, my people have deserted this Qur'an."

25:31 And it is so that We make for every prophet enemies from among the criminals. And your Lord suffices as a Guide and a Victor.

25:32 And those who rejected said: "If only the Qur'an was sent down to him in one go!" It was done as such so We could calm your mind with it, and We arranged it accordingly.

25:33 And for every example they come to you with, We bring you the truth and the best explanation.

25:34 Those who will be gathered to Hell on their faces, these are the most evil and the most strayed from the path.

25:35 And We gave Moses the Book and We made his brother Aaron a minister with him.

25:36 So We said: "Go both of you to the people who have denied Our signs." So We then destroyed them utterly.

25:37 And the people of Noah, when they denied the messengers We drowned them, and We made them a lesson for the people. And

We have prepared for the wicked a painful retribution.

25:38   And 'Aad and Thamud and the dwellers of Arras, and many generations in between.

25:39   And for each one We put forth the examples, and each one We destroyed utterly.

25:40   And they have come upon the town that was showered with a miserable shower. Did they not see it? No, they do not expect any resurrection.

25:41   And if they see you they take you for a mockery: "Is this the one that God sent as a messenger?"

25:42   "He nearly diverted us from our gods had we not been patient for them." They will learn when they see the retribution who is on a path most astray.

25:43   Have you seen the one who has taken his desire as his god? Will you be a caretaker over him?

25:44   Or do you think that most of them hear or comprehend? They are just like hoofed animals. No, they are worse off.

25:45   Did you not see to your Lord how He casts the shadow? And if He wished, He could have made it still, then We would have made the sun as a guide to it.

25:46   Then We retract it to us a simple retraction.

25:47   And He is the One who made for you the night as a cover, and sleep for resting, and He made the day to move about in.

25:48   And He is the One who sent the winds to spread between the hands of His mercy. And We sent down from the sky water which is purifying.

25:49   So that We revive a dead land with it and give drink to many of Our creation of hoofed animals and people.

25:50   And We have dispatched it among them so that they may remember, but most of the people refuse to be anything but rejecters.

25:51   And if We wish, We could send to every town a warner.

25:52   So do not obey the rejecters, and strive against them with it in a great striving.

25:53 And He is the One who merges the two seas; this is fresh and palatable and this is salty and bitter. And He made between them a partition and an inviolable enclosure.

25:54 And He is the One who has created from the water a mortal, so He made him multiply and mate. And your Lord is Capable.

25:55 And they serve besides God what does not benefit them nor harm them. And the rejecter is always set against his Lord.

25:56 And We have not sent you except as a bearer of good news and a warner.

25:57 Say: "I do not ask you for any wage; but for whoever chooses to make a path to his Lord."

25:58 And put your trust in the Living who does not die, and glorify His praise. It is enough for Him that He is Expert in the sins of His servants.

25:59 The One who has created the heavens and the earth and what is between them in six days, then He settled upon the Throne. The Almighty; so ask Him for He is Expert.

25:60 And if they are told: "Prostrate to the Almighty." They say: "And what is the Almighty? Shall we prostrate to what you order us?" And it increases their aversion.

25:61 Blessed is the One who made towers in the heaven and He made in it a lamp and an illuminating moon.

25:62 And He is the One who made the night and the day in succession, for those who wish to remember or wish to be thankful.

25:63 And the servants of the Almighty who walk on the earth in humility and if the ignorant speak to them, they say: "Peace."

25:64 And those who stay awake for their Lord, in prostration and standing.

25:65 And those who say: "Our Lord, avert from us the retribution of Hell. Its retribution is terrible."

25:66 "It is a miserable abode and station."

25:67 And those who when they give they are not excessive nor stingy, but they are in a measure between that.

25:68 And those who do not call on any other god with God; nor do they take the life which God has made forbidden, except in justice; nor do they commit adultery. And whoever does will receive the punishment.

25:69 The retribution will be doubled for him on the Day of Resurrection and he will abide in it in disgrace.

25:70 Except for the one who repents and believes and does good works, for those God will replace their sins with good, and God is Forgiving, Merciful.

25:71 And whoever repents, and does good, then he shall repent towards God a true repentance.

25:72 And those who do not bear false witness, and if they pass by vain talk they pass by with dignity.

25:73 And those who when they are reminded of the revelations of their Lord, they do not fall on them deaf and blind.

25:74 And those who say: "Our Lord, grant us from our mates and our progeny what will be the comfort of our eyes, and make us leaders for the righteous."

25:75 These will be rewarded with a dwelling for what they have been patient for, and they will find in it a greeting and peace.

25:76 In it they will abide, what an excellent abode and station.

25:77 Say: "My Lord would not care about you except for your imploring. But you have denied, so it will be your destiny."

CHAPTER 26

26:0 In the name of God, the Almighty, the Merciful.

26:1 T'SM.

26:2 These are the signs of the Book of Clarity.

26:3 Perhaps you grieve yourself that they do not become believers.

26:4 If We wish, We could send down for them from the heavens a sign, to which they would bend their necks in humility.

26:5 And not a reminder comes to them from the Almighty, except that they turn away from it.

26:6   They have denied, thus the news will come to them of what they used to mock.

26:7   Did they not look to the earth, how many plants have We raised in it, from each a good pair.

26:8   In that is a sign, but most of them are not believers.

26:9   And your Lord is the Noble, the Merciful.

26:10   And when your Lord called to Moses: "Go to the people who are wicked."

26:11   "The people of Pharaoh. Will they not be righteous?"

26:12   He said: "My Lord, I fear that they would deny me."

26:13   "And my chest would become tight, and my tongue would not be able to express; so send for Aaron."

26:14   "And they have charges of a crime against me, so I fear they will kill me."

26:15   He said: "Indeed not! Go both of you with Our signs. I am with you listening."

26:16   "So both of you go to Pharaoh and say: 'We are messengers of the Lord of the worlds.'

26:17   'So send with us the Children of Israel.'"

26:18   He said: "Did we not raise you among us as a new born, and you stayed with us for many of your years?"

26:19   "And you did that deed you did, and you are of the rejecters."

26:20   He said: "I did it, and I was of those misguided."

26:21   "So I ran away from you all, for I feared you. So my Lord granted me judgment, and made me of the messengers."

26:22   "And is it a favor that you taunt me with, so you could continue to enslave the Children of Israel?"

26:23   Pharaoh said: "And what is the Lord of the worlds?"

26:24   He said: "The Lord of the heavens and the earth and what is between them, if you are aware."

26:25   He said to those around him: "Do you hear that?"

26:26 He said: "Your Lord and the Lord of your fathers of old!"

26:27 He said: "This messenger of yours who has been sent to you is crazy!"

26:28 He said: "The Lord of the east and the west, and what is between them, if you comprehend."

26:29 He said: "If you take a god other than me, then I will put you among the prisoners."

26:30 He said: "What if I brought you proof?"

26:31 He said: "Then bring it forth if you are of the truthful ones."

26:32 So he cast his staff, then it manifested into a serpent.

26:33 And he drew out his hand, then it became white to the onlookers.

26:34 He said to the commanders around him: "This is a knowledgeable magician!"

26:35 "He wants to bring you out of your land with his magic. So what will you decide?"

26:36 They said: "Delay him and his brother, and send gatherers to the cities."

26:37 "They will come to you with every knowledgeable magician."

26:38 So the magicians were gathered to a designated day.

26:39 And it was said to the people: "Will you also gather?"

26:40 "Perhaps we can follow the magicians if they are the winners."

26:41 So when the magicians came, they said to Pharaoh: "We should be rewarded if we are the winners."

26:42 He said: "Yes, and you shall also be near to me."

26:43 Moses said to them: "Cast down what it is you will cast."

26:44 So they cast down their ropes and staffs and they said: "By the might of Pharaoh, we will be the winners."

26:45 So Moses cast down his staff, then it was eating up what they fabricated!

26:46 So the magicians went down prostrating.

26:47 They said: "We believe in the Lord of the worlds!"

26:48 "The Lord of Moses and Aaron."

26:49 He said: "Have you believed unto him before I permitted you? He is surely your great one who has taught you magic. So you shall come to know, I will cut off your hands and feet from alternate sides, and I will crucify you all."

26:50 They said: "There is no worry, for we are all returning to our Lord."

26:51 "We hope that our Lord will forgive us our wrongdoings, for we were the first to believe."

26:52 And We inspired Moses: "Take away My servants, for you will be followed."

26:53 So Pharaoh sent gatherers to the cities.

26:54 "These are but a small band."

26:55 "And they have done what has enraged us."

26:56 "And we are all gathered and forewarned."

26:57 So, We evicted them out of gardens and springs.

26:58 And treasures and an honorable station.

26:59 As such, We gave it to the Children of Israel.

26:60 So they were pursued at sunrise.

26:61 But when the two groups saw each other, the companions of Moses said: "We are caught!"

26:62 He said: "No, my Lord is with me and He will guide me."

26:63 So We inspired to Moses: "Strike the sea with your staff." So it split into two, each side like a great mountain.

26:64 And We then brought them to the other side.

26:65 And We saved Moses and all those with him.

26:66 Then We drowned the others.

26:67 In that is a sign, but most of them are not believers.

26:68 And your Lord is the Noble, the Merciful.

26:69 And recite to them the news of Abraham.

26:70 When he said to his father and his people: "What do you worship?"

26:71 They said: "We worship statues; thus we stay devoted to them."

26:72 He said: "Do they hear you when you call to them?"

26:73 "Or do they benefit you or harm you?"

26:74 They said: "No, but we found our fathers doing the same."

26:75 He said: "Do you see that which you have been worshipping."

26:76 "You and your fathers of old."

26:77 "They are enemies to me, except for the Lord of the worlds."

26:78 "The One who has created me, He will guide me."

26:79 "And He is the One who feeds me and gives me to drink."

26:80 "And if I am sick, He is the One who cures me."

26:81 "And the One who will make me die and then bring me to life."

26:82 "And the One whom I hope will forgive my mistakes on the Day of Judgment."

26:83 "My Lord, grant me judgment and join me with the good doers."

26:84 "And give me a tongue that is true for those who will follow."

26:85 "And make me of the inheritors of gardens of bliss."

26:86 "And forgive my father, for he was of those misguided."

26:87 "And do not disgrace me on the Day when they are resurrected."

26:88 "The Day when no money or sons can help."

26:89 "Except for he who comes to God with a pure heart."

26:90 And Paradise was made near for the righteous.

26:91 And Hell was displayed for the wrongdoers.

26:92 And it was said to them: "Where is what you used to worship?"

26:93 "Without God; can they help you or help themselves?"

26:94 So they were thrown in it on their faces, them and the wrongdoers.

26:95   And all the soldiers of Satan.

26:96   They said, while they were disputing therein:

26:97   "By God, we were clearly misguided."

26:98   "For we equated you with the Lord of the worlds!"

26:99   "And none misled us except the criminals."

26:100 "So we have none to intercede for us."

26:101 "Nor a close friend."

26:102 "If only we could have another chance, we would be among the believers."

26:103 In that is a sign, but most of them are not believers.

26:104 And your Lord is the Noble, the Merciful.

26:105 The people of Noah disbelieved the messengers.

26:106 When their brother Noah said to them: "Will you not be righteous?"

26:107 "I am to you a trustworthy messenger."

26:108 "So be aware of God and obey me."

26:109 "And I do not ask you for any wage, for my reward is upon the Lord of the worlds."

26:110 "So be aware of God and obey me."

26:111 They said: "Shall we believe to you when the lowest type of people have followed you?"

26:112 He said: "And what knowledge do I have of what they used to do?"

26:113 "Their judgment is on my Lord, if you could know."

26:114 "And I will not drive away the believers."

26:115 "I am but a clear warner."

26:116 They said: "If you do not cease, O Noah, you will be of those who are stoned."

26:117 He said: "My Lord, my people have denied me!"

26:118 "So open between me and them a rift, and save me and those who are with me of the believers."

26:119 So We saved him and those who were with him in the charged ship.

26:120 Then after that We drowned the rest.

26:121 In that is a sign, but most of them are not believers.

26:122 And your Lord is the Noble, the Merciful.

26:123 'Aad denied the messengers.

26:124 For their brother Hud said to them: "Will you not be righteous?"

26:125 "I am to you a clear messenger."

26:126 "So be aware of God and obey me."

26:127 "And I do not ask you for any wage, for my reward is upon the Lord of the worlds."

26:128 "Do you build on every high place a symbol, for the sake of vanity!"

26:129 "And you take for yourselves strongholds, perhaps you will live forever?"

26:130 "And if you attack, you strike ruthlessly?"

26:131 "So be aware of God and obey me."

26:132 "And be aware of the One who provided you with what you know."

26:133 "He provided you with hoofed animals and sons."

26:134 "And gardens and springs."

26:135 "I fear for you the retribution of a great day."

26:136 They said: "It is the same whether you preach or do not preach."

26:137 "This is nothing except an invention by the people of old."

26:138 "And we are not going to be punished."

26:139 So they denied him, and We destroyed them. In that is a sign, but most are not believers.

26:140 And your Lord is the Noble, the Merciful.

26:141 Thamud denied the messengers.

26:142 For their brother Saleh said to them: "Will you not be righteous?"

26:143 "I am to you a clear messenger."

26:144 "So be aware of God and obey me."

26:145 "And I do not ask you for any wage, for my reward is upon the Lord of the worlds."

26:146 "Will you be left secure in that which you have here?"

26:147 "In gardens and springs."

26:148 "And green crops and palm trees laden with fruit."

26:149 "And you carve homes out of the mountains with great skill?"

26:150 "So be aware of God and obey me."

26:151 "And do not obey the command of the carefree."

26:152 "The ones who corrupt in the land and are not reformers."

26:153 They said: "You are but one of those bewitched!"

26:154 "You are but a mortal like us. So bring a sign if you are of the truthful ones."

26:155 He said: "This is a female camel, for her is a share of water, and for you is a share of water, each on an appointed day."

26:156 "And do not afflict her with harm, else the retribution of a great day will seize you."

26:157 But they slaughtered her, and they became regretful.

26:158 So the retribution took them. In that is a sign, but most of them are not believers.

26:159 And your Lord is the Noble, the Merciful.

26:160 The people of Lot denied the messengers.

26:161 For their brother Lot said to them: "Will you not be righteous?"

26:162 "I am to you a trustworthy messenger."

26:163 "So be aware of God and obey me."

26:164 "And I do not ask you for any wage, for my reward is upon the Lord of the worlds."

26:165 "Do you approach the males of the worlds?"

26:166 "And you leave what your Lord has created for you of mates? You are an intrusive people!"

26:167 They said: "If you do not cease O Lot, you will be among those driven out."

26:168 He said: "I am in severe opposition to your acts!"

26:169 "My Lord, save me and my family from what they do."

26:170 So We saved him and his entire family.

26:171 Except for an old woman who remained.

26:172 Then We destroyed the others.

26:173 And We rained upon them a rain. Miserable was the rain to those who had been warned.

26:174 In that is a sign, but most of them are not believers.

26:175 And that your Lord is the Noble, the Merciful.

26:176 The people of the Sycamore disbelieved the messengers.

26:177 For Shu'ayb said to them: "Will you not be righteous?"

26:178 "I am to you a trustworthy messenger."

26:179 "So be aware of God and obey me."

26:180 "And I do not ask you for any wage, for my reward is upon the Lord of the worlds."

26:181 "Give full measure and do not be of those who cause losses."

26:182 "And weigh with the balance that is straight."

26:183 "And do not defraud the people of their belongings, and do not venture into the land corrupting."

26:184 "And be aware of the One who has created you and the generations of old."

26:185 They said: "You are but one of those bewitched."

26:186 "And you are nothing but a mortal like us, and we think you are one of those who lie."

26:187 "So let pieces from the heaven fall upon us if you are of those who are truthful!"

26:188 He said: "My Lord is most aware of what you do."

26:189 But they denied him, so the retribution of the day of shadow took them. It was the retribution of a terrible day.

26:190 In that is a sign, but most of them are not believers.

26:191 And your Lord is the Noble, the Merciful.

26:192 And this is a revelation from the Lord of the worlds.

26:193 It was sent down with the trusted Spirit.

26:194 Upon your heart, so that you would be of the warners.

26:195 In a clear Arabic tongue.

26:196 And it is in the scriptures of old.

26:197 Was it not a sign for them that the scholars of the Children of Israel knew it?

26:198 And had We revealed it to some of those who did not know Arabic,

26:199 And he read it to them, they would not have believed in it.

26:200 As such, We diverted it from the hearts of the criminals.

26:201 They do not believe in it until they see the painful retribution.

26:202 So it will come to them suddenly, while they do not perceive it.

26:203 Then they would say: "Can we be given more time?"

26:204 Was it not their wish that Our punishment be hastened?

26:205 Do you see that if We gave them luxury for years.

26:206 Then what they were promised came to them.

26:207 All the luxury they were given will not avail them.

26:208 And We have not destroyed any town except after having warners.

26:209 By way of a reminder, and We were never unjust.

26:210 And it is not the devils who have brought this down.

26:211 Nor would they, nor could they.

26:212 They are blocked from overhearing.

26:213 So do not call upon any other god with God, else you will be with those punished.

26:214 And warn your closest kin.

26:215 And lower your wing for any who follow you of the believers.

26:216 But, if they disobey you, say: "I am innocent from what you do."

26:217 And put your trust in the Noble, the Merciful.

26:218 The One who sees you when you stand.

26:219 And your movements among those who prostrate.

26:220 He is the Hearer, the Knowledgeable.

26:221 Shall I inform you on whom the devils come down?

26:222 They come down on every sinful liar.

26:223 They claim to listen, but most of them are liars.

26:224 And the poets, are followed by the strayers.

26:225 Do you not see that they traverse in every valley.

26:226 And that what they say, is not what they do!

26:227 Except for those who believe, and do good works, and remember God greatly, and were victorious after they were wronged. As for those who did wrong, they will know which fate they will meet.

CHAPTER 27

27:0 In the name of God, the Almighty, the Merciful.

27:1 T'S, these are the signs of the Qur'an and a clear Book.

27:2 A guide and good news to the believers.

27:3 Those who hold the Connection, and contribute towards purification, and regarding the Hereafter they are certain.

27:4 As for those who do not believe in the Hereafter, We have made their work appear pleasing to them, so they walk around blind.

27:5 They will have the worst retribution, and in the Hereafter they are the biggest losers.

27:6 And you are receiving the Qur'an from One who is Wise, Knowledgeable.

27:7 And Moses said to his family: "I have seen a fire, I will bring you from there some news or I will bring you a burning piece so that you may be warmed."

27:8 So when he came to it he was called: "Blessed is the One at the fire and whoever is around it, and glory to God, Lord of the worlds."

27:9 "O Moses, it is I, God, the Noble, the Wise."

27:10 "And cast down your staff." So when he saw it vibrate as if it were a Jinn, he ran away and would not turn back. "O Moses, do not fear, for My messengers shall have no fear from Me."

27:11 "Except he who has done wrong. But then if he replaces the evil deed with good, then I am Forgiving, Merciful."

27:12 "And place your hand into your pocket; it will come out white with no blemish, one of nine signs to Pharaoh and his people; for they are a wicked people."

27:13 So when Our signs came to them for all to see, they said: "This is clearly magic!"

27:14 And they rejected them, while their souls knew, out of transgression and arrogance. So see how it ended for the wicked.

27:15 And We bestowed upon David and Solomon knowledge, and they both said: "Praise be to God who preferred us over many of His believing servants."

27:16 And Solomon inherited from David, and he said: "O people, we have been taught how to understand the speech of the creatures that fly, and we have been given from everything. This is indeed an evident grace."

27:17 And the soldiers of Solomon were gathered, comprising of mankind and Jinn and birds, for they were to be spread out.

27:18 Until they came to a valley of ants, a female ant said: "O ants, enter your homes else you will be crushed by Solomon and his soldiers while they do not notice."

27:19 He then smiled, amused by what she said. And he said: "My Lord, help me to be thankful for the blessings You have bestowed upon me and upon my parents, and that I may do good works that pleases You, and admit me by Your mercy with Your righteous servants."

27:20 And he inspected the birds, then said: "Why do I not see the hoopoe, or is he among those absent?"

27:21 "I will punish him severely, or I will kill him, else he should have a clear excuse."

27:22 But he did not stay away too long, then he said: "I know what you do not know, and I have come to you from Sheba with news which is certain."

27:23 "I found a woman was sovereign over them, and she was given all possessions, and she had a great throne."

27:24 "And I found her and her people prostrating to the sun instead of God! And the devil had made their works appear good to them, so he kept them away from the path, for they are not being guided."

27:25 "Will they not prostrate to God who brings out what is hidden in the heavens and the earth, and He knows what you hide and what you declare?"

27:26 "God, there is no god except He, the Lord of the supreme Throne."

27:27 He said: "We will see if you are being truthful or are one of those who lie."

27:28 "Take this letter of mine and cast it to them, then withdraw from them and observe what they respond with."

27:29 She said: "O commanders, a noble letter has been delivered to me."

27:30 "It is from Solomon, and it reads: 'In the name of God, the Almighty, the Merciful.'"

27:31 "'Do not be arrogant towards me and come to me as submitters.'"

27:32 She said: "O commanders, advise me in this matter of mine, for I will not take a decision until you give testimony."

27:33 They said: "We are a people of strength and mighty in power. But the decision is yours, so see what you will command."

27:34 She said: "When the kings enter a town they destroy it and make its most noble people humiliated. It is such that they do."

27:35 "And I will send to them a gift, then I will see with what the messengers will return."

27:36 So when they came to Solomon he said: "Are you providing me with wealth? What God has provided for me is far better than what He has given you. Now you are happy with your gift!"

27:37 "Go back to them. For we shall come to them with soldiers the like of which they have never seen, and we will drive them out humiliated, while they are feeble."

27:38 He said: "O commanders, which of you can bring me her throne before they come to me in submission?"

27:39 A powerful being from among the Jinn said: "I will bring it to you before you rise from your station. For I am strong and trustworthy."

27:40 And one who had knowledge from the Book said: "I will bring it to you before you blink." So when he saw it resting before him, he said: "This is from the grace of my Lord, so that He tests me whether I am thankful or whether I reject. As for he who is thankful, he is thankful for himself, and as for he who rejects, then my Lord is Rich, Bountiful."

27:41 He said: "Disguise her throne so we may see if she will be guided or if she will be of those who are not guided."

27:42 So when she came, it was said: "Is your throne like this?" She said: "It appears to be similar." "And we had the knowledge she did not, and we were submitters."

27:43 And she was prevented by that which she served besides God. She was of the people who were rejecters.

27:44 It was said to her: "Enter the palace." So when she saw it she thought there was a pool, and she uncovered her legs. He said: "It is a palace paved with crystal." She said: "My Lord, I have wronged myself; and I submit with Solomon to God, Lord of the worlds."

27:45 And We have sent to Thamud their brother Saleh: "You shall serve God." But they became two disputing groups.

27:46 He said: "My people, why do you hasten with evil ahead of good?

If you would only seek the forgiveness of God, perhaps you will receive mercy."

27:47 They said: "You have an ill omen with you and those with you." He said: "Your ill omen is with God, but you are a people who are being tested."

27:48 And in the city were nine ruffians who were causing corruption in the land, and they were not reforming.

27:49 They said: "Swear by God to one another that we will attack him and his family at night, and we will then say to his supporters: 'We did not witness who murdered his family, and we are being truthful.'"

27:50 And they schemed a scheme and We schemed a scheme, while they did not notice.

27:51 So see what the result of their planning was! We destroyed them and their people together.

27:52 So these are their homes, ruined, for what they transgressed. In that is a sign for a people who know.

27:53 And We saved those who believed and were righteous.

27:54 And Lot, when he said to his people: "Why do you commit immorality when you can clearly see?"

27:55 "You are approaching the men out of desire instead of the women! Indeed, you are an ignorant people."

27:56 But the reply of his people was that they said: "Expel the family of Lot from your town, for they are a people who make out to be pure!"

27:57 So We saved him and his family, except for his wife; We found her to be of those doomed.

27:58 And We rained down a rain upon them. Miserable was the rain of those warned.

27:59 Say: "Praise be to God, and peace be upon His servants whom He has selected." Is God better, or that which you set up?

27:60 The One who has created the heavens and the earth, and He sent down water from the sky for you, so We cause gardens to grow with it that are full of beauty. It is not your ability that causes the growth of its trees. Is there a god with God? No. But they are a people who ascribe equals!

27:61　The One who made the earth a habitat, and He made in it rivers and He made for it stabilizers, and He made between the two seas a partition. Is there a god with God? No. But most of them do not know.

27:62　The One who answers the distressed when he calls Him, and He removes the evil, and He makes you successors on the earth. Is there a god with God? Little do you remember!

27:63　The One who guides you in the darkness of the land and the sea, and He sends the winds to spread between the hands of His mercy. Is there a god with God? God be exalted above what they set up!

27:64　The One who initiates the creation then He returns it, and He provides for you from the sky and the land. Is there a god with God? Say: "Bring your proof if you are being truthful."

27:65　Say: "None in the heavens or the earth know the unseen except God. And they do not perceive when they will be resurrected."

27:66　No, they have no knowledge of the Hereafter. No, they are in doubt regarding it. No, they are blind to it.

27:67　And those who rejected said: "When we have become dust, as our fathers, shall we be brought out?"

27:68　"We have been promised this, both us and our fathers before. This is nothing except tales of old!"

27:69　Say: "Roam the earth and see how was the end of the criminals."

27:70　And do not be saddened for them, and do not be distraught for what they plot.

27:71　And they say: "When is this promise if you are truthful?"

27:72　Say: "Perhaps He is now sending your way some of that which you hasten."

27:73　And your Lord has given grace to the people, but most of them are not thankful.

27:74　And your Lord knows what is concealed in their chests and what they reveal.

27:75　And there is not a thing hidden in the heavens or the earth, but is in a clear record.

27:76   This Qur'an narrates to the Children of Israel most of that which they are in dispute over.

27:77   And it is a guidance and a mercy for the believers.

27:78   Your Lord decides between them by His judgment. And He is the Noble, the Knowledgeable.

27:79   So put your trust in God, for you are clearly on the truth.

27:80   You cannot make the dead hear, nor can you make the deaf hear the call when they turn their backs and flee.

27:81   Nor can you guide the blind from their misguidance. You can only make those who believe in Our revelations hear you, for they have submitted.

27:82   And when the sentence has fallen upon them, We will bring out for them a creature—of the earth—that speaks to them. Indeed, the people are unaware regarding Our signs.

27:83   And the Day We gather from every nation a party that denied Our revelations, then they will be driven.

27:84   Then, when they have come, He will say: "Have you denied My revelations while you had no explicit knowledge of them? What were you doing?"

27:85   And the punishment was deserved by them for what they transgressed; they shall not speak.

27:86   Did they not see that We made the night for them to reside in, and the day to see in? In that are signs for a people who have faith.

27:87   And on the Day when the horn is blown, then those in the heavens and the earth will be horrified, except for whom God wills. And all shall come to Him humbled.

27:88   And you see the mountains, you think they are solid, while they are passing by like the clouds. The making of God who perfected everything. He is Expert over what you do.

27:89   Whoever comes with a good deed will receive better than it, and from the terror of that Day they will be safe.

27:90   And whoever comes with the bad deed, their faces will be cast in Hell. Are you not being rewarded for what you used to do?

27:91 "I have been ordered to serve the Lord of this land, that He has made restricted, and to Him are all things, and I have been ordered to be of those who submit."

27:92 "And that I recite the Qur'an." He who is guided is guided for himself, and to he who is misguided, say: "I am but one of the warners."

27:93 Say: "Praise be to God, He will show you His signs and you will know them. And your Lord is not unaware of what you do."

CHAPTER 28

28:0 In the name of God, the Almighty, the Merciful.

28:1 T'SM.

28:2 These are the signs of the Book of Clarity.

28:3 We recite to you from the news of Moses and Pharaoh with fact, for a people who believe.

28:4 Pharaoh became mighty in the land, and he turned its people into factions; he oppressed a group of them by killing their children and raping their women. He was of those who corrupted.

28:5 And We wanted to help those who were oppressed in the land, and to make them leaders, and to make them the inheritors.

28:6 And to enable them in the land, and to show Pharaoh and Haamaan and their troops what they had feared.

28:7 And We inspired to Moses' mother: "Suckle him, and if you become fearful for him, then cast him in the running water, and do not fear nor grieve. We will return him to you and We will make him of the messengers."

28:8 Then the family of Pharaoh picked him up, so he would be an enemy to them and a source of sadness. Certainly, Pharaoh and Haamaan and their troops were wrongdoers.

28:9 And the wife of Pharaoh said: "A pleasure to my eye and yours, so do not kill him, perhaps he will benefit us or we may take him as a son;" while they did not perceive.

28:10 And the mind of Moses' mother became anxious, that she nearly revealed her identity. But We strengthened her heart, so that she would be of the believers.

28:11   And she said to his sister: "Follow his path." So she watched him from afar, while they did not notice.

28:12   And We forbade him from accepting all the nursing mothers. Then his sister said: "Shall I lead you to a household that can nurse him for you, and take good care of him?"

28:13   Thus, We returned him to his mother, so that she may be pleased and not be saddened, and to let her know that the promise of God is the truth. However, most of them do not know.

28:14   And when he reached his independence and was established, We gave him judgment and knowledge. We thus reward the good doers.

28:15   And he entered the city unexpectedly, without being noticed by the people. He found in it two men who were fighting, one was from his clan, and the other was from that of his enemy. So the one who was from his clan called on him for help against his enemy, whereby Moses punched him, killing him. He said: "This is from the work of the devil; he is an enemy that clearly misleads."

28:16   He said: "My Lord, I have wronged my soul, so forgive me." He then forgave him, for He is the Forgiver, the Merciful.

28:17   He said: "My Lord, for what blessings you have bestowed upon me, I will never be a supporter for the criminals."

28:18   So he spent the night in the city, afraid and watchful. Then the one who sought his help yesterday, was asking again for his help. Moses said to him: "You are clearly a trouble maker."

28:19   But when he was about to strike their mutual enemy, he said: "O Moses, do you want to kill me, as you killed that person yesterday? Obviously, you wish to be a tyrant on the earth; you do not wish to be of the righteous."

28:20   And a man, from the farthest part of the city, came running saying: "O Moses, the commanders are plotting to kill you, so leave immediately. I am giving you good advice."

28:21   He exited the city, afraid and watchful. He said: "My Lord, save me from the wicked people."

28:22   And as he traveled towards Midyan, he said: "Perhaps my Lord will guide me to the right path."

28:23 When he arrived at the watering hole of Midyan, he found a crowd of people watering, and he found two women waiting on the side. He said: "What is holding you back." They said: "We cannot draw water until the shepherds finish, and our father is an old man."

28:24 So he drew water for them, then he turned to a shaded area, and he said: "My Lord, I am poor, lacking any provisions You may have sent down."

28:25 So one of the two women approached him, shyly, and said: "My father invites you to reward you for watering for us." So when he came to him, and narrated to him the stories, he said: "Do not fear, for you have been saved from the wicked people."

28:26 One of the two women said: "O my father, hire him. For the best to be hired is one who is strong and honest."

28:27 He said: "I wish you to marry one of my two daughters, on condition that you work for me through eight pilgrimage periods; if you complete them to ten, it will be voluntary on your part. I do not wish to make this matter too difficult for you. You will find me, God willing, of the righteous."

28:28 He said: "It is then an agreement between me and you. Whichever period I fulfill, you will not be averse to either one. And God is entrusted over what we said."

28:29 So after Moses fulfilled his obligation and was traveling with his family, he saw a fire on the slope of the mount. He said to his family: "Stay here, I have seen a fire, perhaps I can bring you from there some news or a burning piece of the fire so that you may be warmed."

28:30 So when he reached it, he was called from the edge of the right side of the valley at the blessed area of the tree: "O Moses, it is I, God, Lord of the worlds."

28:31 "And cast down your staff." So when he saw it vibrate as if it were a Jinn, he turned around to flee and would not return. "O Moses, come forward and do not be afraid. You are of those who are safe."

28:32 "Place your hand into your pocket. It will come out white without any blemish, and fold your hand close to your side against fear. These are two proofs from your Lord, to Pharaoh and his commanders; for they are a wicked people."

28:33 He said: "My Lord, I have killed a person from them, so I fear that they will kill me."

28:34 "And my brother Aaron is more eloquent in speech than I. So send him with me to help and to confirm me. For I fear that they will deny me."

28:35 He said: "We will strengthen you with your brother, and We will provide you both with authority. Thus, they will not be able to touch either one of you. With Our signs, the two of you, along with those who follow you, will be the victors."

28:36 So when Moses went to them with Our clear signs, they said: "This is nothing but fabricated magic; nor did we hear of this from our fathers of old!"

28:37 And Moses said: "My Lord is fully aware of who has come with the guidance from Him, and who will have the best deal in the Hereafter. The wicked never succeed."

28:38 And Pharaoh said: "O commanders, I have not known of any god for you other than me. Therefore, O Haamaan, fire-up the bricks and make for me a high platform, so perhaps I may take a look at the god of Moses; though I think he is one of the liars."

28:39 And he and his soldiers were arrogant in the land without any right, and they thought that they would not be returned to Us.

28:40 So We took him and his soldiers, We cast them to the running waters. So see how was the end of the wicked!

28:41 We made them leaders, inviting to the Fire. And on the Day of Resurrection, they will not be supported.

28:42 And We made them followed by a curse in this world, and on the Day of Resurrection they will be despised.

28:43 We had given Moses the Book after We had destroyed the earlier generations; as an example for the people and a guidance and a mercy, perhaps they will take heed.

28:44 And you were not on the western slope when We decreed the command to Moses. You were not a witness.

28:45 And We established many generations, and many ages passed them by. And you were not living among the people of Midyan, reciting Our revelations to them. But We were to send messengers.

28:46 And nor were you on the side of the mount when We called. But it is a mercy from your Lord, so that you may warn a people who received no warner before you, perhaps they may take heed.

28:47　Thus, if any disaster strikes them as a consequence of their own deeds they cannot say: "Our Lord, if only You sent a messenger to us, so that we would follow Your revelations, and we would be of the believers."

28:48　But when the truth came to them from Us, they said: "If only he was given the same that was given to Moses!" Had they not rejected what was given to Moses before? They had said: "Two magicians assisting one another." And they said: "We reject all these things."

28:49　Say: "Then bring forth a book from God that is better than them in guidance so I may follow it, if you are truthful."

28:50　But if they fail to respond to you, then know that they follow only their desires. And who is more astray than he who follows his desire, without guidance from God? God does not guide the wicked people.

28:51　And We have delivered the message, perhaps they may take heed.

28:52　Those to whom We had given the Book before this, they will believe in it.

28:53　And if it is recited to them, they say: "We believe in it. It is the truth from our Lord. Indeed, we had submitted before it."

28:54　To these We grant twice the reward for that they have been patient. And they counter evil with good, and from Our provisions to them, they give.

28:55　And if they come across vain talk, they disregard it and say: "To us are our deeds, and to you are your deeds. Peace be upon you. We do not seek the ignorant."

28:56　You cannot guide whom you love. But it is God who guides whom He wills; and He is fully aware of those who receive the guidance.

28:57　And they said: "If we follow the guidance with you, we will be deposed from our land." Did We not establish for them a safe sanctuary, to which all kinds of fruits are offered, as a provision from Us? Indeed, most of them do not know.

28:58　And how many a town have We destroyed that had become unappreciative of its livelihood. So here are their dwellings, they remained uninhabited after them, except for a few. And We were the inheritors.

28:59 And your Lord does not destroy the towns until He sends to their mother a messenger who recites Our revelations to them. And We do not destroy the towns unless its people are wicked.

28:60 And anything that is given to you is only the materialism of this world, and its glitter. And what is with God is far better, and more lasting. Do you not comprehend?

28:61 Is one whom We promised a good promise, and it will come to pass, equal to one whom We provided with the goods of this life, then on the Day of Resurrection he is of those who will be summoned?

28:62 And on the Day when He calls upon them, saying: "Where are My partners whom you used to claim?"

28:63 Those who have deserved the sentence will say: "Our Lord, these are the ones we misled; we misled them only because we ourselves were misled. We seek to absolve ourselves to You, it was not us that they worshipped."

28:64 And it will be said: "Call upon your partners," but they will not respond to them. And they will see the retribution. If only they were guided!

28:65 On that Day, He will ask them and say: "What was the answer you gave to the messengers?"

28:66 They will be shocked by the news on that Day, they will be speechless.

28:67 As for the one who repents, believes, and does good works; perhaps he will be with the winners.

28:68 And your Lord creates what He wills, and He selects; it is not for them to select. Glory be to God, He is far above the partners they set up.

28:69 And your Lord knows what is concealed in their chests and what they declare.

28:70 And He is God, there is no god except He. To Him belongs all praise in the first and in the last, and judgment belongs with Him, and to Him you will be returned.

28:71 Say: "Have you noted: what if God made the night eternal, until the Day of Resurrection? Which god, other than God, can bring you with light? Do you not listen?"

28:72 Say: "Have you noted: what if God made the daylight eternal, until the Day of Resurrection? Which god, other than God, can provide you with night for you to reside in? Do you not see?"

28:73 And from His mercy is that He created for you the night and the day; that you may reside in it, and that you may seek of His provisions; and perhaps you may be thankful.

28:74 And the Day He will call them and say: "Where are My partners whom you had claimed?"

28:75 And We will extract from every nation a witness, then We will say: "Bring forth your proof." They will then realize that all truth belongs with God, and what they had invented will abandon them.

28:76 Qaroon was from among the people of Moses, but he betrayed them. And We gave him such treasures that the keys thereof were almost too heavy for the strongest person. His people said to him: "Do not glee, for God does not love the gleeful."

28:77 "And seek with the provisions bestowed upon you by God the abode of the Hereafter, and do not forget your share in this world, and do good as God has done good to you. And do not seek corruption in the land. God does not love the corrupters."

28:78 He said: "I have attained all this only because of my own knowledge." Did he not realize that God had annihilated before him generations that were much stronger than he, and greater in riches? The transgressors were not asked about their crimes.

28:79 Then he came out among his people draped in his ornaments. Those who preferred this worldly life said: "Oh, if only we were given similar to what Qaroon has been given. Indeed, he is very fortunate."

28:80 And those who were granted with knowledge said: "Woe to you! The reward from God is far better for those who believe and do good work. And none attains it except the steadfast."

28:81 We then caused the earth to swallow him and his mansion. He had no group that could protect him against God; nor would he be victorious.

28:82 And those who wished they were in his place the day before said: "Indeed it is God who provides or restricts for whoever He chooses from among His servants. Had it not been for the grace of God towards us, He could have caused the earth to swallow us as well. We now realize that the rejecters never succeed."

28:83 Such will be the abode of the Hereafter; We reserve it for those who do not seek prestige on the earth, nor corruption; and the ending will be for the righteous.

28:84 Whoever brings forth a good deed, he will receive a better reward than it. And whoever brings forth a sin then the retribution for their sins will be to the extent of their deeds.

28:85 Surely, the One who decreed the Qur'an to you will summon you to a predetermined appointment. Say: "My Lord is fully aware of who it is that brings the guidance, and who has gone astray."

28:86 Nor did you expect this Book to come your way; but this is a mercy from your Lord. Therefore, you shall not side with the rejecters.

28:87 Nor shall you be diverted from the revelations of God after they have come to you. And invite to your Lord. And do not be of the polytheists.

28:88 And do not call besides God any god, there is no god except He. Everything will fade away except His face. To Him is the judgment, and to Him you will be returned.

CHAPTER 29

29:0 In the name of God, the Almighty, the Merciful.

29:1 ALM.

29:2 Did the people think that they will be left to say: "We believe" without being put to the test?

29:3 We had tested those before them, so that God would distinguish those who are truthful and so that He would know the liars.

29:4 Or did those who sinned think that they would be ahead of Us? Miserable indeed is their judgment!

29:5 Whoever looks forward to meeting God, then the meeting of God will come. And He is the Hearer, the Knowledgeable.

29:6 And whoever strives is only striving for himself; for God is in no need of the worlds.

29:7 And those who believed and did good works, We will cancel their sins and We will reward them in the best for what they did.

29:8 And We instructed the human being to be good to his parents. But if they strive to make you set up partners with Me, then do not obey them. To Me are all your destinies, and I will inform you of what you used to do.

29:9 And those who believed and did good works, We will admit them with the righteous.

29:10 And from among the people are those who say: "We believe in God," but if he is harmed in the sake of God, he equates the persecution inflicted by the people with the punishment of God! And if a victory comes from your Lord, he says: "We were with you!" Is God not fully aware of what is in the chests of the worlds?

29:11 God is fully aware of those who believed, and He is fully aware of the hypocrites.

29:12 And those who rejected said to those who believed: "Follow our path and we will carry your mistakes." But they cannot carry anything from their mistakes, they are liars!

29:13 And they will carry their own burdens, and burdens with their burdens, and they will be asked on the Day of Resurrection regarding what they fabricated.

29:14 And We had sent Noah to his people, so he stayed with them one thousand years, less fifty calendar years. Then the flood took them while they were wicked.

29:15 So We saved him and the people on the ship, and We made it a sign for the worlds.

29:16 And Abraham when he said to his people: "Serve God and be aware of Him, that is better for you if only you knew."

29:17 "You are worshipping nothing except idols besides Him, and you are creating fabrications. Those that you worship besides God do not possess for you any provision, so seek with God the provision and serve Him and be thankful to Him; to Him you will return."

29:18 "And if you disbelieve, then nations before you have also disbelieved." The messenger is only required to deliver clearly.

29:19　Did they not observe how God initiates the creation then He returns it? All that for God is easy to do.

29:20　Say: "Roam the earth and observe how the creation was initiated. Thus God will establish the final creation. God is capable of all things."

29:21　"God will punish whom He wills and He will have mercy on whom He wills, and to Him you will return."

29:22　"And you will not be able to escape this fact, on the earth or in the heavens, nor do you have besides God any ally or victor."

29:23　And those who rejected the revelations of God and in meeting Him; those have forsaken My mercy; and they will have a painful retribution.

29:24　But the only response from his people was their saying: "Kill him, or burn him." But God saved him from the fire. In this are signs for a people who believe.

29:25　And he said: "You have only taken idols besides God so that you may have affection amongst yourselves in this worldly life. But then, on the Day of Resurrection, you will reject one another, and curse one another. Your destiny is Hell, and you will have no victors."

29:26　Lot believed with him and said: "I am emigrating to my Lord. He is the Noble, the Wise."

29:27　And We granted him Isaac and Jacob, and We made within his progeny the prophethood and the Book. And We gave him his reward in this world, and in the Hereafter he is among the righteous.

29:28　And Lot, when he said to his people: "You commit an immorality that no others in the world have done before!"

29:29　"You sexually approach men, and you commit highway robbery, and you bring all vice into your society." But the only response from his people was to say: "Bring us the retribution of God, if you are being truthful!"

29:30　He said: "My Lord, grant me victory over the wicked people."

29:31　And when Our messengers came to Abraham with good news, they said: "We are to destroy the people of such a town, for its people have been wicked."

29:32 He said: "But Lot is in it!" They said: "We are fully aware of who is in it. We will save him and his family, except his wife; she is of those doomed."

29:33 And when Our messengers came to Lot, they were mistreated, and he was embarrassed towards them. And they said: "Do not fear, and do not be saddened. We will save you and your family, except for your wife; she is of those doomed."

29:34 "We will send down upon the people of this town an affliction from the heaven for what wickedness they were in."

29:35 And We left remains of it as a clear sign for a people who comprehend.

29:36 And to Midyan was their brother Shu'ayb. He said: "O my people, serve God and seek the Last Day, and do not roam the earth corrupting."

29:37 But they denied him, so the earthquake took them; thus they became lifeless in their home.

29:38 And 'Aad and Thamud. Much was made apparent to you from their dwellings. The devil had adorned their works in their eyes, thus he diverted them from the path, even though they could see.

29:39 And Qaroon, and Pharaoh, and Haamaan; Moses went to them with clear proofs. But they became arrogant in the land, and they were not the first.

29:40 So each We took by his sins. Some of them We sent upon whom violent winds, and some of them were taken by the scream, and some of them We caused the earth to swallow, and some of them We drowned. God is not the One who wronged them; it is they who wronged themselves.

29:41 The example of those who take allies besides God is like the spider, who takes for itself a home; and the weakest home is the home of the spider, if only they knew.

29:42 God knows that what they are calling on besides Him is nothing. He is the Noble, the Wise.

29:43 Such are the examples We put forth for the people, but none comprehend except the knowledgeable.

29:44 God created the heavens and the earth with truth. In that is a sign for the faithful.

29:45   Recite what is inspired to you of the Book and hold the Connection, for the Connection prohibits immorality and vice; but certainly the remembrance of God is the greatest. God knows everything you do.

29:46   And do not argue with the people of the Book except in that which is better; except for those who are wicked among them; and say: "We believe in what was revealed to us and in what was revealed to you, and our god and your god is the same; to Him we submit."

29:47   And similarly, We have sent down to you the Book. Thus, those whom We have given the Book will believe in it. Also, some of your people will believe in it. The only ones who mock Our revelations are the rejecters.

29:48   You were not reciting any Book before this, nor were you writing one down by your hand. In that case, the doubters would have had reason.

29:49   In fact, it is a clear revelation in the chests of those who have been given knowledge. And it is only the wicked who doubt Our revelations.

29:50   And they said: "If only signs would come down to him from his Lord!" Say: "All signs are with God, and I am but a clear warner."

29:51   Is it not enough for them that We have sent down to you the Book that is being recited to them? In that is a mercy and a reminder for people who believe.

29:52   Say: "God is enough as a witness between me and you. He knows what is in the heavens and the earth. As for those who believe in falsehood and reject God, they are the losers."

29:53   And they hasten you for the retribution! If it were not for an appointed term, the retribution would have come to them. It will come to them suddenly, when they do not expect.

29:54   They hasten you for the retribution; while Hell surrounds the rejecters.

29:55   The Day will come when the retribution overwhelms them, from above them and from beneath their feet; and We will say: "Taste the results of what you used to do!"

29:56   O My servants who believe, My earth is spacious, so serve only Me.

29:57   Every soul will taste death, then to Us you will be returned.

29:58   And those who believe and do good works, We will settle them in mansions in Paradise, with rivers flowing beneath them, abiding therein. Excellent is the reward for the workers.

29:59   The ones who were patient, and put their trust in their Lord.

29:60   And many a creature does not carry its provision; God provides for it, and for you. He is the Hearer, the Knowledgeable.

29:61   And if you ask them: "Who has created the heavens and the earth, and commissioned the sun and the moon?" They will say: "God." Why then did they deviate?

29:62   God expands the provision for whoever He chooses from among His servants, and withholds it. God is fully aware of all things.

29:63   And if you ask them: "Who sends down water from the sky, thus reviving the land after its death?" They will say: "God." Say: "Praise be to God." But most of them do not comprehend.

29:64   And this worldly life is no more than distraction and play, while the abode of the Hereafter is the reality, if only they knew.

29:65   When they ride on a ship, they call on God, devoting the system to Him. But as soon as He saves them to the shore, they set up partners.

29:66   Let them reject what We have given them, and let them enjoy; for they will come to know.

29:67   Have they not seen that We have established a safe sanctuary, while all around them the people are in constant danger? Would they still believe in falsehood, and reject the blessings of God?

29:68   Who is more evil than he who fabricates lies and attributes them to God, or denies the truth when it comes to him? Is there not a place in Hell for the rejecters?

29:69   As for those who strive in Our cause, We will guide them to Our paths. For God is with the pious.

CHAPTER 30

30:0 In the name of God, the Almighty, the Merciful.

30:1 ALM.

30:2 The Romans have won.

30:3 At the lowest part on the earth. But after their victory, they will be defeated.

30:4 In a few more years. The decision before and after is for God, and on that day the believers will rejoice.

30:5 With the victory of God. God gives victory to whom He wishes; He is the Noble, the Merciful.

30:6 Such is the pledge of God, and God does not break His pledge, but most of the people do not know.

30:7 They only know the outside appearance of the worldly life; and regarding the Hereafter, they are ignorant.

30:8 Did they not reflect upon themselves? God did not create the heavens and the earth and what is between them except with truth and an appointed term. But most of the people are in denial regarding their meeting with their Lord.

30:9 Did they not roam the earth and see how it ended for those before them? They were more powerful than them, and they cultivated the land and they built in it far more than these have built, and their messengers came to them with the proofs. God was not to wrong them, but it was they who wronged themselves.

30:10 Then the end of those who did evil was evil, that is because they denied the signs of God, and they used to mock them.

30:11 God initiates the creation, then He repeats it, then to Him you will return.

30:12 And the Day when the Hour will be established, the criminals will be in despair.

30:13 And they did not have any intercessors from the partners they set up, and they will reject such partners.

30:14 And on the Day the Hour is established, they will be separated.

30:15 So, those who believed and did good works, they will be delighted in a luxurious place.

30:16 And as for those who rejected and denied Our revelations and the meeting of the Hereafter, they shall be brought forth for the retribution.

30:17 So glory be to God, when you retire and when you wake.

30:18 And to Him is all praise in the heavens and the earth, and in the evening and when you go out.

30:19 He brings the living out of the dead, and He brings the dead out of the living. And He revives the land after its death. And similarly you will be brought out.

30:20 And from His signs is that He created you from dust, then you became mortals, spreading out.

30:21 And from His signs is that He created for you mates from yourselves that you may reside with them, and He placed between you affection and mercy. In that are signs for a people who reflect.

30:22 And from His signs is the creation of the heavens and the earth, and the difference of your tongues and your colors. In that are signs for the world.

30:23 And from His signs is your sleep by night and day, and your seeking of His bounty. In that are signs for a people who listen.

30:24 And from His signs is that He shows you the lightning, giving you fear and hope, and He sends down water from the sky, and He revives the land with it after its death. In that are signs for a people who comprehend.

30:25 And from His signs is that the heavens and the earth will rise by His command. Then, when He calls you forth from the earth, you will come out.

30:26 And to Him is all that is in the heavens and the earth. All are dutiful to Him.

30:27 And He is the One who initiates the creation, then He repeats it, and this is easy for Him. And to Him is the highest example in the heavens and the earth. And He is the Noble, the Wise.

30:28 An example is put forth for you from among yourselves: are there any from among those who are committed to by your oath that are partners to you in what provisions We have given you that you become equal therein? Would you fear them as you fear each other? It is such that We clarify the revelations for a people who have sense.

30:29   No, those who were wrong followed their desires without knowledge. So who can guide he whom God misguides? And they will have no victors.

30:30   So set your face to the system of monotheism. It is the inclination that God has nurtured the people on. There is no changing in the creation of God. Such is the pure system, but most of the people do not know.

30:31   Turn to Him, and be aware of Him, and hold the Connection, and do not be of the polytheists.

30:32   From those who have divided their system and become sects, each group is happy with what it has.

30:33   And if harm afflicts the people, they call out sincerely to their Lord. But then, when He gives them a taste of His mercy, a group of them set up partners with their Lord!

30:34   So as to reject what We gave them. Enjoy then, for you will come to know.

30:35   Or have We sent down to them an authority, which speaks to them of that which they have set up?

30:36   And if We grant the people a taste of mercy, they become happy with it, but if evil afflicts them for what they have done, they become in despair!

30:37   Did they not see that God grants the provisions for whom He wills, and He is Able? In that are signs for a people who believe.

30:38   So give the relative his due, and the poor, and the wayfarer. That is best for those who seek the face of God, and they are the successful ones.

30:39   And any usury you have taken to grow from the money of the people, it will not grow with God. And any contribution that you have placed seeking the face of God, then those will be multiplied.

30:40   God is the One who has created you, then He provided for you, then He puts you to death, then He brings you to life. Is there any among the partners you set up that can do any of this? Be He glorified and exalted above what they set up.

30:41 Corruption has appeared in the land and the sea at the hands of the people by what they earn. He will make them taste some of what they have done, perhaps they will return.

30:42 Say: "Roam the earth and see how the end was for those before. Most of them were polytheists."

30:43 So set your face to the system which is straight, before a Day comes from God that none can avert. On that Day they shall be separated.

30:44 Whoever rejects, then he will suffer his rejection; and whoever does good works, then it is for themselves that they are preparing a good place.

30:45 So that He will reward those that believe and do good works from His grace. He does not love the rejecters.

30:46 And from His signs is that He sends the winds with glad tidings, and to give you a taste of His mercy, and so that the ships may sail by His command, and that you may seek of His bounty; perhaps you will be thankful.

30:47 And We have sent before you messengers to their people. So they came to them with clear proofs; then We took revenge on those who were criminals. And it is binding upon Us to grant victory to the believers.

30:48 God who sends the winds, so they raise clouds, and He spreads them in the sky as He wishes, then He turns them into joined pieces, then you see the rain drops come forth from their midst. Then when He makes them fall on whoever He wills of His servants, they rejoice!

30:49 Though just before He sent it down to them, they were in despair!

30:50 So look at the effects of the mercy of God, how He revives the land after its death. Such is the One who will revive the dead, and He is capable of all things.

30:51 And if We chose to send a wind and they see it turn yellow, they will continue to be rejecters after it.

30:52 You cannot make the dead listen, nor can you make the deaf hear the call when they have turned their backs.

30:53 Nor can you enlighten the blind from their straying; but you can only make those who believe in Our revelations listen, for they have submitted.

30:54 God is the One who has created you from weakness, then He made strength after the weakness, then He makes after the strength a weakness and grey hair. He creates what He wills and He is the Knowledgeable, the Capable.

30:55 And the Day the Hour is established, the criminals will swear that they have remained only for an hour! Thus they were deluded.

30:56 And those who were given knowledge and faith said: "You have remained according to the decree of God until the Day of Resurrection; so this is now the Day of Resurrection, but you did not know."

30:57 So on that Day, the excuses of those who transgressed will not help them, nor will they be allowed to return.

30:58 And We have put forth for the people in this Qur'an of every example. And if you come to them with a sign, those who rejected will say: "You are bringing falsehood!"

30:59 It is thus that God seals the hearts of those who do not know.

30:60 So be patient, for the promise of God is true, and do not be dissuaded by those who do not have certainty.

CHAPTER 31

31:0 In the name of God, the Almighty, the Merciful.

31:1 ALM.

31:2 These are the signs of the Book of Wisdom.

31:3 A guide and a mercy for the good doers.

31:4 Those who hold the Connection, and contribute towards purification and regarding the Hereafter they are certain.

31:5 These are on a guidance from their Lord, and they are the successful ones.

31:6 And from the people, there are those who will purchase a baseless narrative with which to mislead from the path of God without knowledge, and to make it a mockery. These will have a humiliating retribution.

31:7 And when Our revelations are recited to him, he turns away arrogantly as if he did not hear them, as if there is a deafness in his ears. So give him tidings of a painful retribution.

31:8 Those who believe and do good works, for them will be gardens of bliss.

31:9 Abiding therein, the promise of God is true. And He is the Noble, the Wise.

31:10 He created the heavens without pillars you can see. And He cast in the earth stabilizers so that it would not tumble with you, and He spread on it all kinds of creatures. And We sent down water from the sky, thus We caused to grow all kinds of good plants.

31:11 This is the creation of God, so show me what those besides Him have created? Indeed, the transgressors are far astray.

31:12 And We had given Luqmaan the wisdom: "You shall be thankful to God, and whoever is thankful is being thankful for his own good. As for whoever rejects, then God is Rich, Praiseworthy."

31:13 And Luqmaan said to his son, while he was advising him: "O my son, do not set up any partners with God; for setting up partners is an immense wrongdoing."

31:14 And We enjoined the human being regarding his parents. His mother bore him with hardship upon hardship, and his weaning takes two calendar years. You shall give thanks to Me, and to your parents. To Me is the final destiny.

31:15 If they strive to make you set up any partners besides Me, then do not obey them. But continue to treat them amicably in this world. You shall follow only the path of those who have sought Me. Ultimately, you all return to Me, then I will inform you of everything you have done.

31:16 "O my son, if it be anything, even the weight of a mustard seed, be it deep inside a rock, or be it in the heavens or the earth, God will bring it. God is Sublime, Expert."

31:17 "O my son, hold the Connection and advocate for good and prohibit vice, and be patient to what befalls you. These are the most honorable traits."

31:18 "And do not turn your cheek arrogantly from people, nor shall you walk the earth insolently; for God does not love the arrogant show off."

31:19 "And be humble in how you walk and lower your voice. For the harshest of all voices is the voice of the donkeys."

31:20 Did you not note that God has commissioned in your service what is in the heavens and what is in the earth, and He has showered you with His blessings, both apparent and hidden? Yet from the people are some who argue about God with no knowledge nor guidance nor enlightening Book.

31:21 And if they are told: "Follow that which God has sent down." They say: "No, we will follow what we found our fathers doing." What if the devil had been leading them to the agony of Hell?

31:22 And whoever submits himself completely to God, while he is righteous, indeed he has taken grasp of the strongest hold. And to God is the conclusion of all matters.

31:23 And whoever rejects, then do not be saddened by his rejection. To Us is their ultimate return, then We will inform them of what they had done. God is fully aware of what is in the chests.

31:24 We let them enjoy for a while, then We commit them to a severe retribution.

31:25 And if you ask them: "Who has created the heavens and the earth?" They will say: "God." Say: "Praise be to God." Yet, most of them do not know.

31:26 To God belongs everything in the heavens and the earth. God is the Rich, the Praiseworthy.

31:27 And if all the trees on the earth were made into pens, and the ocean were supplied by seven more oceans, the words of God would not run out. God is Noble, Wise.

31:28 Your creation and your resurrection is all like that of one soul. God is Hearer, Seer.

31:29 Did you not note that God merges the night into the day, and He merges the day into the night, and that He has commissioned the sun and the moon, each running to an appointed term; and that God is expert of everything you do?

31:30 That is because God is the truth, and that which they call on besides Him is falsehood, and that God is the Most High, the

Great.

31:31   Did you not note the ships sailing in the sea by the grace of God, so that He shows you some of His signs? In that are signs for every one who is patient, thankful.

31:32   And when waves surround them like mountains, they call on God, sincerely devoting the system to Him. But when He saves them to the shore, some of them return. None discard Our signs except those who are betrayers, rejecters.

31:33   O people, you shall reverence your Lord, and be concerned of a Day when a father cannot help his child, nor can a child help his father. Certainly, the promise of God is truth. Therefore, do not be deceived by this worldly life; and do not be deceived from God by arrogance.

31:34   With God is the knowledge regarding the Hour. And He sends down the rain, and He knows what is inside the wombs. No soul knows what it may gain tomorrow, nor does any soul know in which land it will die. God is Knowledgeable, Expert.

CHAPTER 32

32:0   In the name of God, the Almighty, the Merciful.

32:1   ALM.

32:2   The sending down of this Book, without a doubt, from the Lord of the worlds.

32:3   Or do they say: "He fabricated it!" No, it is the truth from your Lord, so that you may warn a people who never received a warner before you, in order that they may be guided.

32:4   God is the One who has created the heavens and the earth, and what is between them in six days, then He settled upon the Throne. You do not have besides Him any lord, nor intercessor. Will you not then remember?

32:5   He arranges matters from the heaven to the earth, then it ascends to Him in a day which is equivalent to one thousand of the years which you count.

32:6   Such is the Knower of the unseen and the seen; the Noble, the Merciful.

32:7   The One who perfected everything He created and He began the creation of the human being from clay.

32:8   Then He made his offspring from a structure derived from a lowly liquid.

32:9   Then He evolved him, and blew into him from His Spirit. And He made for you the hearing, the eyesight, and the minds; rarely are you thankful.

32:10   And they said: "When we are buried in the ground, will we be created anew?" Indeed, they reject the meeting of their Lord.

32:11   Say: "Your lives will be terminated by the angel of death that has been assigned to you, then to your Lord you will be returned."

32:12   And if only you could see the criminals when they bow down their heads before their Lord: "Our Lord, we have now seen and we have heard, so send us back and we will do good. We are believers!"

32:13   And if We had wished, We could have given every soul its guidance, but the sentence from Me has taken effect, that I will fill Hell with the Jinn and people all together.

32:14   So taste the consequences of your forgetting this Day; for We have now forgotten you. And taste the eternal retribution in return for what you used to do.

32:15   The only people who believe in Our revelations are those whom when they are reminded by them, they fall prostrating, and they glorify the praise of their Lord, and they are not arrogant.

32:16   Their sides readily forsake their beds, to call on their Lord out of fear and hope, and from Our provisions to them they give.

32:17   No person knows what is being hidden for them of joy, as a reward for what they used to do.

32:18   Is one who is a believer the same as one who is wicked? They are not the same.

32:19   As for those who believe and do good works, for them are eternal gardens as an abode for what they used to work.

32:20   And as for those who were wicked, their abode is the Fire. Every time they try to leave it, they will be put back in it, and it will be said to them: "Taste the retribution of the Fire which you used to deny."

32:21 And We will let them taste the worldly retribution before the greater retribution, perhaps they will return.

32:22 And who is more wicked than he who is reminded of the revelations of his Lord, then he turns away from them? We will exact a punishment from the criminals.

32:23 And We have given Moses the Book; so do not be in any doubt about meeting Him; and We made it a guide for the Children of Israel.

32:24 And We made from them leaders who guided in accordance with Our commandment, for they were patient and had certainty regarding Our revelations.

32:25 Your Lord will separate between them on the Day of Resurrection regarding that which they disputed in.

32:26 Is it not a guide for them how many generations We have annihilated before them in whose dwellings they walk? In that are signs. Do they not listen?

32:27 Have they not seen that We drive the water to the barren lands, and produce with it crops to feed their hoofed animals, and themselves? Do they not see?

32:28 And they say: "When is this victory, if you are being truthful?"

32:29 Say: "On the day of the victory, it will not benefit those who rejected if they believe, nor will they be given respite."

32:30 Therefore, turn away from them and wait, for they too are waiting.

CHAPTER 33

33:0 In the name of God, the Almighty, the Merciful.

33:1 O prophet, you shall be aware of God, and do not obey the rejecters and the hypocrites. God is Knowledgeable, Wise.

33:2 And follow what is being inspired to you by your Lord. God is fully aware of all that you do.

33:3 And put your trust in God. God suffices as an advocate.

33:4 God did not make any man with two hearts in his body. Nor did He make your wives whom you make estranged to be your mothers. Nor did He make your adopted children to be your sons. Such is what you claim with your mouths, but God speaks the truth, and He guides to the path.

33:5   Call them by their fathers. That is more just with God. But if you do not know their fathers, then, as your brothers in the system and your patrons. There is no sin upon you for what mistake you made by it; but you will be responsible for what your hearts deliberately intend. God is Forgiver, Merciful.

33:6   The prophet is closer to the believers than themselves, and his wives are mothers to them. And the decree of God to the believers and the emigrants is that before they help their relatives, they have taken care of their own families first. Such has been decreed in the Book.

33:7   And when We took from the prophets their covenant. And from you, and from Noah, and Abraham, and Moses, and Jesus, son of Mary; We took from them a solemn covenant.

33:8   So that the truthful may be asked about their truthfulness, and He has prepared for the rejecters a painful retribution.

33:9   O you who believe, remember the grace of God upon you when soldiers attacked you and We sent upon them a wind and invisible soldiers. God is Seer of what you do.

33:10   For they came from above you, and from beneath you; and your eyes were terrified, and the hearts reached to the throat, and you harbored doubts about God.

33:11   That is when the believers were truly tested; they were severely shaken up.

33:12   And the hypocrites and those who have a sickness in their hearts said: "God and His messenger promised us nothing but delusion!"

33:13   And a group of them said: "O people of Yathrib, there is no station for you, so come back." And a small party of them sought permission from the prophet, saying: "Our homes are exposed," while they were not exposed. They just wanted to flee.

33:14   And if the enemy had entered at them from all sides, and then they were asked to betray, they would do so with very little hesitation.

33:15   And indeed they had pledged to God before this that they would not turn around and flee; and making a pledge to God brings great responsibility.

33:16 Say: "It will not benefit you to flee away from death or from being killed, for you will only have the enjoyment for a short while."

33:17 Say: "Who can protect you from God if He intends to harm you, or He intends any blessing for you?" They will never find besides God any ally or victor.

33:18 God already knows which of you are the hinderers, and those who say to their brothers: "Come and stay with us." Rarely do they mobilize for battle.

33:19 They are miserable towards you. Then, when fear comes, you see their eyes rolling, as if death had already come to them. But once the fear is gone, they lash out at you with sharp tongues. They are miserable towards doing any good. These have not believed, so God nullifies their works. This is easy for God to do.

33:20 They thought that the Confederates had not yet mobilized. And if the Confederates do appear, they wish that they were out with the Nomads, seeking out news for you. Even if they were among you, they would not have fought except very little.

33:21 Indeed, in the messenger of God a good example has been set for you for he who seeks God and the Last Day and thinks constantly about God.

33:22 And when the believers saw the Confederates, they said: "This is what God and His messenger have promised us, and God and His messenger are truthful." This only increased their faith and their submission.

33:23 From among the believers are men who fulfilled their pledge to God. Thus, some of them have passed away, while some are still waiting; but they never altered in the least.

33:24 That God may recompense the truthful for their truthfulness, and punish the hypocrites if He so wills, or accepts their repentance. God is Forgiver, Merciful.

33:25 And God drove back those who disbelieved with their rage, they left empty handed. God thus spared the believers any fighting. God is Powerful, Noble.

33:26 And He also brought down those who helped support them from among the people of the Book from their secure positions, and He threw terror into their hearts. Some of them you killed, and some you took captive.

33:27 And He made you inherit their lands, and their homes, and their money, and lands you had never stepped on; and God is able to do all things.

33:28 O prophet, say to your wives: "If you are seeking this worldly life and its vanities, then come, I will make a provision for you and release you in an amicable manner."

33:29 "But if you are seeking God and His messenger, and the abode of the Hereafter, then God has prepared for the righteous among you a great reward."

33:30 O women of the prophet, if any of you commits evident immorality, then her retribution will be doubled. This is easy for God to do.

33:31 And any of you who is dutiful to God and His messenger, and does good works, We will grant her double the recompense, and We have prepared for her a generous provision.

33:32 O women of the prophet, you are not like any other women. If you are righteous, then do not speak too softly, lest those with disease in their hearts will move with desire; you shall speak in an honorable manner.

33:33 You shall be content in your homes, and do not show off like in the old days of ignorance. You shall hold the Connection, and contribute towards purification, and obey God and His messenger. God wishes to remove foulness from you, O people of the House, and to purify you a full purification.

33:34 And recall all that is being recited in your homes of the revelations of God and the wisdom. God is Sublime, Expert.

33:35 Surely, the submitting males, and the submitting females, the believing males, and the believing females, the devout males, and the devout females, the truthful males, and the truthful females, the patient males, and the patient females, the humble males, and the humble females, the charitable males, and the charitable females, the fasting males, and the fasting females, the males who maintain their chastity, and the females who maintain, and the males who commemorate God frequently, and the females who commemorate; God has prepared for them a forgiveness and a great recompense.

33:36 It is not for a believing male or believing female, if God and His messenger issue any command, that they have any choice in their decision. And anyone who disobeys God and His messenger, he has gone far astray.

33:37 And you said to the one who was graced by God, and graced by you: "Keep your wife and reverence God," and you hid inside yourself what God wished to proclaim. And you were concerned with the people, while God was more deserving that you be concerned with. So when Zayd ended his relationship with his wife, We had you marry her, to establish that there is no wrongdoing for the believers in marrying the wives of their adopted sons if their relationship is ended. And the command of God is always done.

33:38 There is no blame on the prophet in doing anything that God has decreed upon him. Such was the way of God with the people of old. And the command of God is a determined duty.

33:39 Those who deliver the messages of God, and are concerned towards Him, and they are not concerned towards anyone except God. God suffices as a Reckoner.

33:40 Mohammed is not the father of any of your men, but he is the messenger of God and the seal of the prophets. And God is fully aware of all things.

33:41 O you who believe, you shall remember God frequently.

33:42 And glorify Him morning and evening.

33:43 He is the One who connects upon you, along with His angels, to bring you out of darkness and into the light. And He is ever Merciful towards the believers.

33:44 Their greeting the Day they meet Him is: "Peace" and He has prepared for them a generous recompense.

33:45 O prophet, We have sent you as a witness, and a bearer of good news, and a warner.

33:46 Inviting to God, with His permission, and an illuminating lamp.

33:47 And give good news to the believers, that they have deserved from God a great blessing.

33:48 And do not obey the rejecters and the hypocrites, and ignore their insults, and put your trust in God; for God suffices as an advocate.

33:49 O you who believe, if you marry the believing females, then divorce them before having intercourse with them, then there is no interim required of them. You shall compensate them, and let them go in an amicable manner.

33:50   O prophet, We have made permissible for you the wives to whom you have already given their dowries, and the one committed to by your oath, as granted to you by God; and the daughters of your paternal uncle, and the daughters of your paternal aunts, and the daughters of your maternal uncle, and the daughters of your maternal aunts—those who emigrated with you. Also, the believing woman who had decreed herself to the prophet, the prophet may marry her if he wishes, as a privilege given only to you and not to the believers. We have already decreed their rights in regard to their spouses and those who are committed to by their oath. This is to spare you any hardship. God is Forgiver, Merciful.

33:51   You may postpone whom you will of them, and you may receive whom you will. And whomsoever you seek of those whom you have set aside then there is no sin upon you. Such is best that they may be comforted and not grieve, and that they may all be pleased with what you give them. And God knows what is in your hearts. And God is Knowledgeable, Compassionate.

33:52   No women are permissible to you beyond this, nor that you change them for other wives, even though you may be attracted by their beauty, except what is committed to by your oath. And God is Watcher over all things.

33:53   O you who believe, do not enter the homes of the prophet unless you are invited to a meal, without you forcing such an invitation. But if you are invited, you may enter. And when you finish eating, you shall leave, without staying to wait for a narrative. This used to bother the prophet, and he was shy to tell you. But God does not shy away from the truth. And if you ask his wives for something, ask them from behind a veil. This is purer for your hearts and their hearts. And it is not for you to harm the messenger of God, nor that you should marry his wives after him. This is indeed a gross offence with God.

33:54   If you reveal anything, or hide it, God is fully aware of all things.

33:55   There is no sin upon them before their fathers, or their sons, or their brothers, or the sons of their brothers, or the sons of their sisters, or their women, or those who are committed to by their oath. And be aware of God, for God is witness over all things.

33:56   God and His angels connect upon the prophet. O you who believe, you shall connect upon him, and comply completely.

33:57 Surely those who harm God and His messenger, God will curse them in this world and in the Hereafter; and He has prepared for them a shameful retribution.

33:58 And those who harm the believing males and the believing females, with no just reason, they have brought upon themselves a slander and a gross sin.

33:59 O prophet, tell your wives, your daughters, and the women of the believers that they should lengthen upon themselves their outer garments. That is better so that they will not be recognized and not harmed. God is Forgiver, Merciful.

33:60 If the hypocrites and those with disease in their hearts and those who spread lies in the city do not refrain, then We will let you overpower them, then they will not be able to remain as your neighbors except for a short while.

33:61 They are cursed wherever they are engaged, and they are taken and killed in numbers.

33:62 This is the way of God with those who have passed away before, and you will not find any change in the way of God.

33:63 The people ask you regarding the Hour. Say: "Its knowledge is with God. And for all that you know the Hour may be near!"

33:64 God has cursed the rejecters, and He has prepared for them Hell.

33:65 Abiding therein eternally. They will find no ally, or victor.

33:66 On the Day when their faces will be turned over in the Fire, they will say: "Oh, we wish we had obeyed God, and obeyed the messenger."

33:67 And they will say: "Our Lord, we have obeyed our leaders and our learned ones, but they misled us from the path."

33:68 "Our Lord, give them double the retribution, and curse them with a mighty curse."

33:69 O you who believe, do not be like those who harmed Moses, but then God cleared him of all they said, and he was honorable before God.

33:70 O you who believe, be aware of God and speak only the truth.

33:71 He will then direct your works, and forgive your sins. And whoever obeys God and His messenger has triumphed a great triumph.

33:72 We have offered the trust to the heavens and the earth, and the mountains, but they refused to bear it, and were fearful of it. But the human being accepted it; he was transgressing, ignorant.

33:73 So that God may punish the hypocrite males and the hypocrite females, and the polytheist males and the polytheist females. And God redeems the believing males and the believing females. And God is Forgiver, Merciful.

CHAPTER 34

34:0 In the name of God, the Almighty, the Merciful.

34:1 Praise be to God, to whom belongs everything in the heavens and the earth; and to Him is the praise in the Hereafter. He is the Wise, the Expert.

34:2 He knows what goes into the earth, and what comes out of it, and what comes down from the heaven, and what ascends into it. He is the Merciful, Forgiver.

34:3 And those who rejected said: "The Hour will not come to us!" Say: "Yes, by my Lord, it will come to you." He is the Knower of the unseen; not even the weight of an atom or less than that or greater can be hidden from Him, be it in the heavens or the earth. All are in a clear record.

34:4 That He may reward those who believe and do good works. To them will be a forgiveness and a generous provision.

34:5 As for those who sought against Our revelations to frustrate them, they will have a retribution of painful affliction.

34:6 And those that have been given knowledge will see that what has been sent down to you from your Lord is the truth, and that it guides to the path of the Noble, the Praiseworthy.

34:7 And those who rejected said: "Shall we lead you to a man who will tell you that after you are dismembered you will be created anew?"

34:8 "Has he invented a lie against God, or is there a madness in him?"

Indeed, those who do not believe in the Hereafter will be in a retribution and are far straying.

34:9 Have they not seen all that is before them and behind them, in the heaven and the earth? If We wished, We could cause the earth to swallow them, or cause pieces of the heaven to fall on them. In this is a sign for every obedient servant.

34:10 And We granted David blessings from Us: "O mountains, echo with him, and the birds." And We softened the iron for him.

34:11 That you may make armor, with perfect fittings. And work righteousness, for I am Seer of what you do.

34:12 And for Solomon the wind was given, traveling one month coming and one month going, and We caused a spring of tar to flow for him. And from among the Jinn are those that worked for him with the permission of his Lord; and any one of them who turns from Our commands, We shall cause him to taste the retribution of the Fire.

34:13 They made for him what he desired of enclosures, and images and pools of deep reservoirs, and heavy pots. "O family of David, work to give thanks." Only a few of My servants are thankful.

34:14 Then, when We decreed death for him, nothing informed them of his death until an earth worm kept eating from his staff, so when he fell down, the Jinn realized that if they had known the unseen, they would not have remained in the humiliating retribution.

34:15 There was for Sheba a sign in their homeland, with two gardens on the right and the left. "Eat from the provisions of your Lord, and be thankful to Him." A good land, and a forgiving Lord.

34:16 But they turned away, so We sent them a destructive flash flood, and We substituted their two gardens with two gardens of foul fruits, thorny plants, and a skimpy harvest.

34:17 We thus requited them for what they rejected. And We do not requite except the rejecter.

34:18 And We placed between them and between the towns that We had blessed, towns that were easy to see; and We measured the journey between them: "Travel in them by night and day in complete security."

34:19 But they said: "Our Lord, make the measure between our journeys longer," and they wronged themselves. So We made them narrations and We tore them into pieces. In this are signs for every person who is patient, thankful.

34:20 And Satan was correct in his assumptions of them, for they followed him, except for a group of the believers.

34:21 And he did not have any authority over them except that We might distinguish those who believed in the Hereafter from those who are doubtful about it. And your Lord is Keeper over all things.

34:22 Say: "Call on those whom you have claimed besides God. They do not possess even the weight of an atom in the heavens, or the earth. They possess no partnership therein, nor is there for Him any assistant among them."

34:23 "Nor will intercession be of any help with Him, except for whom He has already given leave." Until when the fear has subsided from their hearts, they ask: "What did your Lord say?" They will say: "The truth!" And He is the Most High, the Great.

34:24 Say: "Who provides for you from the heavens and the earth?" Say: "God! And either we or you are guided, or are clearly astray."

34:25 Say: "You will not be asked about our crimes, nor will we be asked for what you do."

34:26 Say: "Our Lord will gather us together then He will judge between us with the truth. He is the Judge, the Knowledgeable."

34:27 Say: "Show me those whom you have set up as partners with Him! No; He is but God, the Noble, the Wise."

34:28 And We have sent you to all people to be a bearer of good news, and as a warner; but most of the people do not know.

34:29 And they say: "When is this promise, if you are truthful?"

34:30 Say: "You have an appointed Day, which you cannot delay by one hour, nor advance."

34:31 And those who rejected have said: "We will not believe in this Qur'an, nor in what is already with him." And if you could but see these transgressors when they stand before their Lord, how they will accuse one another back and forth. Those who were weak will say to those who were mighty: "If it were not for you, we would have been believers!"

34:32 Those who were mighty will say to those who were weak: "Did we turn you away from the guidance after it had come to you? No, it was you who were criminals."

34:33 And those who were weak will say to those who were mighty: "No, it was your scheming night and day, when you commanded us to reject God and to set up equals to Him." And they are filled with regret when they see the retribution — and We will place shackles around the necks of those who rejected. Are they not being requited for what they used to do?

34:34 And We do not send a warner to any town, except its carefree ones would say: "We reject what you have been sent with."

34:35 And they said: "We have more wealth and more children, and we will not be punished."

34:36 Say: "My Lord gives provisions to whoever He wishes, or He restricts them, but most of the people do not know."

34:37 And it is not your money or your children that will bring you closer to Us, but only those who believe and do good work, they will receive double the reward for their works, and they will reside in the high dwellings in peace.

34:38 As for those who sought against Our revelations, they will be brought to the retribution.

34:39 Say: "My Lord gives provisions for whom He wishes of His servants and He restricts. And anything you spend, He will replace it; and He is the best of providers."

34:40 And on the Day when We gather them all, then We will say to the angels: "Was it you that these people used to serve?"

34:41 They will say: "Be You glorified. You are our Master, not they. No, they were serving the Jinn; most were believers to them."

34:42 So today, none of you can help or harm one another. And We will say to the transgressors: "Taste the retribution of the Fire that you used to deny."

34:43 And when Our clear revelations were recited to them, they said: "This is but a man who wants to turn you away from what your parents were worshiping." And they also said: "This is nothing except a fabricated lie." And those who disbelieved say of the truth when it has come to them: "This is nothing except evident magic!"

34:44   We had not given to them any books to study, nor did We send to them before you any warner.

34:45   And those before them had also denied, while they did not reach one tenth of what We had given them, but they denied My messengers; so how was My retribution?

34:46   Say: "I advise you to do one thing: that you stand to God, in twos and individually, then reflect." There is no madness in your friend, he is only a warner to you in the face of a severe retribution.

34:47   Say: "I have not asked you for any wage; for it will be your own. My wage is from God, and He is Witness over all things."

34:48   Say: "My Lord casts with the truth. He is the Knower of all secrets."

34:49   Say: "The truth has come; while falsehood can neither initiate anything, nor resurrect."

34:50   Say: "If I stray, then I stray to my own loss. And if I am guided, then it is because of what my Lord inspired to me. He is Hearer, Near."

34:51   And if you could but see, when they will be terrified with no escape, and they will be taken from a place that is near.

34:52   And they will say: "We believe in it!" But it will be far too late.

34:53   And they had rejected it in the past; and they made allegations regarding the unseen, from a place far off.

34:54   And a separation was made between them and what they had desired, as was done to their counterparts before. They have been in grave doubt.

CHAPTER 35

35:0   In the name of God, the Almighty, the Merciful.

35:1   Praise be to God, Initiator of the heavens and the earth; Maker of the angels as messengers with wings of two, and three, and four. He increases in the creation as He wishes. God is able to do all things.

35:2   Whatever mercy God opens for the people, none can stop it. And what He holds back none can send it other than He. And He is the Noble, the Wise.

35:3 O people, remember the blessings of God upon you. Is there any creator other than God who provides for you from the heaven and the earth? There is no god besides Him, so why do you deviate?

35:4 And if they deny you, then also messengers before you have been denied. And to God all matters are returned.

35:5 O people, the promise of God is the truth; therefore, do not be overwhelmed by this worldly life, and do not let arrogance overwhelm you from God.

35:6 The devil is an enemy to you, so treat him as an enemy. He only invites his faction to be the dwellers of Hell.

35:7 Those who reject will have a painful retribution, and those who believe and do good works they will have a forgiveness and a great reward.

35:8 As for he whose evil work is adorned for him so he sees it as being good; for God thus misguides whom He wills, and He guides whom He wills. So do not let yourself grieve over them. God is fully aware of what they are doing.

35:9 And God is the One who sends the winds so it stirs up a cloud, then We drive it to a land that is dead, and We revive with it the earth after it had died. Such is the resurrection.

35:10 Whoever is seeking dignity, then know that to God belongs all dignity. To Him ascend the good words, and they are elevated by the good deeds. And as for those who scheme evil, they will have a painful retribution, and their scheming will fail.

35:11 And God created you from dust, then from a seed, then He made you into pairs. And no female becomes pregnant, nor gives birth, without His knowledge. Nor does anyone have his life extended, or his life is shortened, except in a record. This is easy for God.

35:12 Nor are the two seas the same. One is fresh and palatable, good to drink, while the other is salty and bitter. And from each of them you eat tender meat, and you extract jewelry to wear. And you see the ships sailing through them, seeking His provisions; and perhaps you may be thankful.

35:13 He merges the night into the day, and He merges the day into the night. And He has commissioned the sun and the moon, each running for an appointed term. Such is God your Lord; to Him is the sovereignty. And as for those whom you pray to besides Him, they do not possess even the shell of a seed.

35:14   If you pray to them, they cannot hear you. And even if they hear you, they cannot respond to you. And on the Day of Resurrection, they will reject your partnership. And none can inform you like an Expert.

35:15   O people, you are the poor when it comes to God, while God is the Rich, the Praiseworthy.

35:16   If He wishes, He could do away with you and He would bring a new creation.

35:17   And this is not difficult for God.

35:18   And no bearer may carry the burden of another. And if one who is weighed down by his load calls on another to carry it, no part of it may be carried, even if it were a relative. You will only be able to warn those who are concerned towards their Lord while unseen, and they hold the Connection. And whoever contributes, is contributing for himself. And to God is the final destiny.

35:19   The blind and the seer are not equal.

35:20   Nor are the darkness and the light.

35:21   Nor are the shade and the heat.

35:22   Nor equal are the living and the dead; God causes whoever He wills to hear; and you cannot make those who are in the graves hear.

35:23   You are but a warner.

35:24   We have sent you with the truth as a bearer of good news and a warner. There was not a nation that a warner did not come to it.

35:25   And if they deny you, then those before them have also denied. Their messengers went to them with the proofs and the scriptures and the Book of Enlightenment.

35:26   Then I seized those who rejected; so how was My retribution!

35:27   Do you not see that God sends down water from the sky, thus We produce with it fruits of various colors? And of the mountains are peaks that are white, red, or some other color and intense black.

35:28   And from the people, and the creatures, and the hoofed animals, are various colors. Those concerned with God from among His servants are the most knowledgeable. God is Noble, Forgiving.

35:29 Surely, those who recite the Book of God and hold the Connection, and spend secretly and openly from what We have provided them, they are seeking a trade that can never lose.

35:30 He will give them their recompense, and He will increase them from His blessings. He is Forgiving, Thankful.

35:31 And what We inspired to you from the Book, it is the truth, affirming what is between his hands. God is Expert over His servants, Seer.

35:32 Then We inherited the Book to those whom We selected from Our servants. Subsequently, some of them wronged themselves, and others upheld it partly, while others were eager to work righteousness in accordance with the will of God; such is the great benefit.

35:33 They will enter gardens of delight, where they will be adorned with bracelets of gold and pearls, and their garments in it will be of silk.

35:34 And they will say: "Praise be to God who took away our sorrow. Our Lord is Forgiving, Thankful."

35:35 "The One who admitted us into the abode of eternal bliss, out of His grace. In it, no boredom touches us, nor does any fatigue."

35:36 As for those who have rejected, for them is the fire of Hell, where they do not terminate and die, nor is its retribution ever reduced for them. It is such that We requite every rejecter.

35:37 And they will scream in it: "Our Lord, let us out, and we will work righteousness instead of the works we used to do." Did We not give you a long life so that he who would remember would take heed, and a warner came to you? Therefore, taste, for the transgressors will have no supporter.

35:38 God knows the unseen of the heavens and the earth. He is knowledgeable of what is even in the chests.

35:39 He is the One who made you successors on the earth. So, whoever rejects, then to him is his rejection. And the rejection of the rejecters only increases the abhorrence of their Lord towards them. The rejection of the rejecters only increases their loss.

35:40 Say: "Do you see the partners whom you have called on besides

God? Show me what they have created on the earth. Or do they possess any partnership in the heavens?" Or have We given them a book wherein they are taking knowledge from it? Indeed, what the transgressors promise one another is no more than arrogance.

35:41 God is the One who holds the heavens and the earth, lest they cease to exist. And they would certainly cease to exist if anyone else were to hold them after Him. He is Compassionate, Forgiving.

35:42 And they swore by God in their strongest oaths, that if a warner came to them, they would be the most guided of all nations, but when a warner came to them, it only increased their aversion!

35:43 Arrogance on the earth, and evil scheming. And the evil schemes only backfire on those who scheme them. Were they expecting anything different from the ways used on the people of the past? You will not find any change in the way of God, and you will not find any bypass to the way of God.

35:44 Did they not roam the earth and note how was the consequence for those who were before them? And they were even more powerful than they in strength. But nothing can inhibit God be it in the heavens, or the earth. He is Knowledgeable, Omnipotent.

35:45 And if God were to punish the people for what they have earned, He would not leave a single creature standing. But He delays them to an appointed term. So, when their time comes, then God is Seer of His servants.

CHAPTER 36

36:0 In the name of God, the Almighty, the Merciful.

36:1 YS.

36:2 And the Qur'an of wisdom.

36:3 You are one of the messengers.

36:4 Upon a straight path.

36:5 The revelation of the Most Honorable, the Merciful.

36:6 To warn a people whose fathers were not warned, for they are unaware.

36:7 The sentence has been deserved by most of them, for they do not believe.

36:8 We have placed shackles around their necks, up to their chins, so that they are forced in place.

36:9 And We have placed a barrier in front of them, and a barrier behind them, thus We shielded them so they cannot see.

36:10 And whether you warn them or do not warn them, they will not believe.

36:11 You can only warn him who follows the reminder, and is concerned towards the Almighty while unseen. Give him good news of forgiveness and a generous reward.

36:12 It is indeed Us who resurrect the dead, and We record what they have done and left behind. And everything We have counted in a clear guide.

36:13 And put forth for them the example of the people of the town, when the messengers came to it.

36:14 Where We sent two to them, but they disbelieved in them, so We supported them with a third one, thus they said: "We are messengers to you."

36:15 They said: "You are but mortals like us, and the Almighty did not send down anything, you are only telling lies."

36:16 They said: "Our Lord knows that we have been sent to you."

36:17 "And we are only required to give a clear delivery."

36:18 They said: "We have welcomed you better than you deserve. If you do not cease, we will stone you, and you will receive a painful retribution from us!"

36:19 They said: "Keep your welcome with you, for you have been reminded. Indeed, you are a transgressing people."

36:20 And from the farthest part of the city, a man came running, saying: "O my people, follow the messengers."

36:21 "Follow those who do not ask you for any wage, and are guided."

36:22 "And why should I not serve the One who initiated me, and to Him is your ultimate return?"

36:23 "Shall I take gods besides Him? If the Almighty intends any harm for me, their intercession cannot help me in the least, nor can they save me."

36:24 "Then I would be clearly astray."

36:25 "I have believed in your Lord, so listen to me!"

36:26 It was said: "Enter Paradise." He said "Oh, how I wish if only my people knew!"

36:27 "Of what my Lord has forgiven me, and made me of the honored ones."

36:28 And We did not send down upon his people after him soldiers from the heaven; for there was no need to send them down.

36:29 For all it took was one scream, whereupon they were stilled.

36:30 What sorrow for the servants. For every time a messenger went to them, they would mock him.

36:31 Did they not see how many generations We destroyed before them, do they not go back to them?

36:32 And how every one of them will be summoned before Us.

36:33 And a sign for them is the dead land, We revive it and produce from it seeds from which they eat.

36:34 And We made in it gardens of date palms, and grapes, and We cause springs to gush forth therein.

36:35 So that they may eat from its fruits, and what they manufacture with their own hands. Would they be thankful?

36:36 Praise be to the One who has created all pairs from what the earth sprouts out and from themselves, and from what they do not know.

36:37 And a sign for them is the night, We strip the daylight from it, whereupon they are in darkness.

36:38 And the sun runs to a specific destination, such is the design of the Noble, the Knowledgeable.

36:39 And the moon We have measured it to appear in stages, until it returns like an old palm sheath.

36:40 The sun is not required to overtake the moon, nor will the night precede the day; each of them is swimming in its own orbit.

36:41 And a sign for them is that We carried their ancestors on the charged ship.

36:42 And We created for them of its similarity, to ride in.

36:43 And if We wished, We could drown them, so that their screaming would not be heard, nor could they be saved.

36:44 Except through a mercy from Us, and as an enjoyment for awhile.

36:45 And when they are told: "Be aware of your present and your past, that you may attain mercy."

36:46 And no matter what sign comes to them from the signs of their Lord, they turn away from it.

36:47 And when they are told: "Spend from what God has provisioned you." Those who reject say to those who believe: "Shall we feed those whom God could feed, if He so willed? You are clearly misguided!"

36:48 And they say: "When is this promise to come, if you are truthful?"

36:49 They will not realize it when one scream overwhelms them, while they dispute.

36:50 They will not even be able to leave a will, nor will they be able to return to their people.

36:51 And the horn will be blown, whereupon they will rise from the graves massing towards their Lord.

36:52 They will say: "Woe to us! Who has resurrected us from our resting place? This is what the Almighty had promised; and the messengers were truthful!"

36:53 It only took one scream, whereupon they are summoned before Us.

36:54 On this Day, no soul will be wronged in the least. You will be recompensed precisely for whatever you did.

36:55 The dwellers of Paradise will be, on that Day, joyfully busy.

36:56 Both them and their spouses, they will be shaded, reclining on raised couches.

36:57 They will have fruits therein; and they will have all they ask for.

36:58 Saying of: "Peace" from a Merciful Lord.

36:59 "As for you, O criminals, you are singled out."

36:60 "Did I not pledge to you, O Children of Adam, that you should not serve the devil for he is your most ardent enemy?"

36:61 "And that you should serve Me? That is a straight path."

36:62 "He has misled mountain loads of you. Did you not comprehend?"

36:63 "This is Hell that you have been promised!"

36:64 "Burn in it today, as a consequence of your rejection."

36:65 Today, We shall cease their mouths, and their hands will speak to Us, and their feet will bear witness to everything they had done.

36:66 And if We wished, We can blind their eyes, and they would race towards the path, but how would they see?

36:67 And if We wished, We can freeze them in their place; thus, they can neither move forward, nor go back.

36:68 And for whoever We grant a long life, We weaken him in body. Do they not comprehend?

36:69 And We did not teach him poetry, nor does he need it. This is a reminder and a clear Qur'an.

36:70 To warn those who are alive, and so that the retribution will be deserved by the rejecters.

36:71 Did they not see that We created for them with Our own hands hoofed animals which they own?

36:72 And they were subdued by Us for them. So some they ride, and some they eat.

36:73 And they have benefits in them, and to drink. Would they not be thankful?

36:74 And they have taken besides God other gods, perhaps they will help them!

36:75 They cannot help them; while they are soldiers for them.

36:76 So do not be saddened by what they say. We are fully aware of what they conceal and what they declare.

36:77 Has the human being not seen that We have created him from a seed, but he then becomes a clear opponent?

36:78   And he puts forth an example for Us, while forgetting his own creation! He says: "Who can resurrect the bones while they are dust?"

36:79   Say: "The One who has made them in the first place will resurrect them. He is fully aware of every creation."

36:80   The One who initiated for you a forest fire, by which you learned to light.

36:81   Is not the One who has created the heavens and the earth able to create the like of them? Yes indeed; He is the Creator, the Knowledgeable.

36:82   His command, when He wants anything, is to say to it: 'Be,' and it is.

36:83   Therefore, praise be to the One in whose Hand is the sovereignty of all things, and to Him you will be returned.

CHAPTER 37

37:0   In the name of God, the Almighty, the Merciful.

37:1   By the columns in formation.

37:2   By the callers as they call.

37:3   By the remembrance which follows.

37:4   Your god is indeed One.

37:5   The Lord of the heavens and the earth, and what lies between them, and the Lord of the sunrises.

37:6   We have adorned the lower heaven with the decoration of planets.

37:7   And to guard against every rebellious devil.

37:8   They cannot listen to the command up high; and they are bombarded from every side.

37:9   Outcasts; they will have an eternal retribution.

37:10   Any of them who snatches a part, he is pursued by a piercing flame.

37:11 So ask them: "Are they the more powerful creation, or the others We created?" We have created them from a clay that is sticky.

37:12 While you were awed, they simply mocked.

37:13 And when they are reminded, they do not care.

37:14 And when they see a sign, they make fun of it.

37:15 And they said: "This is nothing except evident magic!"

37:16 "Can it be that after we die and become dust and bones, that we are resurrected?"

37:17 "What about our fathers of old?"

37:18 Say: "Yes, and you will be humbled."

37:19 All it takes is one call, then they will be staring.

37:20 And they said: "Woe to us, this is the Day of Judgment!"

37:21 This is the Day of decisiveness that you used to deny.

37:22 Gather the transgressors, and their mates, and all they worshiped.

37:23 Beside God, and guide them to the path of Hell.

37:24 And let them stand and be questioned:

37:25 "Why do you not support one another?"

37:26 No, for today they have totally given up.

37:27 And some of them came to each other, questioning.

37:28 They said: "You used to entice us from the right side."

37:29 They replied: "No, it was you who were not believers."

37:30 "And we never had any power over you, but you were a wicked people."

37:31 "So the sentence of our Lord is now upon us, that we will suffer."

37:32 "We misled you, because we were astray."

37:33 Then, on that Day they will all share in the retribution.

37:34 This is how We deal with the criminals.

37:35 When it was said to them: "There is no god except God," they would be arrogant.

37:36　And they would say: "Shall we leave our gods for a crazy poet?"

37:37　No, he has come with the truth and he has confirmed the messengers.

37:38　You will taste the greatest of retribution.

37:39　And you are only recompensed for what you have done.

37:40　Except for the servants of God who are faithful.

37:41　For them will be known provisions.

37:42　Fruits, and they will be honored.

37:43　In gardens of bliss.

37:44　On beds which are opposite one another.

37:45　They will be served with a cup of pure drink.

37:46　White, delicious for the drinkers.

37:47　There is no bitterness therein, nor do they tire from it.

37:48　And with them are those with a modest gaze, with lovely eyes.

37:49　They are like fragile eggs.

37:50　So then they approached one another, questioning.

37:51　One of them said: "I used to have a friend."

37:52　"Who used to say: 'Are you among those who believe in this?'

37:53　'That if we die and turn into dust and bones, that we would be called to account?'"

37:54　He said: "Can anyone find him?"

37:55　So when he looked, he saw him in the midst of Hell.

37:56　He said: "By God, you nearly ruined me!"

37:57　"And had it not been for the blessing of my Lord, I would have been with you."

37:58　"Are we then not going to die,"

37:59　"Except for our first death, and we will not be punished?"

37:60 Such is the great triumph.

37:61 For this let those who will work endeavor.

37:62 Is that a better destination, or the tree of Bitterness?

37:63 We have made it a punishment for the transgressors.

37:64 It is a tree that grows in the midst of Hell.

37:65 Its shoots are like the devils' heads.

37:66 They will eat from it, so that their bellies are filled up.

37:67 Then they will have with it a drink of boiling liquid.

37:68 Then they will be returned to Hell.

37:69 They had found their parents astray.

37:70 So they too have hastened in their footsteps.

37:71 Most of the previous generations have strayed before them.

37:72 And We had sent to them warners.

37:73 Thus note the consequences for those who were warned.

37:74 Except for the servants of God who are faithful.

37:75 And Noah had called upon Us, for We are the best to respond.

37:76 And We saved him and his family from the great disaster.

37:77 And We made his progeny the one that remained.

37:78 And We kept his history for those who came later.

37:79 Peace be upon Noah among the worlds.

37:80 It is such that We reward the righteous.

37:81 He is of Our believing servants.

37:82 Then We drowned the others.

37:83 And from his clan was Abraham.

37:84 For he came to his Lord with a pure heart.

37:85 When he said to his father and his people: "What are you wor-shiping?"

37:86 "Is it fabricated gods, instead of God, that you want?"

37:87 "What do you say of the Lord of the worlds?"

37:88 Then he looked towards the stars.

37:89 And he said: "I am ill!"

37:90 So they turned away from him and departed.

37:91 He then went to their gods and said: "Can you not eat?"

37:92 "What is the matter, do you not speak?"

37:93 So he then turned on them, striking with his hand.

37:94 Then they approached him outraged.

37:95 He said: "Do you worship what you carve?"

37:96 "While God has created you, and all that you make!"

37:97 They said: "Build for him a structure, then cast him into its fire."

37:98 So they wanted to plan against him, but We made them the losers.

37:99 And he said: "I am going to my Lord; He will guide me."

37:100 "My Lord, grant me from among the righteous."

37:101 So We gave him the good news of a compassionate boy.

37:102 And when he grew enough to work with him, he said: "My son, I am seeing in a dream that I am sacrificing you. What do you think?" He said: "O my father, do what you are commanded to do. You will find me, God willing, patient."

37:103 So when they both had submitted, and he was laid by his forehead.

37:104 And We called him: "O Abraham,"

37:105 "You have carried out the vision." It was such that We rewarded the righteous.

37:106 Surely, this was an exacting test.

37:107 And We ransomed him with a great sacrifice.

37:108 And We kept his history for those who came later.

37:109 Peace be upon Abraham.

37:110 It is thus that We reward the righteous.

37:111 He was of Our believing servants.

37:112 And We gave him the good news of Isaac, a prophet from among the righteous.

37:113 And We blessed him and Isaac. And from among their progeny, some are righteous, and some are clearly wicked.

37:114 And indeed, We have given Our grace to Moses and Aaron.

37:115 And We saved them and their people from the great disaster.

37:116 And We supported them, so that they became the winners.

37:117 And We gave both the clear Book.

37:118 And We guided them to the straight path.

37:119 And We kept their history for those who came later.

37:120 Peace be upon Moses and Aaron.

37:121 We thus reward the righteous.

37:122 Both of them were among Our believing servants.

37:123 And Elias was one of the messengers.

37:124 When he said to his people: "Would you not be righteous?"

37:125 "Would you call on Ba'al and forsake the best Creator?"

37:126 "God is your Lord, and the Lord of your fathers of old!"

37:127 But they denied him. Thus they were called to account.

37:128 Except for God's loyal servants.

37:129 And We kept his history for those who came later.

37:130 Peace be upon the family of Elias.

37:131 We thus reward the righteous.

37:132 He was one of our believing servants.

37:133 And Lot was one of the messengers.

37:134 When We saved him and all his family.

37:135 Except an old woman who remained.

37:136 Then, We destroyed the rest.

37:137 And you pass by them in the morning;

37:138 And in the night. Do you not comprehend?

37:139 And Jonah was one of the messengers.

37:140 When he escaped to the charged ship.

37:141 And he was guilty, so he became among the losers.

37:142 Thus a whale swallowed him, and he was the one to blame.

37:143 And had it not been that he was one of those who implored,

37:144 He would have stayed in its belly until the Day of Resurrection.

37:145 So We threw him on the shore while he was sick.

37:146 And We caused a pumpkin tree to grow on him.

37:147 And We sent him to a hundred thousand, or more.

37:148 And they believed, so We gave them enjoyment for a time.

37:149 So ask them: "Are the daughters for your Lord, while the sons are for them?"

37:150 Or did We create the angels as females while they witnessed?

37:151 Indeed, it is out of their falsehood that they say:

37:152 "The son of God." And they are liars.

37:153 Has He chosen the daughters over the sons?

37:154 What is wrong with you, how do you judge?

37:155 Will you not remember?

37:156 Or do you have a clear proof?

37:157 Bring forth your book, if you are truthful.

37:158 And they invented a kinship between Him and the Jinn. But the Jinn know that they will be gathered.

37:159 God be glorified from what they describe.

37:160 Except for the servants of God who are faithful.

37:161 "As for you and what you worship."

37:162 "You cannot lead away from Him."

37:163 "Except those who are destined to Hell."

37:164 "Every one of us has a destined station."

37:165 "And we are the ones who are in columns."

37:166 "And we are the ones that glorify."

37:167 And they used to say:

37:168 "If only we had received a reminder from the previous generations,"

37:169 "We would have surely been loyal servants of God."

37:170 But they rejected it. They will come to know.

37:171 Our word had been decreed to Our servants who were sent.

37:172 That they would be made victorious.

37:173 And that Our soldiers are the winners.

37:174 So turn away from them for awhile.

37:175 And observe them; for they will see.

37:176 Do they seek to hasten Our retribution?

37:177 When it comes down to their courtyard, dire will be the morning for those who have been warned.

37:178 And turn away from them for awhile.

37:179 And observe; for they will see.

37:180 Glory be to your Lord, the Lord of greatness, for what they have described.

37:181 And peace be upon the messengers.

37:182 And praise be to God, Lord of the worlds.

CHAPTER 38

38:0   In the name of God, the Almighty, the Merciful.

38:1   S', and the Qur'an that contains the remembrance.

38:2   Indeed, those who have disbelieved are in false pride and defiance.

38:3   How many a generation have We destroyed before them. And they called out when it was far too late.

38:4   And they were surprised that a warner has come to them from among themselves. And the rejecters said: "This is a magician, a liar."

38:5   "Has he made the gods into One god? This is indeed a strange thing!"

38:6   And the leaders among them went out: "Walk away, and remain patient to your gods. This thing can be turned back."

38:7   "We never heard of this from the people before us. This is but an innovation."

38:8   "Has the remembrance been sent down to him, from between all of us!" Indeed, they are doubtful of My reminder. Indeed, they have not yet tasted My retribution.

38:9   Or do they have the treasures of mercy of your Lord, the Noble, the Grantor.

38:10   Or do they possess the dominion of the heavens and the earth, and all that is between them? Then let them bring their own solutions.

38:11   The Confederates that have gathered will be defeated.

38:12   Disbelieving before them were the people of Noah, 'Aad, and Pharaoh with the planks.

38:13   And Thamud, and the people of Lot, and the people of the Sycamore; these are the Confederates.

38:14   Each of them disbelieved the messengers, therefore My retribution came to be.

38:15   And what these people are waiting for is a single scream, from which they will not recover.

38:16 And they said: "Our Lord, hasten for us our punishment, before the Day of Reckoning."

38:17 Be patient to what they say, and recall Our servant David, the resourceful. He was obedient.

38:18 We commissioned the mountains to glorify with him, at dusk and sunrise.

38:19 And the birds were gathered; all were obedient to him.

38:20 And We strengthened his kingship, and We gave him the wisdom and the ability to make sound judgment.

38:21 Did the news come to you of the disputing party who came over into the enclosure?

38:22 When they entered upon David, he was startled by them. They said: "Have no fear. We are two who have disputed, and one has wronged the other, so judge between us with the truth, and do not wrong us, and guide us to the right path."

38:23 "This is my brother and he owns ninety-nine lambs, while I own one lamb; so he said to me: 'Let me take care of it' and he pressured me."

38:24 He said: "He has wronged you by asking to combine your lamb with his lambs. And many who mix their properties take advantage of one another, except those who believe and do good works, and these are very few." And David guessed that We had tested him, so he sought forgiveness from his Lord, and fell down kneeling, and repented.

38:25 So We forgave him in this matter. And for him with Us is a near position, and a beautiful abode.

38:26 O David, We have made you a successor on the earth. Therefore, you shall judge among the people with the truth, and do not follow desire, lest it diverts you from the path of God. Indeed, those who stray off the path of God will have a severe retribution for forgetting the Day of Reckoning.

38:27 And We did not create the heaven and the earth, and everything between them, in vain. Such is the thinking of those who rejected. Therefore, woe to those who have rejected from the Fire.

38:28 Or shall We treat those who believe and do good works as We treat those who make corruption on the earth? Or shall We treat the righteous as the wicked?

38:29 A Book that We have sent down to you, that is blessed, so that they may reflect upon its revelations, and so that those who possess intelligence will take heed.

38:30 And to David We granted Solomon. What an excellent and obedient servant.

38:31 When, during dusk, well trained horses were displayed before him.

38:32 He then said: "I have enjoyed the material things over the remembrance of my Lord, until it has become completely veiled!"

38:33 "Send them back." He then rubbed their legs and necks.

38:34 And We had tested Solomon, and slumped a form upon his throne, then he repented.

38:35 He said: "My Lord, forgive me, and grant me a kingship that will never be attained by anyone after me. You are the Grantor."

38:36 So, We commissioned the wind to run by his command, smoothly blowing where he willed it.

38:37 And the devils, building and diving.

38:38 And others, chained in shackles.

38:39 "This is Our gift, so you may spend or withhold, without reckoning."

38:40 And he has a near position with Us, and a wonderful abode.

38:41 And recall Our servant Job, when he called upon his Lord: "The devil has afflicted me with an illness and pain."

38:42 "Rapidly move with your foot, here is a cold spring to wash with and to drink."

38:43 And We restored his family to him along with a group like them, as a mercy from Us; and a reminder for those who possess intelligence.

38:44 "And take in your hand a bundle and go forth with it, and do not break your oath." We found him steadfast. What a good servant! He was obedient.

38:45 And recall Our servants Abraham, Isaac, and Jacob. They were resourceful, and with vision.

38:46 We had chosen them to remind of the Hereafter.

38:47 And with Us, they are of the chosen, the best.

38:48 And recall Ishmael, Elisha, and Isaiah; all are among the best.

38:49 This is a reminder, and the righteous will have a wonderful abode.

38:50 Gardens of delight, whose gates will be open for them.

38:51 Reclining therein, they will be invited to many fruits and drinks.

38:52 And with them are those with a modest gaze, mature in age.

38:53 This is what you have been promised for the Day of Reckoning.

38:54 Such is Our provisions, it does not run out.

38:55 This is so, and for the transgressors is a miserable destiny.

38:56 Hell is where they burn. What a miserable abode!

38:57 This is so, and let them taste what is boiling and dark.

38:58 And others, of the same kind, in pairs.

38:59 Here is another group to be thrown into Hell with you. "We have no welcome for them, for they shall burn in the Fire."

38:60 They said: "No, you are the ones without welcome. It was you who presented this to us, what a miserable result!"

38:61 They said: "Our Lord, whoever brought this upon us, then double their retribution in the Fire!"

38:62 And they said: "Why do we not see some men whom we used to count among the wicked?"

38:63 "Did we mock them erroneously, or have our eyes failed to find them?"

38:64 Surely, this is in truth the feuding of the people of Hell.

38:65 Say: "I am but a warner; and there is no god besides God, the One, the Supreme."

38:66 "The Lord of the heavens and the earth, and everything between them; the Noble, the Forgiving."

38:67   Say: "It is an awesome news."

38:68   "From which you turn away."

38:69   "I had no knowledge of the command up high, that they had quarreled."

38:70   "It is only inspired to me that I am a clear warner."

38:71   For your Lord said to the angels: "I am creating a mortal from clay."

38:72   "So when I have evolved him, and blow of My Spirit in him, then you shall yield to him."

38:73   The angels yielded, all of them,

38:74   Except Satan; he turned arrogant, and became one of the rejecters.

38:75   He said: "O Satan, what prevented you from yielding to what I have created by My hands? Are you too arrogant? Or are you one of those exalted?"

38:76   He said: "I am better than he; You created me from fire, and created him from clay."

38:77   He said: "Therefore exit from it, you are outcast."

38:78   "And My curse will be upon you until the Day of Judgment."

38:79   He said: "My Lord, respite me until the Day they are resurrected."

38:80   He said: "You are respited."

38:81   "Until the appointed Day."

38:82   He said: "By Your majesty, I will mislead them all."

38:83   "Except for Your servants who are loyal."

38:84   He said: "The truth, and the truth is what I say."

38:85   "That I will fill Hell with you and all those who follow you."

38:86   Say: "I do not ask you for any wage, nor am I a fraud."

38:87   "It is but a reminder for the worlds."

38:88   "And you will come to know its news after awhile."

CHAPTER 39

39:0 In the name of God, the Almighty, the Merciful.

39:1 The sending down of the Book is from God, the Noble, the Wise.

39:2 We have sent down to you the Book with the truth, so serve God while devoting the system to Him.

39:3 Absolutely, to God is the true system. And those who set up allies besides Him: "We only serve them so that they may bring us closer to God." God will judge between them in what they dispute. For God does not guide him who is a liar, a rejecter.

39:4 If God wished to take a son, He could have exalted from among His creation what He pleases. Be He glorified; He is God, the One, the Supreme.

39:5 He created the heavens and the earth with the truth. He rolls the night over the day, and He rolls the day over the night. And He commissioned the sun and the moon, each running for an appointed term. Absolutely, He is the Noble, the Forgiving.

39:6 He created you from one person, then He made from it its mate. And He sent down to you—from the hoofed animals—eight, in pairs. He creates you in the wombs of your mothers, a creation after a creation, in darkness that is threefold. Such is God your Lord. To Him belongs the sovereignty. There is no god besides Him. How is it then you deviate?

39:7 If you reject, then know that God is in no need of you, and He is displeased with rejection for His servants. And if you are thankful, He is pleased with it for you. And no bearer may carry the burden of another. Then to your Lord is your return, and He will inform you of everything you had done. He is fully aware of what is in the chests.

39:8 And when the human being is afflicted with adversity, he implores his Lord, turning in repentance to Him. But then, when He grants him a blessing from Him, he forgets his previous imploring, and sets up equals with God, in order to mislead others from His path. Say: "Enjoy your rejection for a while; for you are of the dwellers of the Fire."

39:9 Is one better who is devout during the night, prostrating and standing, fearing the Hereafter, and seeking the mercy of his

Lord? Say: "Are those who know equal to those who do not know?" Only those who possess intelligence will remember.

39:10   Say: "O My servants who believed, be aware of your Lord." For those who worked righteousness in this world will be a good reward, and the earth of God is spacious. Those who steadfastly persevere will receive their recompense fully, without reckoning.

39:11   Say: "I have been commanded to serve God, devoting the system to Him."

39:12   "And I was commanded to be the first of those who submit."

39:13   Say: "I fear, if I disobeyed my Lord, the retribution of a great Day."

39:14   Say: "God is the One I serve, devoting my system to Him."

39:15   "Therefore, serve whatever you wish besides Him." Say: "The losers are those who lose their souls, and their families, on the Day of Resurrection. Indeed, such is the real loss."

39:16   They will have coverings of fire from above them and below them. It is as such that God makes His servants fearful: "O My servants, you shall reverence Me."

39:17   And for those who avoid serving evil, and turn to God in repentance, for them are glad tidings. So give the good news to My servants.

39:18   The ones who listen to what is being said, and then follow the best of it. These are the ones whom God has guided, and these are the ones who possess intelligence.

39:19   As for those who have deserved the retribution; can you save those who are in the Fire?

39:20   But those who reverence their Lord, they will have dwellings constructed upon dwellings, with rivers flowing beneath them. The promise of God, and God does not break the promise.

39:21   Do you not see that God sends down water from the sky, then lets it run as springs in the earth, then He produces with it plants of various colors, then they grow until they turn yellow, then He makes them dry and broken? In this is a reminder for those who possess intelligence.

39:22   If God comforts the chest of a person to submission, then he will be on a light from his Lord. So woe to those whose hearts are hardened against remembering God. They have gone far astray.

39:23 God has sent down the best narrative, a Book that is comparable, but dual. The skins of those who are concerned towards their Lord shiver from it, then their skins and their hearts soften up to the remembrance of God. Such is the guidance of God; He guides with it whoever He wills. And for whoever God misguides, then none can guide him.

39:24 As he who saves his face from the terrible retribution on the Day of Resurrection. And it will be said to the transgressors: "Taste what you have earned."

39:25 Those before them have denied, and thus the retribution came to them from where they did not perceive.

39:26 So God made them taste the humiliation in this worldly life, but the retribution in the Hereafter is far greater, if only they knew.

39:27 And We have put forth for the people in this Qur'an from every example, that they may take heed.

39:28 A Qur'an in Arabic, without any crookedness, that they may be righteous.

39:29 God puts forth the example of a man who has partners that dispute with each other, and a man who has given to dealing with only one man. Are they the same? Praise be to God; most of them do not know.

39:30 You will die, and they will die.

39:31 Then, on the Day of Resurrection, you will quarrel at your Lord.

39:32 Who is more wicked than he who lies about God, and denies the truth when it comes to him? Is there not in Hell an abode for the rejecters?

39:33 And those who came with the truth, and believed in it, these are the righteous.

39:34 They shall have what they wish at their Lord. Such is the reward for the good doers.

39:35 So that God may cancel for them the worst that they did, and He may recompense them their reward for the best of what they used to do.

39:36 Is God not enough for His servant? And they frighten you with others besides Him. And whoever God sends astray, then for him there will be no guide.

39:37   And whoever God guides, then there will be none that can mislead him. Is God not Noble, with Vengeance?

39:38   And if you ask them: "Who has created the heavens and the earth?" They will say: "God." Say: "Do you see what you call on besides God, If God wanted any harm for me, can they alleviate His harm? Or if He wanted a mercy for me, can they hold back his mercy?" Say: "God is sufficient for me; in Him those who trust shall place their trust."

39:39   Say: "O my people, work according to your way, and I will work. You will come to know."

39:40   "To whom the humiliating retribution will come, and on whom a permanent retribution will be cast."

39:41   We have sent down to you the Book for the people with the truth. Then, whoever is guided is guided for himself, and whoever goes astray goes astray to his own loss. And you are not a keeper over them.

39:42   God seizes the souls at the time of their death; and for those that have not died, during their sleep. He then keeps those that have been overtaken by death, and He sends the others back until a predetermined time. In that are signs for a people who will think.

39:43   Or have they taken intercessors besides God? Say: "What if they possessed nothing, nor comprehended?"

39:44   Say: "To God belongs all intercession." To Him belongs the sovereignty of the heavens and the earth, then to Him you will be returned.

39:45   And when God alone is mentioned, the hearts of those who do not believe in the Hereafter are filled with aversion; and when others are mentioned besides Him, they rejoice!

39:46   Say: "Our god, Initiator of the heavens and the earth, Knower of the unseen and the seen, You will judge between Your servants regarding what they disputed in."

39:47   And if those who transgressed owned everything on the earth, and its equivalent again with it, they would ransom it to avoid the terrible retribution on the Day of Resurrection. They will be shown by God what they did not expect.

39:48   And the sinful works they had earned will be shown to them, and they will be surrounded by that which they used to mock.

39:49 So when the human being is touched by adversity, he implores Us, then when We bestow a blessing upon him, he says: "I attained this because of knowledge I had!" Indeed, it is a test, but most of them do not know.

39:50 Those before them have said the same thing, yet what they earned did not help them in the least.

39:51 So, they suffered the evil of what they had earned. And those who transgressed from among these here will suffer the evil of what they earned; they cannot escape.

39:52 Do they not know that God spreads the provision for whomever He chooses, and He restricts? In that are signs for a people who believe.

39:53 Say: "O My servants who transgressed against themselves, do not despair of the mercy of God. For God forgives all sins. He is the Forgiver, the Merciful."

39:54 And repent to your Lord, and submit to Him, before the retribution comes to you. Then you cannot be helped.

39:55 And follow the best of what has been sent down to you from your Lord, before the retribution comes to you suddenly when you least expect it.

39:56 Lest a soul will say: "How sorry I am for disregarding the path of God; and I was certainly one of those who mocked."

39:57 Or say: "Had God guided me, I would have been among the righteous."

39:58 Or say, when it sees the retribution: "If only I could have another chance, I would be among the good doers."

39:59 Yes indeed, My revelations came to you, but you denied them and turned arrogant, and became one of the rejecters.

39:60 And on the Day of Resurrection you will see those who lied about God, their faces will be darkened. Is there not an abode in Hell for the arrogant ones?

39:61 And God will save those who were righteous as their reward. No harm will touch them, nor will they grieve.

39:62 God is the Creator of all things, and He is Guardian over all things.

39:63 To Him belongs the keys of the heavens and the earth. And those who rejected the revelations of God, they are the losers.

39:64 Say: "Do you order me to serve other than God, O you ignorant ones?"

39:65 And He has inspired to you and to those before you, that if you set up partners, He will nullify all your works, and you will be of the losers.

39:66 Therefore, you shall serve God, and be among the thankful.

39:67 And they have not given God His true worth; and the whole earth is within His fist on the Day of Resurrection, and the heavens will be folded in His right hand. Be He glorified and exalted above what they set up.

39:68 And the horn will be blown, whereupon everyone in the heavens and the earth will be struck unconscious, except those spared by God. Then it will be blown another time, whereupon they will all rise up, looking.

39:69 And the earth will shine with the light of its Lord, and the record will be placed, and the prophets and the witnesses will be brought forth; and it will then be judged between them with the truth, and they will not be wronged.

39:70 And every soul will be paid for whatever it did, for He is fully aware of everything they have done.

39:71 And those who rejected will be driven to Hell in groups. When they reach it, and its gates are opened, its guards will say to them: "Did you not receive messengers from among you who recited to you the revelations of your Lord, and warned you about meeting this Day?" They said: "Yes indeed; but the sentence of retribution has come to pass upon the rejecters."

39:72 It was said: "Enter the gates of Hell, abiding therein. What a miserable destiny for the arrogant."

39:73 And those who reverenced their Lord will be driven to Paradise in groups. When they reach it, and its gates are opened, its guards will say to them: "Peace be upon you. You have done well, so enter to abide herein."

39:74 And they said: "Praise be to God who has fulfilled His promise to us, and He made us inherit the land, enjoying Paradise as we please. What a beautiful recompense for the workers!"

39:75 And you will see the angels surrounding the Throne, glorifying the praise of their Lord. And it will be judged between them with the truth, and it will be said: "Praise be to God, Lord of the worlds."

CHAPTER 40

40:0 In the name of God, the Almighty, the Merciful.

40:1 HM.

40:2 The revelation of the Book is from God, the Noble, the Knowledgeable.

40:3 Forgiver of sins, and accepter of repentance, severe in retribution, with ability to reach. There is no god other than Him, to Him is the ultimate destiny.

40:4 None dispute in the revelations of God except those who have rejected. So do not be impressed by their influence in the land.

40:5 Denial had come before them from the people of Noah, and the Confederates after them. And every nation obsessed with their messenger—to take him—and they disputed by means of falsehood to defeat with it the truth. So I took them; how then was My punishment!

40:6 And as such, the word of your Lord has come to pass upon those who rejected, that they are the dwellers of the Fire.

40:7 Those who carry the Throne and all those surrounding it glorify the praise of their Lord, and believe in Him, and they seek forgiveness for those who have believed: "Our Lord, You encompass all things with mercy and knowledge, so forgive those who repented and followed Your path, and spare them the agony of Hell."

40:8 "Our Lord, and admit them into gardens of delight which You had promised for them and for those who did good of their fathers, their spouses, and their progeny. You are the Noble, the Wise."

40:9 "And save them from the sins. And whoever You save from the sins, on that Day, You have granted him mercy. And such is the great triumph."

40:10 Those who had rejected will be told: "The abhorrence of God towards you is greater than your abhorrence of yourselves, for you were invited to believe, but you chose to reject."

40:11 They will say: "Our Lord, You have made us die twice, and You have given us life twice. Now we have confessed our sins. Is there any way out of this state?"

40:12 This is because when God alone was mentioned, you rejected, but when partners were set up with Him, you believed. Therefore, the judgment is for God, the Most High, the Great.

40:13 He is the One who shows you His signs, and He sends down to you provisions from the heaven. But none do remember except those who repent.

40:14 Therefore, call on God while being pure to His system, even if the rejecters hate it.

40:15 Possessor of the highest ranks, the One with the Throne. He sends the Spirit with His command upon whom He wills from His servants, that they may warn of the Day of Summoning.

40:16 The Day when they will be exposed. None of them will hide anything from God. To whom is the sovereignty on this Day? To God, the One, the Supreme.

40:17 Today, every soul will be recompensed for what it had earned. There will be no injustice today. Truly, God is swift in reckoning.

40:18 And warn them of the imminent Day, when the hearts will reach the throats, and many will be remorseful. The transgressors will have no friend nor intercessor to be obeyed.

40:19 He knows what the eyes have seen, and what the chests conceal.

40:20 And God judges with the truth, while those they call on besides Him do not judge with anything. Certainly, God is the Hearer, the Seer.

40:21 Have they not roamed the earth and seen how was the consequence of those who were before them? They used to be stronger than they, and had built more in the land. But God seized them for their sins, and they had no protector against God.

40:22 That is because their messengers used to come to them with proofs, but they rejected. Thus God seized them; for He is Mighty, severe in punishment.

40:23 And We had sent Moses with Our signs, and a clear authority.

40:24   To Pharaoh, Haamaan, and Qaroon. But they said: "A lying magician!"

40:25   Then, when the truth came to them from Us, they said: "Kill the children of those who believed with him, and rape their women." But the planning of the rejecters is always in error.

40:26   And Pharaoh said: "Leave me to kill Moses, and let him call upon his Lord. I fear that he may change your system, or that he will cause evil to spread throughout the land."

40:27   And Moses said: "I seek refuge with my Lord and your Lord from every arrogant one who does not believe in the Day of Reckoning."

40:28   And a believing man from among the people of Pharaoh, who had concealed his belief, said: "Will you kill a man simply for saying: 'My Lord is God', and he has come to you with proofs from your Lord? And if he is a liar, then his lie will be upon him, and if he is truthful, then some of what he is promising you will afflict you. For God does not guide any transgressor, liar."

40:29   "O my people, you have the kingship today throughout the land. But then who will save us against the torment of God, should it come to us?" Pharaoh said: "I am showing you that which I see, and I am guiding you in the right path."

40:30   And the one who believed said: "O my people, I fear for you the same fate as the day of the Confederates."

40:31   "Like the fate of the people of Noah, 'Aad, and Thamud, and those after them. And God does not wish any injustice for the servants."

40:32   "And, O my people, I fear for you the Day of mutual blaming."

40:33   "A Day when you will turn around and flee, you will have no protector besides God, and whoever God sends astray, then there is none who can guide him."

40:34   "And Joseph had come to you before with proofs, but you remained in doubt regarding what he came to you with, until when he died, you said: "God will not send any messenger after him." It is such that God sends astray he who is a transgressor, doubter."

40:35   Those who dispute about the revelations of God without any authority that has come to them, it is greatly abhorred with God and with those who believe. God thus seals the hearts of every arrogant tyrant.

40:36   And Pharaoh said: "O Haamaan, build for me a high platform that I may uncover the secrets."

40:37   "The secrets of the heavens, so that I may take a look at the god of Moses; though I think he is a liar." Thus the evil works of Pharaoh were adorned for him, and he was blocked from the path. And the planning of Pharaoh brought nothing but regret.

40:38   And the one who believed said: "O my people, follow me, and I will guide you to the right path."

40:39   "O my people, this worldly life is but an enjoyment, while the Hereafter is the permanent abode."

40:40   "Whoever does a sin, will not be requited except for its equivalent, and whoever does good, whether male or female, and is a believer, then those will be admitted to Paradise, where they will receive provision without reckoning."

40:41   "And, O my people, why is it that I invite you to salvation, while you invite me to the Fire!"

40:42   "You invite me to reject God, and set up partners besides Him that I have no knowledge of, and I am inviting you to the Noble, the Forgiver."

40:43   "There is no doubt that what you invite me to has no basis in this world, nor in the Hereafter. And our ultimate return will be to God, and that the transgressors will be the dwellers of the Fire."

40:44   "You will come to remember what I am telling you, and I leave my affair in this matter to God; for God is the Seer of the servants."

40:45   So God protected him from the evil of what they schemed, while the people of Pharaoh have incurred the worst retribution.

40:46   The Fire, which they will be exposed to morning and evening, and on the Day when the Hour is established: "Admit the people of Pharaoh into the most severe of the retribution."

40:47   And when they argue in Hell, the weak will say to those who were arrogant: "We used to be your followers, can you take from us any portion of the Fire?"

40:48   Those who were arrogant will say: "We are all in it together, for God has passed judgment upon the servants."

40:49   And those who are in the Fire will say to the guardians of Hell: "Call upon your Lord to reduce for us just one day of the retribution!"

40:50   They will say: "Did your messengers not come to you with proofs?" They will say: "Yes." They will say: "Then implore, but the imploring of the rejecters will be nothing but in vain."

40:51   We will indeed grant victory to Our messengers and to those who believed in the worldly life, and on the Day when the witnesses will rise.

40:52   A Day when excuses will be of no help to the transgressors, and they will be cursed, and they will have the worst abode.

40:53   And We gave Moses the guidance, and We made the Children of Israel inherit the Book.

40:54   A guide and a reminder for those who possess intelligence.

40:55   So be patient, for the promise of God is true, and seek forgiveness for your sin, and glorify with the praise of your Lord evening and morning.

40:56   Surely, those who dispute about the revelations of God without any authority given to them, there is nothing except arrogance in their chests, which they do not perceive. Therefore, seek refuge with God; He is the Hearer, the Seer.

40:57   The creation of the heavens and the earth is greater than the creation of the people, but most of the people do not know.

40:58   And not equal are the blind and the seer, nor those who believe and do good works, and those who do evil. Little do you remember.

40:59   Surely the Hour is coming, there is no doubt in it, but most of the people do not believe.

40:60   And your Lord said: "Call on Me and I will respond to you. Surely, those who are too arrogant to serve Me, they will enter Hell, humbled."

40:61   God, it is He who has made for you the night to reside in and the day to see in. Surely, God provides many blessings upon the people, but most of the people are not thankful.

40:62   That is God, your Lord, Creator of all things. There is no god except He, so why do you deviate?

40:63   Also deviating are those who towards the revelations of God were deniers.

40:64   God is the One who made the earth a habitat for you, and the heaven as a structure, and He designed you, and has perfected your design. And He provided you with good provisions. Such is God your Lord. Most Exalted is God, Lord of the worlds.

40:65   He is the Living; there is no god except He. So call on Him while devoting the system to Him. Praise be to God, Lord of the worlds.

40:66   Say: "I have been prohibited from serving those whom you are calling upon besides God, since the proofs have come to me from my Lord. And I have been commanded to submit to the Lord of the worlds."

40:67   He is the One who has created you from dust, then from a seed, then from an embryo, then He brings you out as a child, then He lets you reach your maturity, then you become old; and some of you will have their lives terminated before this; and that you may reach an appointed term, and perhaps so you may comprehend.

40:68   He is the One who gives life and death. And when He decides upon anything, He simply says to it: 'Be,' and it is.

40:69   Did you not note those who dispute about the revelations of God, how they have deviated?

40:70   Those who deny the Book, and what We have sent Our messengers with. Therefore, they will come to know.

40:71   When the shackles will be around their necks and in chains they will be dragged off.

40:72   Into the boiling water, then into the fire, they are desolate.

40:73   Then it will be said to them: "Where are those that you have set up as partners—"

40:74   "Beside God?" They will say: "They have abandoned us. No, we did not use to call on anything before!" Thus God leads the rejecters astray.

40:75   That was because you used to gloat on the earth without any right, and for what you used to rejoice.

40:76   Enter the gates of Hell, abiding therein. What a miserable abode for the arrogant ones.

40:77   So be patient, for the promise of God is true. So, if We show you some of what We promise them, or We terminate your life, then it is to Us that they will be returned.

40:78 And We have sent messengers before you. Some of them We have narrated to you, and some We did not narrate to you. And it was not given to any messenger that he should bring a sign except with the permission of God. So, when the judgment of God is issued, the matter is decided with the truth, and the followers of falsehood will be lost.

40:79 God is the One who made the hoofed animals for you that you may ride on some of them, and some of them you eat.

40:80 And you have other benefits in them. And that you may reach by them what is desired in your chests. And on them and on the ships, you are carried.

40:81 And He shows you His signs. So which signs of God do you deny?

40:82 Have they not roamed the earth and noted the consequences for those who were before them? They used to be greater in number than them and mightier in strength, and they had built more in the land. Yet, all that they had earned could not avail them.

40:83 Then, when their messengers came to them with clear proofs, they were content with what they already had of knowledge. And they will be surrounded by that which they used to mock.

40:84 So when they saw Our might, they said: "We believe in God alone, and we reject all the partners we used to set up!"

40:85 But their belief could not help them once they saw Our might; such is the way of God that has been established for His servants; and the rejecters were then totally in loss.

CHAPTER 41

41:0 In the name of God, the Almighty, the Merciful.

41:1 HM.

41:2 A revelation from the Almighty, the Merciful.

41:3 A Book whose verses are made detailed—a Qur'an in Arabic for a people who know.

41:4 A bearer of good news, and a warner. But most of them turn away; they do not hear.

41:5   And they said: "Our hearts are sealed from what you invite us to, and in our ears is a deafness, and there is a veil between us and you. So do what you will, and so will we."

41:6   Say: "I am no more than a mortal like you. It is inspired to me that your god is One god, therefore you shall be upright towards Him and seek His forgiveness. And woe to the polytheists."

41:7   "The ones who do not contribute towards purification, and with regards to the Hereafter, they are disbelievers."

41:8   Surely, those who believe and do good works, they will receive recompense that will not end.

41:9   Say: "You are rejecting the One who has created the earth in two days, and you set up equals with Him. That is the Lord of the worlds."

41:10   And He placed in it stabilizers from above it, and He blessed it and established its provisions in proportion in four days, to satisfy those who ask.

41:11   Then He settled to the heaven, while it was still smoke, and He said to it, and to the earth: "Come willingly or unwillingly." They said: "We come willingly."

41:12   Thus, He then made them into seven heavens in two days, and He inspired to every heaven its affair. And We adorned the lowest heaven with lamps, and for protection. Such is the design of the Noble, the Knowledgeable.

41:13   But if they turn away, then say: "I have warned you of a destruction like the destruction of 'Aad and Thamud."

41:14   When the messengers came to them, publicly and privately: "You shall not serve except God." They said: "Had our Lord willed, He would have sent angels. We are rejecting what you have been sent with."

41:15   As for 'Aad, they turned arrogant on the earth, without any right, and they said: "Who is mightier than us in strength?" Did they not see that God, who has created them, was mightier than they in strength? And they were denying Our revelations.

41:16   Consequently, We sent upon them a violent wind, for a few miserable days, that We may let them taste the humiliating retribution in this worldly life, and the retribution of the Hereafter is more humiliating; they can never win.

41:17　And as for Thamud, We gave them the guidance, but they preferred blindness over guidance. Consequently, the blast of humiliating retribution annihilated them, because of what they earned.

41:18　And We saved those who believed and were righteous.

41:19　And the Day when the enemies of God will be gathered to the Fire, forcibly.

41:20　When they come to it, their own hearing, eyes, and skins will bear witness to everything they had done.

41:21　And they will say to their skins: "Why did you bear witness against us?" They will say: "God made us speak; He is the One who causes everything to speak. He is the One who has created you the first time, and to Him you return."

41:22　And there was no way you could hide from the testimony of your own hearing, or your eyes, or your skins. In fact, you thought that God was unaware of much of what you do.

41:23　And this is the kind of thinking about your Lord that has caused you to fail, and thus you became of the losers.

41:24　If they wait, then the Fire will be their destiny, and if they beg to be excused, they will not be excused.

41:25　And We assigned to them associates who adorned their present and past actions—and the sentence was deserved by them—as it was for the nations before them of Jinn and mankind; they were losers.

41:26　And those who rejected said: "Do not listen to this Qur'an and make noise over it that you may succeed."

41:27　We will let those who have rejected taste a severe retribution. And We will recompense them for the evil that they used to do.

41:28　Such is the recompense for the enemies of God. The Fire shall be their eternal abode, as a recompense for their discarding Our revelations.

41:29　And those who have rejected will say: "Our Lord, show us those who have misled us from among the Jinn and mankind so we can trample them under our feet, so that they would be the lowest."

41:30　Those who have said: "Our Lord is God," then they did right, the angels will come down upon them: "You shall not fear, nor shall you grieve. Rejoice in the good news of Paradise that you have been promised."

41:31 "We are your allies in this worldly life and in the Hereafter. In it you will have anything your soul desires, and in it you will have anything you ask for."

41:32 "A dwelling, from a Forgiver, Merciful."

41:33 And who is better in saying than he who invites to God, and does good works, and says: "I am one of those who have submitted."

41:34 And not equal are good and evil. You shall resort to the one which is better. Thus, the one who used to be your enemy, may become your best friend.

41:35 And none can attain this except those who are patient. And none can attain this except those who are extremely fortunate.

41:36 And if bitterness from the devil afflicts you, then seek refuge with God. He is the Hearer, the Knowledgeable.

41:37 And from among His signs are the night and the day, and the sun and the moon. Do not prostrate to the sun, nor the moon; you shall prostrate to God who has created them, if it is truly Him you serve.

41:38 So, if they become arrogant, then those who are with your Lord glorify Him night and day, and they never despair.

41:39 And from among His signs is that you see the land still, then, as soon as We send down the water upon it, it shakes and grows. Surely, the One who revived it can revive the dead. He is capable of all things.

41:40 Those who distort Our revelations are not hidden from Us. Is one who is thrown into Hell better, or one who comes secure on the Day of Resurrection? Do whatever you wish; He is Seer of what you do.

41:41 Those who have rejected the reminder when it came to them; and it is an Honorable Book.

41:42 No falsehood could enter it, presently or afterwards; a revelation from One Most Wise, Praiseworthy.

41:43 What is being said to you is the same that was said to the messengers before you. Your Lord has forgiveness, and He has a painful retribution.

41:44 And had We made it a Qur'an that was non-Arabic, they would have said: "If only its verses were made clear!" Non-Arabic or Arabic, say: "For those who believe, it is a guide and healing. As for those who disbelieve, there is deafness in their ears, and they are blind to it. These will be called from a place far away."

41:45 And We have given Moses the Book, but it was disputed in. And had it not been for the predetermined decision of your Lord, they would have been judged immediately. Indeed, they harbor many doubts about it.

41:46 Whoever does good works does so for his own soul, and whoever works evil shall have the same. Your Lord does not wrong the servants.

41:47 To Him belongs the knowledge regarding the Hour. And no fruit emerges from its sheath, nor does any female conceive or give birth, except by His knowledge. And on the Day He asks them: "Where are My partners?" They will say: "With your permission, none of us will bear witness to such!"

41:48 And they were abandoned by that which they used to call on before, and they realized that there will be no escape.

41:49 The human being does not tire in praying for good things. But if adversity touches him, he is disheartened, desperate!

41:50 And when We let him taste a mercy from Us after hardship had touched him, he will say: "This was by my actions, and I do not think that the Hour will come to pass. And even if I am returned to my Lord, I will find at Him good things for me." Surely, We will inform the rejecters of all they had done, and We will let them taste the severe retribution.

41:51 And when We bless man, he withdraws and turns away, and when he suffers any adversity, then he implores at length!

41:52 Say: "Do you see if this was from God and then you rejected it? Who is further astray than those who are in opposition?"

41:53 We will show them Our signs in the horizons, and within themselves, until it becomes clear to them that this is the truth. Is it not enough that your Lord is witness over all things?

41:54 Indeed, they are in doubt about meeting their Lord; but He is encompassing all things.

CHAPTER 42

42:0   In the name of God, the Almighty, the Merciful.

42:1   HM.

42:2   A'SQ.

42:3   Similarly, inspiring you and those before you, is God, the Noble, the Wise.

42:4   To Him belongs all what is in the heavens and the earth, and He is the Most High, the Great.

42:5   The heavens would nearly shatter from above them, and the angels praise the glory of their Lord, and they ask forgiveness for those on the earth. Surely, God is the Forgiver, the Merciful.

42:6   And those who take allies besides Him, God is responsible for them; and you are not a guardian over them.

42:7   And thus We have inspired to you a Qur'an in Arabic, so that you may warn the mother of towns and all around it, and to warn about the Day of Gathering that is inevitable. A group will be in Paradise, and a group in Hell.

42:8   And if God had willed, He could have made them one nation. But He admits whom He wills into His mercy. And the transgressors will have neither an ally, nor helper.

42:9   Or have they taken allies besides Him? But God is the ally, and He is the One who resurrects the dead, and He is able to do all things.

42:10   And anything you dispute in, then its judgment shall be with God. "Such is God my Lord. In Him I place my trust, and to Him I repent."

42:11   Initiator of the heavens and the earth. He created for you from among yourselves mates, and also mates for the hoofed animals so they may multiply. There is nothing that equals Him. He is the Hearer, the Seer.

42:12   To Him belongs the possessions of the heavens and the earth. He spreads out the provision for whoever He wills, and He measures it. He is fully aware of all things.

42:13   He has decreed for you the same system He ordained for Noah, and what We inspired to you, and what We ordained for Abraham, Moses, and Jesus: "You shall uphold this system, and do not divide in it." Intolerable for the polytheists is what you invite them towards. God chooses for Himself whoever He wills; He guides to Himself those who repent.

42:14 And they only divided after the knowledge had come to them, due to resentment among themselves. And had it not been for a predetermined decision from your Lord, they would have been judged immediately. Indeed, those who inherited the Book after them are full of doubts.

42:15 For that, you shall preach and be upright, as you have been commanded, and do not follow their wishes. And say: "I believe in all that God has sent down as a Book, and I was commanded to be with justice between you. God is our Lord and your Lord. We have our deeds and you have your deeds. There is no argument between us and you. God will gather us all together, and to Him is the ultimate destiny."

42:16 And those who debate about God, after they had been answered, their argument is nullified at their Lord. They have incurred a wrath, and will have a severe retribution.

42:17 God is the One who sent down the Book with the truth, and the balance. And for all that you know, the Hour may be very near.

42:18 Those who do not believe in it seek to hasten it, while those who believe are concerned about it, and they know that it is the truth. Certainly, those who dispute the Hour have gone far astray.

42:19 God is Gracious to His servants; He gives provisions for whoever He wills, and He is the Powerful, the Noble.

42:20 Whoever desires the harvest of the Hereafter, We will increase for him his harvest. And whoever seeks the harvest of this world, We will give him therefrom, and he will have no share in the Hereafter.

42:21 Or do they have partners who decree for them a system which has not been authorized by God? And if it were not for the word already given, they would have been judged immediately. Indeed, the transgressors will have a painful retribution.

42:22 You see the transgressors worried because of what they had done; and it will come back at them. As for those who believed and do good works, they will be in gardens of bliss. They will have what they wish from their Lord. This is the great blessing.

42:23　Such is the good news from God to His servants who believe and do good works. Say: "I do not ask you for any wage, except that you have affection to your relatives." And whoever earns a good deed, We shall increase it for him in goodness. Surely, God is Forgiving, Thankful.

42:24　Or do they say: "He has fabricated lies about God!" Had God willed, He could have sealed your heart. And God erases the falsehood and affirms the truth with His words. He is fully aware of what is in the chests.

42:25　And He is the One who accepts the repentance from His servants, and He forgives the sins. He is fully aware of what you do.

42:26　And those that believe and do good works respond to Him, and He increases for them His blessings. As for the rejecters, they have incurred a severe retribution.

42:27　And if God were to increase the provision for His servants, they would transgress on the earth; but He sends down what He wills in a measure. He is Expert and Seer of His servants.

42:28　And He is the One who sends down the rain after they had despaired, and spreads His mercy. He is the Supporter, the Praiseworthy.

42:29　And from among His signs is the creation of the heavens and the earth, and the creatures He spreads in them. And He is able to gather them, if He wills.

42:30　And any misfortune that happens to you is a consequence of what your hands have earned. And He overlooks much.

42:31　And you can never escape, and you have none besides God as an ally or helper.

42:32　And from His signs are the vessels that sail the sea like flags.

42:33　If He willed, He could still the winds, leaving them motionless on top of it. In that are signs for every one who is patient, thankful.

42:34　Or He may annihilate them, for what they have earned. And He overlooks much.

42:35　And that those who dispute in Our signs may know that they have no place to hide.

42:36　So whatever you are given is simply an enjoyment of the worldly life, and what is with God is far better and more lasting for those who believe and put their trust in their Lord.

42:37   And those who avoid major sins and immorality, and when they are angered, they forgive.

42:38   And those who have responded to their Lord, and they hold the Connection, and their affairs are conducted by mutual consultation among themselves, and from Our provisions to them they give.

42:39   And those who, when injustice befalls them, they seek justice.

42:40   The recompense for a crime shall be its equivalence, but whoever forgives and makes right, then his reward is upon God. He does not like the wrongdoers.

42:41   And for any who demand action after being wronged, those are not committing any error.

42:42   The error is upon those who oppress the people, and they aggress in the land without cause. For these will be a painful retribution.

42:43   And for he who is patient and forgives, then that is an indication of strength.

42:44   And whoever God sends astray will not have any ally after Him. And you will see the transgressors, when they see the retribution, saying: "Is there any way we can go back?"

42:45   And you will see them being displayed to it, in fearful humiliation, and looking, while trying to avoid looking. And those who believed will say: "The losers are those who lost their souls and their families on the Day of Resurrection. The transgressors will be in a lasting retribution."

42:46   And they had no allies to help them against God. And whoever God misguides will never find the way.

42:47   Respond to your Lord before a Day comes from God which cannot be averted. You will have no refuge for you on that Day, nor an advocate.

42:48   But if they turn away, then We did not send you as their guardian. You are only required to deliver. And when We let the human being taste a mercy from Us, he becomes happy with it; and when adversity afflicts them for what their hands have delivered, then the human being becomes rejecting!

42:49   To God is the sovereignty of the heavens and the earth. He creates whatever He wills. He bestows daughters to whoever He wills, and bestows sons to whoever He wills.

42:50   Or, He may bestow them with both sons and daughters, and He makes whom He wills barren. He is Knowledgeable, Capable.

42:51   And it is not for any mortal that God would speak to him, except through inspiration, or from behind a veil, or by sending a messenger to inspire whom He wills with His permission. He is Most High, Wise.

42:52   And thus, We inspired to you a revelation of Our command. You did not know what was the Book, nor what was faith. Yet, We made it a light to guide whoever We wish from among Our servants. Surely, you guide to a straight path.

42:53   The path of God, to whom belongs what is in the heavens and the earth. Ultimately, to God all matters return.

CHAPTER 43

43:0   In the name of God, the Almighty, the Merciful.

43:1   HM.

43:2   And the clarifying Book.

43:3   We have made it a Qur'an in Arabic, perhaps you may comprehend.

43:4   And, in the Mother of the Book with Us, it is held honorable and wise.

43:5   Shall We withdraw the reminder from you, because you are a transgressing people?

43:6   And how many a prophet did We send to the previous generations!

43:7   And every time a prophet went to them, they mocked him.

43:8   We have destroyed those who were even more powerful than these, and the example of the previous generations has already been given.

43:9   And if you asked them: "Who has created the heavens and the earth?" They will say: "They were created by the One who is the Noble, the Knowledgeable."

43:10 He is the One who made the earth a habitat for you, and He made paths in it that you may be guided.

43:11 And He is the One who sends down water from the sky, in exact measure. We then revive with it a dead land. Similarly, you will be brought out.

43:12 And He is the One who has created all the pairs, and He made for you of the ships and the hoofed animals that which you can ride.

43:13 So that you may settle on their backs; then recall the blessing of your Lord once you have settled on them, and say: "Glory to the One who has commissioned this for us, and we could not have done so by ourselves."

43:14 "And we will ultimately return to our Lord."

43:15 And they assigned a share to Him from His own servants! The human being is clearly denying.

43:16 Or has He selected daughters from among His creation, while He has left you with the sons?

43:17 And if one of them is given news of that which he puts forth as an example for the Almighty, his face becomes dark, and he is miserable!

43:18 "What good is an offspring that is brought up to be beautiful, and cannot help in a fight?"

43:19 And they have claimed the angels who are with the Almighty are females! Have they been made witness to their creation? We will record their testimony, and they will be asked.

43:20 And they said: "If the Almighty had willed, we would not have worshipped them." They have no knowledge of this; they only guess.

43:21 Or have We given them a book before this which they are upholding?

43:22 The fact is, they have said: "We found our fathers following a certain way, and we are following in their footsteps."

43:23 And similarly, We did not send a warner to a town, except its carefree ones said: "We found our fathers following a certain way, and we are being guided in their footsteps."

43:24 He said: "What if I brought to you better a guidance than what you found your fathers upon?" They said: "We are disbelievers in that with which you have been sent."

43:25   Consequently, We took revenge upon them. So see how was the consequences of the deniers.

43:26   And when Abraham said to his father and his people: "I am innocent of that which you worship."

43:27   "Except for the One who initiated me, He will guide me."

43:28   And he made it a word to last in his subsequent generations; perhaps they may turn back.

43:29   Indeed, I have given these people and their fathers to enjoy, until the truth came to them, and a clarifying messenger.

43:30   And when the truth came to them, they said: "This is magic, and we reject it."

43:31   And they said: "If only this Qur'an was sent down to a man of greatness from the two towns!"

43:32   Is it they who assign the mercy of your Lord? We have assigned their share in this worldly life, and We raised some of them above others in ranks, so that they would take one another in service. The mercy from your Lord is far better than that which they amass.

43:33   And were it not that all the people would become one nation, We would have provided for those who reject the Almighty silver roofs for their homes, and stairs upon which they could ascend.

43:34   And for their homes, gates, and beds on which they could recline.

43:35   And many ornaments. All these are the pleasures of this worldly life. And the Hereafter with your Lord is for the righteous.

43:36   And whoever turns away from the remembrance of the Almighty, We appoint a devil to be his associate.

43:37   And they hinder from the path, but they think they are guided!

43:38   Until he comes to Us, he will say, "Oh, I wish that between you and me was the distance of the two easts. What a miserable associate!"

43:39   It would not benefit you this Day, for you have transgressed; you are partners in the retribution.

43:40 Can you make the deaf hear, or can you guide the blind and those who are far astray?

43:41 So if We take you away, We may then seek revenge on them.

43:42 Or We may show you that which We promised for them; for We are able to take them.

43:43 You shall hold on to that which is inspired to you; for you are on a straight path.

43:44 And this is indeed a reminder for you and your people; and you will all be questioned.

43:45 And ask those of Our messengers whom We sent before you: "Did We ever appoint gods besides the Almighty to be served?"

43:46 And We sent Moses with Our signs to Pharaoh and his commanders; so he said: "I am a messenger of the Lord of the worlds."

43:47 But when he came to them with Our signs, they laughed at them.

43:48 And every sign We showed them was greater than the one before it, and We seized them with the torment, perhaps they would return.

43:49 And they said: "O you magician, call on your Lord for what pledge He gave you; we will then be guided."

43:50 But when We removed the torment from them, they broke their word.

43:51 And Pharaoh proclaimed among his people: "O my people, do I not possess the kingship of Egypt, and these rivers that flow below me? Do you not see?"

43:52 "Am I not better than this one who is despised and he can barely be understood?"

43:53 "Why then are not golden bracelets bestowed on him, or the angels are accompanying him?"

43:54 He thus convinced his people, and they obeyed him; they were a wicked people.

43:55 So when they persisted in opposing Us, We sought revenge from them, and drowned them all.

43:56 We thus made them a thing of the past, and an example for the others.

43:57 And when the son of Mary was put forth as an example, your people turned away from it.

43:58 And they said: "Our gods are better or is he?" They only put this forth to argue with you. Indeed, they are a quarrelsome people.

43:59 He was no more than a servant whom We graced, and We made him an example for the Children of Israel.

43:60 And if We willed, We could have made some of you angels to be successors on the earth.

43:61 And he was a lesson for the Hour. So have no doubt about it. And follow Me; this is a straight path.

43:62 And let not the devil repel you; he is to you a clear enemy.

43:63 And when Jesus came with the proofs, he said: "I have come to you with the wisdom, and to clarify some of the matters in which you dispute. So be aware of God and obey me."

43:64 "God is my Lord and your Lord. So serve Him. This is a straight path."

43:65 The Confederates disputed among themselves. So, woe to those who have been wicked from the retribution of a painful Day.

43:66 Do they only wait for the Hour to come to them suddenly, while they do not perceive?

43:67 Friends on that Day will become enemies of one another, except for the righteous.

43:68 "O My servants, you will have no fear on this Day, nor will you grieve."

43:69 They are the ones who believed in Our revelations, and had submitted.

43:70 "Enter Paradise, together with your spouses, in happiness."

43:71 They will be served with golden trays and cups, and they will find everything the self desires and the eyes wish for, and you will abide therein.

43:72 And this is Paradise that you have inherited, in return for your works.

43:73 In it you will have all kinds of fruits, from which you eat.

43:74   Surely, the criminals will abide in the retribution of Hell.

43:75   It will not be removed from them; they will be confined therein.

43:76   And We did not wrong them, but it was they who were the wrongdoers.

43:77   And they called out: "O Malek, please let your Lord terminate us!" He will say: "No, you are remaining."

43:78   We have come to you with the truth, but most of you hate the truth.

43:79   Or have they devised some scheme? We will also devise.

43:80   Or do they think that We do not hear their secrets and their private counsel? Yes indeed; and Our messengers are with them, recording.

43:81   Say: "If the Almighty had a son, I would be the first to serve!"

43:82   Glory be to the Lord of the heavens and the earth, the Lord of the Throne, from what they describe.

43:83   So leave them to speak nonsense and play until they meet their Day which they have been promised.

43:84   And He is the One who is a god in the heaven and a god on the earth. And He is the Wise, the Knowledgeable.

43:85   And blessed is the One who possesses the sovereignty of the heavens and the earth, and everything between them; and with Him is the knowledge of the Hour, and to Him you will be returned.

43:86   And those whom they call on besides Him do not possess any intercession; except those who bear witness to the truth, and they fully know.

43:87   And if you asked them who has created them, they would say, "God." Why then do they deviate?

43:88   And it will be said: "O my Lord, these are a people who do not believe."

43:89   So disregard them and say: "Peace." For they will come to know.

CHAPTER 44

44:0 In the name of God, the Almighty, the Merciful.

44:1 HM.

44:2 And the clarifying Book.

44:3 We have sent it down in a blessed night—We were surely to warn.

44:4 In it is a distinction for all decree of wisdom.

44:5 A decree from Us—We were surely to send.

44:6 A mercy from your Lord. He is the Hearer, the Knowledgeable.

44:7 The Lord of the heavens and the earth, and everything between them. If you were certain!

44:8 There is no god except He. He gives life and causes death; your Lord and the Lord of your ancestors.

44:9 No; they are in doubt, playing.

44:10 Therefore, watch for the day when the heaven will bring a visible smoke.

44:11 It will envelop the people: "This is a painful retribution!"

44:12 "Our Lord, remove the retribution from us; we are believers."

44:13 How is it that now they remember, while a clarifying messenger had come to them?

44:14 But then, they turned away from him and said: "Well educated, but crazy!"

44:15 We will remove the retribution in a while; you will then return back.

44:16 On the Day We strike the great strike, We will avenge.

44:17 And We had tested before them the people of Pharaoh, and an honorable messenger came to them.

44:18 "Restore to me the servants of God. I am a trustworthy messenger to you."

44:19 "And, do not transgress against God. I come to you with clear authority."

44:20 "And I seek refuge with my Lord and your Lord, should you stone me."

44:21 "And if you do not believe in me, then have no dealing with me."

44:22 Subsequently, he called on his Lord: "These are a criminal people."

44:23 Travel with My servants during the night; you will be pursued.

44:24 And cross the sea quickly; their troops will be drowned.

44:25 How many gardens and springs did they leave behind?

44:26 And crops and an honorable station?

44:27 And blessings that they enjoyed?

44:28 Thus it was; and We caused another people to inherit it.

44:29 Neither the heaven, nor the earth wept over them, and they were not respited.

44:30 And We saved the Children of Israel from the humiliating agony.

44:31 From Pharaoh; he was a transgressing tyrant.

44:32 And We have chosen them, out of knowledge, over the worlds.

44:33 And We granted them signs, which constituted a great test.

44:34 These people now are saying:

44:35 "There is nothing except our first death; and we will never be resurrected!"

44:36 "So bring back our forefathers, if you are truthful!"

44:37 Are they better or the people of Tubba` and those before them? We destroyed them, they were criminals.

44:38 And We have not created the heavens and the earth, and everything between them, for mere play.

44:39 We did not create them except with the truth, but most of them do not know.

44:40 Surely, the Day of Separation is the designated time for them all.

44:41 That is the Day when no friend can help his friend in any way; nor will they be helped.

44:42 Except him on whom God has mercy. He is the Noble, the Merciful.

44:43 Surely, the tree of Bitterness,

44:44 Will be the food for the sinful.

44:45 Like hot oil, it will boil in the bellies.

44:46 Like the boiling of liquid.

44:47 "Take him and throw him into the midst of Hell."

44:48 "Then pour upon his head the retribution of boiling liquid."

44:49 "Taste this; surely you are the noble, the generous!"

44:50 Surely, this is what you used to doubt!

44:51 The righteous will be in a station of security.

44:52 Among gardens and springs.

44:53 Wearing silk and satin; facing each other.

44:54 So it is, and We married them to wonderful consorts.

44:55 They enjoy in it all kinds of fruits, in perfect peace.

44:56 They do not taste death therein except for the first death, and He has spared them the retribution of Hell.

44:57 As a blessing from your Lord. Such is the great triumph.

44:58 We have thus made it easy in your language, perhaps they may take heed.

44:59 Therefore, watch; for they too will be watching.

CHAPTER 45

45:0 In the name of God, the Almighty, the Merciful.

45:1 HM.

45:2 The revelation of the Book is from God, the Noble, the Wise.

45:3 In the heavens and the earth are signs for the believers.

45:4 And in your creation, and what creatures He puts forth are signs for people who are certain.

45:5 And the alternation of the night and the day, and what God sends down from the heaven of provisions to revive the land after its death, and the dispatching of the winds, are signs for a people who comprehend.

45:6 These are the revelations of God, We recite them to you with the truth. So, in which narrative after God and His revelations do they believe?

45:7 Woe to every sinful fabricator.

45:8 He hears the revelations of God being recited to him, then he persists arrogantly, as if he never heard them. Give him news of a painful retribution.

45:9 And if he learns anything from Our revelations, he takes it in mockery. For these will be a humiliating retribution.

45:10 Waiting for them is Hell. And that which they earned will not help them, nor those whom they have taken as allies besides God, and for them is a terrible retribution.

45:11 This is a guidance. And those who reject the revelations of their Lord, for them is an affliction of a painful retribution.

45:12 God is the One who commissioned the sea in your service, so that the ships can run in it by His command, and that you may seek of His provisions, and that you may be thankful.

45:13 And He commissioned in your service what is in the heavens and what is in the earth; all from Him. In that are signs for a people who reflect.

45:14 Say to those who believed to forgive those who do not look forward to the days of God. He will recompense a people for whatever they have earned.

45:15 Whoever works good does so for himself, and whoever works evil will suffer it. Then to your Lord you will be returned.

45:16 And We had given the Children of Israel the Book, and the judgment, and the prophethood, and We provided them with good provisions; and We preferred them over the worlds.

45:17 And We gave them clarity in the matter, but then they disputed after the knowledge had come to them, out of jealousy among themselves. Your Lord will judge them on the Day of Resurrection regarding everything that they have disputed.

45:18 Then We have established you on the path of things; so follow it and do not follow the desires of those who do not know.

45:19 They cannot help you against God in the least. And the transgressors are allies to one another, while God is the Protector of the righteous.

45:20 This is a physical evidence for the people, and a guidance and a mercy for a people who are certain.

45:21 Or do those who work evil expect that We would treat them the same as those who believe and do good works, in their present life and their death? Miserable is how they judge.

45:22 And God created the heavens and the earth with the truth, and so that every soul may be recompensed for whatever it earned, and they will not be wronged.

45:23 Have you seen the one who took his desire as his god, and God led him astray, despite his knowledge, and He sealed his hearing and his heart, and He made a veil on his eyes? Who then can guide him after God? Will you not remember?

45:24 And they said: "There is nothing except this worldly life; we die and we live and nothing destroys us except the passing of time!" And they have no knowledge about this; they only conjecture.

45:25 And when Our clear revelations are recited to them, their only argument is to say: "Then bring back our forefathers, if you are truthful."

45:26 Say: "God gives you life, then He puts you to death, then He will gather you to the Day of Resurrection, in which there is no doubt. But most of the people do not know."

45:27 And to God is the sovereignty of the heavens and the earth. And on the Day the Hour comes to pass, on that Day the falsifiers will lose.

45:28 And you will see every nation kneeling. Every nation will be called to its book. "Today, you will be recompensed for everything you have done."

45:29 "This is Our record; it utters the truth about you. We have been recording everything you did."

45:30 As for those who believed and did good works, their Lord will admit them into His mercy. Such is the clear triumph.

45:31 As for those who disbelieve: "Were not My revelations recited to you, but you turned arrogant and were a criminal people?"

45:32 And when it was said: "Surely the promise of God is the truth, and there is no doubt about the coming of the Hour," you said: "We do not know what the Hour is! We are full of conjecture about it; we are not certain."

45:33 And the evils of their works will become evident to them, and they will be surrounded by that which they used to mock.

45:34 And it will be said to them: "Today We will forget you, just as you forgot the meeting of this Day. And your abode is the Fire, and you will have no helpers."

45:35 "This is because you took the revelations of God in mockery, and you were deceived by the worldly life." So from this Day, they will never exit therefrom, nor will they be excused.

45:36 To God belongs all praise; the Lord of the heavens, and the Lord of the earth; the Lord of the worlds.

45:37 And to Him belongs all majesty in the heavens and the earth. He is the Noble, the Wise.

CHAPTER 46

46:0 In the name of God, the Almighty, the Merciful.

46:1 HM.

46:2 The revelation of the Book from God, the Noble, the Wise.

46:3 We did not create the heavens and the earth, and everything between them except with the truth, and for an appointed time. And those who disbelieve turn away from what they are being warned with.

46:4 Say: "Do you see those that you call on besides God? Show me what they have created on the earth, or do they have a share in the heavens? Bring me a book before this, or any trace of knowledge, if you are truthful."

46:5 And who is more astray than he who calls on others besides God that do not respond to him even until the Day of Resurrection? And they are totally unaware of the calls to them!

46:6 And at the time when the people are gathered, they will be enemies for them, and they will reject their worship.

46:7 And when Our clear revelations are recited to them, those who rejected said of the truth that came to them: "This is evidently magic!"

46:8 Or do they say: "He fabricated this!" Say: "If I fabricated this, then you cannot protect me at all from God. He is fully aware of what you say. He suffices as a witness between me and you. He is the Forgiver, the Merciful."

46:9 Say: "I am no different from the other messengers, nor do I know what will happen to me or to you. I only follow what is inspired to me. I am no more than a clear warner."

46:10 Say: "Do you see that if it were from God, and you rejected it, and a witness from the Children of Israel gave testimony to its similarity, and he has believed, while you have turned arrogant? Surely, God does not guide the wicked people."

46:11 And those who had rejected said regarding those who had believed: "If it were any good, they would not have beaten us to it." And when they are not able to be guided by it, they will say: "This is an old fabrication!"

46:12 And before it was the Book of Moses, a beacon and a mercy. And this is an affirming Book, in an Arabic tongue, so that you may warn those who have transgressed, and to give good news to the righteous.

46:13 Those who said: "Our Lord is God," then they lead a righteous life, there is no fear for them, nor will they grieve.

46:14 These are the dwellers of Paradise, abiding therein, a reward for what they used to do.

46:15 And We enjoined the human being to do good to his parents. His mother bore him with hardship, gave birth to him in hardship, and his bearing and weaning lasts thirty months. So that, when he has reached his independence, and he has reached forty years, he says: "My Lord, direct me to appreciate the blessings You have bestowed upon me and upon my parents, and to do good work that pleases You. And let my progeny be righteous. I have repented to You; I am of those who have submitted."

46:16 It is from these that We accept the best of their deeds, and We shall overlook their sins, among the dwellers of Paradise. This is the promise of truth that they had been promised.

46:17 And the one who says to his parents: "Enough of you! Are you promising me that I will be resurrected, when the generations who died before me never came back?" While they both will implore God: "Woe to you; believe! For the promise of God is the truth." He would say: "This is nothing except tales of old!"

46:18 These are the ones against whom the sentence has been deserved in nations who had come before them of mankind and Jinn; they are the losers.

46:19 And to each will be degrees according to what they did, and He will recompense them and they will not be wronged.

46:20 And on the Day when those who disbelieved will be displayed to the Fire: "You have wasted the good things given to you during your worldly life, and you took pleasure in it. Consequently, today you will be recompensed with a shameful retribution for your arrogance in the land without any right, and for what wickedness you were in."

46:21 And recall the brethren of `Aad, when he warned his people at the dunes—while warnings had been given before him and with him: "You shall not serve except God. For I fear for you the retribution of a great day!"

46:22 They said: "Have you come to us to divert us away from our gods? Then bring us what you are promising us, if you are truthful!"

46:23 He said: "The knowledge is only with God; and I deliver to you what I was sent with. However, I see that you are a people who are ignorant."

46:24 But when they saw a storm cloud heading towards their valleys, they said: "This is a storm cloud that will bring to us much needed rain!" No, this is what you had asked to be hastened; a violent wind wherein there is a painful retribution.

46:25 It destroys everything by the command of its Lord. Thus they became such that nothing could be seen except their dwellings. We thus requite the criminal people.

46:26 And We had established them in the same way as We established you, and provided them with hearing, and eyesight, and minds. But their hearing, eyesight, and minds did not help them at all. This is because they used to disregard the revelations of God, and they will be surrounded by that which they used to mock.

46:27 And We destroyed the towns around you and We had dispatched the signs, perhaps they would repent.

46:28 They were to be supported by those who had established offerings to gods instead of God. Alas, they abandoned them. Such was their lie, and what they fabricated.

46:29 And We dispatched to you a company of Jinn, in order to let them listen to the Qur'an. So when they arrived there, they said: "Pay attention." Then, when it was finished, they returned to their people, to warn them.

46:30 They said: "O our people, we have heard a Book that was sent down after Moses, affirming what is between his hands. It guides to the truth; and to a straight path."

46:31 "O our people, respond to the caller to God, and believe in Him. He will then forgive your sins, and spare you a painful retribution."

46:32 And whoever does not respond to the caller to God will not escape in the land, and he will not have besides Him any allies. Such have gone far astray.

46:33 Did they not see that God, who has created the heavens and the earth and was not tired by their creation, is able to revive the dead? Yes indeed; He is able to do all things.

46:34 And the Day those who rejected are displayed to the Fire: "Is this not the truth?" They will say: "Yes indeed, by our Lord." He will say: "Then taste the retribution for what you had rejected."

46:35 Therefore, be patient like the messengers of strong-will did before you and do not be in haste regarding them. On the Day they will see what they have been promised, it will be as if they had not remained except for one hour of a single day—a directive—are any destroyed except for the wicked people?

CHAPTER 47

47:0   In the name of God, the Almighty, the Merciful.

47:1   Those who rejected and repelled from the path of God, He will mislead their works.

47:2   And those who believe and do good works, and believe in what was sent down to Mohammed, for it is the truth from their Lord, He cancels for them their sins, and relieves their concern.

47:3   That is because those who reject followed falsehood, while those who believe followed the truth from their Lord. God thus puts forth for the people their examples.

47:4   So, if you encounter those who have rejected, then strike the necks; until you overpower them, then bind them securely. You may thereafter either set them free or ransom them, until the burden of war ends. That, and if God had willed, He alone could have beaten them, but He thus tests you by one another. As for those who get killed in the cause of God, He will never let their deeds be put to waste.

47:5   He will guide them, and relieve their concerns.

47:6   And He will admit them into Paradise, which He has described to them.

47:7   O you who believe, if you support God, He will support you, and make your foothold firm.

47:8   And those who rejected, for them is destruction; and He has misled their works.

47:9   That is because they hated what God sent down, thus He nullifies their works.

47:10   Did they not roam the earth and note how was the end for those before them? God destroyed them; and for the rejecters in a similar fate.

47:11   This is because God is the Master for those who believe, while the rejecters have no master.

47:12   God admits those who believe and do good works to gardens with rivers flowing beneath them. And those who reject, they are enjoying and eating as the hoofed animals eat, and the Fire will be their abode.

47:13   And many a town was stronger than your own town, which drove you out. We destroyed them, and there was none who could help them.

47:14   Is he who is based on proof from his Lord, as he for whom his evil works have been adorned for him and they followed their desires?

47:15   Is the example of Paradise; that the righteous have been promised with rivers of pure water, and rivers of milk whose taste does not change, and rivers of intoxicants that are delicious for the drinkers, and rivers of strained honey, and for them in it are all kinds of fruits, and a forgiveness from their Lord; like that of those who abide in the Fire, and are given to drink boiling water that cuts-up their intestines?

47:16   And some of them listen to you, until when they go out from you, they say to those who have been given the knowledge: "What did he say?" Those are the ones whom God has sealed their hearts, and they followed their desires.

47:17   And those who are guided, He increases their guidance, and grants them their righteousness.

47:18   So are they waiting until the Hour comes to them suddenly? For its conditions have already been met. But once it comes to them, how will they benefit from their message?

47:19   So know that there is no god besides God, and ask forgiveness of your sins and also for the believing males and the believing females. And God knows your movements and your place of rest.

47:20   And those who believe say: "If only a chapter is sent down!" But when a fixed chapter is sent down, and fighting is mentioned in it, you see those who have a disease in their hearts look at you, as if death had already come to them. It thus revealed them.

47:21   Obedience and to speak righteousness until the matter is decided, then if they trust God it would be better for them.

47:22   So do you plan that when you turn away, that you will corrupt the land and sever your family ties?

47:23   These are the ones whom God has cursed and thus He made them deaf and blinded their sight.

47:24 Do they not reflect upon the Qur'an? Or are there locks on the hearts?

47:25 Surely, those who returned back, after the guidance has been made clear to them, the devil has enticed them and has led them on.

47:26 That is because they said to those who hated what God had sent down: "We will obey you in certain matters." And God knows their secrets.

47:27 So how will it be when their lives are terminated by the angels, while striking their faces and their backs?

47:28 That is because they followed that which angered God, and they hated that which pleased Him. Thus, He nullified their works.

47:29 Or did those who harbor a disease in their hearts think that God would not bring out their evil thoughts?

47:30 And if We wished, We would show them to you so you would recognize them by their looks. However, you can recognize them by their speech. And God is fully aware of your works.

47:31 And We will test you for We know those who strive among you and those who are patient. And We will bring out your qualities.

47:32 Those who have rejected and repelled from the path of God, and stood against the messenger; after the guidance has been made clear for them; they will not harm God in the least, and He will nullify their works.

47:33 O you who believe, obey God, and obey the messenger. And do not render your works in vain.

47:34 Surely, those who rejected and repelled from the path of God, then they died while still rejecting, God will never forgive them.

47:35 Therefore, do not be weak and ask for peace, for you are on a higher moral ground, and God is with you. And He will not waste your efforts.

47:36 The worldly life is no more than play and distraction. But if you believe and lead a righteous life, He will reward you, and He will not ask you for your wealth.

47:37 If He were to ask you for it, to the extent of creating a hardship for you, you would become stingy, and your hidden evil will be exposed.

47:38 Here you are being invited to spend in the cause of God, but some among you turn stingy. And whoever is stingy is only being stingy on himself. And God is the Rich, while you are the poor. And if you turn away, He will substitute another people instead of you, then they will not be like you.

CHAPTER 48

48:0 In the name of God, the Almighty, the Merciful.

48:1 We have given you a clear conquest.

48:2 That God may forgive your present sins, and those past, and so that He may complete His blessings upon you, and guide you on a straight path.

48:3 And God will support you with a victory which is noble.

48:4 He is the One who sends down tranquility into the hearts of the believers, so that they may increase in faith along with their present faith. And to God belongs the soldiers of the heavens and the earth, and God is Knowledgeable, Wise.

48:5 That He may admit the believing males and believing females into gardens with rivers flowing beneath them, abiding therein, and He will forgive their sins for them. And with God this is a great triumph.

48:6 And He will punish the hypocrite males and the hypocrite females, and the polytheist males and the polytheist females; they think evil thoughts about God. Their evil will come back to them, and God was angry with them, and He has cursed them and prepared for them Hell. What a miserable destiny!

48:7 And to God belongs the soldiers of the heavens and the earth. And God is Noble, Wise.

48:8 We have sent you as a witness, a bearer of good news, and a warner.

48:9 That you may believe in God and His messenger, and that you may support Him, honor Him, and glorify Him, morning and evening.

48:10 Those who pledge to you, are in fact pledging to God; the hand of God is above their hands. Those of them who violate such a pledge, are violating it only for themselves. And whoever fulfills what he has pledged to God, then He will grant him a great reward.

48:11   The Nomads who lagged behind will say to you: "We were preoccupied with our money and our family, so ask forgiveness for us." They say with their tongues what is not in their hearts. Say: "Who then would possess any power for you against God if He wanted harm to afflict you or if He wanted benefit for you?" God is fully Aware of everything you do.

48:12   Alas, you thought that the messenger and the believers would not return to their families, and this was deemed pleasant in your hearts, and you thought the worst thoughts; you were a wicked people!

48:13   Anyone who does not believe in God and His messenger, then We have prepared for the rejecters a Fire.

48:14   And to God is the sovereignty of the heavens and the earth. He forgives whoever He wills, and punishes whoever He wills. God is Forgiver, Merciful.

48:15   Those who lagged behind will say, when you venture out to collect the spoils: "Let us follow you!" They want to change the words of God. Say: "You will not follow us; this is what God has decreed beforehand." They will then say: "No, you are envious of us." Alas, they rarely understood anything.

48:16   Say to those Nomads who lagged behind: "You will be called on to fight a people who are very powerful in warfare, unless they surrender. Then if you obey, God will grant you a good reward, but if you turn away as you turned away before, He will punish you with a painful retribution."

48:17   There is no burden on the blind, nor is there any burden on the cripple, nor is there any burden on the sick. And whoever obeys God and His messenger, He will admit them into gardens with rivers flowing beneath them; and whoever turns away, He will punish him with a painful retribution.

48:18   God is pleased with the believers who pledged to you under the tree. He knew what was in their hearts, so He sent down tranquility upon them, and rewarded them with a victory that is near.

48:19   And abundant spoils that they will take. God is Noble, Wise.

48:20   God has promised you abundant spoils that you will take. Thus

He has hastened this for you, and He has withheld the hands of the people against you; that it may be a sign for the believers, and that He may guide you to a straight path.

48:21 And the other group which you could not vanquish, God took care of them. And God was capable of all things.

48:22 And if the rejecters had fought you, they would have turned and ran, then they would have found neither an ally nor a victor.

48:23 Such is the way of God with those who have passed away before, and you will not find any change in the way of God.

48:24 And He is the One who withheld their hands against you, and your hands against them in the interior of Mecca, after He had made you victorious over them. God is Seer of what you do.

48:25 They are the ones who rejected and barred you from the restricted Temple, and barred your offerings from reaching their destination. And there had been believing men and believing women whom you did not know, and you may have hurt them, and on whose account you would have incurred a sin unknowingly. God will admit into His mercy whoever He wills. Had they become separated, We would then have punished those from them who rejected with a painful retribution.

48:26 Those who rejected had put in their hearts the rage of the days of ignorance. Thus, God sent down tranquility upon His messenger and the believers, and He attached to them the word of righteousness; and they were well entitled to it and worthy of it. And God is fully aware of all things.

48:27 God has affirmed His messenger's vision shall come true: "You will enter the restricted Temple, God willing, secure, with your heads shaven and shortened, having no fear." Thus, He knew what you did not know. And He has ordained, after this, a conquest close at hand.

48:28 He is the One who sent His messenger with the guidance and the system of truth, so that it would expose all other systems. And God is enough as a witness.

48:29 Mohammed is the messenger of God, and those with him are severe against the rejecters, merciful between themselves. You see them kneeling and prostrating, seeking the blessings and approval of God. Their distinction is in their faces, as a result of prostrating. Such is their example in the Torah. And their example in the Gospel is like a plant which shoots out and becomes strong and thick and it stands straight on its trunk, pleasing to the farmers. That He may enrage the rejecters with them. God promises those among them who believe and do good works forgiveness and a great reward.

CHAPTER 49

49:0 In the name of God, the Almighty, the Merciful.

49:1 O you who believe, do not place your opinion above that of God and His messenger. And be aware of God. God is Hearer, Knowledgeable.

49:2 O you who believe, do not raise your voices above the voice of the prophet, nor shall you speak loudly to him as you would speak loudly to each other, lest your works become nullified while you do not perceive.

49:3 Surely, those who lower their voices with the messenger of God, they are the ones whose hearts have been tested by God for righteousness. They have deserved forgiveness and a great recompense.

49:4 Surely, those who call on you from behind the lodgings, most of them do not comprehend.

49:5 And if they had only been patient until you came out to them, it would have been better for them. God is Forgiver, Merciful.

49:6 O you who believe, if a wicked person comes to you with any news, then you shall investigate it. Lest you harm a people out of ignorance, then you will become regretful over what you have done.

49:7 And know that among you is the messenger of God. If he were to obey you in many things, you would have deviated. But God made you love faith and He adorned it in your hearts, and He made you hate disbelief, wickedness, and disobedience. These are the rightly guided ones.

49:8 Such is the grace from God and a blessing. God is Knowledgeable, Wise.

49:9 And if two parties of believers battle with each other, you shall reconcile them; but if one of them aggresses against the other, then you shall fight the one aggressing until it complies with the command of God. Once it complies, then you shall reconcile the two groups with justice, and be equitable; for God loves those who are equitable.

49:10 The believers are brothers; so reconcile between your brothers, and be aware of God, that you may receive mercy.

49:11 O you who believe, let not any people ridicule other people, for they may be better than they. Nor shall any women ridicule other women, for they may be better than they. Nor shall you mock one another, or insult each other with nicknames; miserable indeed is the name of wickedness after attaining faith. And anyone who does not repent, then these are the transgressors.

49:12 O you who believe, you shall greatly avoid suspicion—some suspicion is sinful. And do not spy on one another, nor shall you backbite. Would any of you enjoy eating the flesh of his dead brother? You certainly would hate this. You shall observe God. God is Redeemer, Merciful.

49:13 O people, We created you from a male and female, and We made you into nations and tribes, that you may know one another. Surely, the most honorable among you in the sight of God is the most righteous. God is Knowledgeable, Expert.

49:14 The Nomads said: "We believe." Say: "You have not believed; but you should say: 'We have submitted;' until belief enters into your hearts." And if you obey God and His messenger, He will not put any of your works to waste. God is Forgiver, Merciful.

49:15 Believers are those who believe in God and His messenger, then they became without doubt, and they strive with their money and their lives in the cause of God. These are the truthful ones.

49:16 Say: "Are you teaching God about your system while God knows everything in the heavens and the earth? God is knowledgeable of all things."

49:17 They think they are doing you a favor by having submitted! Say: "Do not think you are doing me any favors by your submission. For it is God who is doing you a favor that He has guided you to the faith, if you are being true."

49:18 Surely, God knows all the unseen in the heavens and the earth; God is Seer of what you do.

CHAPTER 50

50:0   In the name of God, the Almighty, the Merciful.

50:1   Q, and the Qur'an of glory.

50:2   Are they surprised that a warner has come to them from amongst them, so the rejecters said: "This is something strange!"

50:3   "Can it be that when we are dead and we become dust, that we come back later?"

50:4   We know which of them has become consumed with the earth; and We have with Us a record which keeps track.

50:5   But they denied the truth when it came to them, so they are in a confused state.

50:6   Did they not look to the heaven above them, how We built it, and adorned it, and how it has no openings?

50:7   And the land We extended it, and placed in it stabilizers, and We gave growth in it to every pair that is pleasing.

50:8   Something to see and a reminder for every pious servant.

50:9   And We sent down from the sky blessed water, and We gave growth with it to gardens and grain that is harvested.

50:10   And the palm trees, emerging with clustering fruit.

50:11   A provision for the servants, and We gave life with it to the land which was dead. Such is the resurrection.

50:12   Before their denial was that of the people of Noah, and the dwellers of Al-Raas, and Thamud.

50:13   And 'Aad, and Pharaoh, and the brethren of Lot.

50:14   And the people of the Sycamore, and the people of Tubba`. All of them disbelieved the messengers, so the promise came to pass.

50:15   Did We have any difficulty in making the first creation? No, they are in confusion about the next creation.

50:16   And We have created the human being and We know what his soul whispers to him, and We are closer to him than his jugular vein.

50:17   When the two receivers meet on the right and on the left.

50:18   He does not utter a word except a watcher is constantly with him.

50:19   And the moment of death came with truth: "This is what you have been trying to avoid!"

50:20   And the horn is blown on the promised Day.

50:21   And every soul is brought, being driven, and with a witness.

50:22   "You were heedless of this, so now We have removed your cover, and your sight today is iron!"

50:23   And his associate said: "Here is one who is a transgressor."

50:24   "Cast in Hell every stubborn rejecter."

50:25   "Denier of good, transgressor, doubter."

50:26   "The one who has set up with God another god; so cast him into the severe retribution."

50:27   His associate said: "Our Lord, I did not corrupt him, but he was already far astray."

50:28   He said: "Do not argue with each other before Me, I have already presented you with My promise."

50:29   "The sentence will not be changed with Me, and I do not wrong the servants."

50:30   The Day We say to Hell: "Are you full?" And it says: "Is there not more?"

50:31   And Paradise is brought near to the righteous, not far off.

50:32   This is what you have been promised, for every obedient, steadfast.

50:33   Who is concerned towards the Almighty while unseen, and came with a repenting heart.

50:34   Enter it in peace. This is the Day of eternal life.

50:35   In it they will have what they wish, and We have even more.

50:36   And how many a generation before them have We destroyed? They were stronger in power, and they had dominated the land. Did they find any refuge?

50:37   In that is a reminder for whoever has a heart, or cares to listen while he is heedful.

50:38 And We have created the heavens and the earth and what is between them in six days, and no fatigue touched Us.

50:39 So be patient to what they are saying, and glorify the grace of your Lord before the rising of the sun and before the setting.

50:40 And from the night glorify Him, and after prostrating.

50:41 And listen to the Day when the caller will call from a near place.

50:42 The Day they hear the scream with the truth. That is the Day of coming out.

50:43 We are the Ones who give life and bring death, and to Us is the destiny.

50:44 The Day when the earth will rapidly crumble away from them; that will be a gathering which is easy for Us.

50:45 We are fully aware of what they say; and you are not a tyrant over them. So remind with the Qur'an those who fear My promise.

CHAPTER 51

51:0 In the name of God, the Almighty, the Merciful.

51:1 By the winds that blow.

51:2 Carrying rain.

51:3 Traveling easily.

51:4 Distributing as commanded.

51:5 What you are being promised is true.

51:6 And the Judgment will come to pass.

51:7 By the heaven that is woven.

51:8 You are saying what is different.

51:9 To mislead those who are misled.

51:10 Woe to the deceitful.

51:11 Who are in mischief, unaware.

51:12 They ask: "When is the Day of Judgment?"

51:13 The Day they ordeal upon the Fire.

51:14 "Taste this ordeal of yours; this is what you asked to be hastened."

51:15 The righteous are in gardens and springs.

51:16 Receiving what their Lord has bestowed to them, for they were before that pious.

51:17 They used to rarely sleep the whole night.

51:18 And before dawn, they would seek forgiveness.

51:19 And in their money was a portion for the beggar and the needy.

51:20 And on the earth are signs for those who comprehend.

51:21 And within yourselves; do you not see?

51:22 And in the heaven is your provision, and what you are promised.

51:23 By the Lord of the heaven and the earth, this is truth just as the fact that you speak.

51:24 Has the narrative of the noble guests of Abraham come to you?

51:25 When they entered upon him, they said: "Peace." He said: "Peace to a people unknown!"

51:26 Then he went to his family and brought a fat calf.

51:27 He offered it to them, he said: "Do you not eat?"

51:28 He then became fearful of them. They said: "Do not fear," and they gave him glad tidings of a knowledgeable boy.

51:29 His wife approached in a daze; she slapped upon her face, and said: "An old barren woman!"

51:30 They said: "It was such that your Lord has said. He is the Wise, the Knowledgeable."

51:31 He said: "What is your undertaking, O messengers?"

51:32 They said: "We have been sent to a criminal people."

51:33 "To send down upon them rocks of clay."

51:34   "Prepared by your Lord for the transgressors."

51:35   We then vacated from it all the believers.

51:36   But We only found in it one house of those who had submitted.

51:37   And We left in it a sign for those who fear the painful retribution.

51:38   And also Moses, for We sent him to Pharaoh with a clear authority.

51:39   But he and his camp turned away, and said: "A magician, or crazy."

51:40   So We took him and his soldiers, We cast them to the running waters; and he was to blame.

51:41   And also 'Aad, for We sent upon them the barren wind.

51:42   Anything that it came upon was utterly destroyed.

51:43   And also Thamud, for it was said to them: "Enjoy for a while."

51:44   But they rebelled against the command of their Lord. So the thunderbolt took them while they were looking.

51:45   They were unable to rise up, nor could they win.

51:46   And the people of Noah before; they were a wicked people.

51:47   And the heaven We constructed with resources, and We are expanding it.

51:48   And the earth We have spread out; graced is the making.

51:49   And of everything We created a pair, perhaps you may remember.

51:50   So turn towards God. I am to you from Him a clear warner.

51:51   And do not make any other god with God. I am to you from Him a clear warner.

51:52   Likewise, when a messenger went to those before them, they said: "A magician, or crazy."

51:53   Have they passed down this saying to each other? Indeed, they are a wicked people.

51:54   So turn away from them; you will not be blamed.

51:55   And remind, for the reminder benefits the believers.

51:56   I did not create the Jinn and mankind except to serve Me.

51:57   I need no provisions from them, nor do I need them to give food.

51:58   God is the Provider, the One with Power, the Supreme.

51:59   The transgressors will have the same fate as their previous friends; so let them not be hasty.

51:60   So woe to those who rejected from the Day that is waiting for them.

CHAPTER 52

52:0   In the name of God, the Almighty, the Merciful.

52:1   By the mount.

52:2   And a recorded Book.

52:3   In parchment published.

52:4   And the frequented House.

52:5   And the vaulted ceiling.

52:6   And the desolate sea.

52:7   The retribution of your Lord is unavoidable.

52:8   Nothing can stop it.

52:9   The Day when the heaven will violently thunder.

52:10   And the mountains will be wiped out.

52:11   Woe on that Day to the deniers.

52:12   Who are in their recklessness, playing.

52:13   The Day they will be called into Hell, forcibly:

52:14   "This is the Fire which you used to deny!"

52:15   "Is this magic, or do you not see?"

52:16   "Enter it, whether you are patient or impatient, it will be the same for you. You are only being requited for what you used to do."

52:17   The righteous are in gardens and bliss.

52:18   Delighted by what their Lord has granted them; and their Lord has spared them the retribution of Hell.

52:19 Eat and drink happily because of what you used to do.

52:20 They recline on arranged beds, and We married them to wonderful consorts.

52:21 And those who believed, and their progeny also followed them in belief; We will have their progeny join them. We never fail to reward them for any work. Every person is paid for what he did.

52:22 We will supply them with fruit and meat such as they desire.

52:23 They will enjoy drinks therein, from which there is no nonsense, nor blame.

52:24 And serving them are boys who are like protected pearls.

52:25 And they came to one another asking.

52:26 They said: "We used to be compassionate among our people."

52:27 "So God has graced us, and has spared us the agony of the fierce hot winds."

52:28 "We used to implore Him before; He is the Kind, the Merciful."

52:29 Therefore, you shall remind. For by the grace of your Lord, you are neither a soothsayer, nor crazy.

52:30 Or do they say: "He is a poet; so let us just wait until a disaster befalls him."

52:31 Say: "Continue waiting; for I will wait along with you."

52:32 Or do their dreams dictate this to them, or are they a transgressing people?

52:33 Or do they say: "He made it all up"? No, they simply do not believe.

52:34 Let them produce a narrative like this, if they are truthful.

52:35 Or were they created from nothing? Or was it them who have created?

52:36 Or did they create the heavens and the earth? No, they do not comprehend.

52:37 Or do they possess the treasures of your Lord? Are they in control?

52:38 Or do they have a stairway that enables them to listen? Then let their listeners show their proof.

52:39 Or to Him belongs the daughters, and to you belong the sons?

52:40 Or do you ask them for a wage, so they are burdened by the fine?

52:41 Or do they know the future, thus they have it recorded?

52:42 Or do they want to make a plan? Indeed, it is the rejecters who are being planned against.

52:43 Or do they have another god besides God? God be glorified above what they set up.

52:44 And if they see a portion from the heaven falling, they will say: "Piled clouds!"

52:45 So disregard them until they meet their Day in which they are stricken.

52:46 The Day when their scheming will not protect them in the least, nor will they be helped.

52:47 And for those who transgressed will be a retribution beyond this, but most of them do not know.

52:48 You shall be patient for the judgment of your Lord, for you are in Our sights; and glorify the praise of your Lord when you rise.

52:49 Also from the night glorify Him, and at the fading of the stars.

CHAPTER 53

53:0 In the name of God, the Almighty, the Merciful.

53:1 As the star descended.

53:2 Your friend was not astray, nor was he deceived.

53:3 Nor does he speak from personal desire.

53:4 It is a divine inspiration.

53:5 He has been taught by the One mighty in power.

53:6 Free from any defect, he became stable.

53:7 While he was at the highest horizon.

53:8 Then he drew nearer by moving down.

53:9 Until he became as near as two bow-lengths or nearer.

53:10 He then inspired to His servant what He inspired.

53:11 The mind did not invent what it saw.

53:12 Do you doubt him in what he saw?

53:13 And indeed, he saw him in another descent.

53:14 At the ultimate point.

53:15 Near it is the eternal Paradise.

53:16 The whole place was overwhelmed.

53:17 The eyes did not waver, nor go blind.

53:18 He has seen from the great signs of his Lord.

53:19 Have you considered Allaat and Al-`Uzzah?

53:20 And Manaat, the third one?

53:21 Do you have the males, while He has the females?

53:22 What a strange distribution!

53:23 These are but names that you made up, you and your forefathers. God never authorized such. They only follow conjecture, and personal desire, while the guidance has come to them from their Lord.

53:24 Or shall the human being have what he wishes?

53:25 To God belongs the end, and the beginning.

53:26 And there are many an angel in the heavens, whose intercession does not benefit in the least, unless God gives permission for whom He wishes and is pleased with him.

53:27 Those who disbelieve in the Hereafter name the angels with feminine names.

53:28 While they had no knowledge about this; they only followed conjecture. And conjecture is no substitute for the truth.

53:29 So disregard he who turns away from Our reminder, and only desires this worldly life.

53:30 This is the extent of their knowledge. Your Lord is fully aware of those who strayed away from His path, and He is fully aware of those who are guided.

53:31 And to God belongs everything in the heavens and everything on the earth. He will requite those who commit evil for their works, and will reward the righteous for their righteousness.

53:32 They avoid major sins and immorality, except for minor offences. Your Lord is with vast forgiveness. He has been fully aware of you since He initiated you from the earth, and while you were embryos in the wombs of your mothers. Therefore, do not ascribe purity to yourselves; He is fully aware of the righteous.

53:33 Have you noted the one who turned away?

53:34 And he gave very little, then he stopped.

53:35 Did he possess knowledge of the future? Could he see it?

53:36 Or was he not informed of the teachings in the scripts of Moses?

53:37 And of Abraham who fulfilled?

53:38 That no bearer may carry the burden of another.

53:39 And the human being will have what he sought.

53:40 And his works will be shown.

53:41 Then he will be paid fully for such works.

53:42 And to your Lord is the final destiny.

53:43 And He is the One who makes laughter and tears.

53:44 And He is the One who takes life and gives it.

53:45 And He is the One who has created the pair, the male and the female.

53:46 From a seed that is put forth.

53:47 And He will effect the recreation.

53:48 And He is the One who makes you rich or poor.

53:49 And He is the Lord of the brightest star.

53:50 And He is the One who destroyed ʿAad the first.

53:51 And from Thamud He left none.

53:52 And the people of Noah before that; they were evil transgressors.

53:53 And the overthrown city was made to fall.

53:54 So it was covered by that which covers.

53:55 So which powers of your Lord do you doubt?

53:56 This is a warning like the old warnings.

53:57 That which is inevitable draws near.

53:58 None besides God can unveil it.

53:59 Are you surprised by this narrative?

53:60 And you are laughing, while you should be crying?

53:61 And you are indulging yourselves?

53:62 So, prostrate yourselves to God, and serve.

CHAPTER 54

54:0 In the name of God, the Almighty, the Merciful.

54:1 The Hour has drawn near, and the moon is reached.

54:2 And if they see a sign, they turn away and say: "Ongoing magic!"

54:3 And they disbelieved, and followed their desires, and every old tradition.

54:4 While the news had come to them in which there was sufficient warning.

54:5 A perfect wisdom; but the warnings are of no benefit.

54:6 So turn away from them; the Day will come when the caller will call to a terrible disaster.

54:7 With their eyes humiliated, they come out of the graves like a swarm of locusts.

54:8 Hastening towards the caller, the rejecters will say: "This is a difficult Day."

54:9   The people of Noah disbelieved before them. They disbelieved Our servant and said: "He is crazy!" And he was oppressed.

54:10   So he called on his Lord: "I am beaten, so grant me victory."

54:11   So We opened the gates of the sky with pouring water.

54:12   And We caused springs to gush out of the earth. Thus the waters met to a command which had been measured.

54:13   We carried him on a craft made of slabs and mortar.

54:14   It ran under Our watchful eyes; a reward for one who was rejected.

54:15   And We have left it as a sign. Are there any who want to learn?

54:16   So how was My retribution after the warnings!

54:17   And We made the Qur'an easy to remember. Are there any who want to learn?

54:18   'Aad disbelieved. So how was My retribution after the warnings!

54:19   We sent upon them a violent wind, on a day of continuous misery.

54:20   It uprooted the people as if they were decayed palm tree trunks.

54:21   So how was My retribution after the warnings!

54:22   And We made the Qur'an easy to remember. Are there any who will learn?

54:23   Thamud rejected the warnings.

54:24   They said: "Shall we follow one of us; a mortal? We will then go astray, and be in Hell."

54:25   "Has the reminder come down to him, of all people amongst us? He is an evil liar."

54:26   They will find out tomorrow who the evil liar is.

54:27   We are sending the camel as a test for them. So watch them and be patient.

54:28   And inform them that the water shall be divided between them; each shall be allowed to drink in turn.

54:29   But they called on their friend, and he was paid to slaughter.

54:30   So how was My retribution after the warnings!

54:31   We sent upon them one scream, whereupon they became like harvested hay.

54:32   And We made the Qur'an easy to remember. Are there any who will learn?

54:33   The people of Lot rejected the warners.

54:34   We sent upon them projectiles. Except for the family of Lot, We saved them at dawn.

54:35   A blessing from Us; it is thus that We reward the thankful.

54:36   And he warned them about Our punishment, but they ridiculed the warnings.

54:37   And they sought to remove him from his guests; so We diverted their eyes. "Taste My retribution; you have been warned."

54:38   And in the early morning, a devastating retribution struck them.

54:39   "Taste My retribution; you have been warned."

54:40   And We made the Qur'an easy to remember. Are there any who will learn?

54:41   And the warnings had come to the people of Pharaoh.

54:42   They rejected all Our signs. So We took them, the taking of the Noble, the Able.

54:43   Are your rejecters better than those? Or have you been absolved by the scriptures?

54:44   Or do they say: "We are a large group and we will win."

54:45   The large group will be defeated; they will turn around and flee.

54:46   The Hour is their appointed time, and the Hour is far worse and more painful.

54:47   The criminals are in error and will burn.

54:48   The Day when they will be dragged upon their faces into the Fire: "Taste the agony of the scorching heat!"

54:49   Everything We have created in measure.

54:50   And Our commands are done at once with the blink of an eye.

54:51   And We have destroyed your counterparts. Do any of you wish to learn?

54:52   And everything they had done, is in the scriptures.

54:53   And everything, small or large, is written down.

54:54   The righteous will be in gardens and rivers.

54:55   In a position of honor, at an Omnipotent King.

CHAPTER 55

55:0   In the name of God, the Almighty, the Merciful.

55:1   The Almighty.

55:2   He has taught the Qur'an.

55:3   He has created man.

55:4   He taught him how to distinguish.

55:5   The sun and the moon are perfectly calculated.

55:6   And the stars and the trees are yielding.

55:7   And He raised the heaven and He established the balance.

55:8   Do not transgress in the balance.

55:9   And observe the weight with equity, and do not fall short in the balance.

55:10   And the earth He has made for all creatures.

55:11   In it are fruits, and date palms with their hanging fruit.

55:12   And the grain covered with husk and the spices.

55:13   So which of the favors of your Lord will you deny?

55:14   He created the human being from a sludge, like pottery.

55:15   And the Jinn He created from a smokeless fire.

55:16   So which of the favors of your Lord will you deny?

55:17   The Lord of the two easts and the two wests.

55:18 So which of the favors of your Lord will you deny?

55:19 He merges the two seas where they meet.

55:20 A screen is placed between them, which they do not cross.

55:21 So which of the favors of your Lord will you deny?

55:22 Out of both of them comes pearls and coral.

55:23 So which of the favors of your Lord will you deny?

55:24 And to Him are the ships that roam the sea like flags.

55:25 So which of the favors of your Lord will you deny?

55:26 Everyone upon it will fade away.

55:27 And the face of your Lord will remain; One with Majesty and Honor.

55:28 So which of the favors of your Lord will you deny?

55:29 Those in the heavens and the earth ask Him, everyday He is in some matter.

55:30 So which of the favors of your Lord will you deny?

55:31 We will call you to account, both of you beings.

55:32 So which of the favors of your Lord will you deny?

55:33 O assembly of Jinn and mankind, if you can penetrate the boundaries of the heavens and the earth, then go ahead and penetrate. You will not penetrate without might.

55:34 So which of the favors of your Lord will you deny?

55:35 He sends against both of you projectiles of fire, and of copper; so you will not succeed.

55:36 So which of the favors of your Lord will you deny?

55:37 When the heaven is torn, and turns like a rose colored paint.

55:38 So which of the favors of your Lord will you deny?

55:39 On that Day, no human being or Jinn will be asked of his sins.

55:40 So which of the favors of your Lord will you deny?

55:41 The guilty will be recognized by their features; they will be taken by the forelocks and the feet.

55:42 So which of the favors of your Lord will you deny?

55:43 This is Hell that the criminals used to deny.

55:44 They will move between it and a boiling liquid.

55:45 So which of the favors of your Lord will you deny?

55:46 And for he who feared the station of his Lord, will be two gardens.

55:47 So which of the favors of your Lord will you deny?

55:48 Full of provisions.

55:49 So which of the favors of your Lord will you deny?

55:50 In them are two springs, flowing.

55:51 So which of the favors of your Lord will you deny?

55:52 In them will be of every fruit, in pairs.

55:53 So which of the favors of your Lord will you deny?

55:54 While reclining upon furnishings lined with satin, the fruits of the two gardens are within reach.

55:55 So which of the favors of your Lord will you deny?

55:56 In them are those with a modest gaze, untouched before by any human being or Jinn.

55:57 So which of the favors of your Lord will you deny?

55:58 They look like rubies and coral.

55:59 So which of the favors of your Lord will you deny?

55:60 Is there any reward for goodness except goodness?

55:61 So which of the favors of your Lord will you deny?

55:62 And besides these will be two other gardens.

55:63 So which of the favors of your Lord will you deny?

55:64 Dark green in color.

55:65 So which of the favors of your Lord will you deny?

55:66 In them, two springs which gush forth.

55:67 So which of the favors of your Lord will you deny?

55:68 In them are fruits, date palms, and pomegranate.

55:69 So which of the favors of your Lord will you deny?

55:70 In them is what is good and beautiful.

55:71 So which of the favors of your Lord will you deny?

55:72 Consorts, inside grand pavilions.

55:73 So which of the favors of your Lord will you deny?

55:74 No human being has ever touched them, nor Jinn.

55:75 So which of the favors of your Lord will you deny?

55:76 Reclining on green carpets, in beautiful surroundings.

55:77 So which of the favors of your Lord will you deny?

55:78 Glorified be the name of your Lord, possessor of Majesty and Honor.

CHAPTER 56

56:0 In the name of God, the Almighty, the Merciful.

56:1 When the inevitable comes to pass.

56:2 Nothing can stop it from happening.

56:3 It will bring low, and raise up.

56:4 When the earth will be shaken a terrible shake.

56:5 And the mountains will be wiped out.

56:6 So that they become dust in the wind.

56:7 And you will be in three groupings.

56:8 So those on the right, who will be from those on the right?

56:9 And those on the left, who will be from those on the left?

56:10 And the forerunners, the forerunners.

56:11   They will be the ones who are brought near.

56:12   In gardens of bliss.

56:13   Many from the first generations.

56:14   And a few from the later generations.

56:15   Upon luxurious beds.

56:16   Reclining in them, facing each other.

56:17   Moving among them will be immortal children.

56:18   With cups, pitchers, and a cup of pure drink.

56:19   They do not get a headache from it, nor do they tire.

56:20   And fruits of their choice.

56:21   And meat of birds that they desire.

56:22   And wonderful consorts.

56:23   Like pearls which are sheltered.

56:24   A reward for their works.

56:25   They will not hear in it any nonsense, nor blame.

56:26   Only the utterances of: "Peace. Peace."

56:27   And those on the right, who will be with those on the right?

56:28   In lush orchards.

56:29   And fruit trees which are ripe.

56:30   And extended shade.

56:31   And flowing water.

56:32   And many fruits.

56:33   Neither ending; nor disallowed.

56:34   And raised furnishings.

56:35   We have developed them completely.

56:36   And made them never previously touched.

56:37   Perfect, mature in age.

56:38   For those on the right side.

56:39   Many from the early generations.

56:40   And many from the later generations.

56:41   And those on the left, who will be from those on the left?

56:42   In fierce hot winds and boiling water.

56:43   And a shade that is unpleasant.

56:44   Neither cool, nor helpful.

56:45   They used to be indulged in luxury before this.

56:46   And they persisted in the great oathbreaking.

56:47   And they used to say: "After we die and turn to dust and bones, we will get resurrected?"

56:48   "And also our fathers of old?"

56:49   Say: "The people of old and the later generations,"

56:50   "Will be gathered to a designated day."

56:51   "Then you, O rejecting strayers,"

56:52   "Will eat from the tree of Bitterness,"

56:53   "Filling your bellies therefrom,"

56:54   "Then drinking on top of it boiling water,"

56:55   "So you will drink like diseased camels!"

56:56   Such is their share on the Day of Judgment.

56:57   We have created you, if you could only believe!

56:58   Have you noted the semen that you produce?

56:59   Did you create it, or were We the Ones who have created it?

56:60   We have predetermined death for you. Nothing can stop Us,

56:61   From transforming your forms, and establishing you in what you do not know.

56:62   You have come to know about the first creation. If only you would remember.

56:63 Have you noted the crops you reap?

56:64 Did you grow them, or was it We who grew them?

56:65 If We wished, We can turn them into hay. Then you will be left in wonderment:

56:66 "We are lost."

56:67 "No, we are deprived!"

56:68 Have you noted the water you drink?

56:69 Did you send it down from the clouds, or is it We who sent it down?

56:70 If We wished, We can make it salty. If only you would give thanks.

56:71 Have you noted the fire you kindle?

56:72 Did you establish its tree, or is it We who established it?

56:73 We rendered it a reminder, and a useful tool for the users.

56:74 You shall glorify the name of your Lord, the Great.

56:75 I do swear by the positions of the stars.

56:76 This is an oath, if only you knew, that is great.

56:77 It is an honorable Qur'an.

56:78 In a protected Book.

56:79 None can grasp it except those purified.

56:80 A revelation from the Lord of the worlds.

56:81 Are you disregarding this narrative?

56:82 And you have your provisions, yet you are denying?

56:83 So when the time comes and it reaches your throat.

56:84 And at that moment you look around.

56:85 We are closer to it than you are, but you do not see.

56:86 So if you do not owe any account.

56:87 Then return it, if you are truthful?

56:88 So, if he is one of those who are made near.

56:89 Then joy, and rose buds, and gardens of bliss.

56:90 And if he is one of the people of the right.

56:91 Then: "Peace" from the people of the right.

56:92 But if he is one of the deniers, the strayers.

56:93 Then an abode of boiling water.

56:94 And a burning in Hell.

56:95 This is the absolute truth.

56:96 You shall glorify the name of your Lord, the Great.

CHAPTER 57

57:0 In the name of God, the Almighty, the Merciful.

57:1 Glorifying God is everything in the heavens and the earth. He is the Noble, the Wise.

57:2 To Him is the kingship of the heavens and the earth. He brings life and death. And He is capable of all things.

57:3 He is the First and the Last, the Evident and the Innermost. And He is fully aware of all things.

57:4 He is the One who has created the heavens and the earth in six days, then He settled upon the Throne. He knows everything that enters within the earth, and everything that comes out of it, and everything that comes down from the heaven, and everything that ascends into it. And He is with you wherever you may be. God is Seer of what you do.

57:5 To Him is the kingship of the heavens and the earth, and to God all matters are returned.

57:6 He merges the night into the day, and He merges the day into the night. He is fully aware of what is in the chests.

57:7 Believe in God and His messenger, and spend from what He has made you successors to. Those among you who believe and spend have deserved a great recompense.

57:8 Why should you not believe in God when the messenger is inviting you to believe in your Lord? And He has already taken a covenant from you, if you are believers.

57:9 He is the One who sends down to His servant clear revelations, to bring you out of the darkness and into the light. God is Compassionate towards you, Merciful.

57:10 And why do you not spend in the cause of God, when God possesses all wealth in the heavens and the earth? Not equal among you are those who spent before the victory and fought. They attained a greater rank than those who spent after the victory and fought. And for each, God promises goodness. And God is Expert in everything you do.

57:11 Who will lend God a loan of righteousness that He may multiply it for him, and he will have a generous recompense?

57:12 The Day will come when you see the believing males and the believing females with their light radiating around them and to their right. "Good news is yours today, you will have estates with rivers flowing beneath them; abiding therein. This is the great triumph!"

57:13 On that Day, the hypocrite males and the hypocrite females will say to those who believed: "Wait for us! Let us absorb some of your light." It will be said: "Go back behind you, and seek light." So a wall will be put forth between them, whose gate separates mercy on the inner side, from retribution on the outer side.

57:14 They will call upon them: "Were we not with you?" They will reply: "Yes, but you led yourselves into temptation, and you hesitated, and doubted, and became misled by wishful thinking, until the judgment of God came. You were diverted from God by arrogance."

57:15 "This Day, no ransom can be taken from you, nor from those who disbelieved. Your abode is the Fire, it is your patron; what a miserable abode."

57:16 Has not the time come for those who believed to open up their hearts for the remembrance of God, and the truth that is revealed herein? And they should not be like those who were given the Book before, and the waiting became long for them, so their hearts became hardened, and many of them were wicked.

57:17 Know that God revives the land after it had died. We have made clear to you the signs, perhaps you may comprehend.

57:18 Surely, the charitable males and charitable females, who lend God a loan of righteousness, He will multiply their reward, and they will have a generous recompense.

57:19 And those who believed in God and His messengers are the truthful ones. And the martyrs at their Lord will have their reward and their light. As for those who disbelieved and denied Our revelations, they are the dwellers of Hell.

57:20 Know that the worldly life is no more than play and distraction and adornments, and boasting among you, and to increase in wealth and children. It is like plants that are supplied by an abundant rain, which appear pleasing to the rejecters. But then they dry up and turn yellow, and become useless hay. And in the Hereafter there is severe retribution, and forgiveness from God and acceptance. This worldly life is no more than a deceiving enjoyment.

57:21 You shall race towards forgiveness from your Lord, and a Paradise whose width is as the width of the heaven and the earth, prepared for those who believed in God and His messengers. Such is the grace of God that He bestows upon whoever He wills. God is the Possessor of Infinite Grace.

57:22 No misfortune can happen on the earth, or in yourselves, except it is decreed in a record, before We bring it about. This is easy for God to do.

57:23 In order that you do not despair over anything that has passed you by, nor be happy of anything He has bestowed upon you. God does not love those who are boastful, proud.

57:24 They are stingy, and order the people to be stingy. And for anyone who turns away, then know that God is the Rich, the Praiseworthy.

57:25 We have sent Our messengers with clear proofs, and We sent down with them the Book and the balance, so that the people may uphold justice. And We sent down the iron, wherein there is great strength, and many benefits for the people. So that God would distinguish those who would support Him and His messengers in the unseen. God is Powerful, Noble.

57:26 And We had sent Noah and Abraham, and We placed in their progeny the prophethood and the Book. Some of them were guided, while many were wicked.

57:27 Then We sent in their tracks Our messengers. And We sent Jesus, son of Mary, and We gave him the Gospel, and We ordained in the hearts of his followers kindness and mercy. But they invented

Monasticism which We never decreed for them. They wanted to please God, but they did not observe it the way it should have been observed. Consequently, We gave those who believed among them their recompense, while many of them were wicked.

57:28 O you who believe, you shall reverence God and believe in His messenger. He will then grant you double the reward from His mercy, and He will make for you a light by which you shall walk, and He will forgive you. And God is Forgiving, Merciful.

57:29 So that the followers of the Book should know that they have no power over the grace of God, and that all grace is in the hand of God. He bestows it upon whoever He wills. God is Possessor of Infinite Grace.

CHAPTER 58

58:0 In the name of God, the Almighty, the Merciful.

58:1 God has heard the woman who has argued with you regarding her husband, and she complained to God. And God hears the argument between you. God is Hearer, Seer.

58:2 Those among you who have estranged their women; they can never be made as their mothers, for their mothers are those who gave birth to them. Indeed, they are uttering what is strange and a falsehood. And God is Pardoner, Forgiver.

58:3 Those who had estranged their women, then they retracted what they had said, they shall free a slave before they have sexual contact between them. This is to enlighten you. God is well aware of everything you do.

58:4 If he cannot find any, then the fasting of two consecutive months before any sexual contact between them. If he cannot, then he shall feed sixty poor people. That is so you would believe in God and His messenger. And these are the boundaries set by God. The disbelievers have incurred a painful retribution.

58:5 Those who oppose God and His messenger will be disgraced, like their previous counterparts were disgraced. We have sent down clear proofs, and the rejecters have incurred a shameful retribution.

58:6 The Day when God resurrects them all, then He informs them of what they had done. God has recorded it, while they have forgotten it. God witnesses all things.

58:7   Do you not realize that God knows everything in the heavens and everything on the earth? No three people can meet secretly without Him being their fourth, nor five without Him being the sixth, nor less than that, nor more, without Him being there with them wherever they may be. Then, on the Day of Resurrection, He will inform them of everything they had done. God is fully aware of all things.

58:8   Have you noted those who were prohibited from holding meetings in secret, but then they go back to what they have been prohibited from? They meet secretly to commit sin, transgression, and disobedience of the messenger. When they come to you, they greet you with a greeting other than that which God greets you with. They say to themselves: "Why does God not punish us for our utterances?" Hell will be sufficient for them, wherein they burn; what a miserable destiny.

58:9   O you who believe, if you must meet secretly, then you shall not meet to commit sin, transgression, and to disobey the messenger. You shall meet to work righteousness and piety. And be aware of God, before whom you will be summoned.

58:10   Secret meetings are from the devil, to cause grief to those who believed. However, he cannot harm them except if God wills. In God the believers shall put their trust.

58:11   O you who believe, if you are told to make room in the assemblies, then make room; God will make room for you. And if it is said, arise, then arise. God will raise those among you who believe, and those who acquire knowledge to higher ranks; and God is fully aware of all you do.

58:12   O you who believe, if you wish to hold a private meeting with the messenger, you shall offer a charity before you do so. This is better for you, and purer. If you cannot do so, then God is Forgiver, Merciful.

58:13   Are you reluctant to offer a charity before such meeting? If you cannot do such, and God has forgiven you; then you shall hold the Connection, and contribute towards purification, and obey God and His messenger. God is fully aware of everything you do.

58:14   Have you noted those who befriended people with whom God is angry? They are now neither from you nor from them. And they deliberately swear to lies while they know!

58:15   God has prepared for them a severe retribution. Miserable indeed is what they used to do.

58:16   They used their oaths as a means of repelling from the path of God. Consequently, they have incurred a shameful retribution.

58:17   Neither their money nor their children will avail them anything from God. These are the dwellers of the Fire, in it they will abide.

58:18   The Day will come when God resurrects them all. Then they will swear to Him, just as they swear to you, thinking that they are actually right! Indeed, they are the liars.

58:19   The devil has overtaken them, and has caused them to forget the remembrance of God. These are the party of the devil. Absolutely, the party of the devil are the losers.

58:20   Surely, those who oppose God and His messenger, they will be with the lowliest.

58:21   God has decreed: "I and My messengers will be the victors." God is Powerful, Noble.

58:22   You will not find any people who believe in God and the Last Day leaning towards those who oppose God and His messenger, even if they were their parents, or their children, or their siblings, or their kin. For these, He decrees faith into their hearts, and supports them with a Spirit from Him, and He admits them into estates with rivers flowing beneath them; abiding therein. God is pleased with them, and they are pleased with Him. These are the party of God. Most assuredly, the party of God are the winners.

CHAPTER 59

59:0   In the name of God, the Almighty, the Merciful.

59:1   Glorifying God is everything in the heavens and the earth; and He is the Noble, the Wise.

59:2   He is the One who drove out those who disbelieved among the people of the Book from their homes at the very first mobilization. You never thought that they would leave, and they thought that their fortresses would protect them from God. But then God came to them from where they did not expect, and He cast terror into their hearts. They destroyed their homes with their own hands and the hands of the believers. So learn from this, O you who possess vision.

59:3 And had God not decreed to banish them He would have punished them in this world; and in the Hereafter they will face the retribution of the Fire.

59:4 This is because they challenged God and His messenger. And whoever challenges God, then God is severe in punishment.

59:5 Whether you cut down a tree or left it standing on its root, it was with the permission of God. He will surely humiliate the wicked.

59:6 And what God provided to His messenger, without you having to battle for it on horses or on foot, was because God sends His emissaries against whoever He wills. And God is capable of all things.

59:7 Whatever God bestowed upon His messenger from the people of the towns, then it shall be to God and His messenger, and the relatives, and the orphans, and the poor, and the wayfarer. Thus, it will not remain monopolized by the rich among you. And you may take what the messenger gives you, but do not take what he prohibits you from taking. And be aware of God, for God is mighty in retribution.

59:8 For the immigrants who are poor and were driven out of their homes and deprived of their properties; they were seeking a grace from God and acceptance, and they supported God and His messenger; these are the truthful ones.

59:9 And those who provided them with shelter, and were believers before them; they love those who immigrated to them, and they find no hesitation in their hearts in helping them, and they readily give them priority over themselves, even when they themselves need what they give away. Indeed, those who overcome their desires are the successful ones.

59:10 And those who came after them saying: "Our Lord, forgive us and our brothers who preceded us to the faith, and do not place in our hearts any animosity towards those who believed. Our Lord, You are Compassionate, Merciful."

59:11 Have you noted those who are hypocrites, they say to their brothers who have rejected among the people of the Book: "If you are driven out we will go out with you, and we will never obey anyone who opposes you. And if anyone fights you, we will support you." God bears witness that they are liars.

59:12 If they were driven out, they would not have gone out with them, and if anyone fought them, they would not have supported them. And even if they supported them, they would have turned around and fled. They could never win.

59:13 Indeed, you strike more terror in their hearts than their fear of God. This is because they are people who do not understand.

59:14 They will not fight you all together unless they are in fortified towns, or from behind walls. Their might appears formidable among themselves. You would think that they are united, but their hearts are divided. This is because they are a people who do not comprehend.

59:15 Like the example of those who preceded them. They suffered the consequences of their decisions. They have incurred a painful retribution.

59:16 Like the example of the devil, when he says to man: "Reject," then as soon as he rejects, he says: "I am innocent of you. I fear God, Lord of the worlds."

59:17 So the destiny for both of them is the Fire, abiding therein. And such is the recompense for the wicked.

59:18 O you who believe, be aware of God, and let every soul examine what it has put forth for tomorrow. And be aware of God; for God is fully aware of everything you do.

59:19 And do not be like those who forgot God, so He made them forget themselves. These are the wicked.

59:20 Not equal are the dwellers of the Fire and the dwellers of Paradise; the dwellers of Paradise are the winners.

59:21 Had We sent down this Qur'an to a mountain, you would have seen it trembling, crumbling, out of concern from God. And such are the examples We put forth for the people, that they may reflect.

59:22 He is God; there is no other god besides Him. Knower of all secrets and declarations. He is the Almighty, the Merciful.

59:23 He is God; there is no other god besides Him. The King, the Holy, the Peace, the Faithful, the Supreme, the Noble, the Powerful, the Dignified. God be glorified; far above what they set up.

59:24 He is God; the Creator, the Initiator, the Designer. To Him belongs the most beautiful names. Glorifying Him is everything in the heavens and the earth. He is the Noble, the Wise.

CHAPTER 60

60:0 In the name of God, the Almighty, the Merciful.

60:1 O you who believe, do not take My enemy and your enemy as allies. You extend affection to them, while they have rejected the truth that has come to you. They drive you and the messenger out, simply because you believe in God, your Lord. While you have gone forth to strive in My cause, and are seeking My blessings, then why do you still harbor affection for them? I am fully aware of everything you conceal and what you declare. And whoever of you does this, then he has gone astray from the right path.

60:2 If there is an engagement, then they will be your enemies, and they will extend their hands and tongues against you to hurt you. They desire that you reject.

60:3 Neither your relatives nor your children will benefit you; on the Day of Resurrection He will separate between you. And God is Seer of what you do.

60:4 There has been a good example set for you by Abraham and those with him, when they said to their people: "We are innocent from you and what you serve besides God. We have rejected you, and it appears that there shall be animosity and hatred between us and you until you believe in God alone." Except for the saying of Abraham to his father: "I will ask forgiveness for you, but I do not possess any power to protect you from God." "Our Lord, we have put our trust in You, and we turn to You, and to You is the final destiny."

60:5 "Our Lord, do not let us become a test for those who rejected, and forgive us. Our Lord, You are the Noble, the Wise."

60:6 Certainly, a good example has been set by them for those who seek God and the Last Day. And whoever turns away, then God is the Rich, the Praiseworthy.

60:7 Perhaps God will place affection between you and those you consider enemies. And God is Capable; and God is Forgiving, Merciful.

60:8 God does not prohibit you from those who have not fought you because of your system, nor drove you out of your homes, that you deal kindly and equitably with them. For God loves the equitable.

60:9 But God does prohibit you regarding those who fought you because of your system, and drove you out of your homes, and helped to drive you out. You shall not ally with them. Those who ally with them, then such are the transgressors.

60:10 O you who believe, if the believing females come emigrating to you, then you shall test them. God is fully aware of their belief. Thus, if you establish that they are believers, then you shall not return them to the rejecters. They are no longer permissible for one another. And return the dowries that were paid. And there is no sin upon you to marry them, if you have paid their dowries to them. And do not keep disbelieving wives, and ask back what dowries you paid. And let them ask back what dowries they had paid. Such is the judgment of God; He judges between you. God is Knowledgeable, Wise.

60:11 And if any of your wives have gone over to the camp of the rejecters, and you are granted victory over them, then you shall compensate those whose wives have gone over, to the equivalent of what dowry they spent. And be aware of God, in whom you believe.

60:12 O prophet, if the believing females come to pledge to you that they will not set up anything besides God, nor steal, nor commit adultery, nor kill their children, nor fabricate any falsehood, nor disobey you in any matter which is righteous, then you shall accept their pledge, and ask God to forgive them. God is Forgiver, Merciful.

60:13 O you who believe, do not ally a people with whom God is angry; for they have given up regarding the Hereafter, just like the rejecters have given up on the people who are already in the graves.

CHAPTER 61

61:0 In the name of God, the Almighty, the Merciful.

61:1 Glorifying God is everything in the heavens and everything on the earth. And He is the Noble, the Wise.

61:2 O you who believe, why do you say what you do not do?

61:3 It is most despicable with God that you would say what you do not do.

61:4 God loves those who fight in His cause as one column; they are like bricks in a wall.

61:5 And when Moses said to his people: "O my people, why do you harm me, while you know that I am a messenger of God to you?" But when they deviated, God diverted their hearts. And God does not guide the wicked people.

61:6 And when Jesus, son of Mary, said: "O children of Israel, I am a messenger of God to you, affirming what is between my hands of the Torah and bringing good news of a messenger to come after me whose name will be 'most acclaimed.'" But when he showed them the clear proofs, they said: "This is clearly magic."

61:7 And who is more evil than he who invents lies about God, while he is being invited to submission? And God does not guide the wicked people.

61:8 They want to extinguish the light of God with their mouths. But God will continue with His light, even if the rejecters hate it.

61:9 He is the One who sent His messenger with the guidance and the system of truth, so that it will expose all other systems, even if the polytheists hate it.

61:10 "O you who believe, shall I lead you to a trade that will save you from a painful retribution?"

61:11 "That you believe in God and His messenger and strive in the cause of God with your money and your lives. This is best for you, if only you knew."

61:12 He will then forgive your sins, and admit you into estates with rivers flowing beneath them, and beautiful mansions in gardens of delight. This is the great triumph.

61:13 And also you will receive what you love: a triumph from God and a victory that is close at hand. And give good news to the believers.

61:14 O you who believe, be God's supporters, as Jesus, son of Mary, said to his disciples: "Who are my supporters towards God?" The disciples said: "We are God's supporters." Thus, a group from the Children of Israel believed, and another group rejected. So We supported those who believed against their enemy, and they were successful.

CHAPTER 62

62:0   In the name of God, the Almighty, the Merciful.

62:1   Glorifying God is everything in the heavens and everything on the earth; the King, the Holy, the Noble, the Wise.

62:2   He is the One who sent to the gentiles a messenger from among themselves, to recite to them His revelations, and to purify them, and teach them the Book and the wisdom. And before this, they were clearly astray.

62:3   And to other generations subsequent to them. He is the Noble, the Wise.

62:4   Such is the grace of God, which He bestows upon whoever He wills. God is Possessor of Infinite Grace.

62:5   The example of those who were given the Torah, but then failed to uphold it, is like the donkey that is carrying a cargo of books. Miserable indeed is the example of the people who denied the revelations of God. And God does not guide the wicked people.

62:6   Say: "O you who are Jewish, if you claim that you are the chosen of God, to the exclusion of all other people, then you should long for death if you are truthful!"

62:7   But they will never long for it, because of what their hands have delivered. God is fully aware of the wicked.

62:8   Say: "The death that you are fleeing from, it will come to find you. Then you will be returned to the Knower of all secrets and declarations, then He will inform you of everything you had done."

62:9   O you who believe, if the Connection is called to on the day of congregation, then you shall hasten towards the remembrance of God, and cease all selling. This is better for you, if only you knew.

62:10   Then, once the Connection is complete, you shall disperse through the land and seek the provisions of God, and remember God frequently that you may succeed.

62:11   And if they come across any trade, or some entertainment, they rush to it and leave you standing! Say: "What God possesses is far better than entertainment or trade. And God is the best Provider."

CHAPTER 63

63:0   In the name of God, the Almighty, the Merciful.

63:1   When the hypocrites come to you they say: "We bear witness that you are the messenger of God." And God knows that you are His messenger, and God bears witness that the hypocrites are liars.

63:2   They have chosen their oath as a deceit, thus they repel from the path of God. Miserable indeed is what they do.

63:3   That is because they believed, then disbelieved. Hence, their hearts are sealed; they do not understand.

63:4   And when you see them, you are impressed by their physical stature; and when they speak, you listen to their eloquence. They are like blocks of wood propped-up. They think that every call is intended for them. These are the enemies, so beware of them. May God condemn them; they have deviated.

63:5   And if they are told: "Come and let the messenger of God ask for your forgiveness," they turn aside their heads, and you see them shun away in pride.

63:6   It is the same for them, whether you ask for their forgiveness, or do not ask for their forgiveness; God will not forgive them. For God does not guide the wicked people.

63:7   They are the ones who say: "Do not spend on those who are with the messenger of God, unless they abandon him!" And to God belongs the treasures of the heavens and the earth, but the hypocrites do not understand.

63:8   They say: "When we go back to the city, the noble therein will evict the lowly." But all nobility belongs to God and His messenger, and the believers. However, the hypocrites do not know.

63:9   O you who believe, do not be distracted by your money and your children from the remembrance of God. And those who do this, then they are the losers.

63:10   And give from what We have provided to you, before death comes to one of you, then he says: "My Lord, if only You would delay me for a short while, I would then be charitable and join the righteous!"

63:11   And God will not delay any soul if its time has come. And God is Expert in all that you do.

CHAPTER 64

64:0   In the name of God, the Almighty, the Merciful.

64:1   Glorifying God is everything in the heavens and everything on the earth. To Him is all kingship, and to Him is all praise, and He is capable of all things.

64:2   He is the One who has created you, then among you there is the rejecter, and among you there is the believer. And God is Seer of what you do.

64:3   He created the heavens and the earth with the truth, and He designed you and perfected your design, and to Him is the final destiny.

64:4   He knows what is in the heavens and the earth, and He knows what you conceal and what you declare. And God is aware of what is in the chests.

64:5   Did the news not come to you of those who had rejected before? They had tasted the consequences of their decision and they incurred a painful retribution.

64:6   That was because their messengers came to them with clear proofs, but they said: "Shall mere mortals guide us?" So they rejected and turned away. And God had no need. And God is Rich, Praiseworthy.

64:7   Those who rejected claim that they will not be resurrected. Say: "Yes, by my Lord, you will be resurrected, then you will be informed of everything you have done, and this is easy for God to do."

64:8   Therefore, you shall believe in God and His messenger, and the light that We have sent down. And God is Expert over what you do.

64:9   The Day when He will gather you; the Day of Gathering; that is the Day of mutual blaming. And whoever believes in God and does good works, He will forgive his sins, and will admit him into estates with rivers flowing beneath them, abiding therein eternally. Such is the great triumph.

64:10   As for those who reject and deny Our revelations, they are the dwellers of the Fire; they will abide therein. What a miserable destiny!

64:11   No misfortune strikes except with the permission of God. And whoever believes in God, He will guide his heart. And God is fully aware of all things.

64:12 Obey God and obey the messenger. And if you turn away, then it is only required of Our messenger to deliver clearly.

64:13 God, there is no god besides Him. In God the believers shall put their trust.

64:14 O you who believe, from among your spouses and your children are enemies to you; so beware of them. And if you pardon, and overlook, and forgive, then God is Forgiver, Merciful.

64:15 Your money and children are a test, and with God is a great recompense.

64:16 Therefore, be aware of God as much as you can, and listen, and obey, and give for your own good. And whoever is protected from his own stinginess, then these are the successful ones.

64:17 If you lend God a loan of righteousness He will multiply it for you, and forgive you. God is Thankful, Compassionate.

64:18 The Knower of all secrets and declarations; the Noble, the Wise.

CHAPTER 65

65:0 In the name of God, the Almighty, the Merciful.

65:1 O prophet, if any of you divorce the women, then divorce them while ensuring their required interim is fulfilled, and keep count of the interim. You shall reverence God your Lord, and do not evict them from their homes, nor should they leave, unless they commit an evident immorality. And these are the boundaries of God. And anyone who transgresses the boundaries of God has wronged his soul. You never know; perhaps God will make something come out of this.

65:2 Then, once the interim is fulfilled, either you remain together equitably, or part ways equitably and have it witnessed by two just people from among you; and give the testimony for God. This is to enlighten those who believe in God and the Last Day. And whoever reverences God, He will create a solution for him.

65:3 And He will provide for him whence he never expected. Anyone who puts his trust in God, then He suffices him. The commands of God will be done. God has decreed for everything its fate.

65:4 As for those who have reached menopause from your women, if you have any doubts, their interim shall be three months. As for those whose menstruation has ceased, and are already pregnant, their interim is until they give birth. And anyone who reverences God, He makes his matters easy for him.

65:5 This is the command of God that He sends down to you. And anyone who is aware of God, He will forgive his sins, and will improve his reward.

65:6 You shall let them reside in the dwelling you were in when you were together, and do not coerce them to make them leave. And if they are pregnant, you shall spend on them until they give birth. Then, if they nurse the infant, you shall give them their due payment. And you shall maintain the amicable relations between you. If you disagree, then another woman may nurse the child.

65:7 The rich shall provide support in accordance with his means, and the poor shall provide according to the means that God bestowed upon him. God does not burden any soul more than He has given it. God will provide ease after difficulty.

65:8 Many a town rebelled against the command of its Lord and His messengers. Thus, We called them to account severely, and We punished them a terrible punishment.

65:9 They tasted the result of their actions, and the consequence of their actions was a total loss.

65:10 God has prepared for them a severe retribution. Therefore, you shall be aware of God, O you who possess intelligence and believed. God has sent down to you a remembrance.

65:11 A messenger who recites to you the revelations of God, which are clear, to lead those who believe and work righteousness out of the darkness and into the light. Anyone who believes in God and does good works, He will admit him into estates with rivers flowing beneath them; abiding therein eternally. God has granted for him an excellent reward.

65:12 God who has created seven heavens and the same number of earths; the command is sent down between them; that you may know that God is capable of all things, and that God has encompassed all things with His knowledge.

CHAPTER 66

66:0   In the name of God, the Almighty, the Merciful.

66:1   O prophet, why do you make forbidden what God has made permissible for you, seeking to please your wives? God is Forgiver, Merciful.

66:2   God has already decreed for you regarding the cancellation of oaths. And God is your Lord, and He is the Knowledgeable, the Wise.

66:3   And when the prophet confided a narrative to some of his wives, then one of them spread it, and God revealed it to him, he recognized part of it and denied part. So when he informed her, she said: "Who informed you of this?" He said: "I was informed by the Knowledgeable, the Expert."

66:4   If the two of you repent to God, then your hearts have listened. But if you band together against him, then God is his ally, and so are Gabriel and the righteous believers. Also, the angels are his helpers.

66:5   It may be that he would divorce you, then his Lord will substitute other wives in your place who are better than you; submitting, believing, devout, repentant, serving, active—previously married or virgins.

66:6   O you who believe, protect yourselves and your families from a Fire whose fuel is people and rocks. Guarding it are stern and powerful angels who do not disobey God in what He commanded them; and they carry out what they are commanded to.

66:7   O you who have rejected, do not apologize today. You are being requited only for what you did.

66:8   O you who believe, you shall repent to God a sincere repentance. It may be that your Lord will forgive your sins and admit you into estates with rivers flowing beneath them. On that Day, God will not disappoint the prophet and those who believed with him. Their light will radiate around them and to their right. They will say: "Our Lord, keep perfect our light for us, and forgive us; You are able to do all things."

66:9   O prophet, strive against the rejecters and the hypocrites and be stern with them. Their abode is Hell, and a miserable destiny.

66:10   God puts forth as examples of those who have rejected, the wife of Noah and the wife of Lot. They were married to two of Our righteous servants, but they betrayed them and, consequently, they could not help them at all against God. And it was said: "Enter the Fire, both of you, with those who will enter it."

66:11 And God puts forth as an example of those who believed the wife of Pharaoh. She said: "My Lord, build a home for me near You in Paradise, and save me from Pharaoh and his works; and save me from the transgressing people."

66:12 And Mary, the daughter of Imran, who safeguarded her chastity, so We blew into it from Our Spirit, and she believed in the words of her Lord and His Books; and she was of those who were devout.

CHAPTER 67

67:0 In the name of God, the Almighty, the Merciful.

67:1 Most exalted is the One in whose hands is all sovereignty, and He is capable of all things.

67:2 The One who has created death and life, that He may test you, which of you will do better works? He is the Noble, the Forgiving.

67:3 The One who has created seven heavens in layers. You do not see any imperfection in the creation by the Almighty. Look again; do you see any flaw?

67:4 Then look again twice; your eyes will come back humiliated and tired.

67:5 And We have adorned the lower heaven with lamps, and We made it with projectiles against the devils; and We prepared for them the retribution of the blazing Fire.

67:6 And for those who rejected their Lord will be the retribution of Hell. What a miserable destiny.

67:7 When they are cast therein, they hear its furor as it boils.

67:8 It almost explodes from rage. Whenever a group is thrown therein, its keepers would ask them: "Did you not receive a warner?"

67:9 They said: "Yes indeed; a warner did come to us, but we disbelieved and said: God did not reveal anything, you are being led astray."

67:10 And they said: "If we had listened or understood, we would not be among the dwellers of the blazing Fire!"

67:11 Thus, they confessed their sins. So away with the dwellers of the blazing Fire.

67:12 As for those who are concerned towards their Lord while unseen, they have attained forgiveness and a great reward.

67:13 And whether you keep your utterances secret, or declare them, He is fully aware of what is in the chests.

67:14 Should He not know what He created? And He is the Sublime, the Expert.

67:15 He is the One who made the earth subservient for you. So roam its paths, and eat from His provisions; and to Him is the final summoning.

67:16 Are you secure that the One in the heaven will not cause the earth to swallow you when it shakes?

67:17 Or are you secure that the One in the heaven will not send upon you a violent storm? Then you will know the value of the warning.

67:18 And those before them have disbelieved; so how was the requital!

67:19 Have they not looked to the birds lined-up together above them, and they contract? It is the Almighty who holds them. He is Seer of all things.

67:20 Where is this army of yours to grant you victory without the Almighty? Indeed, the disbelievers are deceived.

67:21 Where is this who can give you provisions if He holds back His provisions? Indeed, they have plunged deep into transgression and aversion.

67:22 Is one who walks while his face is slumped better guided, or one who walks straight on the right path?

67:23 Say: "He is the One who initiated you, and made for you the hearing, the eyes, and the minds. Little do you give thanks."

67:24 Say: "He is the One who placed you on the earth, and to Him you will be gathered."

67:25 And they say: "When will this promise come to pass, if you are being truthful?"

67:26 Say: "The knowledge is with God, and I am but a clear warner."

67:27 So when they see it near, the faces of those who rejected will be miserable, and it will be proclaimed: "This is what you had called for!"

67:28 Say: "Do you see? If God annihilates me and those with me, or He bestows mercy upon us, who is there to protect the rejecters from a painful retribution?"

67:29 Say: "He is the Almighty; we believe in Him, and we put our trust in Him. You will come to find out who is clearly astray."

67:30 Say: "What if your water becomes deep underground, who then can provide you with pure water?"

CHAPTER 68

68:0 In the name of God, the Almighty, the Merciful.

68:1 N, the pen, and what they write.

68:2 You are not, by the blessing of your Lord, crazy.

68:3 And you will have a reward that will not end.

68:4 And you are of a high moral character.

68:5 So you will see, and they will see.

68:6 Which of you are condemned.

68:7 Your Lord is fully aware of those who strayed off His path, and He is fully aware of those who are guided.

68:8 So do not obey those who deny.

68:9 They wish that you compromise, so they too can compromise.

68:10 And do not obey every lowly swearer.

68:11 A slanderer, a backbiter.

68:12 Forbidder of charity, a transgressor, a sinner.

68:13 Unappreciative, and greedy.

68:14 Because he possessed money and sons.

68:15 When Our revelations are recited to him, he says: "Tales of old!"

68:16   We will mark him on the path.

68:17   We have tested them like We tested those who owned the farm, when they swore that they will harvest it in the morning.

68:18   They were without doubt.

68:19   So a passing sent from your Lord came to it while they all were asleep.

68:20   Thus, it became barren.

68:21   They called on one another when they awoke.

68:22   "Let us go this morning to harvest the crop."

68:23   So they went, while conversing.

68:24   That from today, none of them would ever be poor.

68:25   And they went, ready to harvest.

68:26   But when they saw it, they said: "We have gone astray!"

68:27   "Now, we have nothing!"

68:28   The most balanced among them said: "If only you had glorified!"

68:29   They said: "Glory be to our Lord. We have transgressed."

68:30   Then they started to blame each other.

68:31   They said: "Woe to us. We sinned."

68:32   "Perhaps our Lord will grant us better than it. We repent to our Lord."

68:33   Such was the punishment. But the retribution of the Hereafter is far worse, if only they knew.

68:34   The righteous have deserved, at their Lord, gardens of bliss.

68:35   Should We treat those who submitted the same as those who are criminals?

68:36   What is wrong with you, how do you judge?

68:37   Or do you have a book which you study?

68:38   In it, you can find what you wish?

68:39   Or do you have an oath from Us, extending until the Day of Resurrection, that you can judge as you please?

68:40   Ask them: "Who of them will make such a claim?"

68:41   Or do they have partners? Then let them bring their partners, if they are truthful.

68:42   The Day will come when they will be exposed, and they will be required to prostrate, but they will be unable to.

68:43   With their eyes subdued, humiliation will cover them. They were invited to prostrate when they were whole and able.

68:44   Therefore, let Me deal with those who reject this narrative; We will entice them from where they do not perceive.

68:45   And I will lead them on; for My planning is formidable.

68:46   Or do you ask them for a wage, so they are burdened by the fine?

68:47   Or do they know the future? So they have it recorded?

68:48   You shall be patient for the judgment of your Lord. And do not be like the companion of the whale who called out while he was in sorrow.

68:49   Had it not been for the grace of his Lord, he would have remained trapped, while he was to be blamed.

68:50   But his Lord selected him, and made him righteous.

68:51   And those who have rejected almost attack you with their eyes when they hear the reminder, and they say: "He is crazy!"

68:52   And it is but a reminder for the worlds.

CHAPTER 69

69:0   In the name of God, the Almighty, the Merciful.

69:1   The reality.

69:2   What is the reality?

69:3   Absolutely, do you know what is the reality?

69:4   Thamud and 'Aad disbelieved in the Shocker.

69:5   As for Thamud, they were annihilated by the devastation.

69:6   And as for 'Aad, they were annihilated by a furious violent wind.

69:7   He commissioned it upon them for seven nights and eight days, in succession. You could see the people destroyed in it, as if they are decayed palm trunks.

69:8   Do you see any legacy for them?

69:9   And Pharaoh, and those before him, and the sinners, came with wrongdoing.

69:10   They disobeyed the messenger of their Lord. So He took them with a devastating requital.

69:11   And when the water flooded, We carried you on the vessel.

69:12   That We would make it as a reminder for you, and so that any listening ear may understand.

69:13   And when the horn is blown once.

69:14   And the earth and the mountains will be removed from their place and crushed with a single crush.

69:15   On that Day the unavoidable event will come to pass.

69:16   And the sky will be torn, and on that Day it will be flimsy.

69:17   And the angels will be on its borders; and the Throne of your Lord will be carried, above them on that Day, by eight.

69:18   On that Day, you will be exposed, nothing from you can be hidden.

69:19   As for the one who is given his record in his right, he will say: "Here, come and read my record!"

69:20   "I knew that I was going to be held accountable."

69:21   So he shall be in a life, well-pleasing.

69:22   In a lofty Paradise.

69:23   Its fruits are within reach.

69:24   "Eat and drink merrily in return for your works in days past."

69:25   As for him who is given his record in his left, he will say: "Oh, I wish I never received my record,"

69:26   "And that I never knew my account,"

69:27   "I wish the end had been final,"

69:28   "My money cannot help me,"

69:29   "All my power is gone."

69:30   Take him and shackle him.

69:31   Then to Hell cast him.

69:32   Then, in a chain that is the length of seventy arms, tie him up.

69:33   For he did not believe in God, the Great.

69:34   Nor did he advocate the feeding of the poor.

69:35   Consequently, he has no friend here today.

69:36   Nor any food, except from pollutants.

69:37   Food for the wrongdoers.

69:38   So I do swear by what you see.

69:39   And what you do not see.

69:40   This is the utterance of an honorable messenger.

69:41   It is not the utterance of a poet; rarely do you believe.

69:42   Nor the utterance of a soothsayer; rarely do you take heed.

69:43   A revelation from the Lord of the worlds.

69:44   And had he attributed anything falsely to Us.

69:45   We would have seized him by the right.

69:46   Then, We would have severed his life-line.

69:47   None of you would be able to prevent it.

69:48   And this is a reminder for the righteous.

69:49   And We know that some of you are deniers.

69:50   And that it is a distress for the rejecters.

69:51   And it is the absolute truth.

69:52   Therefore, you shall glorify the name of your Lord, the Great.

CHAPTER 70

70:0   In the name of God, the Almighty, the Merciful.

70:1   Someone asked about the inevitable retribution.

70:2   For the rejecters, there is nothing that will stop it.

70:3   From God, Possessor of the ascending portals.

70:4   The angels and the Spirit ascend to Him in a day which is equivalent to fifty thousand years.

70:5   So be patient with a good patience.

70:6   They see it as far away.

70:7   And We see it as near.

70:8   On the Day the heaven is like molten copper.

70:9   And the mountains are like wool.

70:10   And no friend will ask about his friend.

70:11   When they see it, the criminal will wish he can ransom his children against the retribution.

70:12   And his mate and his brother.

70:13   And his relatives who sheltered him.

70:14   And all who are on the earth, so that he can be saved!

70:15   No, it is a torching flame.

70:16   Eager to roast.

70:17   It calls on those who turned away.

70:18   And who hoarded and counted.

70:19   Indeed, the human being was created anxious.

70:20   When adversity touches him he is miserable.

70:21   And when good touches him he is stingy.

70:22   Except for those who connect.

70:23   Who are always maintaining their connection.

70:24 And they set aside part of their wealth.

70:25 For the seeker and the denied.

70:26 And they believe in the Day of Judgment.

70:27 And they are fearful of the retribution of their Lord.

70:28 The retribution of their Lord is not to be taken for granted.

70:29 And they maintain their chastity.

70:30 Except around their spouses or those committed to by their oath, there is no blame.

70:31 Whoever seeks anything beyond this, they are the transgressors.

70:32 And they are trustworthy and keep their pledges.

70:33 And they uphold their testimonies.

70:34 And they maintain their connecting.

70:35 They will be honored in gardens.

70:36 So what is wrong with the rejecters staring at you?

70:37 From the right and the left, in crowds?

70:38 Does every one of them hope to enter a garden of bliss?

70:39 No, We have created them from what they know.

70:40 So I do swear by the Lord of the east and the west, that We are able.

70:41 To replace them with better people, We can never be defeated.

70:42 So let them talk in vain and play, until they meet their Day which they are promised.

70:43 When they will come out of the graves in a rush, as if they are racing towards a goal.

70:44 Their eyes are cast down, with shame covering them. This is the Day which they were promised.

CHAPTER 71

71:0 In the name of God, the Almighty, the Merciful.

71:1 We have sent Noah to his people: "Warn your people before a painful retribution comes to them."

71:2 He said: "My people, I am to you a clear warner."

71:3 "That you shall serve God and be aware of Him and obey me."

71:4 "He shall forgive your sins and delay you to a predetermined time. When the time of God comes, it cannot be delayed, if you know."

71:5 He said: "My Lord, I have called on my people night and day."

71:6 "But my calling only drove them away!"

71:7 "And every time I called on them so that You may forgive them, they put their fingers in their ears and they covered their heads with their outer garments and they insisted, and they became greatly arrogant."

71:8 "Then I called to them publicly."

71:9 "Then I declared to them, and I spoke to them in secret."

71:10 "And I said: Seek forgiveness from your Lord, for He is forgiving."

71:11 "He sends the sky to you abundantly."

71:12 "And He provides you with wealth and sons, and He makes for you gardens, and He makes for you rivers."

71:13 "Why do you not seek God humbly."

71:14 "While He created you in stages?"

71:15 "Did you not note how God created seven heavens in layers?"

71:16 "And He made the moon to illuminate in them, and He made the sun to be a lamp?"

71:17 "And God made you grow from the earth as plants."

71:18 "Then He returns you to it, and He brings you out totally?"

71:19 "And God made the land for you as a plain."

71:20 "So that you may seek in it ways and paths?"

71:21 Noah said: "My Lord, they have disobeyed me and have followed he whose money and children only increased him in loss."

71:22 And they plotted a great plotting.

71:23 And they said: "Do not abandon your gods; nor abandon Destroyer, nor Fertility; nor Lion, Steed and Eagle."

71:24 And they have misguided many. And do not increase the wicked, except in misguidance.

71:25 Because of their wrongdoing they were drowned, then they were admitted to the Fire, and they could not find besides God any victor.

71:26 And Noah said: "My Lord, do not leave on the earth any of the rejecters at all."

71:27 "If you are to leave them, then they will misguide Your servants and they will only give birth to a wicked rejecter."

71:28 "My Lord, forgive me, and my parents, and whoever enters my home as a believer, and the believing males, and the believing females; and do not increase the wicked except in destruction."

CHAPTER 72

72:0 In the name of God, the Almighty, the Merciful.

72:1 Say: "It has been inspired to me that a group of Jinn were listening." They said: "We have heard a magnificent Qur'an!"

72:2 "It guides to what is correct, so we believed in it, and we will not set up anyone with our Lord."

72:3 "And Exalted is the Majesty of our Lord, He has not taken a wife nor a son."

72:4 "And the foolish one among us used to say lies about God."

72:5 "And we had thought that neither mankind nor the Jinn would ever utter a lie against God."

72:6 "And there were men from among mankind who used to seek help from the men among the Jinn, but they only increased them in sin."

72:7 "And they thought as you thought, that God would not send anyone."

72:8   "And we touched the heavens, but found it full of powerful guards and projectiles."

72:9   "And we used to sit in it in places of listening, but anyone who sits now finds a projectile seeking him."

72:10   "And we do not know, is it evil that is intended for those on the earth, or does their Lord want them to be guided?"

72:11   "And among us are those who are good doers, and some of us are opposite to that, we are in many paths."

72:12   "And we acknowledge that we cannot escape God on the earth, nor can we escape Him if we run."

72:13   "And when we heard the guidance, we believed in it. So whoever believes in his Lord, then he will not fear a decrease in reward, nor a burdensome punishment."

72:14   "And among us are those who submitted, and among us are the inequitable." As for those who have submitted, they have sought what is correct.

72:15   And as for the inequitable, they are firewood for Hell.

72:16   And those who remain on the right path, We will provide them with abundant water.

72:17   To test them with it. And whoever turns away from the remembrance of his Lord, He will enter him a severe retribution.

72:18   And the temples are for God, so do not call on anyone with God.

72:19   And when the servant of God stood up to call on Him, they nearly banded to oppose him.

72:20   Say: "I only call on my Lord, and I do not set up anyone with Him."

72:21   Say: "I have no power to harm you nor to show you what is right."

72:22   Say: "No one can protect me from God, and I will not find any refuge except with Him."

72:23   "To simply proclaim from God, and His messages." And whoever disobeys God and His messenger, then he will have the fire of Hell to dwell eternally therein.

72:24   Until they see what they are promised, then they will know who has the weakest ally and is least in number.

72:25 Say: "I do not know if what you are promised is near, or if my Lord will delay it for a while."

72:26 Knower of the unseen, He does not reveal His unseen to anyone.

72:27 Except to whom He has accepted as a messenger, then He reveals from the past and the future.

72:28 So as to make manifest that they have delivered the messages of their Lord, and He surrounds all that is with them, and He has counted the number of all things.

CHAPTER 73

73:0 In the name of God, the Almighty, the Merciful.

73:1 O you who are cloaked.

73:2 Stand the night except for a little.

73:3 Half of it, or a little less than that.

73:4 Or a little more, and arrange the Qur'an in its arrangement.

73:5 We will place upon you a saying which is heavy.

73:6 The time of the night is more effective and better for study.

73:7 For you have many duties during the day.

73:8 And remember the name of your Lord, and devote to Him completely.

73:9 The Lord of the east and the west, there is no god except He, so take Him as a protector.

73:10 And be patient over what they say, and abandon them in a good manner.

73:11 And leave Me to deal with the deniers who have been given the good things, and give them time for a while.

73:12 We have with Us restraints and a raging fire.

73:13 And food that chokes, and a painful retribution.

73:14 The Day the earth and the mountains shake, and the mountains become a crumbling pile.

73:15   We have sent to you a messenger as a witness over you, as We have sent to Pharaoh a messenger.

73:16   But Pharaoh disobeyed the messenger, so We took him in a severe manner.

73:17   So how can you be righteous when you have rejected? A Day which will turn the children white haired!

73:18   The heavens will crack with it. His promise is always delivered.

73:19   This is a reminder, so let he who wishes take a path to his Lord.

73:20   Your Lord knows that you rise a little less than two thirds of the night, and half of it, and one third of it; and a group of those who are with you. And God measures the night and the day. He knows that you will not be able to keep up, so He pardons you. So read what is made easy of the Qur'an. He knows that there will be sick among you, and others that go forth in the land seeking from the bounty of God, and others who are fighting in the cause of God, so read what you can of it. And hold the Connection and contribute towards purification and lend God a loan of righteousness. And whatever you put forth yourselves, you will find it with God, for it is better and a greater reward. And seek the forgiveness of God, for God is Forgiving, Merciful.

CHAPTER 74

74:0   In the name of God, the Almighty, the Merciful.

74:1   O you who are blanketed.

74:2   Stand and warn.

74:3   And your Lord magnify.

74:4   And purify your garments.

74:5   And abandon that which afflicts.

74:6   And do not give for a return.

74:7   And to your Lord be patient.

74:8   Then, when the piercing sound is made.

74:9   That will be a very difficult Day.

74:10   Upon the rejecters it will not be easy.

74:11   So leave Me alone with he whom I have created.

74:12   And I gave him abundant wealth.

74:13   And sons to bear witness.

74:14   And I made everything comfortable for him.

74:15   Then he is greedy, wanting that I give more.

74:16   No. He was stubborn to Our revelations.

74:17   I will exhaust him in ascending.

74:18   He thought and he analyzed.

74:19   So woe to him for how he thought.

74:20   Then woe to him for how he thought.

74:21   Then he looked.

74:22   Then he frowned and became bad tempered.

74:23   Then he turned away and was arrogant.

74:24   So he said: "This is nothing except the magic of old."

74:25   "This is nothing except the saying of a mortal."

74:26   I will cast him in the scorching heat.

74:27   And do you know what is the scorching heat?

74:28   It does not spare nor leave anything.

74:29   A signal to mortals.

74:30   Upon it is nineteen.

74:31   And We have made the guardians of the Fire to be angels; and We did not make their number except as a test for those who have rejected, so that those who were given the Book would understand, and those who have faith would be increased in faith, and so that those who have been given the Book and the believers do not have doubt, and so that those who have a sickness in their hearts and the rejecters would say: "What did God mean with an example such as this?" It is such that God misguides whom He wishes, and He guides whom He wishes. And none know the soldiers of your

Lord except He; and it is but a reminder for mortals.

74:32   No, by the moon.

74:33   And by the night when it withdraws.

74:34   And by the morning when it brightens.

74:35   It is one of the great ones.

74:36   A warning to mortals.

74:37   For any among you who wishes to advance or regress.

74:38   Every soul is held by what it earned.

74:39   Except for the people of the right.

74:40   In gardens, they will inquire.

74:41   About the criminals.

74:42   "What has caused you to be in the scorching heat?"

74:43   They said: "We were not of those who connected."

74:44   "And we did not feed the poor person."

74:45   "And we used to participate with those who spoke falsehood."

74:46   "And we used to deny the Day of Judgment."

74:47   "Until the certainty came to us."

74:48   So no intercession of intercessors could help them.

74:49   Why did they turn away from being reminded?

74:50   They are like fleeing zebras.

74:51   Running from the lion.

74:52   Alas, every one of them wants to be given separate scripts.

74:53   No, they do not fear the Hereafter.

74:54   No, it is a reminder.

74:55   So whoever wishes will remember it.

74:56   And none will remember except if God wills. He is the source of righteousness and the source of forgiveness.

CHAPTER 75

75:0   In the name of God, the Almighty, the Merciful.

75:1   I do swear by the Day of Resurrection.

75:2   And I do swear by the soul which is self blaming.

75:3   Does the human being think that We will not gather his bones?

75:4   Indeed, We were able to make his fingertips.

75:5   No, the human being desires that he continues committing sins.

75:6   He asks: "When is the Day of Resurrection?"

75:7   So, when the sight is dazzled.

75:8   And the moon collapses.

75:9   And the sun and the moon are joined together.

75:10   The human being will say on that Day: "Where can I escape!"

75:11   No. There is no refuge.

75:12   To your Lord on that Day is the abode.

75:13   The human being will be told on that Day what he has put forward, and what he has done.

75:14   Indeed, the human being will testify against himself.

75:15   Even though he puts forth his excuses.

75:16   Do not move your tongue with it to hasten it.

75:17   It is for Us to gather it into its Qur'an.

75:18   Thus, when We read it, you shall follow such a Qur'an.

75:19   Then it is for Us to explain it.

75:20   Alas, you all like this world.

75:21   And neglect the Hereafter.

75:22   Faces on that Day will be shining.

75:23   Looking at their Lord.

75:24 And faces on that Day will be gloomy.

75:25 Thinking that a punishment is coming to them.

75:26 Alas, when it reaches the throat.

75:27 And it will be said: "Who can save him?"

75:28 And he assumes it is the time of passing.

75:29 And the leg is buckled around the other leg.

75:30 To your Lord on that Day he will be driven.

75:31 For he did not regard truth, nor did he connect.

75:32 But he denied and turned away.

75:33 Then he went to his family admiring himself.

75:34 Woe to you, woe to you.

75:35 Then woe to you, woe to you.

75:36 Did the human being think that he will be left neglected?

75:37 Was he not a seed from sperm put forth?

75:38 Then he was an embryo, so he was created and developed.

75:39 Then He made from it the pair, the male and the female.

75:40 Is One as such then not able to resurrect the dead?

CHAPTER 76

76:0 In the name of God, the Almighty, the Merciful.

76:1 Was there not a time when the human being was nothing to even be mentioned?

76:2 We have created the human being from a mixed seed; We test him, so We made him hear and see.

76:3 We have guided him to the path, either to be thankful or to reject.

76:4 We have prepared for the rejecters chains and shackles and a blazing Fire.

76:5 As for the pious, they will drink from a cup which has the scent of musk.

76:6 A spring from which the servants of God drink, it gushes forth abundantly.

76:7 They fulfill their vows, and they fear a Day whose consequences are widespread.

76:8 And they give food out of love to the poor and the orphan and the captive.

76:9 "We only feed you seeking the face of God; we do not desire from you any reward or thanks."

76:10 "We fear from our Lord a Day, which will be horrible and difficult."

76:11 So God shielded them from the evil of that Day, and He cast towards them a look and a smile.

76:12 And He rewarded them for their patience with a paradise and silk.

76:13 They are reclining in it on raised couches, they do not have in it excessive sun nor bitter cold.

76:14 And the shade is close upon them, and the fruit is hanging low within reach.

76:15 And they are served upon with bowls of silver and glasses of crystal.

76:16 Crystal laced with silver, measured accordingly.

76:17 And they are given to drink in it from a cup which has the scent of ginger.

76:18 A spring therein which is called 'Salsabeel.'

76:19 And they are surrounded by imortal children. If you see them you will think they are pearls which have been scattered about.

76:20 And if you look, then you will see a blessing and a great dominion.

76:21 They will have garments of fine green silk, and necklaces and bracelets from silver, and their Lord will give them a purifying drink.

76:22 "This is the reward for you, and your struggle is appreciated."

76:23 We have sent down to you the Qur'an in stages.

76:24 So be patient to the judgment of your Lord, and do not obey from them any sinner or rejecter.

76:25 And remember the name of your Lord morning and evening.

76:26 And from the night you shall prostrate to Him and praise Him throughout.

76:27 These people like the current life, and they put behind them a heavy Day.

76:28 We have created them, and established them, and if We wished, We could replace their kind completely.

76:29 This is a reminder, so let whoever wills take a path to his Lord.

76:30 And you cannot will unless God wills. God is Knowledgeable, Wise.

76:31 He admits whom He wills to His mercy. And as for the wicked, He has prepared for them a painful retribution.

CHAPTER 77

77:0 In the name of God, the Almighty, the Merciful.

77:1 By those sent with knowledge.

77:2 So they drive the wind.

77:3 And they stir up clouds.

77:4 So they distribute provisions.

77:5 So the remembrance is brought down.

77:6 As an excuse or a warning.

77:7 What you are being promised will come to pass.

77:8 So when the stars are plunged.

77:9 And when the heaven is opened.

77:10 And when the mountains are obliterated.

77:11 And when the messengers are gathered.

77:12 For what day has it been delayed?

77:13 For the Day of Separation.

77:14 And do you know what is the Day of Separation?

77:15 Woe on that Day to the disbelievers!

77:16 Did We not destroy the ancient people?

77:17 Then We made others to succeed them.

77:18 It is such that We do to the criminals.

77:19 Woe on that Day to the disbelievers!

77:20 Did We not create you from a fragile water,

77:21 Then We made it in a place of protection,

77:22 Until a time that is predetermined?

77:23 So We measured, and We are the best to measure.

77:24 Woe on that Day to the disbelievers!

77:25 Did We not make the earth an abode,

77:26 Living and dead.

77:27 And We made massive stabilizers in it, and We gave you to drink fresh water?

77:28 Woe on that Day to the disbelievers!

77:29 Away with you towards what you have disbelieved.

77:30 Away with you to a shadow with three columns.

77:31 Neither does it shade, nor does it avail from the flames.

77:32 It throws sparks as huge as logs.

77:33 As if they were yellow camels.

77:34 Woe on that Day to the disbelievers!

77:35 This is a Day when they shall not speak.

77:36 Nor will it be permitted for them so they can make excuses.

77:37 Woe on that Day to the disbelievers!

77:38 This is the Day of Separation where We have gathered you with the ancient people.

77:39 So if you have a plan, then make use of it.

77:40 Woe on that Day to the disbelievers!

77:41 The righteous are among shades and springs.

77:42 And fruit from what they desire.

77:43 "Eat and drink comfortably for what you used to do."

77:44 It is such that We reward the good doers.

77:45 Woe on that Day to the disbelievers!

77:46 "Eat and enjoy for a little while, for you are criminals."

77:47 Woe on that Day to the disbelievers!

77:48 And when they are told "kneel," they do not kneel.

77:49 Woe on that Day to the disbelievers!

77:50 So in what narrative, after it, will they believe?

CHAPTER 78

78:0 In the name of God, the Almighty, the Merciful.

78:1 What are they inquiring about?

78:2 About the significant news.

78:3 The one which they are in disagreement about.

78:4 No, they will come to know.

78:5 No, then again, they will come to know.

78:6 Did We not make the earth a habitat?

78:7 And the mountains as pegs?

78:8 And We created you in pairs?

78:9 And We made your sleep for resting?

78:10 And We made the night as a covering?

78:11 And We made the day to work in?

78:12 And We constructed above you seven mighty ones?

78:13 And We made a blazing lamp?

78:14 And We sent down from the clouds abundant water,

78:15 To bring out with it seeds and plants,

78:16 And gardens of thick growth?

78:17 The Day of Separation is the designated time.

78:18 The Day when the horn is blown and you come in crowds.

78:19 And the heaven is opened, so it becomes gates.

78:20 And the mountains will be moved as if they were a mirage.

78:21 For Hell is in wait.

78:22 For the transgressors it is a dwelling.

78:23 They will be in it for eons.

78:24 They will not taste any coolness in it nor drink.

78:25 Except that which is boiling and dark.

78:26 An exact recompense.

78:27 They did not expect the reckoning.

78:28 And they denied Our revelations greatly.

78:29 And everything We have counted in a record.

78:30 So taste it, for no increase will come to you from Us except in retribution.

78:31 As for the righteous, they will have triumph.

78:32 Gardens and vineyards.

78:33 And bunches that are ripe.

78:34 And a cup that is full.

78:35 They do not hear in it any vain talk or lies.

78:36 A reward from your Lord, in recognition for what is done.

78:37 The Lord of the heavens and the earth and what is between them, the Almighty. They do not possess any authority besides Him.

78:38 The Day the Spirit and the angels stand in line, none will speak unless the Almighty permits him and he speaks what is true.

78:39 That is the Day of truth, so let whoever wills seek refuge to his Lord.

78:40 We have warned you of a retribution which is close, the Day when the human being will look at what he has brought forth and the rejecter will say: "I wish I were dust!"

CHAPTER 79

79:0 In the name of God, the Almighty, the Merciful.

79:1 By those that take the person forcibly.

79:2 And those that take the person gently.

79:3 And those that swim along.

79:4 And those that press forward in a race.

79:5 So as to carry out a command.

79:6 On the Day the ground shakes.

79:7 It will be followed by the second blow.

79:8 Hearts on that Day will be terrified.

79:9 Their eyes cast down.

79:10 They say: "Shall we be returned to live our lives."

79:11 "Even after we were crumbled bones?"

79:12 They said: "This is an impossible recurrence."

79:13 All it takes is one call.

79:14 Whereupon they will rise up.

79:15 Did the narrative of Moses come to you?

79:16 His Lord called him at the holy valley of Tuwa.

79:17 "Go to Pharaoh, for he has transgressed."

79:18 Tell him: "Would you not be purified?"

79:19 "And I will guide you to your Lord, that you may be concerned."

79:20 He then showed him the great sign.

79:21 But he disbelieved and rebelled.

79:22 Then he turned away in a hurry.

79:23 So he gathered and proclaimed.

79:24 He said: "I am your lord, the most high."

79:25 So God seized him, restrained for the Hereafter, and the first life.

79:26 In that is a lesson for those who are concerned.

79:27 Are you a more powerful creation than the heaven which He built?

79:28 He raised its height, and perfected it.

79:29 And He covered its night and brought out its morning.

79:30 And the land after that He spread out.

79:31 He brought forth from it its water and pasture.

79:32 And the mountains He set firmly.

79:33 All this to be a provision for you and your hoofed animals.

79:34 Then, when the great blow comes.

79:35 The Day when the human being remembers all that he strove for.

79:36 And Hell will be made apparent for all who can see.

79:37 As for he who transgressed.

79:38 And was preoccupied with the worldly life.

79:39 Then Hell will be the abode.

79:40 And as for he who feared the station of his Lord, and prohibited the self from desire.

79:41 Paradise will be the abode.

79:42 They ask you about the Hour: "When is its appointed time?"

79:43 You have no knowledge of it.

79:44 To your Lord is its term.

79:45 You are simply to warn those who are concerned by it.

79:46 For the Day they see it, it will be as if they had remained an evening or half a day.

CHAPTER 80

80:0 In the name of God, the Almighty, the Merciful.

80:1 He frowned and turned away.

80:2 When the blind one came to him.

80:3 And what makes you know, perhaps he is seeking to purify?

80:4 Or to remember, so the remembrance will benefit him?

80:5 As for the one who was rich.

80:6 You were addressing yourself to him.

80:7 And why does it concern you that he does not want to purify?

80:8 And as for the one who came to you seeking.

80:9 While he was concerned.

80:10 You were too occupied for him.

80:11 No, this is but a reminder.

80:12 For whoever wills to remember.

80:13 In scripts which are honorable.

80:14 Raised and pure.

80:15 By the hands of scribes.

80:16 Honorable and righteous.

80:17　The human being is killed for his rejection.

80:18　From what did He create him?

80:19　From a seed He created him and molded him.

80:20　Then the path He made easy for him.

80:21　Then He made him die, and buried him.

80:22　Then if He wishes He resurrects him.

80:23　Alas, when what has been ordained is complete.

80:24　Let the human being look to his provisions.

80:25　We have poured the water abundantly.

80:26　Then We breached the land with cracks.

80:27　And We made grow in it seeds.

80:28　And grapes and pasture.

80:29　And olives and palm trees.

80:30　And gardens in variety.

80:31　And fruits and vegetables.

80:32　An enjoyment for you and your hoofed animals.

80:33　So when the screaming shout comes.

80:34　The Day when a person will run from his brother.

80:35　And his mother and his father.

80:36　And his mate and his children.

80:37　For every person on that Day is a matter that concerns him.

80:38　Faces on that Day which are openly displayed.

80:39　Laughing and seeking good news.

80:40　And faces on that Day with dust on them.

80:41　Being burdened by remorse.

80:42　Those are the rejecters, the wicked.

Chapter 81

81:0   In the name of God, the Almighty, the Merciful.

81:1   When the sun expands.

81:2   And when the stars cannot be seen.

81:3   And when the mountains are moved.

81:4   And when the reproduction is ended.

81:5   And when the beasts are herded.

81:6   And when the seas are made desolate.

81:7   And when the souls are paired.

81:8   And when the girl killed in infancy is asked,

81:9   "For what crime was she killed?"

81:10   And when the scripts are displayed.

81:11   And when the sky is removed.

81:12   And when Hell is ignited.

81:13   And when Paradise is made near.

81:14   Every soul will know what it had done!

81:15   So I do swear by the collapsing stars.

81:16   Running in their orbits.

81:17   And the night when it passes.

81:18   And the morning when it breathes.

81:19   It is the saying of an honorable messenger.

81:20   With power and influence from the One upon the Throne.

81:21   Obeyed, and trustworthy.

81:22   And your friend is not crazy.

81:23   And he saw him by the clear horizon.

81:24   And he has no knowledge of the future.

81:25 And it is not the saying of an outcast devil.

81:26 So where will you go?

81:27 It is but a reminder for the worlds.

81:28 For whoever of you wishes to go straight.

81:29 And you cannot will anything except if it is also willed by God, Lord of the worlds.

CHAPTER 82

82:0 In the name of God, the Almighty, the Merciful.

82:1 When the heaven is cracked.

82:2 And when the planets are scattered.

82:3 And when the seas burst.

82:4 And when the graves are disturbed.

82:5 The soul will know what it has brought forth and what it has left behind.

82:6 O man, what made you arrogant against your Lord, the Generous?

82:7 The One who created you, then evolved you, then made you upright?

82:8 In any which picture He chooses, He places you.

82:9 No, you are but deniers of the system.

82:10 And over you are those who watch.

82:11 Honorable scribes.

82:12 They know what you do.

82:13 The pious are in Paradise.

82:14 And the wicked are in Hell.

82:15 They will enter it on the Day of Judgment.

82:16 And they will not be absent from it.

82:17 And do you know what is the Day of Judgment?

82:18 Then again, do you know what is the Day of Judgment?

82:19 The Day when no soul possesses anything for any other soul, and the decision on that Day is to God.

CHAPTER 83

83:0 In the name of God, the Almighty, the Merciful.

83:1 Woe to the defrauders.

83:2 Those who when they are receiving any measure from the people, they take it in full.

83:3 And when they are the ones giving measure or weight, they give less than due.

83:4 Do these not assume that they will be resurrected?

83:5 To a great Day?

83:6 The Day the people will stand before the Lord of the worlds.

83:7 No! The record of the wicked is in 'Sijjeen.'

83:8 And do you know what is 'Sijjeen?'

83:9 A numbered record.

83:10 Woe on that Day to the deniers.

83:11 Those who deny the Day of Judgment.

83:12 And none will deny it, except every transgressor, sinner.

83:13 When Our revelations are recited to him, he says: "Tales of old!"

83:14 No! A covering has been placed on their hearts for what they have earned.

83:15 No! They will be veiled from their Lord on that Day.

83:16 Then they will be entered into Hell.

83:17 Then it will be said: "This is what you used to deny!"

83:18 No! The record of the pious is in 'Elliyeen.'

83:19 And do you know what is 'Elliyeen?'

83:20 A numbered record.

83:21 To be witnessed by those brought near.

83:22 The pious are in Paradise.

83:23 Upon raised couches, they are looking.

83:24 You will recognize in their faces the look of bliss.

83:25 They are given to drink from a pure sealed vial.

83:26 Its seal is musk, so in that let those who are in competition compete.

83:27 And its taste will be special.

83:28 From a spring which those who are brought near will drink.

83:29 Those who were criminals used to laugh at those who had believed.

83:30 And when they passed by them they used to wink to each other.

83:31 And when they returned to their people, they would return jesting.

83:32 And if they see them they say: "These are indeed misguided!"

83:33 But they were not sent over them as caretakers.

83:34 And today, those who had believed are laughing at the rejecters!

83:35 Upon raised couches, they are looking.

83:36 Have the rejecters not been rewarded for what they used to do?

CHAPTER 84

84:0 In the name of God, the Almighty, the Merciful.

84:1 When the heaven is torn.

84:2 And it admits its Lord, and is ready.

84:3 And when the earth is stretched.

84:4 And it spits out what is in it and becomes empty.

84:5 And it permits its Lord, and is ready.

84:6 O man, you will be moving towards your Lord and meeting Him.

84:7 So whoever is given his record in his right.

84:8 He will then receive an easy reckoning.

84:9 And he will return to his family in joy!

84:10 And as for he who is given his record behind his back.

84:11 He will invoke his destruction.

84:12 And he will enter a blazing Fire.

84:13 He used to be joyful among his people!

84:14 He thought he would not be returned.

84:15 No, He is ever seeing of him.

84:16 So I do swear by the redness of dusk.

84:17 And the night and what it is driven on.

84:18 And the moon when it is full.

84:19 You will ride a platform upon a platform.

84:20 So what is the matter with them that they do not believe?

84:21 And when the Qur'an is read over them, they do not prostrate.

84:22 No, those who have rejected are in denial.

84:23 And God is more aware of what they gather.

84:24 So inform them of a painful retribution.

84:25 Except for those who believe and do good works, they will have a reward that will not end.

CHAPTER 85

85:0 In the name of God, the Almighty, the Merciful.

85:1 By the heaven laden with towers.

85:2 And the appointed Day.

85:3 And a witness and a witnessed.

85:4 Destroyed will be the people of the pit!

85:5   The fire they supplied with fuel.

85:6   Which they then sat around.

85:7   And they were witness to what they did to the believers.

85:8   And they hated them simply because they had asked them to believe in God, the Noble, the Praiseworthy!

85:9   The One to whom belongs the kingship of the heavens and the earth, and God is witness over everything.

85:10   Those who have persecuted the believing males and the believing females, and then did not repent, they will have the retribution of Hell, and they will have the retribution of the burning.

85:11   Those who believe and do good works, they will have estates with rivers flowing beneath them. Such is the great reward.

85:12   The punishment of your Lord is severe.

85:13   It is He who initiates and then returns.

85:14   And He is the Forgiver, the Most Kind.

85:15   Possessor of the Throne, the Glorious.

85:16   Doer of what He wills.

85:17   Has narrative of the soldiers come to you?

85:18   Pharaoh and Thamud?

85:19   No, those who rejected are in denial.

85:20   And God after them is encompassing.

85:21   No, it is a glorious Qur'an.

85:22   In a tablet, preserved.

CHAPTER 86

86:0   In the name of God, the Almighty, the Merciful.

86:1   By the heaven and the herald.

86:2   And do you know what the herald is?

427

86:3   The pulsing star.

86:4   Every soul has a recorder over it.

86:5   So let the human being see from what he was created.

86:6   He was created from a water that spurts forth.

86:7   It comes out from between the spine and the testes.

86:8   For He is able to bring him back.

86:9   The Day when all is revealed.

86:10   Then he will not have any power or victor.

86:11   And the sky which gives rain.

86:12   And the land with cracks.

86:13   This is the word that separates matters.

86:14   And it is not a thing for amusement.

86:15   They are planning a plan.

86:16   And I am planning a plan.

86:17   So respite the rejecters, respite them for a while.

Chapter 87

87:0   In the name of God, the Almighty, the Merciful.

87:1   Glorify the name of your Lord, the Most High.

87:2   The One who has created and developed.

87:3   And the One who measured and then guided.

87:4   And the One who brought out the pasture.

87:5   So He made it dry up into hay.

87:6   We will let you read, so do not forget.

87:7   Except for what God wills, He knows what is declared and what is hidden.

87:8 And We will make easy for you the way.

87:9 So remind, perhaps the reminder will help.

87:10 He who is concerned will remember.

87:11 And he who is wicked will avoid it.

87:12 He will enter the great Fire.

87:13 Then he will neither die in it nor live.

87:14 Whoever purifies will succeed.

87:15 And mentions the name of his Lord, so he connects.

87:16 No, you desire the worldly life.

87:17 But the Hereafter is better and more lasting.

87:18 This has been revealed in the previous scripts.

87:19 The scripts of Abraham and Moses.

CHAPTER 88

88:0 In the name of God, the Almighty, the Merciful.

88:1 Has the narrative of that which will overwhelm come to you?

88:2 Faces on that Day which will be shamed.

88:3 Laboring and weary.

88:4 They will enter a blazing Fire.

88:5 And be given to drink from a boiling spring.

88:6 They will have no food except from a thorny plant.

88:7 It does not nourish nor avail against hunger.

88:8 And faces on that Day which are soft.

88:9 For their pursuit they are content.

88:10 In a high paradise.

88:11 You will not hear in it any nonsense.

88:12   In it is a running spring.

88:13   In it are raised beds.

88:14   And cups that are set.

88:15   And cushions arranged in rows.

88:16   And rich carpets spread out.

88:17   Will they not look at the camels, how were they created?

88:18   And to the sky, how was it raised?

88:19   And to the mountains, how were they set?

88:20   And to the land, how was it flattened?

88:21   So remind, for you are but a reminder.

88:22   You have no power over them.

88:23   Except for he who turns away and rejects.

88:24   Then God will punish him with the great retribution.

88:25   Indeed, to Us is their return.

88:26   Then to Us is their judgment.

CHAPTER 89

89:0   In the name of God, the Almighty, the Merciful.

89:1   By the dawn.

89:2   And ten nights.

89:3   And the even and the odd.

89:4   And the night when it passes.

89:5   Is there in that an oath for one with intelligence?

89:6   Did you not note what your Lord did to 'Aad?

89:7   Irum, with the great columns?

89:8   The one which was like no other in the land?

89:9   And Thamud who carved the rocks in the valley?

89:10   And Pharaoh with the planks?

89:11   They all transgressed in the land.

89:12   And made much corruption therein.

89:13   So your Lord poured upon them a measure of retribution.

89:14   Your Lord is ever watchful.

89:15   As for man, if his Lord tests him and is generous to him, then he says: "My Lord is generous to me!"

89:16   And if his Lord tests him and gives him little wealth, then he says: "My Lord has humiliated me!"

89:17   No—you are not generous to the orphan.

89:18   And you do not look to feeding the poor.

89:19   And you consume others inheritance, all with greed.

89:20   And you love money, a love that is excessive.

89:21   Alas, when the earth is pounded into rubble.

89:22   And your Lord comes with the angels row after row.

89:23   And Hell on that Day is brought. On that Day the human being will remember, but how will the remembrance now help him?

89:24   He says: "I wish I had worked towards my life!"

89:25   On that Day, no other will bear his punishment.

89:26   And none will be able to free his bonds.

89:27   "O you soul which is peaceful."

89:28   "Return to your Lord happy and content."

89:29   "And enter in among My servants."

89:30   "And enter My Paradise."

CHAPTER 90

90:0   In the name of God, the Almighty, the Merciful.

90:1   I do swear by this land.

90:2   And you are a dweller in this land.

90:3   And a father and what he begets.

90:4   We have created the human being in struggle.

90:5   Does he think that no one is able to best him?

90:6   He says: "I spent so much money!"

90:7   Does he think that no one sees him?

90:8   Did We not make for him two eyes?

90:9   And a tongue and two lips?

90:10   And We guided him to dual paths?

90:11   He should choose the difficult path.

90:12   Do you know which is the difficult path?

90:13   The freeing of a slave,

90:14   Or feeding on a day of great hardship,

90:15   An orphan of relation,

90:16   Or a poor person in need;

90:17   Then becoming one of those who believe, and exhort one another to patience, and exhort one another to kindness.

90:18   Those are the people of the right.

90:19   And those who rejected Our revelations, they are the people of misery.

90:20   Upon them is a Fire closed over.

CHAPTER 91

91:0 In the name of God, the Almighty, the Merciful.

91:1 By the Sun and its brightness.

91:2 And the Moon that comes after it.

91:3 And the day when it reveals.

91:4 And the night when it covers.

91:5 And the heaven and what He built.

91:6 And the earth and what He sustains.

91:7 And a soul and what He made.

91:8 So He gave it its evil and good.

91:9 Successful is the one who betters it.

91:10 And failing is the one who hides it.

91:11 Thamud denied their transgression.

91:12 They followed the worst among them.

91:13 So the messenger of God said to them: "This is the camel of God and her place of drinking."

91:14 But they disbelieved him, and they killed her. So their Lord repaid them for their sin and leveled it.

91:15 Yet, those who came after remain heedless.

CHAPTER 92

92:0 In the name of God, the Almighty, the Merciful.

92:1 By the night when it covers.

92:2 And by the day when it appears.

92:3 And by what He has created, the male and female.

92:4 Your works are various.

92:5   As for he who gives and is righteous.

92:6   And trusts in goodness.

92:7   We will make for him the easy path.

92:8   And as for he who is stingy and holds back.

92:9   And denies goodness.

92:10   We will make for him the difficult path.

92:11   And his wealth will not avail him when he demises.

92:12   It is upon Us to guide.

92:13   And to Us is the end and the beginning.

92:14   I have warned you of a fire that is blazing.

92:15   None shall have it but the wicked.

92:16   The one who denies and turns away.

92:17   As for the righteous, he will be spared it.

92:18   The one who gives his money to purify.

92:19   Seeking nothing in return.

92:20   Except the face of his Lord, the Most High.

92:21   And he will be pleased.

CHAPTER 93

93:0   In the name of God, the Almighty, the Merciful.

93:1   By the late morning.

93:2   And the night when it falls.

93:3   Your Lord has not left you, nor did He forget you.

93:4   And the Hereafter is better for you than the first.

93:5   And your Lord will give you and you will be pleased.

93:6   Did he not find you an orphan and He sheltered you?

93:7   And He found you lost, and He guided you?

93:8   And He found you in need, so He gave you riches?

93:9   As for the orphan, you shall not make him sad.

93:10   And as for the beggar, you shall not reprimand.

93:11   And you shall proclaim the blessings from your Lord.

CHAPTER 94

94:0   In the name of God, the Almighty, the Merciful.

94:1   Did We not comfort your chest,

94:2   And take from you your burden,

94:3   Which had put strain on your back?

94:4   And We have raised your remembrance,

94:5   So with hardship comes ease.

94:6   With hardship comes ease.

94:7   So when you have free time, then stand.

94:8   And to your Lord you shall seek.

CHAPTER 95

95:0   In the name of God, the Almighty, the Merciful.

95:1   By the fig and the olive.

95:2   And the mount of ages.

95:3   And this secure land.

95:4   We have created the human being in the best form.

95:5   Then We returned him to the lowest of the low ones.

95:6   Except those who have believed and done good works, they will have a reward that will not end.

95:7   So what would make you deny the system after that?

95:8   Is God not the Wisest of the wise ones?

CHAPTER 96

96:0   In the name of God, the Almighty, the Merciful.

96:1   Read in the name of your Lord who has created.

96:2   He created the human being from an embryo.

96:3   Read, and your Lord is the Generous One.

96:4   The One who taught by the pen.

96:5   He taught the human being what he did not know.

96:6   No! The human being is bound to transgress.

96:7   When he achieves, he no longer has need!

96:8   To your Lord is the return.

96:9   Did you see the one who prohibits,

96:10 A servant from connecting

96:11 Did you see if he was being guided,

96:12 Or that he advocated righteousness?

96:13 Did you see that he denied and turned away?

96:14 Does he not realize that God can see?

96:15 No! If he does not cease, We will take him by the forelock.

96:16 A forelock which lies and errs.

96:17 So let him call on his supporter.

96:18 We will call on the guardians.

96:19 No! Do not obey him; but prostrate and come near.

CHAPTER 97

97:0 In the name of God, the Almighty, the Merciful.

97:1 We have sent it down in the Night of Decree.

97:2 And do you know what is the Night of Decree?

97:3 The Night of Decree is better than one thousand months.

97:4 The angels and the Spirit come down in it with the permission of their Lord to carry out every matter.

97:5 Peaceful it is until the emergence of dawn.

CHAPTER 98

98:0 In the name of God, the Almighty, the Merciful.

98:1 Those who rejected among the people of the Book and the polytheists would not leave until a proof came to them.

98:2 A messenger from God reciting purified scripts.

98:3 In them are valuable books.

98:4 And those who had previously received the Book did not divide except after the proof came to them.

98:5 And they were not commanded except to serve God and be loyal to His system, monotheists, and hold the Connection and contribute towards purification. Such is the valuable system.

98:6 Those who rejected from the people of the Book and the polytheists are in the fires of Hell abiding therein, those are the worst of creation.

98:7 As for those who believe and do good works, they are the best of creation.

98:8 Their reward with their Lord are gardens of delight with rivers flowing beneath them, abiding therein eternally. God is satisfied with them, and they are satisfied with Him. That is for whoever is concerned towards his Lord.

CHAPTER 99

99:0 In the name of God, the Almighty, the Merciful.

99:1 When the earth rumbles and shakes.

99:2 And the earth brings out its load.

99:3 And the human being will say: "What is wrong with her?"

99:4 On that Day it will inform its news.

99:5 That your Lord had inspired her to do so.

99:6 On that Day, the people will be brought out in throngs to be shown their works.

99:7 So whoever does the weight of an atom of good will see it.

99:8 And whoever does the weight of an atom of evil will see it.

CHAPTER 100

100:0 In the name of God, the Almighty, the Merciful.

100:1 By the fast gallopers.

100:2 Striking sparks.

100:3 Charging in the morning.

100:4 Forming clouds of dust.

100:5 Penetrating to the midst together.

100:6 Surely, the human being is unappreciative to his Lord.

100:7 And he will indeed bear witness to this.

100:8 And he loves the material things excessively.

100:9 Does he not realize that the contents of the graves will be disturbed?

100:10 And what is inside the chests will be collected.

100:11 They will realize then, that their Lord was fully cognizant of them.

Chapter 101

101:0 In the name of God, the Almighty, the Merciful.

101:1 The Shocker.

101:2 What is the Shocker?

101:3 And how would you know what the Shocker is?

101:4 The Day when people come out like swarms of butterflies.

101:5 And the mountains will be like fluffed up wool.

101:6 As for him whose weights are heavy.

101:7 He will be in a happy life.

101:8 As for him whose weights are light.

101:9 His destiny is the lowest.

101:10 And how would you know what it is?

101:11 A blazing Fire.

Chapter 102

102:0 In the name of God, the Almighty, the Merciful.

102:1 Hoarding has distracted you.

102:2 Until you visit the graves.

102:3 No, you will find out.

102:4 Then again, you will find out.

102:5 No, if only you had the knowledge of certainty.

102:6 You would then see Hell.

102:7 Then you would see it with the eye of certainty.

102:8 Then you would be questioned, on that Day, about the blessings.

CHAPTER 103

103:0 In the name of God, the Almighty, the Merciful.

103:1 By time.

103:2 The human being is indeed in loss.

103:3 Except those who believe, and do good works, and support one another with the truth, and support one another with perseverance.

CHAPTER 104

104:0 In the name of God, the Almighty, the Merciful.

104:1 Woe to every backbiter, slanderer.

104:2 Who gathered his wealth and counted it.

104:3 He thinks that his wealth will make him eternal.

104:4 Never! He will be thrown into the Destroyer.

104:5 And do you know what is the Destroyer?

104:6 The kindled Fire of God.

104:7 Which reaches the inside of the minds.

104:8 It will confine them therein.

104:9 In extended columns.

CHAPTER 105

105:0 In the name of God, the Almighty, the Merciful.

105:1 Did you not note what your Lord did to the companions of the elephant?

105:2 Did He not cause their plans to go astray?

105:3 And He sent upon them a flying swarm.

105:4 Striking them with fiery projectiles.

105:5 Until He made them like chewed up hay.

CHAPTER 106

106:0 In the name of God, the Almighty, the Merciful.

106:1 This should be cherished by Quraysh.

106:2 The way they cherish the journey of the winter and summer.

106:3 So let them serve the Lord of this House.

106:4 The One who fed them from hunger, and protected them from fear.

CHAPTER 107

107:0 In the name of God, the Almighty, the Merciful.

107:1 Have you seen he who is denying in the system?

107:2 It is the one who mistreats the orphan,

107:3 And the one who does not encourage the feeding of the poor.

107:4 So woe to those who connect,

107:5 But, to their connecting they are absent minded.

107:6 They only want to be seen,

107:7 And they refuse to aid.

CHAPTER 108

108:0 In the name of God, the Almighty, the Merciful.

108:1 We have given you plenty.

108:2 Therefore, you shall connect towards your Lord, and sacrifice.

108:3 Indeed your rival will be the loser.

CHAPTER 109

109:0 In the name of God, the Almighty, the Merciful.

109:1 Say: "O rejecters,"

109:2 "I do not serve what you serve,"

109:3 "Nor do you serve what I serve,"

109:4 "Nor will I serve what you serve,"

109:5 "Nor will you serve what I serve,"

109:6 "To you is your system, and to me is mine."

CHAPTER 110

110:0 In the name of God, the Almighty, the Merciful.

110:1 When the victory of God and conquest comes.

110:2 And you see the people entering into the system of God in flocks.

110:3 You shall glorify the grace of your Lord, and seek His forgiveness; for He is the Redeemer.

CHAPTER 111

111:0 In the name of God, the Almighty, the Merciful.

111:1 Condemned are the hands of the firebrand; condemned.

111:2 His money will not avail him, nor what he has earned.

111:3 He will be sent to a flaming fire.

111:4 And his wife who carries the logs.

111:5 Within her collar, is a rope of thorns.

CHAPTER 112

112:0 In the name of God, the Almighty, the Merciful.

112:1 Say: "He is God, the One,"

112:2 "God, the Indivisible,"

112:3 "He does not beget, nor was He begotten,"

112:4 "And there is none who is His equal."

CHAPTER 113

113:0 In the name of God, the Almighty, the Merciful.

113:1 Say: "I seek refuge with the Lord of the rising dawn,"

113:2 "From the evil among His creation,"

113:3 "And from the evil of darkness as it falls,"

113:4 "And from the evil of those who blow on knots,"

113:5 "And from the evil of an envier when he envies."

CHAPTER 114

114:0 In the name of God, the Almighty, the Merciful.

114:1 Say: "I seek refuge with the Lord of the people,"

114:2 "The King of the people,"

114:3 "The god of the people,"

114:4 "From the evil of the sneaking whisperer,"

114:5 "Who whispers into the chests of the people."

114:6 "From the Jinn and the people."

QUR'AN INDEX BY TOPIC

A

'AAD 7:65, 7:74, 9:70, 11:50-60, 22:42, 25:38, 26:123-140, 29:38, 38:12, 41:15-16, 46:21-26, 50:13, 51:41, 53:50, 54:18-21, 69:4, 69:6, 89:6

AARON 2:248, 4:163, 6:84, 7:122, 7:142, 10:75, 19:28, 19:53, 20:30, 20:70, 20:90-92, 21:48, 23:45, 25:35, 26:13, 26:48, 28:34, 37:114, 37:120

ABLUTION 4:43, 5:6

ABORTION 6:151, 31:14, 46:15

ABRAM 2:124-140, 2:258-260,

ABRAHAM 3:33, 3:65-68, 3:84, 3:95-97, 4:54, 4:125, 4:163, 6:74-75, 6:83, 6:161, 9:70, 9:114, 11:69, 11:74-76, 12:6, 12:38, 14:35, 15:51, 16:120-123, 19:41-46, 19:58, 21:51-69, 22:26, 22:43, 22:78, 26:69, 29:16, 29:31, 33:7, 37:83, 37:104-109, 38:45, 42:13, 43:26, 51:24, 53:37, 57:26, 60:4, 87:19

ABU-LAHAB 111:1-3

ADAM 2:31-37, 3:33, 3:59, 5:27, 7:11-35, 7:172, 17:61, 17:70, 18:50, 19:58, 20:115-121, 36:60

ADOPTION 33:4-5

ADULTERY 4:25, 17:32, 24:2-9, 25:68, 60:12

INTOXICANTS 2:219, 4:43, 5:90-91, 12:36, 12:41, 16:67, 47:15

ALLIANCES 4:88-89, 4:139, 4:144, 5:51, 8:72, 9:7, 9:23

ANGELS 2:30-34, 2:97-98, 2:210, 2:285, 4:97, 7:12, 8:50, 13:23, 15:7-8, 16:2, 21:108, 22:75, 25:22, 25:25, 26:194, 32:11, 33:43, 33:56, 34:40, 35:1, 37:150, 38:71, 38:76, 39:75, 41:14, 41:30, 42:5, 43:19, 43:53, 43:60, 47:27, 53:26-27, 66:4, 66:6, 69:17, 70:4, 74:30-31, 82:10-12, 86:4, 89:22, 97:4

ANGER 3:134

ANTS 27:18

APES 5:60, 2:65, 7:166

ARABIC 12:2, 13:37, 16:103, 20:113, 26:195, 39:28, 41:3, 41:44, 42:7, 43:3, 46:12

ARAFAAT 2:198

ARK "COVENANT" 2:248

ARK "NOAH" 7:64, 10:73, 11:37-38, 23:27-28, 26:119, 29:15, 36:41, 54:13

ARMOR 21:80, 34:11

ART 34:13

ARRAS 25:38

ASTRONOMY 6:96-97, 7:54, 10:5, 13:2, 14:33, 15:16, 16:12, 16:16, 21:33, 22:18, 22:65, 25:45, 25:61, 29:61, 31:29, 34:9, 35:13, 35:41, 36:38-40, 37:5-6, 37:88, 39:5, 41:12, 41:37, 44:39, 45:22, 46:3, 51:7, 53:49, 54:1, 55:5, 55:17, 64:3, 67:5, 70:40, 71:16, 74:32, 78:13, 79:1-4, 81:1-2, 81:15-16, 84:16, 84:18, 85:1, 86:3, 86:11, 91:1-2

AZAR 6:74

B

BAAL 37:125

BABYLON 2:102

BAKK'A 3:96

BEES 16:68

BELIEVERS 2:2-5, 2:285, 8:2-4, 8:24, 9:18, 9:71, 24:23, 33:58, 85:10

BIOLOGY 11:7, 21:30, 24:45, 25:54

BIRDS 6:38, 16:79, 21:41, 27:16, 27:17, 27:20, 34:10, 38:19, 67:19

BORDERS 8:72

BRIBERY 2:188

BURIAL 5:31

C

Camel 7:40, 7:73, 7:77, 11:64, 17:59, 26:155, 54:27, 91:13

Captives 2:85, 8:67, 8:70, 33:26, 76:8

Cave "People of" 18:9-25

Charity 2:43, 2:83, 2:110, 2:177, 2:215, 2:219, 2:262-265, 2:267-268, 2:270-274, 2:277, 3:92, 3:134, 3:180, 4:37-39, 5:12, 5:55, 9:5, 9:18, 9:34-35, 9:58, 9:60, 9:71, 9:76, 9:121, 16:71, 21:73, 22:36-38, 22:41, 22:78, 24:22, 24:37, 24:61, 25:67, 27:3, 30:38-39, 31:4, 36:47, 41:7, 47:36-38, 51:19, 52:40, 57:7, 57:10-12, 57:24, 58:12-13, 63:10, 64:16-17, 73:20, 76:8, 89:18, 92:8, 92:18-19, 98:5, 107:3, 107:7

Children 16:72, 17:64, 18:46, 19:77, 26:133, 34:35, 34:37, 40:67, 46:15, 57:20, 58:17, 63:9, 64:14, 64:15, 65:7, 68:14, 71:12, 71:22, 74:13, 80:36

Clothing 7:26, 16:81, 23:5, 24:30-31, 24:33, 70:29

Confession 16:106, 26:18-20

Conservation "Game" 5:1-5, 5:94-97, 56:63-74

Contract 5:1, 16:91

Credit 2:280-282

Custody "Children" 2:233

D

David 2:251, 4:163, 5:78, 6:84, 17:55, 21:78, 21:79, 27:15-16, 34:10, 34:13, 38:17, 38:21-26, 38:30

Death 2:154, 3:169, 3:185, 3:193, 3:195, 4:78, 4:100, 6:131, 9:115, 10:47, 11:117, 15:4, 16:119, 17:15, 21:35, 22:58, 28:59, 32:11, 33:16, 33:19, 33:23, 44:56, 47:4, 47:27, 56:60, 56:84-87, 63:10, 75:29

Defense 42:41

Divorce 2:226-232, 33:49, 65:1-6

Dogs 5:4, 7:176, 18:18, 18:22

Donkeys 2:259, 16:8, 31:19, 62:5

Dreams 8:43, 12:36-41, 12:43-49, 37:102

E

Earth 3:190, 7:54, 10:3, 10:6, 11:7, 13:3, 14:33, 14:48, 22:61, 25:62, 39:5, 41:9-10, 41:37, 45:5, 50:38, 51:20, 51:48, 57:4, 57:6, 79:30, 91:6

Earthquake 22:1, 99:1

Egypt 2:61, 10:87, 12:21, 12:99, 43:51

Eight 6:143, 18:22, 28:27, 39:6, 69:7, 69:17

Eighty 24:4

Elephant 105:1

Eleven 12:4

Elisha 6:86, 38:48

Embezzle 3:161

Embryology 22:5, 23:14, 35:11, 40:67, 75:37-39

Enoch "Idris" 19:56-57, 21:85

Etiquette 4:86, 3:133-134, 3:159, 4:94, 6:108, 13:22, 14:24-26, 16:125, 25:63, 31:18-19, 41:34, 49:6, 49:11-13

Evil 13:22, 28:54, 41:34

Evolution 71:14, 71:18

Ezra 9:30

F

Falsehood 49:6

Family 8:75

Fasting 2:183-187, 2:196, 4:92, 5:89, 5:95, 19:26, 33:35, 58:4

Fighting 9:14, 9:123, 22:39, 47:4, 48:16

Fire 56:71, 100:2

Food 2:61, 2:168, 2:173, 3:93, 4:160, 5:3-4, 6:118, 6:121, 6:138, 6:145-146, 10:59-60, 16:115, 35:12, 40:79, 80:24

FORBIDDEN "HARAM" 2:173, 2:275, 3:93, 4:23, 4:160, 5:1-3, 5:72, 5:87, 5:95-96, 6:119, 6:138, 6:140, 6:146, 6:148, 6:150, 6:151-153, 7:32-33, 7:50, 7:157, 9:29, 9:37, 16:35, 16:115, 16:118, 17:33, 24:3, 25:68, 66:1

FULL MOON "BADR" 3:123

FUTURE 5:3, 5:90, 15:18, 37:8, 72:9

G

GABRIEL 2:97-98, 66:4

GENITALIA 23:5, 24:30-31, 33:35, 70:29

GINGER 76:12

GOD 2:26, 2:98, 2:106, 2:115, 2:117, 2:142, 2:177, 2:255, 2:259, 3:6, 3:64, 3:108, 3:151, 3:165, 3:189, 3:191, 4:40, 4:66-68, 4:78, 4:95-96, 4:103, 4:125-126, 4:133, 4:171, 5:54, 5:101, 6:35-36, 6:59, 6:73, 6:125, 6:140, 6:148, 7:32, 7:180, 8:30, 8:36, 8:41, 8:70, 9:51, 9:94, 9:105, 9:116, 9:120, 10:12, 10:18, 11:4, 11:7, 13:9, 14:4, 14:19, 16:8, 16:40, 16:57, 16:93, 16:104, 16:119, 17:40, 17:71, 17:110, 20:8, 21:47, 22:10, 22:47, 25:64, 26:209, 28:56, 29:65, 32:5-6, 33:42, 34:48, 35:16, 35:38, 36:23, 36:67, 39:3, 39:38, 39:46, 40:31, 40:68, 41:46, 42:49, 43:16, 43:81-82, 43:86, 44:8, 45:22, 49:9, 49:15, 49:18, 50:29, 52:39, 53:19-22, 53:43-44, 57:2-3, 57:22, 59:22, 59:24, 61:11, 62:8, 64:11, 64:18, 67:2, 67:12, 70:4, 72:3, 72:26, 74:31, 87:7, 93:3, 95:8, 112:3, 113:1-5, 114:1-6

GOG & MAGOG 18:94, 21:96

GOLD 3:14, 3:91, 9:34, 18:31, 22:23, 35:33, 43:53, 43:71

GOLDEN CALF 2:51, 2:54-55, 4:153, 7:148, 7:152, 20:88

GOLIATH 2:249, 2:251

GOVERNMENT 3:159, 42:38

GRAIN 36:33, 55:12

GRAVE 9:84, 22:7, 35:22, 60:13, 80:21, 82:4, 100:9, 102:2

GREETING 4:86, 25:63

GUARDIANSHIP 4:5-6, 4:10, 6:151

H

HAAMAAN 28:6, 28:8, 28:38, 29:39, 40:24, 40:36

HANDICAPPED 24:61

HAROOT 2:102

HEARING 41:22

HEAVEN 2:25, 2:29, 2:164, 3:15, 3:129, 3:136, 3:181, 3:195, 3:198, 4:57, 6:73, 6:101, 13:23, 17:44, 36:56, 37:48-49, 38:52, 40:8, 43:70, 52:21, 55:30, 55:56, 55:72-74, 56:17, 56:22, 56:34-36, 65:12, 67:3, 71:15, 72:8, 76:19, 78:12, 78:33

HELL 2:24, 2:119, 2:161, 2:166, 2:201, 3:10, 3:12, 3:116, 3:131, 3:151, 3:162, 3:192, 4:55-56, 4:93, 4:97, 4:114, 4:121, 4:169, 5:10, 5:37, 5:72, 5:86, 6:27, 6:70, 6:128, 7:18, 7:36, 7:38, 7:41, 7:50, 7:179, 8:16, 8:36, 8:50, 9:17, 9:35, 9:49, 9:63, 9:68, 9:73, 9:81, 9:95, 9:109, 9:113, 10:8, 10:27, 11:16, 11:17, 11:98, 11:106, 11:113, 11:119, 13:5, 13:18, 13:35, 14:16, 14:49, 15:43, 16:29, 16:62, 17:8, 17:18, 17:39, 17:63, 17:97, 18:29, 18:53, 18:100, 18:106, 19:68, 19:70, 19:86, 20:74, 21:39, 21:98, 22:4, 22:9, 22:19-22, 22:51, 22:72, 23:103-104, 24:57, 25:11-13, 25:34, 25:65, 26:91, 26:94, 27:90, 28:41, 29:25, 29:54, 29:68, 31:21, 32:13, 32:20, 33:64, 33:66, 34:12, 34:42, 35:6, 35:36, 36:63, 37:10, 37:23, 37:55, 37:63, 37:68, 37:163, 38:27, 38:56, 38:57, 38:59, 38:61, 38:64, 38:85, 39:8, 39:16, 39:19, 39:32, 39:60, 39:71, 39:72, 40:6, 40:7, 40:41, 40:43, 40:46, 40:47, 40:49,

40:60, 40:72, 40:76, 41:19, 41:24, 41:28, 41:40, 42:7, 43:74, 44:47, 44:56, 45:10, 45:34, 45:35, 46:20, 46:34, 47:12, 47:15, 48:6, 48:13, 50:24, 50:30, 51:13, 52:13-16, 52:18, 54:48, 55:43, 56:94, 57:15, 57:19, 58:8, 58:17, 59:3, 59:17, 59:20, 64:10, 66:6, 66:9, 66:10, 67:5-10, 69:31-32, 70:15, 71:25, 72:15, 72:23, 73:12-13, 74:26-31, 74:42, 76:4, 77:31, 78:21, 78:23, 79:36, 79:39, 81:12, 82:14, 83:16, 84:12, 85:10, 87:12-13, 88:4, 89:23, 90:20, 92:14, 98:6, 101:9-11, 102:6, 104:6-9, 111:3

HISTORY 3:137, 12:110-111, 14:5

HONEY 16:69, 47:15

HOOFED ANIMALS 3:14, 4:119, 6:136, 6:138, 6:139, 6:142, 7:179, 10:24, 16:5, 16:66, 16:80, 20:54, 22:30, 23:21, 25:44, 25:49, 26:133, 32:27, 35:28, 36:71, 39:6, 40:79, 42:11, 43:12, 47:12 , 79:33, 80:32

HOOFED ANIMALS (DOMESTICATED) 5:1, 22:28, 22:34

HORSES 3:14, 8:60, 16:8, 17:64, 59:6

HUD 7:65-72, 11:50-57, 11:89, 26:124-138, 46:21-25

HUNAYN 9:25

HUNDRED(S) 2:259, 2:261, 8:65, 8:66, 18:25, 24:2, 37:147

HUNTING 5:4

HYPOCRITES 3:167, 4:61, 4:88, 4:138, 4:140, 4:142, 4:145, 8:49, 9:64, 9:67, 9:68, 9:73, 9:77, 9:97, 9:101, 29:11, 33:1, 33:12, 33:24, 33:48, 33:60, 33:73, 48:6, 57:13, 59:11, 63:1, 63:7, 63:8, 66:9

I

IMMIGRATION "HIJRA" 2:218, 3:195, 4:89, 4:97, 4:100, 8:72, 8:74-75, 9:20, 9:100, 9:117, 16:41, 16:110, 22:58, 24:22, 29:26, 33:6, 59:8-9, 60:10

IMMORALITY 2:169, 2:268, 4:15-16, 7:28, 12:24, 16:90, 24:21, 26:165-166, 27:55, 29:28-29, 29:45

IMPLORE 2:186, 3:38, 6:40-41, 7:29, 7:55-56, 7:180, 7:189, 10:12, 10:22, 10:106, 17:11, 17:67, 17:110, 26:213, 27:62, 28:88, 29:65, 30:33, 31:32, 39:8, 39:49, 40:12, 40:14, 40:60, 40:65, 44:22, 54:10

IMRAN 3:33, 3:35, 66:12

INHERITANCE 4:7-8, 4:11-12, 4:176

INJEEL "GOSPEL" 3:3, 3:48, 3:65, 5:46-47, 5:66, 5:68, 5:110, 7:157, 9:111, 48:29, 57:37

INTOXICANT 4:43, 15:72, 16:67, 22:2

IRON 17:50, 18:96, 22:21, 34:101, 50:22, 57:25

IRUM 89:7

ISAAC 2:136, 2:140, 3:84, 4:163, 6:84, 11:71, 12:5, 12:6, 12:38, 14:39, 21:72, 37:112-113, 38:45

ISAIAH 21:85, 38:48

ISHMAEL 2:125-127, 2:133, 2:136, 2:140, 3:84, 4:163, 6:86, 14:39, 19:54, 21:85, 38:48

ISRAEL "CHILDREN OF" 2:40, 2:47, 2:83, 2:122, 2:211, 2:246, 3:49, 3:93, 5:12, 5:32, 5:70-72, 5:78, 5:110, 7:105, 7:134-138, 10:90-93, 17:2-4, 17:101, 17:104, 20:47, 20:80, 20:94, 26:17, 26:22, 26:59, 26:197, 27:76, 32:23, 40:53, 43:59, 44:30, 45:16, 46:10, 61:6, 61:14

ISRAEL "JACOB" 3:93, 19:58

J

JACOB 2:132-140, 3:84, 4:164, 6:84, 11:71, 12:6, 12:38, 12:68, 19:6, 19:49, 21:72, 29:27, 38:45

JESUS 2:87, 2:136, 2:252, 3:45-49, 3:52, 3:55, 3:59, 4:157-159, 4:163, 4:171-172, 5:17, 5:72, 5:75, 5:110, 5:116,

9:30, 9:31, 10:68, 19:22, 19:30-34, 21:91, 23:50, 33:7, 43:61, 43:65, 61:6, 61:14

JEWS 2:42-43, 2:61-62, 2:75, 2:84-85, 2:88, 2:91, 2:94, 2:111, 2:113, 2:120, 2:136, 2:139-140, 2:146, 2:159, 2:174, 3:21, 3:23, 3:71, 3:75, 3:112, 3:114, 3:181, 3:183, 4:44, 4:46-47, 4:51, 4:155, 4:157, 4:160-161, 5:13, 5:15, 5:18, 5:32, 5:41, 5:43, 5:45, 5:48, 5:64-66, 5:68-70, 5:82, 5:85, 6:91, 6:146, 7:157, 9:30, 9:34-35, 15:90, 22:17, 57:29, 61:6, 62:6

JIHAD 2:218, 3:142, 4:95, 5:35, 5:54, 8:72, 8:74-75, 9:16, 9:20, 9:24, 9:41, 9:73, 9:81, 9:86, 9:88, 16:110, 22:78, 25:52, 29:8, 29:69, 31:15, 47:31, 49:15, 60:1, 66:9

JINN 6:100, 6:112, 6:128, 6:130, 7:38, 7:179, 15:27, 17:88, 18:50, 27:10, 27:17, 27:39, 28:31, 34:12-14, 34:41, 41:25, 41:29, 46:18, 46:29, 51:56, 55:15, 55:33, 55:39, 55:56, 55:74, 72:1-6

JOB 4:163, 6:84, 21:83, 38:41-44,

JOHN 3:38-40, 6:85, 6:86, 19:7-15, 21:90

JONAH 4:163, 6:86, 10:98, 21:87, 37:139

JOSEPH 6:84, 12:4-101, 40:34

JUDGMENT DAY 2:123, 2:177, 2:254, 3:9, 3:25, 3:106, 3:114, 4:41 4:59, 4:136, 5:69 5:119, 6:15-16, 6:31, 6:40, 6:128, 6:151, 7:8, 7:53, 7:187, 9:29, 9:35, 9:44, 9:45, 9:77, 9:99, 10:15, 10:28, 10:51-52, 11:3, 11:8, 11:25, 11:84, 11:103, 11:105, 12:107, 14:21, 14:29, 14:30, 14:41, 14:42, 14:44, 14:48, 14:49, 15:36, 15:38, 16:77, 16:84, 16:87, 16:89, 16:111, 17:71, 17:104, 18:99, 18:100, 19:37-39, 19:75, 19:85, 20:15, 20:105-112, 21:49, 21:103-104, 22:2-7, 22:55-56, 24:37, 25:8, 25:11, 25:25, 26:82, 27:83, 30:12, 30:14,

30:55, 31:33, 32:14, 33:21, 33:44, 33:63, 33:66, 34:3, 36:53, 37:20, 38:16, 38:26, 38:53, 39:13, 39:68, 40:9, 40:27, 40:33, 40:51, 40:59, 40:85, 42:7, 43:66, 43:83, 43:85, 44:10, 44:40, 45:27, 45:32, 45:34, 45:35, 47:18, 49:6, 49:12, 50:20, 50:44, 51:12, 52:10, 52:45, 54:1, 54:46, 54:48, 55:35, 55:37, 56:4-5, 56:8-11, 56:15-38, 56:41-55, 56:56, 56:88-89, 56:90-94, 58:22, 60:6, 64:9, 69:13-37, 70:8-9, 70:26, 73:14, 73:17-18, 74:8, 74:46, 76:7, 77:8-11, 77:13-14, 77:38, 78:17-20, 78:38, 79:6-14, 81:1-14, 82:1, 82:3, 82:15, 82:19, 83:11, 84:1, 84:3, 84:7-12, 89:21-22, 99:1-8, 101:1, 101:5-6

JUDGMENT 4:58, 5:8, 6:151-152, 37:53, 40:78, 45:21, 50:29, 51:6, 60:10, 69:18, 76:24, 82:9, 95:8

K

KA'ABA "QUADRANGLE" 5:95, 5:97

KILLING 4:92-93, 6:151, 17:33, 18:74, 18:80, 25:68, 48:25

KINGS 2:246-247, 5:20, 12:43, 12:50, 12:54, 12:72, 12:76, 18:79, 27:34

L

LANGUAGE 14:4, 16:103, 19:97, 26:195, 30:22, 44:58, 46:12

LAW "GOD ALONE" 2:170-171, 5:48-50, 5:101, 6:19, 6:114-115, 6:151-153, 10:15-18, 10:59-60, 16:89, 18:57, 39:45, 45:6-11

LION 74:15

LOCUSTS 54:7, 105:3

LOT 6:86, 7:80-84, 11:70, 11:74, 11:77-83, 11:89, 15:59-72, 21:71, 21:74, 22:43, 29:28, 29:32-33, 37:153, 38:13, 50:13, 54:33-39, 66:10

Luqmaan 31:13-19

M

Malek 43:77
Manna 2:57, 7:160, 20:80
Maroot 2:102
Marriage 2:229-230, 2:235, 4:22-25, 5:5, 24:32-33, 26:165-166, 28:27
Mary 3:36-45, 4:156, 4:171, 5:17, 5:110, 5:116, 19:16-27, 23:50, 66:12

Mecca 48:24
Menstruation 2:222, 65:4
 3:45, 4:157, 4:171-172, 5:17, 5:72, 5:75, 9:30-31
Metallurgy 13:17, 18:96-97, 34:2, 57:25
Michael 2:98
Median 7:85-93, 9:70, 11:84-96, 15:78, 20:40, 22:44, 26:176, 26:160-173, 27:54-57, 28:22-23, 28:45, 29:36, 50:14
Milk 16:66, 47:15
Miracle "Sign" 2:118, 2:164, 2:219, 2:248, 2:259, 3:41, 3:190, 5:114, 6:25, 6:37, 6:109, 6:158, 7:73, 7:132-133, 7:146, 7:175, 10:92, 10:101, 11:64, 11:96, 12:7, 13:38, 17:1, 17:12, 17:101, 19:10, 19:21, 20:22, 20:42, 20:56, 21:32, 21:91, 23:45, 27:12-13, 28:36, 29:15, 29:35, 30:20-25, 30:46, 31:31, 34:15, 36:33, 36:37, 40:23, 40:78, 40:81, 41:53, 42:29, 43:46-48, 45:3-5, 48:20, 51:20, 51:37, 53:18, 54:15, 79:20
Mohammed 3:144, 33:40, 47:2, 48:29
Monkeys 2:65, 5:60, 7:166
Month(s) 2:185, 2:194, 2:197, 2:217, 2:226, 2:234, 4:92, 5:2, 5:97, 9:2, 9:5, 9:36, 34:12, 46:15, 58:4, 65:4, 97:3
Moses 2:51, 2:60, 2:136, 2:248, 3:84, 5:21, 6:84, 6:91, 7:103-162, 7:160,

7:163, 10:75-93, 11:96, 11:110, 14:5, 14:6, 14:8, 17:2, 17:101-104, 18:60-82, 19:51-53, 20:9-98, 21:48, 22:44, 23:45-49, 25:35, 26:10-66, 27:7-14, 28:3-43, 28:44, 28:48, 28:76, 29:39, 32:23, 33:7, 33:69, 37:114-120, 40:23-27, 40:53, 41:45, 42:13, 43:46-55, 44:17-36, 46:12, 46:30, 51:38-40, 53:37, 61:5, 79:14-25, 87:19
Mountains 15:19, 16:15, 16:81, 17:37, 20:105-107, 27:61, 31:10, 33:72, 34:10, 38:18, 41:10, 42:32, 50:7, 77:27, 78:7, 79:32, 81:3, 88:19, 95:2
Mules 16:8
Murder 4:92, 5:45

N

Nazarenes "Christians" 2:62, 2:111, 2:113, 2:120, 2:135, 2:140, 3:67, 5:14, 5:18, 5:51, 5:69, 5:82, 9:30, 22:17
Night 25:47
Nineteen 74:30
Noah 3:33, 4:163, 6:84, 7:59, 7:69, 9:70, 10:71, 11:25-48, 11:89, 14:9, 17:3, 17:17, 19:58, 21:76, 22:42, 23:23, 25:37, 26:105-120, 29:14, 33:7, 37:75-79, 38:12, 40:5, 40:31, 42:13, 50:12, 51:46, 53:52, 54:9, 57:26, 66:10, 71:1-28
Nomads 9:90, 9:97-99, 9:101, 9:120, 33:2048:11, 48:16, 49:14
Noise 31:19

O

Oaths 2:224, 5:89, 16:91, 16:92, 16:94, 23:8, 48:10, 70:32
Olives 6:99, 6:141, 16:11, 24:35, 80:29, 95:1
Oppression 2:191, 2:193, 2:217, 8:39, 42:42, 42:39

ORPHANS 2:83, 2:220, 4:2-6, 4:10, 4:127, 6:152, 17:34, 93:7

P

PARENTS 2:83, 6:151, 31:14-15
PATRIARCHS 33:5
PEACEKEEPING 49:9-10
PEARLS 35:33, 52:24, 55:22, 55:58, 56:23, 76:19
PEN 68:1, 96:4
PHARAOH 2:49-50, 3:11, 7:103-141, 8:52-54, 10:75-92, 11:97, 14:6, 17:101-102, 20:24-79, 23:46, 26:11-53, 27:12, 28:3-38, 29:29, 38:12, 40:24-46, 43:46-51, 44:17, 44:31, 50:13, 51:38, 54:41, 66:11, 69:9, 73:15-16, 79:17, 85:18, 89:10
PILGRIMAGE "HAJJ" 2:126, 2:158, 2:189, 2:196-203, 3:96-97, 5:2, 9:2-5, 22:27-29, 22:32-33, 22:36-38, 95:1-3
POET 21:5, 26:224, 27:36, 36:69, 52:30, 69:41
POLLUTION 30:41
POMEGRANATES 6:99, 61:68, 55:68
POOR 2:43, 2:83
Pornography 7:26, 24:30-31
PREGNANCY 7:189, 22:2, 31:14, 35:11, 41:47, 46:15, 65:4-6
PRISONERS 12:36
PRIVACY 24:27-29, 24:58-59
PROPERTY 21:78, 38:22-24
PSALMS 4:163, 17:55, 21:105

Q

QAROON 28:76, 28:79, 29:39, 40:24
QIBLA 2:142-145, 10:87
QUAIL 2:57, 7:160, 20:80
QURAISH 106:1
QUR'AN (READING) 2:185, 4:82, 5:101, 6:19, 7:204, 9:111, 10:15, 10:37, 10:61, 12:2, 12:3, 13:31, 15:1, 15:87, 15:91, 16:98, 17:9, 17:41, 17:45, 17:46, 17:60, 17:78, 17:82, 17:88, 17:89, 17:106, 18:54, 20:2, 20:113, 20:114, 25:30, 25:32, 27:1, 27:6, 27:76, 27:92, 28:85, 30:58, 34:31, 36:2, 36:69, 38:1, 39:27, 39:28, 41:3, 41:26, 41:44, 42:7, 43:3, 43:31, 46:29, 47:24, 50:1, 50:45, 54:17, 54:22, 54:32, 54:40, 55:2, 56:77, 59:21, 72:1, 73:4, 73:20, 76:23, 84:21, 85:21

R

RAPE 12:25, 12:42
REBELLION 5:33-34
RECONNAISSANCE 27:22
RELIGION 2:256, 3:19, 3:65, 3:85, 3:103, 4:162, 6:21, 6:70, 6:116, 6:119, 7:51, 8:22, 16:116, 22:78, 29:61-65, 42:13-14, 43:22, 45:17, 47:36, 51:8, 78:3, 98:4, 110:2
REPENT 2:37, 2:54, 2:160, 2:187, 3:89-90, 4:16-18, 4:26, 4:92, 4:146, 5:34, 5:39, 5:74, 6:54, 7:143, 7:153, 9:5, 9:11, 9:74, 9:104, 9:112, 9:126, 11:3, 11:61, 16:119, 19:60, 20:82, 24:31, 25:70-71, 28:67, 40:3, 42:25, 46:15, 66:8, 85:10
RESURRECTION 10:4, 10:34, 21:104, 27:64, 30:27, 34:49, 83:4
REVELATION 2:97, 13:38, 18:24, 26:194, 42:51-52, 43:4, 45:16, 46:12, 47:20, 52:2-3, 53:2-11, 56:80, 57:16, 57:25, 57:26, 66:12, 69:43, 74:31, 74:52, 80:13, 98:1, 98:4, 98:6
REVENGE 42:40
ROME 30:1-6
RUBY 55:58

S

SABBATH 2:65, 4:47, 4:145, 7:163, 16:124

SABIANS 2:62, 5:69, 22:17

SACRIFICE 2:196, 5:27, 22:36-37, 108:2

SALAT (CONNECTION) 2:3, 2:43, 2:45, 2:83, 2:110, 2:125, 2:153, 2:177, 2:238, 2:277, 3:39, 4:43, 4:77, 4:101-103, 4:142, 4:162, 5:6, 5:12, 5:55, 5:58, 5:91, 5:106, 6:72, 6:92, 6:162, 7:170, 8:3, 8:35, 9:5, 9:11, 9:18, 9:54, 9:71, 9:84, 9:103, 10:87, 11:87, 11:114, 13:22, 14:31, 14:37, 14:40, 17:78, 17:110, 19:31, 19:55, 19:59, 20:14, 20:132, 21:73, 22:35, 22:41, 22:78, 23:2, 24:37, 24:41, 24:56, 24:58, 27:3, 29:45, 30:31, 31:4, 31:17, 33:33, 33:43, 33:56, 35:18, 35:29, 42:38, 58:13, 62:9, 62:10, 70:22-23, 70:34, 73:20, 74:43, 75:31, 87:15, 96:10, 98:5, 107:4-5, 108:2

SALEH 7:73-77, 11:61-66, 11:89, 26:142, 27:45

SAMARITAN 20:85-87, 20:95

SATAN "IBLEES" 2:34, 3:155, 3:175, 4:38, 4:60, 4:76, 4:116, 4:119-120, 4:140, 4:145, 5:90, 5:91, 6:38, 6:43, 6:68, 7:11-12, 7:20, 7:21, 7:27, 7:175, 7:200, 7:201, 8:11, 8:48, 12:5, 12:42, 12:100, 14:22, 15:31-40, 16:63, 16:98, 17:27, 17:53, 17:61, 17:64, 18:50, 18:63, 19:44, 19:45, 20:116, 20:120, 22:52, 22:53, 24:21, 25:29, 26:95, 27:24, 28:15, 29:38, 31:21, 34:20-21, 35:6, 36:60, 37:65, 38:41, 38:74-85, 41:36, 43:62, 47:25, 58:10, 58:19, 59:16

SAUL 2:247-249

SEA 2:50, 2:164, 5:96, 6:59, 6:63, 7:138, 7:163, 10:22, 10:90, 14:32, 16:14, 17:66, 17:67, 17:70, 18:60, 18:61, 18:63, 18:79, 18:109, 20:77,

22:65, 24:40, 26:63, 27:63, 30:41, 31:27, 31:31, 42:33, 45:12, 52:6, 55:24, 81:6

SEVEN 2:29, 2:196, 2:261, 12:43, 12:46-48, 15:44, 15:87, 17:44, 18:22, 23:17, 23:86, 31:27, 41:12, 65:12, 67:3, 69:7, 71:15, 78:12

SEVENTY 7:155, 9:80, 69:32

SEX 2:187, 2:222-223, 4:19, 24:33,

SHEBA 27:22, 34:15

SHIPS 2:164, 10:22, 14:32, 16:14, 17:66, 18:71, 18:79, 22:65, 23:22, 29:15, 29:65, 30:46, 31:31, 35:12, 37:140, 40:80, 43:12, 45:12

SHU'AYB 7:85-92, 11:84-94, 26:177, 29:36

SIGHT 41:22

SILK 22:23, 44:53, 76:12, 76:21

SILVER 3:14, 9:34, 43:33, 76:15-16, 76:21

SIN 3:16, 3:31, 3:135, 3:147, 3:193, 4:31, 4:111, 4:112, 12:97, 14:10, 33:71, 39:53, 40:3, 40:11, 40:55, 46:31, 47:19, 48:2, 61:12, 71:4

SINAI 23:20

SKIN 2:187, 41:22

SKY 41:11, 88:18

SLAVERY "FREEING" 4:92, 5:89, 58:3, 90:12-13

SLEEP 2:255, 7:97, 25:47, 30:23, 39:42, 68:19, 78:9

SOLOMON 2:102, 4:163, 6:84, 21:78-81, 27:15-18, 27:30, 27:36, 27:44, 34:12, 38:30, 38:34

SORCERY 2:102, 5:110, 6:7, 7:109-116, 10:2, 10:63, 10:76-81, 11:7, 20:57-73, 21:3, 26:34-35, 26:49, 27:13, 28:36, 34:43, 37:15, 38:4, 40:24, 43:30, 43:49, 46:7, 51:39, 51:52, 52:15, 54:2, 61:6, 74:24

SPIDER 29:41

SPOUSES 64:14

SUICIDE 4:29-30

SWINE 2:173, 5:3, 5:60, 6:145, 16:115

SYNAGOGUE 22:40

T

TAX 8:41
TELEPORTATION 27:40
TEMPLE(S) 2:114, 2:187, 7:29, 7:31, 9:17-18, 9:107-108, 18:21, 22:40, 72:18
TEMPLE "RESTRICTED" 2:144, 2:149-150, 2:191, 2:196, 2:217, 5:2, 8:34, 9:7, 9:19, 9:28, 17:1, 17:7, 22:25, 48:25, 48:27
TEN(S) 2:196, 2:234, 5:89, 6:160, 7:142, 8:65, 11:13, 20:103, 28:27, 89:2
THAMUD 7:73-78, 9:70, 11:61-67, 11:95, 14:9, 15:80-82, 17:59, 22:42, 25:38, 26:141-158, 27:45-52, 29:38, 38:13, 40:31, 41:13, 41:17, 50:12, 51:43, 53:51, 54:23-31, 69:4, 69:5, 85:18, 89:9, 91:11-14
THEFT 5:38, 12:70-77, 12:81, 60:12
THOUSAND(S) 2:96, 3:124-125, 8:9, 8:65-66, 22:47, 29:14, 32:5, 37:147, 70:4, 97:3
TIME 103:1
TORAH 3:3, 3:48, 3:50, 3:65, 3:93, 5:43, 5:44, 5:46, 5:66, 5:68, 5:110, 7:157, 9:111, 48:29, 61:6, 62:5
TREACHERY 4:105, 4:107, 8:27, 8:58, 8:71, 22:38
TREE 2:35, 7:19, 7:20, 7:22, 14:24, 14:26, 16:10, 16:68, 17:60, 20:120, 22:18, 23:20, 24:35, 27:60, 28:30, 31:27, 36:80, 37:62, 37:64, 37:146, 44:43, 48:18, 55:6, 56:52
TRINITY 4:171, 5:73
TRUTH 2:42
TWELVE 2:60, 5:12, 7:160, 9:36
TWO 2:282, 4:3, 4:11, 4:176, 5:106, 6:143-144, 9:40, 11:40, 13:3, 15:87, 16:51, 23:27, 34:46, 35:1, 36:14, 39:23, 40:11

TUBBA` 44:37, 50:14
TUNNEL 6:35

U

USURY 2:275-278, 3:130, 4:161, 30:39

V

VOICES 17:64, 20:108, 31:19, 49:2-3
VOLCANO 11:40, 23:27

W

WAR 2:190-193, 2:216, 3:165, 4:75, 4:94, 8:1, 8:15-19, 8:57-67, 8:72, 9:12, 22:38-39, 47:4
WATER 25:53, 27:61, 35:12, 47:15, 55:19, 55:21, 56:31, 56:68, 67:30, 77:27, 88:17
WEATHER 2:163-164, 2:265, 4:102, 6:99, 7:57, 7:160, 8:11, 10:24, 13:12-13, 13:17, 14:18, 14:32, 15:22, 16:65, 17:68-69, 18:45, 20:53, 21:81, 22:5, 22:63, 23:18, 24:40, 24:43, 25:25, 25:48, 27:60, 27:63, 29:40, 29:63, 30:24, 30:46, 30:48, 30:51, 31:10, 33:9, 34:12, 35:9, 35:27, 35:9, 38:36, 39:21, 40:13, 41:16, 41:39, 42:28, 42:33, 43:11, 45:5, 46:24, 50:9, 51:1-4, 51:41, 52:27, 52:44, 54:19, 56:69, 57:20, 52:44, 67:17, 69:6, 78:14, 80:25
WIDOWS 2:234-235, 2:240
WILLS 2:180-181, 5:106-108
WINE 47:15, 83:25
WITNESSING 2:282, 4:6, 4:15, 4:41, 4:135, 5:107, 6:150, 7:172, 11:54, 12:26, 21:61, 24:2, 24:4-8, 24:13, 27:32, 46:10, 63:1, 65:2
WOMEN 4:15-16, 4:34, 24:60, 60:10-12, 66:3-6

Wool 16:80

Y

Yathrib 33:13

Z

Zechariah 3:37-38, 6:85, 19:2, 19:7, 21:89
Zayd 33:37
Zebra 74:50
Zul-Qarnain (two horned one) 18:83, 18:86, 18:94

**Please report any errors or
comments to
free@free-minds.org**